ANNUAL EDITIONS

Developing World 09/10
Nineteenth Edition

EDITOR
Robert J. Griffiths
University of North Carolina

Robert J. Griffiths is Associate Professor of Political Science at the University of North Carolina at Greensboro. His teaching and research interests are in the field of comparative and international politics with a focus on Africa. He teaches courses on the politics of the non-western world, African politics, international law and organization, international security, and international political economy. His publications include articles on parliamentary oversight of defense in South Africa, South African civil-military relations and democratic consolidation, and the developing world and global commons negotiations.

Higher Education

Boston   Burr Ridge, IL   Dubuque, IA   New York   San Francisco   St. Louis
Bangkok   Bogotá   Caracas   Kuala Lumpur   Lisbon   London   Madrid   Mexico City
Milan   Montreal   New Delhi   Santiago   Seoul   Singapore   Sydney   Taipei   Toronto

Higher Education

ANNUAL EDITIONS: DEVELOPING WORLD, NINETEENTH EDITION

Annual Editions® is a registered trademark of the McGraw-Hill Companies, Inc.
Annual Editions is published by the **Contemporary Learning Series** group within the McGraw-Hill Higher Education division.

1 2 3 4 5 6 7 8 9 0 QPD/QPD 0 9 8

ISBN 978–0–07–339782–5
MHID 0–07–339782–2
ISSN 1096–4215

Managing Editor: *Larry Loeppke*
Senior Managing Editor: *Faye Schilling*
Developmental Editor: *Debra Henricks*
Editorial Coordinator: *Mary Foust*
Editorial Assistant: *Nancy Meissner*
Production Service Assistant: *Rita Hingtgen*
Permissions Coordinator: *Lenny J. Behnke*
Senior Marketing Manager: *Julie Keck*
Marketing Communications Specialist: *Mary Klein*
Marketing Coordinator: *Alice Link*
Project Manager: *Sandy Wille*
Design Specialist: *Tara McDermott*
Senior Production Supervisor: *Laura Fuller*
Cover Graphics: *Kristine Jubeck*

Compositor: Laserwords Private Limited
Cover Image: © Mark Downey/Getty (inset); © 2006 Glowimages, Inc. All rights reserved (background)

Library of Congress Cataloging-in-Publication Data
Main entry under title: Annual Editions: Developing World. 2009/2010.
  1. Developing World—Periodicals. I. Griffiths, Robert J., *comp.* II. Title: Developing World.
658'.05

www.mhhe.com

Editors/Advisory Board

Members of the Advisory Board are instrumental in the final selection of articles for each edition of ANNUAL EDITIONS. Their review of articles for content, level, currentness, and appropriateness provides critical direction to the editor and staff. We think that you will find their careful consideration well reflected in this volume.

Preface

The developing world continues to play an increasingly important role in world affairs.

It is home to the vast majority of the world's population and it has an increasingly significant impact on the international economy. From the standpoint of international security, developing countries are not only sites of frequent conflicts and humanitarian crises, but also a source of continuing concern related to international terrorism. Developing countries also play a critical role in the efforts involved to protect the global environment.

The developing world demonstrates considerable ethnic, cultural, political, and economic diversity, making generalizations about such a diverse group of countries difficult. Increasing differentiation among developing countries further complicates our comprehension of the challenges of modernization, development, and globalization that they face. A combination of internal and external factors shape the current circumstances throughout the developing world; and issues of peace and security, international trade and finance, debt, poverty, the environment, human rights, and gender illustrate the complexity of these challenges as well as the effects of globalization and the growing interdependence between nations. The ways in which these issues interrelate suggest the need for greater understanding of the connections between developing and industrialized countries. There continues to be significant debate about the best way to address the challenges faced by the developing world.

The developing world competes for attention on an international agenda that is often dominated by relations between the industrialized nations. Moreover, the domestic concerns of the industrial countries frequently overshadow the plight of the developing world. The nineteenth edition of *Annual Editions: Developing World* seeks to provide students with an understanding of the diversity and complexity of the developing world and to acquaint them with the challenges that these nations confront. I remain convinced of the need for greater awareness of the problems that confront the developing world and that the international community must make a commitment to effectively address these issues, especially in the era of globalization. I hope that this volume contributes to students' knowledge and understanding of current trends and their implications, and serves as a catalyst for further discussion.

Over fifty percent of the articles in this edition are new. I chose articles that I hope are both interesting and informative, and that can serve as a basis for further student research and discussion. The units deal with what I regard as the major issues facing the developing world. In addition, I have attempted to suggest the similarities and differences between developing countries, the nature of their relationships with the industrialized nations, and the different perspectives that exist regarding the causes of and approaches to meet the issues.

I would again like to thank McGraw-Hill for the opportunity to put together a reader on a subject that is the focus of my teaching and research. I would also like to thank those who have sent in the response forms with their comments and suggestions. I have tried to take these into account in preparing the current volume. No book on a topic as broad as the developing world can be completely comprehensive. There certainly are additional and alternative readings that might be included. Any suggestions for improvement are welcome. Please complete and return the postage-paid article rating form at the end of the book with your comments.

Robert J. Griffiths
Editor

Contents

UNIT 1
Understanding the Developing World

Unit Overview   xvi

1. **The New Face of Development,** Carol Lancaster, *Current History,* January 2008

   The nature and emphasis of development has shifted as some progress on reducing poverty has been achieved. While poverty continues to be a challenge, especially in sub-Saharan Africa, development has increasingly come to be identified with human development, civil and political rights, security, and sustainability. Government to government aid programs are increasing through the efforts of civil society organizations, philanthropists, and multinational corporations. Technology has also helped shift development emphases.   **2**

2. **The Ideology of Development,** William Easterly, *Foreign Policy,* July/August 2007

   William Easterly argues that the development model advocated by international financial institutions and the UN amounts to a discredited ideology. He criticizes the view that development is a problem that can be solved by externally-imposed technical plans, which often fail to take the local politics and economics into account. Instead, development should rely on the ability of people to make their own choices, benefit from their successes and learn from the failures.   **6**

3. **Africa's Village of Dreams,** Sam Rich, *Wilson Quarterly,* Spring 2007

   Economist Jeffrey Sachs has initiated an ambitious program to alleviate poverty in Africa. The Millennium Villages Project is an effort to help people out of poverty by injecting large sums of aid into villages to boost agricultural production, improve health care, and provide schooling. The effort is controversial and critics question its sustainability over the long run.   **9**

4. **Today's Golden Age of Poverty Reduction,** Surjit S. Bhalla, *The International Economy,* Spring 2006

   Contrary to prevailing views, Surjit Bhalla argues that an emphasis on economic growth has resulted not in growing inequality, but rather in unprecedented poverty reduction. Market emphases have been behind this success, but Bhalla claims that political correctness coupled with efforts to protect the interests of international financial institutions prevent the recognition of this trend.   **14**

5. **Devising a Shared Global Strategy for the MDGs,** Sha Zukang, *UN Chronicle,* No. 4, 2007

   The Millennium Development Goals were formulated to cut extreme poverty in half by 2015. Just past the halfway point to that goal, UN Under-Secretary for Economic and Social Affairs Sha Zukang says that success is still possible. *Meeting the MDGs will require a cooperative effort that includes effective national development strategies combined with adequate international support.*   **18**

6. **Development as Poison,** Stephen A. Marglin, *Harvard International Review,* Spring 2003

   The West's conception of development emphasizes on markets and assumes that following its lead will result in development. In reality, Western culture undermines indigenous cultures, especially that of communities. *The West should realize that the values underlying its culture are not necessarily universal.*   **20**

7. **Why God Is Winning,** Timothy Samuel Shah and Monica Duffy Toft, *Foreign Policy,* July/August 2006

   Although modernization was originally thought to lead to an increase in secularization, in many instances the opposite has occurred. Globalization and democratization have facilitated an increase in religious activism among Muslims, Christians, and Hindus. Political liberalization has allowed for the expression of religious beliefs and has also led to organizing political action. This trend has been reinforced by access to communication technology, which makes it possible to reach a broader audience.   **25**

The concepts in bold italics are developed in the article. For further expansion, please refer to the Topic Guide.

UNIT 2
Political Economy and the Developing World

The concepts in bold italics are developed in the article. For further expansion, please refer to the Topic Guide.

UNIT 3
Conflict and Instability

The concepts in bold italics are developed in the article. For further expansion, please refer to the Topic Guide.

UNIT 4
Political Change in the Developing World

The concepts in bold italics are developed in the article. For further expansion, please refer to the Topic Guide.

UNIT 5
Population, Resources, Environment, and Health

The concepts in bold italics are developed in the article. For further expansion, please refer to the Topic Guide.

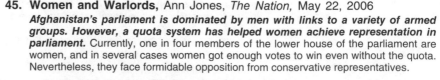

UNIT 6
Women and Development

The concepts in bold italics are developed in the article. For further expansion, please refer to the Topic Guide.

Correlation Guide

The *Annual Editions* series provides students with convenient, inexpensive access to current, carefully selected articles from the public press. **Annual Editions: Developing World 09/10** is an easy-to-use reader that presents articles on important topics such as *democracy, foreign aid, human rights,* and many more. For more information on *Annual Editions* and other *McGraw-Hill Contemporary Learning Series* titles, visit www.mhcls.com.

This convenient guide matches the units in **Annual Editions: Developing World 09/10** with the corresponding chapters in two of our best-selling McGraw-Hill Political Science textbooks by Boyer and Rourke.

Annual Editions: Developing World 09/10	International Politics on the World Stage, Brief, 8/e by Boyer/ Rourke	International Politics on the World Stage, 12/e by Rourke
Unit 1: Understanding the Developing World	**Chapter 1:** Thinking and Caring about World Politics **Chapter 2:** The Evolution of World Politics **Chapter 4:** Nationalism: The Traditional Orientation **Chapter 5:** Globalization and Transnationalism: The Alternative Orientation	**Chapter 1:** Thinking and Caring about World Politics **Chapter 2:** The Evolution of World Politics **Chapter 4:** Nationalism: The Traditional Orientation **Chapter 5:** Globalism: The Alternative Orientation
Unit 2: Political Economy and the Developing World	**Chapter 3:** Level of Analysis **Chapter 5:** Globalization and Transnationalism: The Alternative Orientation **Chapter 11:** Global Economic Competition and Cooperation	**Chapter 3:** Levels of Analysis and Foreign Policy **Chapter 5:** Globalism: The Alternative Orientation **Chapter 12:** National Economic Competition: The Traditional Road **Chapter 13:** International Economic Cooperation: The Alternative Road
Unit 3: Conflict and Instability	**Chapter 9:** Pursuing Security	**Chapter 8:** National Power and Statecraft: The Traditional Approach **Chapter 10:** National Security: The Traditional Road **Chapter 11:** International Security: The Alternative Road
Unit 4: Political Change in the Developing World	**Chapter 6:** Power and the National States: The Traditional Structure **Chapter 7:** International Organization: An Alternative Structure	**Chapter 6:** National States: The Traditional Structure **Chapter 7:** Intergovernmental Organization: Alternative Governance
Unit 5: Population, Resources, Environment, and Health	**Chapter 8:** International Law and Human Rights: An Alternative Approach **Chapter 10:** Globalization in the World Economy **Chapter 12:** Preserving and Enhancing the Global Commons	**Chapter 12:** National Economic Competition: The Traditional Road **Chapter 14:** Preserving and Enhancing Human Rights and Dignity **Chapter 15:** Preserving and Enhancing the Biosphere
Unit 6: Women and Development	**Chapter 8:** International Law and Human Rights: An Alternative Approach	**Chapter 14:** Preserving and Enhancing Human Rights and Dignity

Topic Guide

This topic guide suggests how the selections in this book relate to the subjects covered in your course. You may want to use the topics listed on these pages to search the Web more easily.

On the following pages a number of Web sites have been gathered specifically for this book. They are arranged to reflect the units of this Annual Editions reader. You can link to these sites by going to *http://www.mhcls.com.*

All the articles that relate to each topic are listed below the bold-faced term.

Internet References

The following Internet sites have been selected to support the articles found in this reader. These sites were available at the time of publication. However, because Web sites often change their structure and content, the information listed may no longer be available. We invite you to visit http://www.mhcls.com for easy access to these sites.

AE: Developing World 09/10

General Sources

Foreign Policy in Focus (FPIF): Progressive Response Index
http://fpif.org/progresp/index_body.html

This index is produced weekly by FPIF, a "think tank without walls," which is an international network of analysts and activists dedicated to "making the U.S. a more responsible global leader and partner by advancing citizen movements and agendas." This index lists volume and issue numbers, dates, and topics covered by the articles.

People & Planet
http://www.peopleandplanet.org

People & Planet is an organization of student groups at universities and colleges across the United Kingdom. Organized in 1969 by students at Oxford University, it is now an independent pressure group campaigning on world poverty, human rights, and the environment.

United Nations System Web Locator
http://www.unsystem.org

This is the Web site for all the organizations in the United Nations family. According to its brief overview, the United Nations, an organization of sovereign nations, provides the machinery to help find solutions to international problems or disputes and to deal with pressing concerns that face people everywhere, including the problems of the developing world, through the UN Development Program at *http://www.undp.org* and UNAIDS at *http://www.unaids.org*.

United States Census Bureau: International Summary Demographic Data
http://www.census.gov/ipc/www/idb/

The International Data Base (IDB) is a computerized data bank containing statistical tables of demographic and socioeconomic data for all countries of the world.

World Health Organization (WHO)
http://www.who.ch

The WHO's objective, according to its Web site, is the attainment by all peoples of the highest possible level of health. Health, as defined in the WHO constitution, is a state of complete physical, mental, and social well-being and not merely the absence of disease or infirmity.

UNIT 1: Understanding the Developing World

Africa Index on Africa
http://www.afrika.no/index/

A complete reference source on Africa is available on this Web site.

African Studies WWW (U. Penn)
http://www.sas.upenn.edu/African_Studies/AS.html

The African Studies Center at the University of Pennsylvania supports this ongoing project that lists online resources related to African Studies.

UNIT 2: Political Economy and the Developing World

Center for Third World Organizing
http://www.ctwo.org/

The Center for Third World Organizing (CTWO, pronounced "C-2") is a racial justice organization dedicated to building a social justice movement led by people of color. CTWO is a 20-year-old training and resource center that promotes and sustains direct action organizing in communities of color in the United States.

ENTERWeb
http://www.enterweb.org

ENTERWeb is an annotated meta-index and information clearinghouse on enterprise development, business, finance, international trade, and the economy in this age of cyberspace and globalization. The main focus is on micro-, small-, and medium-scale enterprises, cooperatives, and community economic development both in developed and developing countries.

International Monetary Fund (IMF)
http://www.imf.org

The IMF was created to promote international monetary cooperation, to facilitate the expansion and balanced growth of international trade, to promote exchange stability, to assist in the establishment of a multilateral system of payments, to make its general resources temporarily available under adequate safeguards to its members experiencing balance of payments difficulties, and to shorten the duration and lessen the degree of disequilibrium in the international balances of payments of members.

TWN (Third World Network)
http://www.twnside.org.sg/

The Third World Network is an independent, nonprofit international network of organizations and individuals involved in issues relating to development, the Third World, and North-South issues.

U.S. Agency for International Development (USAID)
http://www.usaid.gov

USAID is an independent government agency that provides economic development and humanitarian assistance to advance U.S. economic and political interests overseas.

Internet References

The World Bank
http://www.worldbank.org

The International Bank for Reconstruction and Development, frequently called the World Bank, was established in July 1944 at the UN Monetary and Financial Conference in Bretton Woods, New Hampshire. The World Bank's goal is to reduce poverty and improve living standards by promoting sustainable growth and investment in people. The bank provides loans, technical assistance, and policy guidance to developing country members to achieve this objective.

UNIT 3: Conflict and Instability

The Carter Center
http://www.cartercenter.org

The Carter Center is dedicated to fighting disease, hunger, poverty, conflict, and oppression through collaborative initiatives in the areas of democratization and development, global health, and urban revitalization.

Center for Strategic and International Studies (CSIS)
http://www.csis.org/

For four decades, the Center for Strategic and International Studies (CSIS) has been dedicated to providing world leaders with strategic insights on, and policy solutions to, current and emerging global issues.

Conflict Research Consortium
http://conflict.colorado.edu/

The site offers links to conflict- and peace-related Internet sites.

Institute for Security Studies
http://www.iss.co.za

This site is South Africa's premier source for information related to African security studies.

Institute for Global communications
http://www.igc.org/peacenet/

PeaceNet promotes dialogue and sharing of information to encourage appropriate dispute resolution, highlights the work of practitioners and organizations, and is a proving ground for ideas and proposals across the range of disciplines within the conflict resolution field.

Refugees International
http://www.refintl.org

Refugees International provides early warning in crises of mass exodus. It seeks to serve as the advocate of the unrepresented—the refugee. In recent years, Refugees International has moved from its initial focus on Indochinese refugees to global coverage, conducting almost 30 emergency missions in the last 4 years.

UNIT 4: Political Change

Latin American Network Information Center—LANIC
http://www.lanic.utexas.edu

According to Latin Trade, LANIC is "a good clearinghouse for Internet-accessible information on Latin America."

ReliefWeb
http://www.reliefweb.int/w/rwb.nsf

ReliefWeb is the UN's Department of Humanitarian Affairs clearinghouse for international humanitarian emergencies.

World Trade Organization (WTO)
http://www.wto.org

The WTO is promoted as the only international body dealing with the rules of trade between nations. At its heart are the WTO agreements, the legal ground rules for international commerce and for trade policy.

UNIT 5: Population, Resources, Environment, and Health

Earth Pledge Foundation
http://www.earthpledge.org

The Earth Pledge Foundation promotes the principles and practices of sustainable development—the need to balance the desire for economic growth with the necessity of environmental protection.

EnviroLink
http://envirolink.org

EnviroLink is committed to promoting a sustainable society by connecting individuals and organizations through the use of the World Wide Web.

Greenpeace
http://www.greenpeace.org

Greenpeace is an international NGO (nongovernmental organization) that is devoted to environmental protection.

Linkages on Environmental Issues and Development
http://www.iisd.ca/linkages/

Linkages is a site provided by the International Institute for Sustainable Development. It is designed to be an electronic clearinghouse for information on past and upcoming international meetings related to both environmental issues and economic development in the developing world.

Population Action International
http://www.populationaction.org

According to its mission statement, Population Action International is dedicated to advancing policies and programs that slow population growth in order to enhance the quality of life for all people.

The Worldwatch Institute
http://www.worldwatch.org

The Worldwatch Institute advocates environmental protection and sustainable development.

UNIT 6: Women and Development

WIDNET: Women in Development NETwork
http://www.focusintl.com/widnet.htm

This site provides a wealth of information about women in development, including the Beijing '95 Conference, WIDNET statistics, and women's studies.

Women Watch/Regional and Country Information
http://www.un.org/womenwatch/

The UN Internet Gateway on the Advancement and Empowerment of Women provides a rich mine of information.

UNIT 1

Understanding the Developing World

Unit Selections

1. **The New Face of Development,** Carol Lancaster
2. **The Ideology of Development,** William Easterly
3. **Africa's Village of Dreams,** Jeffrey Sachs
4. **Today's Golden Age of Poverty Reduction,** Surjit S. Bhalla
5. **Devising a Shared Global Strategy for the MDGs,** Sha Zukang
6. **Development as Poison,** Stephen A. Marglin
7. **Why God Is Winning,** Timothy Samuel Shaw and Monica Duffy Toft

Key Points to Consider

- How has the emphasis of development changed?

- What is the ideology of development?

- What are the criticisms of the Millennium Villages Project?

- What will it take to meet the Millennium Development Goals?

- What constitutes the Western model of development?

- Is the Western model of development transferable to the developing world?

- What accounts for the increase in religious activism?

Student Web Site
www.mhcls.com/online

Internet References
Africa Index on Africa
http://www.afrika.no/index/
African Studies WWW (U. Penn)
http://www.sas.upenn.edu/African_Studies/AS.html

The diversity of the countries that make up the developing world has made it difficult to characterize and understand these countries and their role in international affairs. The task has become even more difficult as further differentiation among developing countries has occurred. "Developing world" is a catch-all term that lacks precision and explanatory power. It is used to describe societies that range from those that are desperately poor to the ones that are rich in resource, the traditional to the modern, and the authoritarian to the democratic nations. To complicate things even further, there is also controversy over what actually constitutes development. For some, it is economic growth or progress towards democracy, while for others it involves greater empowerment and dignity. There are also differing views on why progress toward development has been uneven. The West tends to see the problem as stemming from poor governance, institutional weakness and failure to embrace free-market principles. Critics from the developing world cite the legacy of colonialism and the nature of the international political and economic structures as the reasons for the lack of development. Not only are there differing views on the causes of lagging development, but there is considerable debate on how best to tackle these issues. The Millennium Development Goals seek to eradicate extreme poverty and hunger, and address issues of education, health, gender, and the environment. Progress so far has been uneven, and this has contributed to the debate on the best way to achieve development goals. The emphasis of development has shifted as well; it now extends beyond the traditional focus on poverty reduction, to include issues like civil and political rights, human security, and environmental sustainability. Reflecting this broader emphasis is a growing list of actors that includes non-governmental organizations and philanthropic organizations involved in development efforts. Critics question these broad goals and are skeptical about the traditional top-down approach advocated by international institutions. In any case, lumping together the 120-plus nations that make up the developing world obscures the disparities in size, population, resources, forms of government, level of industrialization, distribution of wealth, ethnicity, and a host of other indicators that makes it difficult to categorize and generalize this large, diverse group of countries.

Despite their diversity, most nations of the developing world share some characteristics. Developing countries often have large populations, with annual growth rates that often exceed two percent. Although there has been some improvement, poverty continues to be widespread in both rural and urban areas, with rural areas often containing the poorest of the poor. While the majority of the developing world's inhabitants continue to live in the countryside, there is a massive rural-to-urban migration under way, cities are growing rapidly, and some developing countries are approaching urbanization at the same rate as industrialized countries. Wealth is unevenly distributed, making education, employment opportunities, and access to health care luxuries that only a few enjoy. Corruption and mismanagement are too common. With

© Royalty-Free/Corbis

very few exceptions, these nations share a colonial past that has affected them both politically and economically. Moreover, critics charge that the present neocolonial structure of the international economy and the West's political, military, and cultural links with the developing world amount to continued domination.

The roots of the diverging views between the rich and the poor nations on development emerged shortly after the beginning of the independence era. The basis for this difference in view is the opinion that the industrialized world continued to dominate and exploit the developing countries. This viewpoint encouraged efforts to alter the international economic order during the 1970s. While the New International Economic Order (NIEO) succumbed to neoliberalism in the 1980s, developing countries still seek solidarity in their interactions with the West. The efforts to extract concessions from the industrialized countries in the negotiations on the Doha Trade Round illustrate this effort. Moreover, developing countries still view Western prescriptions for development skeptically and chafe under the Washington Consensus, which dictates the terms for the access to funds from international financial institutions and foreign aid. Some critics suggest that Western development models are detrimental and result in inequitable development and give rise to cultural imperialism. In contrast to the developing world's criticism of the West, industrial countries continue to maintain the importance of institution-building and following the Western model that emphasizes a market-oriented approach to development. There is a clear difference of opinion between the industrialized countries and the developed world on issues ranging from economic development to governance. Ultimately the development process will be shaped primarily by the countries experiencing it. The industrialized countries can, however, contribute to this process through trade liberalization, and by providing access to technology, and more innovative and effective aid.

The New Face of Development

"As the traditional development challenge of reducing poverty is increasingly met, a new challenge for the twenty-first century emerges: that of ensuring a livable, peaceful, and prosperous world."

CAROL LANCASTER

A number of trends in international development that were already emerging at the end of the last millennium—including the introduction of new actors and technologies, the increasing role of private investment, and the remarkable reduction in poverty in countries such as China and India—have become even more apparent as we approach the end of the current decade. These trends go to the core of what development is, how it is achieved, and who is involved in promoting it. In combination, they suggest that international development in the future will likely be very different from what it has been in the past.

The world first turned its attention to the challenge of international development in the decades immediately after World War II, as the cold war began and decolonization got under way. How, the international community asked itself, could growth be accelerated and poverty reduced in newly independent, less developed nations? Wealthy countries increasingly engaged in promoting economic progress in developing countries (primarily through foreign aid), and also established professional agencies, both bilateral and multilateral, to allocate and manage development assistance. The motives for the developed countries' actions, of course, were not purely altruistic. They sought to promote their national interests (such as the containment of Soviet influence); to ensure that decolonization proceeded smoothly; to preserve spheres of influence in former colonies; to expand their own exports; and to secure sources of raw materials abroad.

During the 40 years between 1960 and 2000, the international aid and development regime depended on rich countries' providing concessional economic assistance. They provided such assistance either directly to recipient governments, or indirectly, through international institutions. The aid was targeted toward agreed-upon projects like roads, government-provided agricultural services, primary education, and health care. Rich countries' trade and investment policies were understood to be an important part of the development equation, but they tended to be much less prominent than development aid itself, since trade and investment usually involved powerful domestic interests within rich countries, a circumstance that constrained their use for development purposes.

Over the same period, the ways in which aid was used to promote development underwent an evolution. In the 1960s, the primary emphasis was on encouraging economic growth by providing funds for infrastructure and other projects meant to expand national production. In the 1970s, the main focus was direct action to alleviate poverty, with aid devoted to projects that would meet the basic needs of the poor in developing countries (including basic education, primary health care, and development of small farms). In the 1980s, the emphasis was on fostering growth through budgetary support for economic reforms and "structural adjustment."

The 1990s turned out to be a transition decade for development. With the end of the cold war and the breakup of the Soviet Union, many of the former communist bloc countries began a transition to free markets and democratic governance. Aid-giving governments turned their attention, and their aid, to furthering this transition. A wave of democratization washed over other parts of the world as well, including sub-Saharan Africa, and democracy became increasingly linked with development in the minds of many development practitioners. Democracy, it was now argued, was a key facilitator of development, and thus foreign aid was increasingly used to promote political development.

At the same time, rising concerns over transnational problems, such as environmental deterioration and infectious diseases (especially HIV/AIDS), expanded the development discourse. Conflict prevention and mitigation became part of the broadening framework of international development as civil conflicts erupted in a number of countries, especially in Africa, and it became obvious that economic progress required peaceful conditions. Finally, the development dialogue renewed its emphasis on poverty reduction, partly because of the "associational revolution"—an explosion of civil society organizations, in both rich and poor countries. Many of these organizations were interested in bettering the human condition.

The continued evolution of information technologies will empower the poor, probably in ways we cannot foresee.

And so, between the postwar period and the year 2000, much changed. In particular, the notion of development expanded to include a much wider range of issues. Yet the core focus remained poverty reduction, and the primary instrument for achieving it remained government-based economic assistance.

An Elastic Idea

Today, international development has become an even more elastic concept, as ideas about what constitutes development, how it is best achieved, and who should be part of the process continue to evolve. Starting from the early years of the international development era a half-century ago, development was thought of as a means to improve the material conditions of life. That is, public and private investment would promote growth, which in turn would eventually reduce or even eliminate poverty. This basic concept remains at the heart of development, but there have been some important additions.

"Human development" is now part of the equation, meaning that education, health, life expectancy, and other indicators of well-being are given greater attention. Political rights are also considered a key aspect of development, in part to ensure that the poor and excluded have a political voice. Some have incorporated "human security," as well, including security against economic deprivation and against physical violence, actual or threatened. "Sustainable development," or economic progress that does not affect the environment too harshly, is another element in the welter of ideas that currently define development. Some in recent years have defined development as the freedom to choose a fulfilling life.

This trend is likely to continue. Development will have at its core the reduction of severe poverty as long as that problem endures; but it will also continue to evolve to reflect changing global beliefs about the basic requirements of a decent human life and about how to meet those requirements.

Western economists have always believed that the driver of development is private investment—on the theory that because it increases productivity, production, growth, incomes, and jobs, it will ultimately eliminate poverty. Others, however, have taken the view that the market is unable to create equitable development and that state intervention is necessary to direct and hasten economic progress. This state-versus-market tension was evident during the cold war, with the socialist and capitalist models doing battle. The same philosophical difference is part of the debate between those who emphasize macroeconomic growth (for example, through structural adjustment) and those who emphasize direct interventions to reduce poverty. From an institutional perspective, this tension has been reflected in the often differing approaches of the World Bank and nongovernmental organizations (NGOs) toward promoting development.

In recent years, something of a consensus has emerged. It is now broadly accepted that private investment and well functioning markets are essential to sustaining long-term growth, and that the state cannot do it alone. But it is also generally recognized that without a well-functioning state, markets cannot produce sustained growth and reduce poverty.

When the era of international development began, the major actors were states, along with international institutions like the World Bank. Rich states shaped world trade policies and the special trade arrangements (for example, the Generalized System of Preferences) that affected the trade of poor countries. Not much foreign investment in poor countries was carried out, and even then it was sometimes unwelcome. Essentially, the governments of rich countries provided aid to the governments of poor countries. It was, in the language of telecommunications, a "one-to-one" world.

This has changed. Governments still play a major role but they are joined by civil society organizations, both in developed and developing countries. These groups deliver services, funded both by governments and through private giving, and advocate for more action to improve the lives of the poor. Growing numbers of corporations are investing large amounts in poor countries. They are also funding development activities on their own, often in public-private partnerships that also involve governments of rich countries and NGOs. These activities are part of corporate social responsibility programs, or even part of businesses' marketing strategies.

The scale of global philanthropy has grown over time, and the number of philanthropic organizations funding development activities has also grown. The Gates Foundation is the most prominent of the new foundations but there are many others. Countless so-called social entrepreneurs have come on the scene as well. These are individuals in developed and developing countries who create NGOs to tackle development problems—as well as "venture philanthropists" who create enterprises with double and triple bottom lines, enterprises that aim to do good while doing well. (An example would be an equity fund that combines investing with providing technical assistance to small enterprises that have few alternatives for capital or training.)

These actors have created a "many-to-many" development space that promises to grow in the coming decades. Also contributing to many-to-many development is the growing flow of remittances from immigrants working in rich countries to their families in poor countries. Indeed, the flow of remittances exceeds the global total of foreign aid by a considerable amount.

The Technology Revolution

All these trends have been facilitated by new information technologies. We are living, in fact, in the midst of several technology revolutions—information technology, biotechnology, nano-technology, and materials technology. All of these hold the promise of radically changing not only our lives but also the lives of the poor in developing countries.

Information technology is already connecting many inhabitants of developing nations to the internet, as computers become increasingly affordable in poor countries. Cell phones are being used for banking, medical investigations, market updates, and obtaining all manner of otherwise out-of-reach information (as well as for political networking). The continued evolution of information technologies will empower the poor, probably in ways we cannot foresee. It has already provided new means for financial support to reach the poor through NGOs operating in developing countries, as wealthy people contribute through internet portals. This innovation cuts out middlemen and encourages direct giving. The internet has also facilitated the transfer of remittances from rich to poor countries. And it permits the poor to network as never before, an opportunity that will surely be seized even more in the future as cell phones come to resemble computers and become more affordable for all.

The biological revolution promises gains in medicine and agriculture, though these are not without controversy. The benefits have not yet reached a large enough scale to have a major impact on the lives of the poor, but this seems only a matter of time. Nanotechnology fosters miniaturization that, among other things, will make more powerful and cheaper cell phones possible. And advances in materials technology could lead to the production of commodities especially designed for difficult environments, an encouraging prospect for the poor living in those environments.

The Third World's End

During much of the past 40 years, people spoke and wrote about the "Third World"—the many developing countries that were an arena of competition between the United States and the Soviet Union. The Soviet Union, of course, is gone. But so is any semblance of shared poverty among the 150 or so countries comprising Asia, Africa, and Latin America. China has provided the most dramatic example of a poor country achieving rapid growth through manufacturing and exporting. In the past 25 years, China's development has lifted a quarter of a billion people out of poverty. This is a degree of economic progress, even with all of its accompanying problems, that is historically unprecedented. China is in fact now a major source of trade, aid, and investment for countries in Africa, Latin America, and elsewhere in Asia.

Economic progress in India—the other country with large-scale poverty and a population in excess of a billion—is increasingly evident as well. There, development is based to a large extent on the export of services. Poverty has fallen somewhat in Latin America, too, as many economies there diversify and grow. This means that the world's hard-core poverty and development problem is now concentrated in sub-Saharan Africa.

In many countries in sub-Saharan Africa, little economic progress has been achieved since independence. The difficulties standing in the way of the region's advancement include a difficult climate and the heavy disease load that comes with being located in the tropics. Also, many sub-Saharan nations are small and landlocked. Others are resource-rich but have found these resources to be a curse (Nigeria with its oil; Sierra Leone with its diamonds; the Democratic Republic of Congo [DRC] with its copper, cobalt, and other minerals).

One discerns a real opportunity—for the first time in history—to eradicate severe poverty worldwide.

Governments in these countries have long exhibited incompetence and corruption, and their resources have made it possible for them to provide little accountability to their citizens. Discontent has often led to violent conflict, which has been further stoked by competition for the control of resources. Civil conflicts in the DRC, Sierra Leone, and elsewhere have killed large numbers of people, created even more refugees and displaced persons, and destroyed national assets. Nigeria continues to teeter on the brink of a political abyss, the DRC continues to be plagued by internal war, and Somalia is still a collapsed state—with predictable effects on development.

But not all the news out of Africa is gloomy. Economic growth in India and China has increased demand, and thus prices, for the raw materials that many African countries export. Economic management in Africa, at least in most places, is better than it has been in several decades. Democratic development—or political openness, anyway—is greater than it has been during much of the period since independence.

Corruption, on the other hand, remains a major problem in many African countries. Additionally, China's extraordinary success in producing cheap manufactured goods appears to have left African countries—which lack the cheap, productive labor that China has—with few opportunities to attract the investment that might lead them into world manufacturing markets. In short, Africa is experiencing some new economic opportunities but also some new challenges.

Global Challenges

Beginning in the 1990s, major powers began to take greater note of global and transnational problems when they calculated their foreign policy and foreign aid policies. For much of that decade, the focus of this set of concerns, known as global public goods, was the environment—pollution, loss of plant and animal species, and loss of the ozone layer. While these transnational concerns (other than the ozone layer) have not abated, two more have joined them: infectious disease (above all HIV/AIDS) and climate change (which was not yet such a prominent concern in the 1990s).

The Bush administration has promised an extraordinary amount of aid to fight HIV/AIDS worldwide—$30 billion over the coming five years. Concern over this disease has risen in the United States as its global impact has become ever more evident, above all in Africa. The American religious right—long skeptical of the appropriateness and efficacy of foreign aid—has embraced fighting HIV/AIDS as the duty of Christians to aid those, especially women and children, who are suffering through no fault of their own. Although allocations of assistance so far have not kept pace with pledges, it is possible that fighting this disease will become the largest element in US foreign aid in the future.

But the next US president will also need to confront the issue of climate change, the reality and probable impact of which can no longer be ignored. That impact, incidentally, is expected to be particularly damaging to many of the world's poor countries. It seems likely, given that the governments of rich countries only have so much money to spend on development, that some development money will be shifted over the coming decades to fund activities intended to combat global warming—perhaps some of it as incentive payments to encourage governments to reduce greenhouse gas emissions.

Beyond climate change, two other trends may produce major development challenges in decades to come: the continuing growth of the world's population and the economic growth in China, India, and elsewhere. Global population is expected to continue expanding over the coming years—with nearly all of the growth taking place in the world's poor countries. Increased population will mean additional greenhouse gas emissions, as well as additional pressure on supplies of food, water, and energy. Economic growth, though it is hoped for and expected, will exacerbate those pressures, especially as demand for superior foods—meats instead of grains—increases. (A widely observed growth pattern is that as people's incomes rise they demand more protein in their diets in the form of meat and fish. But producing one pound of beef requires eight pounds of grain, and this increases pressures on food production systems.)

As for water, pressures on supply are already evident in Africa, the Middle East, northern China, and the Indian subcontinent. Where adequate water supplies cannot be procured, threats to human health and well-being emerge, along with threats to peace, stability, and income growth. Severe tensions over water already exist in the Middle East, and such situations are likely to become more common as population continues to increase. Meanwhile, a growing world population will use more fossil fuels, which will not only lead to progressively higher petroleum prices but will also exacerbate global warming.

These trends suggest that the combination of worldwide population growth and income growth needs to be managed carefully if the planet is to remain livable for our children and grandchildren. This challenge may prove the greatest of the twenty-first century.

An additional problem affecting development worldwide will be movements of people. The populations of many rich countries, and China as well, are growing at or below the replacement rate (with the United States, for reasons that are not entirely clear, a notable exception). The average age of people in these countries is rising, and this means that the dependency ratio is rising as well—each worker is in effect supporting more people. Unsurprisingly, the demand for additional workers is growing in these economies, and immigration from poorer countries to richer ones—from China to Japan, from North Africa and sub-Saharan Africa to Europe, and from Latin America to the United States—has exploded. Much of this immigration is illegal.

This movement of people has delivered benefits both to host countries and to countries of origin. It allows necessary work to be carried out in host countries while immigrants are able to send home remittances that finance consumption and investment there. This seems like a win-win arrangement—except that some citizens of the host countries experience the arrangement as a threat to their identities and ways of life. Even in the United States, where national identity is based on the idea of republican democracy rather than ethnicity, religion, or language, tensions surrounding immigration are increasingly evident.

Such tensions, in the United States and also in Japan and Europe, threaten sometimes to erupt into social strife (as indeed has occurred in recent years in France). It is not clear what will happen as the irresistible force of immigration continues to collide with the immovable object of host-country resistance, but certainly if the remittance economy and access to labor are constrained, international development will suffer a setback.

After Poverty

Since the end of the cold war, because we no longer live in a bipolar world, we have lacked a certain clarity that allowed us to order our international relations and forge domestic consensus on urgent problems. Today's world has a single major power—and many complex problems that are beyond that power's ability to resolve. International development is one of them.

Nevertheless, within this complex and fluid world, one discerns a real opportunity—for the first time in history—to eradicate severe poverty worldwide. The resources and know-how are available and much progress has already been made, especially in China and, increasingly, in India. It will not be easy to "make poverty history" over the coming decades. A great deal needs to be achieved in education, investment, and governance, and in addition we must address the issue of migrations of people away from areas of the world with too few resources to sustain a minimally acceptable standard of living. The obstacles may be insuperable in some cases. But the opportunities are there.

Meanwhile, as the traditional development challenge of reducing poverty is increasingly met, a new development challenge for the twenty-first century emerges: that of ensuring a livable, peaceful, and prosperous world. This will require addressing the global problems that arise when growing populations and rising incomes collide with limited resources.

CAROL LANCASTER is an associate professor at Georgetown University's Walsh School of Foreign Service and director of the university's Mortara Center for International Studies. A former deputy administrator of the US Agency for International Development, she is author of the forthcoming *George Bush's Foreign Aid: Revolution or Chaos?* (Center for Global Development, 2008).

The Ideology of Development

The failed ideologies of the last century have come to an end. But a new one has risen to take their place. It is the ideology of Development—and it promises a solution to all the world's ills. But like Communism, Fascism, and the others before it, Developmentalism is a dangerous and deadly failure.

WILLIAM EASTERLY

A dark ideological specter is haunting the world. It is almost as deadly as the tired ideologies of the last century—communism, fascism, and socialism—that failed so miserably. It feeds some of the most dangerous trends of our time, including religious fundamentalism. It is the half-century-old ideology of Developmentalism. And it is thriving.

Like all ideologies, Development promises a comprehensive final answer to all of society's problems, from poverty and illiteracy to violence and despotic rulers. It shares the common ideological characteristic of suggesting there is only one correct answer, and it tolerates little dissent. It deduces this unique answer for everyone from a general theory that purports to apply to everyone, everywhere. There's no need to involve local actors who reap its costs and benefits. Development even has its own intelligentsia, made up of experts at the International Monetary Fund (IMF), World Bank, and United Nations.

The power of Developmentalism is disheartening, because the failure of all the previous ideologies might have laid the groundwork for the opposite of ideology—the freedom of individuals and societies to choose their destinies. Yet, since the fall of communism, the West has managed to snatch defeat from the jaws of victory, and with disastrous results. Development ideology is sparking a dangerous counterreaction. The "one correct answer" came to mean "free markets," and, for the poor world, it was defined as doing whatever the IMF and the World Bank tell you to do. But the reaction in Africa, Central Asia, Latin America, the Middle East, and Russia has been to fight against free markets. So, one of the best economic ideas of our time, the genius of free markets, was presented in one of the worst possible ways, with unelected outsiders imposing rigid doctrines on the xenophobic unwilling.

The backlash has been so severe that other failed ideologies are gaining new adherents throughout these regions. In Nicaragua, for instance, IMF and World Bank structural adjustments failed so conspicuously that the pitiful Sandinista regime of the 1980s now looks good by comparison. Its leader, Daniel Ortega,

is back in power. The IMF's actions during the Argentine financial crisis of 2001 now reverberate a half decade later with Hugo Chávez, Venezuela's illiberal leader, being welcomed with open arms in Buenos Aires. The heavy-handed directives of the World Bank and IMF in Bolivia provided the soil from which that country's neosocialist president, Evo Morales, sprung. The disappointing payoff following eight structural adjustment loans to Zimbabwe and $8 billion in foreign aid during the 1980s and 1990s helped Robert Mugabe launch a vicious counterattack on democracy. The IMF-World Bank-Jeffrey Sachs application of "shock therapy" to the former Soviet Union has created a lasting nostalgia for communism. In the Middle East, $154 billion in foreign aid between 1980 and 2001, 45 structural adjustment loans, and "expert" advice produced zero per capita GDP growth that helped create a breeding ground for Islamic fundamentalism.

This blowback against "globalization from above" has spread to every corner of the Earth. It now threatens to kill sensible, moderate steps toward the freer movement of goods, ideas, capital, and people.

Development's Politburo

The ideology of Development is not only about having experts design your free market for you; it is about having the experts design a comprehensive, technical plan to solve all the problems of the poor. These experts see poverty as a purely technological problem, to be solved by engineering and the natural sciences, ignoring messy social sciences such as economics, politics, and sociology.

Sachs, Columbia University's celebrity economist, is one of its main proprietors. He is now recycling his theories of overnight shock therapy, which failed so miserably in Russia, into promises of overnight global poverty reduction. "Africa's problems," he has said, "are . . . solvable with practical and proven technologies." His own plan features hundreds of expert interventions to solve every last problem of the poor—from green manure, breast-feeding education, and bicycles to solar-energy systems, school uniforms for aids orphans, and windmills. Not to mention such critical interventions as "counseling and information services for men to address their reproductive health needs." All this will be done, Sachs says, by "a united and effective United Nations country team, which coordinates in one place the work of the U.N. specialized agencies, the IMF, and the World Bank."

Under Developmentalism, an end to starvation, tyranny, and war are thrown in like a free toaster.

So the admirable concern of rich countries for the tragedies of world poverty is thus channeled into fattening the international aid bureaucracy, the self-appointed priesthood of Development. Like other ideologies, this thinking favors collective goals such as national poverty reduction, national economic growth, and the global Millennium Development Goals, over the aspirations of individuals. Bureaucrats who write poverty-reduction frameworks outrank individuals who actually reduce poverty by, say, starting a business. Just as Marxists favored world revolution and socialist internationalism, Development stresses world goals over the autonomy of societies to choose their own path. It favors doctrinaire abstractions such as "market-friendly policies," "good investment climate," and "pro-poor globalization" over the freedom of individuals.

Development also shares another Marxist trait: It aspires to be scientific. Finding the one correct solution to poverty is seen as a scientific problem to be solved by the experts. They are always sure they know the answer, vehemently reject disagreement, and then later change their answers. In psychiatry, this is known as Borderline Personality Disorder. For the Development Experts, it's a way of life. The answer at first was aid-financed investment and industrialization in poor countries, then it was market-oriented government policy reform, then it was fixing institutional problems such as corruption, then it was globalization, then it was the Poverty Reduction Strategy to achieve the Millennium Development Goals.

One reason the answers keep changing is because, in reality, high-growth countries follow a bewildering variety of paths to development, and the countries with high growth rates are constantly changing from decade to decade. Who could be more different than successful developers such as China and Chile, Botswana and Singapore, Taiwan and Turkey, or Hong Kong and Vietnam? What about the many countries who tried to emulate these rising stars and failed? What about the former stars who have fallen on hard times, like the Ivory Coast, which was one of the fastest developers of the 1960s and 1970s, only to become mired in a civil war? What about Mexico, which saw rapid growth until 1980 and has had slow growth ever since, despite embracing the experts' reforms?

The experts in Developmentalism's Politburo don't bother themselves with such questions. All the previous answers were right; they were just missing one more "necessary condition" that the experts have only just now added to the list. Like all ideologies, Development is at the same time too rigid to predict what will work in the messy real world and yet flexible enough to forever escape falsification by real-world events. The high church of Development, the World Bank, has guaranteed it can never be wrong by making statements such as, "different policies can yield the same result, and the same policy can yield different results, depending on country institutional contexts and underlying growth strategies." Of course, you still need experts to figure out the contexts and strategies.

Resistance Is Futile

Perhaps more hypocritical yet is Development's simple theory of historical inevitability. Poor societies are not just poor, the experts tell us, they are "developing" until they reach the final stage of history, or "development," in which poverty will soon end. Under this historiography, an end to starvation, tyranny, and war are thrown in like a free toaster on an infomercial. The experts judge all societies on a straight line, per capita income, with the superior countries showing the inferior countries the image of their own future. And the experts heap scorn on those who resist the inevitabilities on the path to development.

One of today's leading Developmentalists, *New York Times* columnist Thomas Friedman, can hardly conceal his mockery of those who resist the march of history, or "the flattening of the world." "When you are Mexico," Friedman has written, "and your claim to fame is that you are a low-wage manufacturing country, and some of your people are importing statuettes of your own patron saint from China, because China can make them and ship them all the way across the Pacific more cheaply than you can produce them . . . you have got a problem. [T]he only way for Mexico to thrive is with a strategy of reform . . . the more Mexico just sits there, the more it is going to get run over." Friedman seems blissfully unaware that poor Mexico, so far from God yet so close to American pundits, has already tried much harder than China to implement the experts' "strategy of reform."

The self-confidence of Developmentalists like Friedman is so strong that they impose themselves even on those who accept their strategies. This year, for instance, Ghana celebrated its 50th anniversary as the first black African nation to gain independence. Official international aid donors to Ghana told its allegedly independent government, in the words of the World Bank: "We Partners are here giving you our pledge to give our best to make lives easier for you in running your country." Among the things they will do to make your life easier is to run your country for you.

Unfortunately, Development ideology has a dismal record of helping any country actually develop. The regions where the ideology has been most influential, Latin America and Africa, have done the worst. Luckless Latins and Africans are left chasing yesterday's formulas for success while those who ignored the Developmentalists found homegrown paths to success. The nations that have been the most successful in the past 40 years did so in such a variety of different ways that it would be hard to argue that they discovered the "correct answer" from development ideology. In fact, they often conspicuously violated whatever it was the experts said at the time. The East Asian tigers, for instance, chose outward orientation on their own in the 1960s, when the experts' conventional wisdom was industrialization for the home market. The rapid growth of China over the past quarter century came when it was hardly a poster child for either the 1980s Washington Consensus or the 1990s institutionalism of democracy and cracking down on corruption.

What explains the appeal of development ideology despite its dismal track record? Ideologies usually arise in response to tragic situations in which people are hungry for clear and comprehensive solutions. The inequality of the Industrial Revolution bred Marxism, and the backwardness of Russia its Leninist offshoot. Germany's defeat and demoralization in World War I birthed Nazism. Economic hardship accompanied by threats to identity led to both Christian and Islamic fundamentalism. Similarly, development ideology appeals to those who want a definitive, complete answer to the tragedy of world poverty and inequality. It answers the question, "What is to be done?" to borrow the title of Lenin's 1902 tract. It stresses collective social outcomes that must be remedied by collective, top-down action by the intelligentsia, the revolutionary vanguard, the development expert. As Sachs explains, "I have . . . gradually come to understand through my scientific research and on the ground advisory work the awesome power in our generation's hands to end the massive suffering of the extreme poor . . . although introductory economics textbooks preach individualism and decentralized markets, our safety and prosperity depend at least as much on collective decisions."

Freeing the Poor

Few realize that Americans in 1776 had the same income level as the average African today. Yet, like all the present-day developed nations, the United States was lucky enough to escape poverty before there were Developmentalists. In the words of former IMF First Deputy Managing Director Anne Krueger, development in the rich nations "just happened." George Washington did not have to deal with aid partners, getting structurally adjusted by them, or preparing poverty-reduction strategy papers for them. Abraham Lincoln did not celebrate a government of the donors, by the donors, and for the donors. Today's developed nations were free to experiment with their own pragmatic paths toward more government accountability and freer markets. Individualism and decentralized markets were good enough to give rise to penicillin, air conditioning, high-yield corn, and the automobile—not to mention better living standards, lower mortality, and the iPod.

The opposite of ideology is freedom, the ability of societies to be unchained from foreign control. The only "answer" to poverty reduction is freedom from being told the answer. Free societies and individuals are not guaranteed to succeed. They will make bad choices. But at least they bear the cost of those mistakes, and learn from them. That stands in stark contrast to accountability-free Developmentalism. This process of learning from mistakes is what produced the repositories of common sense that make up mainstream economics. The opposite of Development ideology is not anything goes, but the pragmatic use of time-tested economic ideas—the benefits of specialization, comparative advantage, gains from trade, market-clearing prices, trade-offs, budget constraints—by individuals, firms, governments, and societies as they find their own success.

History proves just how much good can come from individuals who both bear the costs and reap the benefits of their own choices when they are free to make them. That includes local politicians, activists, and businesspeople who are groping their way toward greater freedom, contrary to the Developmentalists who oxymoronically impose freedom of choice on other people. Those who best understood the lessons of the 20th century were not the ideologues asking, "What is to be done?" They were those asking, "How can people be more free to find their own solutions?"

The ideology of Development should be packed up in crates and sent off to the Museum of Dead Ideologies, just down the hall from Communism, Socialism, and Fascism. It's time to recognize that the attempt to impose a rigid development ideology on the world's poor has failed miserably. Fortunately, many poor societies are forging their own path toward greater freedom and prosperity anyway. That is how true revolutions happen.

WILLIAM EASTERLY is professor of economics at New York University.

Africa's Village of Dreams

A small Kenyan village is the laboratory for celebrity economist Jeffrey Sachs's ambitious scheme to lift Africa out of poverty. Can big money buy the continent's poorest people a better future?

SAM RICH

Sauri must be the luckiest village in Africa. The maize is taller, the water cleaner, and the schoolchildren better fed than almost anywhere else south of the Sahara.

Just two years ago, Sauri was an ordinary Kenyan village where poverty, hunger, and illness were facts of everyday life. Now it is an experiment, a prototype "Millennium Village." The idea is simple: Every year for five years, invest roughly $100 for each of the village's 5,000 inhabitants, and see what happens.

The Millennium Villages Project is the brainchild of economist Jeffrey Sachs, the principal architect of the transition from state-owned to market economies in Poland and Russia. His critics and supporters disagree about the success of those efforts, often referred to as "shock therapy," but his role in radical economic reform in the two countries vaulted him to fame. Now he has a new mission: to end poverty in Africa.

Africa has been drip-fed aid for decades, Sachs writes in his 2005 book The End of Poverty, but it has never received enough to make a difference. What money has trickled in has been wasted on overpriced consultants and misspent on humanitarian relief and food aid, not directed at the root causes of poverty. The average African, Sachs says, is caught in a "poverty trap." He farms a small plot for himself and his family, and simply doesn't have enough assets to make a profit. As the population grows, people have less and less land, and grow poorer. When the farmer has to pay school fees for his children or buy medication, he is forced to sell the few assets he has or else go into debt. But if he had some capital, he could invest in his farm, grow enough to harvest a surplus, sell it, and start making money.

It's not this diagnosis of Africa's problems that makes Sachs's theories contentious, but his proposed solution, which might be called shock aid—huge, sudden injections of money into poor areas. Over five years, $2.75 million is being invested in the single village of Sauri, and an equal amount will be sunk into each of another 11 Millennium Village sites that are being established in 10 African countries.

The project is structured around the Millennium Development Goals that the United Nations laid out in 2000 as part of an ambitious plan to reduce global poverty. The UN wants poor countries to meet these benchmarks in health, education, and other sectors by 2015. Halfway there, most countries appear unlikely to meet these targets. However, the first two Millennium Villages—Sauri, which was so designated in 2004, and Koraro, Ethiopia, where efforts were launched in 2005—are on track to surpass them.

Sachs has persuaded Western governments, local governments, businesses, and private donors such as Hollywood stars and international financiers to foot the bill. Under the auspices of the Earth Institute, the project he heads at Columbia University, he has gathered specialists in fields from HIV/AIDS research to soil science to work out master plans for these dozen villages.

Never before has so much money been invested in an African community as small as Sauri. If Sauri succeeds, it could usher in a new era for development in Africa. The hope of Sachs as well as those who head the United Nations Millennium Project, with which he has partnered, is that by 2015, when the Millennium Development Goals still seem far away, these villages will be seen as models whose success can be duplicated across Africa. But if Sauri fails, the West may become yet more disillusioned with aid, and perhaps even reduce what it presently contributes. This is a defining moment in the aid debate.

Last year I paid a visit to Sauri, this village on which so much appears to hang. I'd just finished reading The End of Poverty, and I'll admit I was skeptical about the soundness of spending vast amounts of money in a single small village. But most of all, I was looking for early indications of what this exhibit in the aid argument might show.

I was carried on a bicycle taxi through the dusty streets of Kisumu, Kenya, past vendors selling barbecued maize in front of shacks cobbled together from tin cans beaten flat and nailed onto wooden struts. Occasionally I could make out the faded logo of the U.S. Agency for International Development on the rusted shell of an old vegetable-oil can. As I neared my destination I caught a glimpse of Lake Victoria's shore, where vendors in stalls sell fried tilapia and chunks of boiled maize meal.

Inside a concrete compound at the headquarters of the Millennium Villages Project, development experts sat at computer monitors in glass-walled offices. As I entered, the receptionist at the front desk was on the phone: "You need notebooks? . . . How many? . . .Three hundred, is that all? Right, I'll order them for you tomorrow. You'll get them in a few days."

I've spent the last five years in Africa, where I've worked with outfits ranging from big international nongovernmental organizations to tiny one-man-band agencies, but I've never seen an order made as breezily as this. At most NGOs, the procurement even of stationery entails filling out forms in triplicate and long delays.

There was a tour leaving on the 30-mile trip to Sauri the next day. I imagined trekking around the model village with one of Sachs's celebrity protégés, perhaps Angelina Jolie or Bono, or maybe a millionaire altruist the likes of George Soros, so I was slightly disappointed to find myself at the appointed hour in a Toyota Land Cruiser beside a couple of unglamorous American professors on a brief visit to advise the project.

The air conditioning purred as our driver bumped the Toyota over potholes on the single-lane highway that runs inland from the Kenyan coast through the capital, Nairobi, toward Uganda. Sauri itself lies just off the road, some 200 miles from Nairobi, and the sight of tall, strong stalks of maize was the first indication that we'd arrived. Women in brightly colored headscarves and second-hand clothes imported from America and Europe sold homemade snacks and Coca-Cola from wooden shacks dotting the sides of the red-brown dirt road. The grass behind them was a lush green, giving way to a wall of maize plants beneath a sky heavy with the clouds that hang in the rainy season.

Our four-by-four negotiated footpaths through the maize fields and under acacias. The first stop was Sauri's health clinic, which provided stark reminders of the depth of Sauri's problems and the benefits money can bring. The nurse there told us that each household received mosquito nets at the start of the project, when a sample test of villagers revealed that more than 40 percent had malaria. Now that figure has dropped to 20 percent. Malaria, a debilitating and sometimes deadly disease, is being treated free of charge with Coartem, an expensive drug unavailable in most parts of Kenya. The clinic provides condoms and Depo-Provera contraceptive injections, and there are plans to introduce tests for HIV, thought to afflict one in four villagers, and to administer anti-retroviral therapy. Outside the clinic was a covered waiting area furnished with benches. It wasn't big enough to accommodate the burden of the clinic's success: a queue of 50 people waiting to see the facility's sole doctor. More than 200 patients arrive for treatment every day. Most walk from villages miles away.

Minutes later, we arrived at the green courtyard of Bar Sauri Primary School. The red-brick buildings with holes for doors and windows house classrooms for more than 600 children. One of the buildings lacked a roof. The teacher seemed embarrassed to tell us that it had blown off in a storm just days before. He knew roofs don't blow off schoolrooms where we come from.

But he was enthusiastic about the school's innovative feeding program. Ten percent of the village's harvest goes toward school lunches for the children, he said. In addition, the Mil-

lennium Villages Project buys fruit, meat, and fish to provide students with necessary vitamins and protein. The project has built upon Sauri's own school feeding program, established five years ago for students in the top year. Now the entire student body receives nourishing meals. Since Sauri began the program, its school ranking has risen from just inside the top 200 in the district into the top 10. Improved nutrition means that the students can concentrate better, and they're also healthier and more energetic. Sauri won everything at the regional sports day, the teacher told us. With a proud smile, he recalled, "And not one of our children fainted!"

The next stop was the information technology center. It was just a shack with a nice sign on the outside and a few books inside. One day, when the village is connected to the electricity grid, computers will be bought and Internet access provided. Bridging the digital divide may seem a low priority when Sauri has so many pressing problems. But textbooks are a rare commodity, and an Internet connection will allow students access to unlimited information; their parents will be able to obtain up-to-date reports on crop prices, pesticides, and fertilizers.

We returned to the Land Cruiser and set off to visit another ramshackle brick building with a crude dirt floor. Here, the dozen men and women who constitute the village's agriculture committee make decisions key to the success of the whole project. Improved harvests can support the school feeding program and provide income for farmers. Successful farming should enable the village to continue to grow after the five-year project finishes in 2009.

The project's major contribution to agriculture has been the purchase of fertilizer to increase maize production. Maize, which has been grown for as long as anyone can remember, is the main subsistence crop here, as it is in large parts of Africa. Synthetic fertilizers are far too expensive for the average farmer, but in Sauri the project spends $50,000 a year on them. The chairman of the committee said the maize harvest has increased two and a half times as a result. Now the question is how to store the surplus so that villagers can sell it in the dry season when prices are high.

At the tour's final stop, the professors stayed in the Land Cruiser to apply more sunscreen. Outside, I found a cement block with a tap jutting out of it. A water and sanitation expert at the site explained that this was an outlet for a filtered spring, and that purified drinking water is supplied to 50 taps around the village. In neighboring villages, long queues form by a single borehole that slops out murky water, which must be boiled over a charcoal stove before it is potable.

The tour over, the professors drove off, but I decided to stay. Clearly, the Millennium Villages Project has achieved some great things, but I didn't feel I'd seen the full picture. As the light fell, I walked toward the guesthouse by the main highway. A woman was handing out cobs of corn to some kids, and offered me one too. We sat on a bench to eat it and watched the steady stream of lorries roll by, carrying imported goods from the Kenyan port of Mombasa into Uganda, 40 miles up the road. The returning lorries moved faster: They were usually empty. None of them stopped in Sauri.

There are two schools of thought about development. The "macro" school, with its emphasis on national-level economic policy, aims at developing an entire society by changing government policies and encouraging investment. This is often called a top-down approach, because people at the top are making decisions for the benefit of those at the grass roots. This is the work of many economists and other academic specialists as well as organizations such as the World Bank and the International Monetary Fund.

Then there's the "micro" school, oriented toward community development, which advocates working with one group of people at a time, trying to solve particular problems by providing training and minimal investment. This bottom-up approach is the domain of most NGOs and charities.

Though these two schools have the same general objectives, their adherents rarely interact and seemingly speak different languages. What's interesting about the Millennium Villages Project is that it is essentially a micro project run by experts from the macro school, such as Sachs.

But Sachs is no ordinary economist. His charisma and fundraising ability are legendary. He convinced Bono, the lead singer of U2 and a well-known activist in his own right, to write the introduction to The End of Poverty. In it, Bono describes traveling with Sachs as the economist enthused about development. Bono modestly portrays himself as the smart, clean-cut geek hanging on the words of the wild-haired creative guy.

It was Sachs's influence and initiative that spawned the Millennium Villages Project. In 2004, after a visit to Sauri as a special adviser to Kofi Annan, then secretary-general of the UN, he wrote an open letter in which he outlined a plan of action for the village that he had developed with the Earth Institute and the UN Millennium Project. He called on donors to support the plan: "The rich world needs to wake from its slumber."

Even Sachs's harshest critic, New York University professor and former World Bank economist William Easterly, has described Sachs as "the economist as rock star." But Sachs's fan base doesn't rescue his theories, in Easterly's opinion. He points out that the idea of investing vast sums of money to close the poverty gap in Africa was tried in the 1950s and '60s, and failed. He says that Sachs's book peddles an "administrative central plan" in which the UN secretary-general "would supervise and coordinate thousands of international civil servants and technocratic experts to solve the problems of every poor village and city slum everywhere." The solutions Easterly favors instead include measures designed to improve accountability and reduce corruption, and specific investments aimed at tackling one problem at a time. In his eyes, Sachs is a utopian. Sachs dismisses Easterly as a "can't do" economist.

But economists aren't Sachs's only critics; others within the micro school he wants to win over are asking questions, too. They want to make sure communities such as Sauri are not simply passive recipients of handouts from donors and lectures from experts, but are actively involved in making decisions about their own development. This is what they mean when they talk about empowerment. Any development project can bring temporary benefits. The trick is to ensure that a community is not enjoying a honeymoon that ends when the project does, but is making changes on which it can continue to build. They want sustainability.

When I tried to ask questions on the tour about these issues, I received some evasive answers. Millennium Villages staffers and Sauri residents seemed reluctant to criticize the project. This is a common problem in areas that receive a good deal of aid: Workers on the project don't want to criticize their employers, and villagers don't want to bite the hand that's feeding them. Would the crop yields and health care in Sauri be better in 10 years' time? Did the villagers believe the changes the project had bought were valuable? Would they be able to keep them up when the money ran out, and did they want to? I decided to spend a few more days in Sauri and talk to the villagers themselves.

I crossed the highway and walked into the village to meet one of Sachs's graduate students, a researcher from Columbia University. When I caught up with him, he was wearing a yellow T-shirt that said "Jeff Sachs Is My Home Boy." I'd run into him earlier in the day, and he had offered to take me to the home of a Sauri resident, Ben Bunde.

When we arrived at Bunde's house, he and his friends were seated under a tree on wooden benches that seemed to grow from the soil in which they were planted. The group was hunched over bits of scrap paper densely covered in handwriting. They had decided to start up a publication called The Sauri Times, and the Millennium Villages Project had helped fund the first print run.

"There are so many stories to be told about Sauri," Bunde said. "The problem is which ones to tell."

When I asked him how Sauri had changed in the last two years, he leaned back, laughing, and said, "The girls have better haircuts now." There are more hair salons, he said, warming to his subject, and the girls are all getting braids. For the first time, people are selling French fries on the side of the highway. People are more generous, too. "A funeral is a big event in the village, with lots of food. In the old days we would get rice and beans, but now we get meat and soup too." There was so much excitement when the project started that mothers named their babies "Millennium."

I mentioned the elections that took place at the start of the project. Committees of about a dozen villagers for health, education, agriculture, and other key sectors were elected on the advice of project coordinators. The committees' role is to decide how the Millennium Villages money should be spent, and to empower Sauri as a result. But Bunde didn't seem to have confidence in the elections or the committees.

"Few people took part, and they didn't know who to vote for. . . . What would Sachs say if he knew about the witchcraft that took place before the elections? The Kalanya were scaring people to vote for them. In Kenya, we have the Kikuyu factor—the Kikuyu are the dominant tribe. Here in Sanri, we have the Kalanya factor. The Kalanya are the dominant clan. Kalanya elders head all the committees, and yet many of them are uneducated and illiterate. And yet here," he said, gesturing at the young journalists around him, "we have some clever, educated people."

Bunde argued that "clanism" was fostering nepotism and other forms of favoritism. As an example, he cited one of the buildings at the new clinic, which was so badly constructed that it has been condemned. And he hinted at other forms of corruption.

There were rumors that the clinic was charging patients from outside Sauri. Civil servants and police in neighboring villages were allegedly using their influence to get their children into Sauri's school.

There was fighting both within and between committees, he continued, and this had delayed development in the village. In the early days of the project, he said, Sachs had ceremoniously handed over the keys to a truck that was to be used to take goods to market and as an ambulance. But because of power struggles over it, the truck hadn't been used or seen in the village since.

Bunde said that there wasn't enough education of Sauri's people at the start of the project. After receiving free fertilizer and mosquito nets, some villagers sold them to people in the surrounding communities the very next day and then conspired to get more fertilizer and nets.

When I asked if he planned to put any of these stories in The Sauri Times, he shook his head. "No, we don't want the donors to pull out!"

In the end, Bunde questioned whether outside experts really understand the problems in Sauri. While life had improved in the years since the Millennium Village experiment began, Bunde wondered fearfully what will happen when the project ends, "because we have become so dependent." Change, he said, needs to be led from inside the village. "As we say here, only the wearer knows where the shoe pinches."

At breakfast the next morning in the courtyard of the guest-house, I ran into one of the project coordinators, who agreed to chat with me if he could remain anonymous.

On the tour, our guide had emphasized that the elected committees make all the decisions about how Sauri is run and how aid money is spent. I asked the coordinator if there was tension between what the project's representatives wanted to do with the money and what the committees wanted.

"Yes," he said. "We provided the inputs like the fertilizers, and so the committees just sat back. There were mistakes made on entry to Sauri. There was not enough sensitization. . . . Now the problem is [that] the project is moving so fast, the committees can't keep up."

Lack of education, or "sensitization," both within the committees and in the village generally, has caused problems, the project coordinator observed. The villagers often disappoint their benefactors. When project officials want to implement a change, they advise the committees. But the committees sometimes move slowly, because there's not enough support for a particular proposal either within the committee or in the village as a whole. In the surrounding villages to which the project has been expanded, there has been more education, but he doubted that there has been enough.

The basic inputs of the project have also changed. In Sauri, he said, the amount of fertilizer given to farmers was based on plot size. But this scheme was contrary to traditional community practice because its effects were thought to exacerbate existing inequalities and were often divisive. At the new Millennium Villages Project sites, each farmer will be given the same amount of fertilizer.

From Sauri, I walked half a mile down some railway tracks to the neighboring village of Yala, passing the old, dilapidated train station. Even though only one train passes by a week, the station's colonial-era ornamental gardens are still tended with care.

The local government is based in Yala, and I wanted to find out how its members viewed the new Sauri. A hand-painted sign pointed to a small, spare room, where the paint peeled under a corrugated-iron roof. There I found Richard Odunga, a resident of Sauri and Yala's town clerk. His secretary sat next door in front of a typewriter.

Odunga owns a big plot, uses the fertilizer, and has sold a lot of maize. When I asked him if he'd been able to save money, he sighed. He has been forced to support family members who live outside of Sauri. They ask him for help with school fees and medication, and have drained all his maize profits.

He said relations between the local government and project organizers have been strained. "At first, there was no consultation with government. Later, they realized we were a stakeholder and they needed our assistance." Project leaders initially wanted to build not just a clinic but a hospital in Sauri, before the government pointed out that there was already a hospital just a few kilometers away. The project wanted help from government in electrifying Sauri and grading its roads. Two years on, work has started on the roads, but there is still no connection to the national power grid.

Odunga wondered what will remain after the project finishes. When I asked if the community had started contributing to the project yet, he said, "There is some cost sharing, but it's at a minimum level." Who will pay for the clinic after the project ends? he asked. But villagers will at least benefit from the training they've received: "Skills. That's the most important thing."

A couple of days later, I met a senior official working on the Millennium Villages Project for the UN who has a background in community development, as Sachs, he noted, does not. This official, too, would only talk if he were not identified.

The Millennium Villages Project, he said, "has made all the classic development mistakes. . . . If you give away tons of fertilizer, it's predictable that much of it will end up on the open market. If you put millions [of dollars] in a small place, you're going to have problems."

Encouraging farmers to grow maize is the wrong strategy, he argued. "It just means you move from being food insecure for 11 months of the year to food insecure for just nine months of the year."

Growing only maize year after year depletes the soil. It's also a high-risk strategy, he said, as the entire crop may fail. The price of maize has dropped dramatically around Sauri, he noted, as the village's crop yields have improved and supply has increased. Maize is a subsistence crop that has fed Sauri families for years, but, he contended, its price is too low to make it a cash crop. He is trying to push the project to spend more time touting vegetable crops that fetch good prices at market, such as onions, tomatoes, and cabbages.

In this official's opinion, the project could be more effective if it pushed for some macroeconomic changes, rather than concentrate all its efforts in the village. For instance, farmers in Kenya don't buy fertilizer because it costs three times as much as it does in Europe, he said. If the Kenyan government eased taxes and import duties on fertilizer, "a lot more farmers would buy it."

Many UN officials I spoke to criticized the Sauri project, but none would speak openly. It was clear that dissenting voices were not welcomed, as an e-mail I received from one made plain: "Unfortunately I'm already in a lot of trouble for talking about what every good scientist should be talking about. The current environment is one in which scientists can no longer speak openly and expect to keep their jobs."

The Millennium Villages Project is being launched in locations in Kenya, Ethiopia, Ghana, Malawi, Mali, Nigeria, Senegal, Tanzania, Rwanda, and Uganda. Each cluster of villages will be transformed thanks to the investment of nearly $3 million over five years. The sheer scale of investment in the Millennium Villages Project is difficult to convey. The sums involved are not just bigger than those for other community development projects in Africa; they are hundreds of times bigger.

But is this level of investment really plausible for all of Africa? In Kenya alone, aid from abroad would need to increase 10 times, from $100 million to $1 billion, to blanket the whole of the country with the amounts equivalent to what is spent in Millennium Villages.

Sachs says that if the West spent the 0.7 percent of its gross national product on aid set as a goal by the Monterrey Consensus in 2002, this could start to become a reality. This assumes that all the additional aid would go to Africa, and not, as is often the case, to projects in more developed countries such as those of the former Soviet bloc. Currently, only a few countries, such as Denmark, Sweden, and the Netherlands, are reaching the 0.7 percent mark; the United States gives about 0.2 percent of GNP in aid. It justifies its contribution by pointing out that it's still giving more in absolute terms than any other nation—in fact, it gives more than the world's next two biggest economies, Germany and Japan, put together.

The scale of the Millennium Villages Project makes it seem a different breed entirely from most micro programs, which go into a village with modest funds to achieve a specific goal. They may give a farmer a single cow bred in the West for its high milk yield, and train him to look after it. The farmer passes his first calves on to a neighbor and trains him, and gradually the benefits extend to the wider community. The idea is to create a cycle of development that doesn't require extra money. The progress in this kind of program may be slow, but it's much easier to pinpoint what's working and what's not, to figure out why, and to adapt as necessary.

Sauri has achieved more than such projects could ever reasonably hope to, but it's not yet a model village. Instead, Sauri remains Africa in microcosm. All the fundamental problems that exist in Africa still exist in Sauri; in some cases, these problems are magnified.

The village's political framework is confused. Sauri now has two governments in conflict with each other: the committees and the existing local government. The project's committees have introduced a new layer of bureaucracy, and their vastly superior resources have weakened the local government's power. Further, committees are accused of working against each other, and of being corrupt, slow, and unwieldy. Their representatives are said to have been chosen for their ethnic ties and standing in society, rather than their political acumen. As in many parts of Africa, it's unclear which decisions are made by government and which by donors.

Sauri faces the same economic challenges it always has. Most farmers are still growing subsistence crops and depleting their soils. They could instead be growing crops for market or investing in livestock. Low-cost improvements in farming techniques, such as the use of manure and other organic methods that are more sustainable in the long run, are only beginning to be promoted. Growth will be slow because taxation, bad roads, and a lack of electricity need to be addressed at a national level.

Villagers are clearly enjoying better health as a result of the project. The simple extension of a school feeding program has improved students' performance and could serve as a model for schools across Africa. The clinic has transformed health care: The incidence of malaria has decreased, family planning has increased, and soon anti-retroviral treatments will be available to people with HIV and AIDS. But when the project ends, the funds for the clinic and the doctor, the mosquito nets, and the anti-retrovirals will dry up. In three years, the Kenyan government will face the difficult choice between continuing to fund one model clinic in Sauri or cutting the budget considerably.

And Sauri still must contend with the divisions that are typical throughout Kenya: between ethnic groups, men and women, young and old. Witchcraft was employed to influence the outcome of the elections. The practice of wife inheritance remains common, indicative of a wider set of gender issues. These kinds of cultural problems can't be solved with handouts, but only with subtler interventions.

This is not to say that Sauri cannot change, or that investment in the village is wasted. But if Sauri is to become a useful model for development on a bigger scale, and not just another development expert's white elephant, Sachs and others working on the project must acknowledge that they are still learning about Africa. Sauri is not yet a success.

Lasting changes in Sauri will come about not through distribution of commodities, but through education for children and training for adults. To put it another way, give a man a mosquito net, and when it rips, he'll come and ask for another one. But show him how using a mosquito net benefits his health and how it will save him money on medication in the long run, and he might just go out and buy one for himself.

SAM RICH is a development consultant who has worked on community and international development projects in East Africa for nongovernmental organizations, governments, and the World Bank.

Today's Golden Age of Poverty Reduction

The story the World Bank and other agencies don't want you to know.

SURJIT S. BHALLA

Have we just witnessed history? The last twenty years have been good for growth in the developing countries and have been very good for poverty reduction—indeed, the best ever. More than a billion people have been moved out of poverty, defined according to the dollar a day measure. From about 1.3 billion poor in 1980, poverty in 2000 was close to 500 million. In no other period in history has the number of poor people declined, let alone declined by such historic proportions.

Calculations of poverty reduction go back to at least 1820, but calculations of the decline in the number of poor are unfair to history. Because of health improvements, life expectancy has improved enormously over the last two hundred years. This has enhanced population growth for all levels of income, poor and rich alike. With each succeeding generation, reductions in poverty have become more difficult. A better index, therefore, of historical performance is the fraction of people in poverty. Chart 1 compares the pace of poverty reduction since 1820. The share of population in absolute poverty has declined at a rate of approximately 4 percentage points every twenty years for the 130-year period, 1820 to 1950. Between 1950 and 1980, the pace increased to a rate of 14 percentage points for each twenty years. But the golden age for the poor has been the period post-1980. During this age, the record is of an astonishingly large 20 percentage point plus decline.

What happened? In large part, Asia, the continent given up for "dead" by most economists, came alive. (Gunnar Myrdal won a Nobel prize for his pessimistic work on Asian poverty, *Asian Drama: An Inquiry into the Poverty of Nations*.) More accurately, the two population giants, India and China, reversed course on economic policy. The China conversion story is well known. Not as well known is the fact that until about 1980, the Indian policy regime was as "controlled" as China. So both economies changed at approximately the same time (1978–1980); both started to open up, reduce tariffs, and embrace markets. The rest is history. In 1980, the poverty head count ratio in India and China was 50 and 60 percent, respectively. By 2000,

the poverty ratios in both economies were in the range 10 to 25 percent. The number of people moved out of poverty in these two countries alone was about a billion. This is history—an upliftment of 20 percent of the developing world's population. That is approximately the entire population share of the two other continents where poor people reside, Latin America and sub-Saharan Africa.

> **The golden age for the poor has been the period post-1980. The record is of an astonishingly large 20 percentage point plus decline . . . This is history.**

What has made this possible? Though detractors remain, there were at least three important developments in the world economy: first, more than 1.5 billion individuals in the developing world witnessed an increase in political liberties, as measured by Freedom House. This means that governments today have a lesser chance of survival if they pursue anti-growth policies. For some time now, the confusing "Confucian" hypothesis has prevailed in the world, positing that East Asian economies such as Korea and China grew fast because they had able dictatorships (an oxymoron). This correlation conveniently ignores the fact that most African and Latin American countries also had dictatorships and have not grown particularly fast. Political liberties enhance growth prospects because they limit the tenure of bad governments.

The second important development has been in terms of reversing ostrich-like closed tendencies. Tariff rates in developing economies are less than a third of the levels prevailing in 1980, and the absolute level of such tariffs today is less than 10 percent. This means that industrialists have to earn profits the old-fashioned way—by being efficient. Less chances for bribery of politicians and bureaucrats means better allocation of resources. Low tariffs means pressure from international and domestic consumers for higher efficiency and lower prices that lead to higher growth. How bad was it before and how much has policy changed? Well, the magnitude of change can be appreciated from the fact that as late as 1991, India proudly announced that the peak tariff rate had been reduced to 180 percent!

As late as 1991, India proudly announced that the peak tariff rate had been reduced to 180 percent!

The increased efficiency in production leads to increased trade, which in turn leads to faster growth, and the cycle continues. This is the third happy happening in poor countries. The share of trade in developing economies expanded; this share (fraction of GDP accounted for by exports and imports) was 20 percent in 1960, 30 percent in 1980 and 53 percent in 2000.

Developing (and all) world income inequality not only has improved over the last twenty years, but done so for the first time ever.

It is believed that history would have been even better if somehow the poor countries had been able to control population growth. This belief no longer reflects the recent transformation. A centuries-old phenomenon, associated with all countries, is that with development, fertility rates (number of children

ever born per woman) decline, and labor force participation of women increases, and both fuel each other. This is indeed what has happened in China. India, and most poor Bangladesh is today less than three, and in China and Iran less than two. The population growth rate in India today is close to 1.4 percent annually. The new story in the world today is not population growth, but the great fertility decline. It is coming soon to your favorite poor country.

What's Wrong with Markets?

The "practice" of markets has been the major factor behind historical rates of poverty reduction. But the practice of capitalism and/or enhancement of markets is widely considered a four-letter word (according to those professing political correctness).

The basic complaint against capitalism or "markets" is that while it can and does generate extra growth, it does leave a lot to be desired in terms of inequality. The much-too-often-heard and erroneous refrain is that under capitalism, the rich get richer and the poor get poorer. But like the invisible hand, this deemed politically correct adversity is nowhere to be seen. Indeed, the data are consistent with the alternate explanation—growth is good for poverty reduction. An old truism, but somewhat surprisingly, one that needs to be emphasized every second day.

Just last year, the two leading development institutions in the world came out with reports on the importance of inequality change for reduction of poverty. The presumption, and conclusion, was that inequality deterioration had led to considerable welfare loss for the poor, i.e., if inequality had not worsened, world poverty would have been reduced more. The first part of the statement is wrong—developing (and all) world income inequality not only has improved over the last twenty years, but done so for the first time ever (Chart 2). Over the long 130-year period from 1820 to 1980, developing world inequality increased

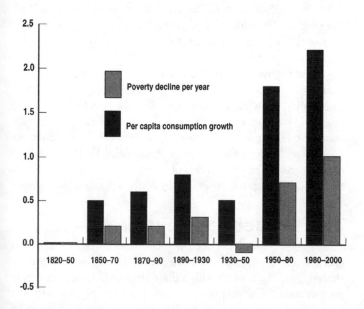

Note: The figures represent annual averages.

Figure 1 Consumption growth and the pace of poverty reduction.

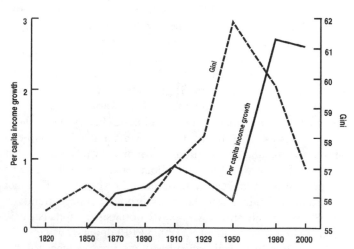

Note: The Gini represents the level of inequality in the designated years; per capita growth is average annual growth between two periods.

Figure 2 Developing world: Inequality and per capita income growth.

(consumption inequality peaks in 1980); only in the last twenty years has it shown some decline. Not incoincidentally, inequality started declining when average per capita growth in the poorest countries (such as India and China) started exceeding average growth in the rich countries around 1980.

Political liberties enhance growth prospects because they limit the tenure of bad governments.

Yet another (and more heuristic) indicator of inequality change is the excess growth experienced by the bottom 40 percent of the population. When this "excess" growth is negative, inequality has worsened. For example, between 1950 and 1980, average per capita consumption growth in developing economies was 1.8 percent annually: the bottom 40 percent had an average growth rate of 1.6 percent per year. So excess growth for this group was –0.2 percent per year (Chart 3). But globalization during the 1980–2000 period (the one severely criticized for worsening inequality) actually shows the poor reflecting a higher growth than average; 3.1 percent annually versus 2.2 percent, an excess growth of 0.9 percent per year.

The new story in the world today is not population growth, but the great fertility decline. It is coming soon to your favorite poor country.

Fast poverty reduction and improving inequality is not the news one obtains from a cursory perusal of major international newspapers, or the outpourings of international organizations dedicated to the removal of absolute poverty. The chorus: poverty reduction, especially in the last twenty years, has been a failure. Indeed, according to the World Bank, the number of poor in the world barely budged between 1.2 billion in 1990 and 1.1 billion in 2001. This deemed lack of poverty reduction has been the mantra (see Joseph Stiglitz's book, *Globalization and Its Discontents*), and the cause has been variously but mostly attributed to "capitalistic growth" models. History shows these conclusions as false. In my view, poverty reduction has been of such gargantuan proportions (as indicated in Chart 1) that it is time for the world to think about relative poverty. Most of the present poor, and future poor, are relatively poor. This fact should be recognized, and the absolute poverty line, currently at $1.08 1993 purchasing power parity dollars per capita per day, needs to be raised to about $2 (2005 PPP) dollars a day.

Given this historical and miraculous improvement for the world's poor, the question remains: Why isn't this one of the biggest stories of our time? There are several reasons, some good, some perverse, for this disconnect between rock band political correctness and economic reality. It could be argued that by constantly downplaying the success in poverty reduc-

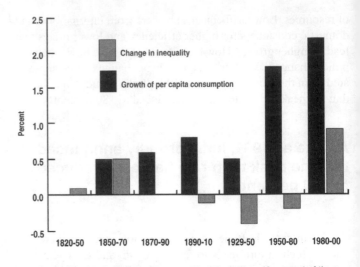

Note: Inequality change is the excess growth of the bottom 40 percent of the population relative to average growth.

Figure 3 Inequality and consumption.

tion, the poor of the world would actually gain more resources to redress their poverty. Extended, this argument means that agencies such as the World Bank can actually lobby the rich governments to give more money for poverty alleviation.

The average sub-Saharan/Latin America per capita growth (two continents that witnessed near zero growth for the long two decades 1981 to 2002) since 2002 has been over 2.5 percent annually.

Extended further, the assumption is that aid monies will be "correctly" allocated to the needy in poor countries. Even if all this is done, the extra money gained due to drawing attention to the world's poor by down-playing poverty achievements has still not reached the poor. That involves the assumption that developing country governments will actually deliver money meant for the poor to the poor. Anybody who buys this sequence of probabilities is "knowledge-proof" about the political reality in the developing world. There maybe such buyers of snake oil in rich countries, but developing country practitioners know better. As far back as 1985, the then-Indian Prime Minister Rajiv Gandhi announced that only 15 percent of every rupee meant for the poor ever reached the poor, the reality has only worsened since then.

The Present and Future

The last few years have been witness to a resurgence in world growth; and both Latin America and sub-Saharan Africa have shared in it. The average sub-Saharan/Latin America per capita growth (two continents that witnessed near zero growth for the long two decades 1981 to 2002) since 2002 has been over 2.5 percent annually; for Asian (and eastern European economies), the growth has been in excess of 6 percent annually! For developed economies the growth has been close to 2 percent. Surely, this is the golden age for poverty reduction.

But such an age is not recognized by most analysts and most definitely not by international organizations like the World Bank and United Nations. The question does arise: was the growth made possible by state interventions or by the "capitalistic market"? Phrased differently, what are the lessons for Africa from all of this history? Is it Communism that did it? Or was it dictatorship? Or was it enlightened state intervention as argued by some? In all of this heartburning, let us also not forget about the "bad" globalization period—so "bad" that it has helped move close to a billion people out of poverty in the last twenty sweet years. The growth did it, not government intervention, benign or otherwise. And growth for the poor was helped by a decline in world inequality, as poor countries grew faster than rich countries.

Sources

Bhalla, Surjit S. 2002. *Imagine There's No Country: Poverty. Inequality and Growth in the Era of Globalization.* Institute for International Economics.

Bhalla, Surjit S. 2006. *Second Among Equals: The Middle Class Kingdoms of India and China.* Forthcoming.

Bourguignon, François, and Christian Morrisson. 2002. Inequality Among World Citizens: 1820–1992. *American Economic Review,* September, 727–44.

SURJIT S. BHALLA is the head of the hedge fund Oxus Research & Investments in New Delhi, India. He has previously worked for the World Bank, Goldman Sachs and Deutsche Bank.

Devising a Shared Global Strategy for the MDGs

Building on Successes Towards 2015

Sha Zukang

Seven years on and halfway towards 2015—the deadline set for the achievement of the Millennium Development Goals—success is still possible. The MDGs, which set quantitative benchmarks to halve extreme poverty in all its forms, are achievable if countries implement national development strategies and receive adequate support from the international community.

The annual progress report of the United Nations on the MDGs, released in June 2007, shows that remarkable progress has been made even in regions where the challenges are greatest. These accomplishments testify to the unprecedented degree of commitment by developing countries and their development partners to the Millennium Declaration, as well as to some success in building the global partnership embodied in the Declaration.

Based on the estimates produced by the World Bank in 2007, the number of people living on less than one dollar a day appears to have fallen from 1.25 billion in 1990 to some 980 million in 2004. Even in sub-Saharan Africa, the earlier relentless increase in the number of the poor appears to have been halted and their proportion has begun to decline, from 46 to 41 per cent of the population. The share of children attending primary school increased from 80 per cent in 1991 to 88 per cent in 2005. Child mortality—an age-old scourge of humanity—has also declined, thanks to effective and inexpensive interventions against measles, malaria, diarrhea and other causes of child deaths.

The commonly-held view that sub-Saharan Africa remains afflicted by war and corrupt Governments, making development impossible, is a misconception. Tremendous progress has been made in improving economic policies and fighting corruption. Many African countries are leading the way in developing national programmes that have yielded big results in a short time. For example, agricultural productivity has been dramatically raised in Malawi; more children are going to primary schools in Ghana, Kenya, the United Republic of Tanzania and Uganda; malaria is being brought under control in Niger, Togo and Zambia; land is being reforested on a large scale in Niger;

and Senegal is on track to halving the proportion of people without access to clean water and sanitation.

These successes demonstrate that the MDGs can be achieved even in very poor countries, when strong government commitment and good strategies are backed up with adequate financing from donors. It is now time to take these successes to scale by supporting government leadership in Africa and other parts of the world still afflicted by severe poverty. These targets are not ambitious, but aim to ensure the fulfillment of basic needs and human rights. If we fail, the consequences will be devastating: 30 million more malnourished children by 2015; 10 million children dying each year of easily preventable causes; millions of HIV-infected people dying because of lack of access to drugs that are easily available in rich countries; over 70 million children without an education; and 600 million people without basic sanitation.

Shortfalls are most severe is sub-Saharan Africa, but even regions that have made substantial progress, including parts of Asia, face challenges in such areas as health and environmental sustainability. More generally, the lack of employment opportunities for young people, gender inequalities, rapid and unplanned urbanization, deforestation, increasing water scarcity and high HIV-prevalence are pervasive obstacles. In addition, insecurity and instability in conflict and post-conflict countries make long-term development efforts extremely difficult. In turn, failure to achieve the MDGs can further heighten the risk of instability and conflict. Yet, in spite of a consensus that development and security are mutually dependent, international efforts all too often treat them as independent from one another.

For countries to be able to see progress, disparities across different groups of the population will have to be addressed. Often, those living in rural areas, children, women with no formal education or the poorest households, do not make enough progress to meet the targets. This is particularly evident in the lack of access to health services and education. In order to achieve the MDGs, countries will need to mobilize additional resources and target public investments that benefit the poor. With guidance from the United Nations, many developing countries, particularly in Africa, have advanced in preparing strategies to achieve the MDGs. As of mid-2007, 41 sub-Saharan African countries have started the process of preparing national development strategies aligned with the MDGs and other development goals agreed upon through the United Nations.

In general, strategies should adopt a wide-ranging approach that seeks to achieve pro-poor economic growth, including through the creation of a large number of additional opportunities for decent work. This, in turn, will require comprehensive programmes for human development, particularly in education and health, as well as building productive capacity and improved physical infrastructure. In each case, an effort should be made to quantify the resources required to implement these programmes. Implementation should be based on a medium-term approach to public expenditure. A sound national statistical system and enhanced public accountability are necessary to support all these efforts.

The MDGs should also be systematically integrated into post-conflict recovery strategies, by coordinating security and humanitarian operations with long-term development efforts. They provide outcome objectives that countries can use as benchmarks for the transition from relief and recovery to long-term development. But success in achieving the MDGs in the poorest and most disadvantaged countries cannot be achieved without international aid. Rich nations need to meet the long-standing target of devoting 0.7 per cent of their gross national income to official development assistance. The leading industrialized countries at the G8 Summit 2005 in Gleneagles (Scotland) pledged to double aid to Africa by 2015, and reaffirmed their commitment at the G8 Summit 2007 in Heiligendamm (Germany). Since 2005, however, aid to the African continent and to the poorest countries overall, excluding debt relief and humanitarian assistance, has barely increased.

It is essential that donor countries renew their efforts to increase development aid. Moreover, to ensure good governance on their part, donors need to inform every country how much aid it will receive in the coming years so that Governments can plan for the increased investments needed to achieve the MDGs. As a further element of their development partnership, and as agreed to in the Fourth World Trade Organization (WTO) Ministerial Conference in Doha in 2001, all Governments should redouble their efforts to reach a successful and equitable conclusion of the present trade negotiations—an outcome that ensures that the international trading system and global trading arrangements become more conducive to progress in all developing countries.

Addressing the challenge of climate change has to be a new but integral element of each country's development strategy. More importantly, however, it should become an enhanced part of the international development agenda. All development partners should collaborate intensively in devising a shared global strategy to address this global problem.

SHA ZUKANG became UN Under-Secretary-General for Economic and Social Affairs on 1 July 2007. He heads the UN Department responsible for the follow-up to major United Nations summits and conferences. The Department also services the Economic and Social Council, as well as the Second and Third Committees of the General Assembly. Prior to assuming his current position, he held a number of posts in the diplomatic service of the People's Republic of China. Mr. Sha also chairs the UN Executive Committee on Economic and Social Affairs.

Development as Poison
Rethinking the Western Model of Modernity

Stephen A. Marglin

A *t the beginning of Annie Hall, Woody Allen tells a story about two women returning from a vacation in New York's Catskill Mountains. They meet a friend and immediately start complaining: "The food was terrible," the first woman says, "I think they were trying to poison us." The second adds, "Yes, and the portions were so small." That is my take on development: the portions are small, and they are poisonous. This is not to make light of the very real gains that have* come with development. In the past three decades, infant and child mortality have fallen by 66 percent in Indonesia and Peru, by 75 percent in Iran and Turkey, and by 80 percent in Arab oil-producing states. In most parts of the world, children not only have a greater probability of surviving into adulthood, they also have more to eat than their parents did—not to mention better access to schools and doctors and a prospect of work lives of considerably less drudgery.

Nonetheless, for those most in need, the portions are indeed small. Malnutrition and hunger persist alongside the tremendous riches that have come with development and globalization. In South Asia almost a quarter of the population is undernourished and in sub-Saharan Africa, more than a third. The outrage of anti-globalization protestors in Seattle, Genoa, Washington, and Prague was directed against the meagerness of the portions, and rightly so.

But more disturbing than the meagerness of development's portions is its deadliness. Whereas other critics highlight the distributional issues that compromise development, my emphasis is rather on the terms of the project itself, which involve the destruction of indigenous cultures and communities. This result is more than a side-effect of development; it is central to the underlying values and assumptions of the entire Western development enterprise.

The White Man's Burden

Along with the technologies of production, healthcare, and education, development has spread the culture of the modern West all over the world, and thereby undermined other ways of seeing, understanding, and being. By culture I mean something more than artistic sensibility or intellectual refinement. "Culture" is used here the way anthropologists understand the term, to mean the totality of patterns of behavior and belief that characterize a specific society. Outside the modern West, culture is sustained through community, the set of connections that bind people to one another economically, socially, politically, and spiritually. Traditional communities are not simply about shared spaces, but about shared participation and experience in producing and exchanging goods and services, in governing, entertaining and mourning, and in the physical, moral, and spiritual life of the community. The culture of the modern West, which values the market as the primary organizing principle of life, undermines these traditional communities just as it has undermined community in the West itself over the last 400 years.

The West thinks it does the world a favor by exporting its culture along with the technologies that the non-Western world wants and needs. This is not a recent idea. A century ago, Rudyard Kipling, the poet laureate of British imperialism, captured this sentiment in the phrase "White Man's burden," which portrayed imperialism as an altruistic effort to bring the benefits of Western rule to uncivilized peoples. Political imperialism died in the wake of World War II, but cultural imperialism is still alive and well. Neither practitioners nor theorists speak today of the white man's burden—no development expert of the 21st century hankers after clubs or golf courses that exclude local folk from membership. Expatriate development experts now work with local people, but their collaborators are themselves formed for the most part by Western culture and values and have more in common with the West than they do with their own people. Foreign advisers—along with their local collaborators—are still missionaries, missionaries for progress as the West defines the term. As our forbears saw imperialism, so we see development.

There are in fact two views of development and its relationship to culture, as seen from the vantage point of the modern West. In one, culture is only a thin veneer over a common, universal behavior based on rational calculation and maximization of individual self interest. On this view, which is probably the view of most economists, the Indian subsistence-oriented peasant is no less calculating, no less competitive, than the US commercial farmer.

> **Cultural imperialism is still alive and well. . . . Foreign advisers ... are still missionaries, missionaries for progress as the West defines the term. As our forebears saw imperialism, so we see development.**

There is a second approach which, far from minimizing cultural differences, emphasizes them. Cultures, implicitly or explicitly, are ranked along with income and wealth on a linear scale. As the West is richer, Western culture is more progressive, more developed. Indeed, the process of development is seen as the transformation of backward, traditional, cultural practices into modern practice, the practice of the West, the better to facilitate the growth of production and income.

What these two views share is confidence in the cultural superiority of the modern West. The first, in the guise of denying culture, attributes to other cultures Western values and practices. The second, in the guise of affirming culture, posits an inclined plane of history (to use a favorite phrase of the Indian political psychologist Ashis Nandy) along which the rest of the world is, and ought to be, struggling to catch up with us. Both agree on the need for "development." In the first view, the Other is a miniature adult, and development means the tender nurturing by the market to form the miniature Indian or African into a full-size Westerner. In the second, the Other is a child who needs structural transformation and cultural improvement to become an adult.

Both conceptions of development make sense in the context of individual people precisely because there is an agreed-upon standard of adult behavior against which progress can be measured. Or at least there was until two decades ago when the psychologist Carol Gilligan challenged the conventional wisdom of a single standard of individual development. Gilligan's book *In A Different Voice* argued that the prevailing standards of personal development were male standards. According to these standards, personal development was measured by progress from intuitive, inarticulate, cooperative, contextual, and personal modes of behavior toward rational, principled, competitive, universal, and impersonal modes of behavior, that is, from "weak" modes generally regarded as feminine and based on experience to "strong" modes regarded as masculine and based on algorithm.

Drawing from Gilligan's study, it becomes clear that on an international level, the development of nation-states is seen the same way. What appear to be universally agreed upon guidelines to which developing societies must conform are actually impositions of Western standards through cultural imperialism. Gilligan did for the study of personal development what must be done for economic development: allowing for difference. Just as the development of individuals should be seen as the flowering of that which is special and unique within each of us—a process by which an acorn becomes an oak rather than being obliged to become a maple—so the development of peoples should be conceived as the flowering of what is special

and unique within each culture. This is not to argue for a cultural relativism in which all beliefs and practices sanctioned by some culture are equally valid on a moral, aesthetic, or practical plane. But it is to reject the universality claimed by Western beliefs and practices.

Of course, some might ask what the loss of a culture here or there matters if it is the price of material progress, but there are two flaws to this argument. First, cultural destruction is not necessarily a corollary of the technologies that extend life and improve its quality. Western technology can be decoupled from the entailments of Western culture. Second, if I am wrong about this, I would ask, as Jesus does in the account of Saint Mark, "[W]hat shall it profit a man, if he shall gain the whole world, and lose his own soul?" For all the material progress that the West has achieved, it has paid a high price through the weakening to the breaking point of communal ties. We in the West have much to learn, and the cultures that are being destroyed in the name of progress are perhaps the best resource we have for restoring balance to our own lives. The advantage of taking a critical stance with respect to our own culture is that we become more ready to enter into a genuine dialogue with other ways of being and believing.

The Culture of the Modern West

Culture is in the last analysis a set of assumptions, often unconsciously held, about people and how they relate to one another. The assumptions of modern Western culture can be described under five headings: individualism, self interest, the privileging of "rationality," unlimited wants, and the rise of the moral and legal claims of the nation-state on the individual.

Individualism is the notion that society can and should be understood as a collection of autonomous individuals, that groups—with the exception of the nation-state—have no normative significance as groups; that all behavior, policy, and even ethical judgment should be reduced to their effects on individuals. All individuals play the game of life on equal terms, even if they start with different amounts of physical strength, intellectual capacity, or capital assets. The playing field is level even if the players are not equal. These individuals are taken as given in many important ways rather than as works in progress. For example, preferences are accepted as given and cover everything from views about the relative merits of different flavors of ice cream to views about the relative merits of prostitution, casual sex, sex among friends, and sex within committed relationships. In an excess of democratic zeal, the children of the 20th century have extended the notion of radical subjectivism to the whole domain of preferences: one set of "preferences" is as good as another.

Self-interest is the idea that individuals make choices to further their own benefit. There is no room here for duty, right, or obligation, and that is a good thing, too. Adam Smith's best remembered contribution to economics, for better or worse, is the idea of a harmony that emerges from the pursuit of self-interest. It should be noted that while individualism is a prior condition for self-interest—there is no place for self-interest

Insurance

Spending on Insurance Premiums

Region	Percent of Global Premium Market
North America	**37.32**
Canada	1.91
United States	35.41
Latin America	**1.67**
Brazil	0.51
Mexico	0.4
Europe	**31.93**
France	4.99
Germany	5.06
UK	9.7
Asia	**26.46**
China	0.79
India	0.41
Japan	20.62
Africa	**1.03**
South Africa	0.87
Oceania	**1.59**
Australia	1.46

http://www.internationalinsurance.org

without the self—the converse does not hold. Individualism does not necessarily imply self-interest.

The third assumption is that one kind of knowledge is superior to others. The modern West privileges the algorithmic over the experiential, elevating knowledge that can be logically deduced from what are regarded as self-evident first principles over what is learned from intuition and authority, from touch and feel. In the stronger form of this ideology, the algorithmic is not only privileged but recognized as the sole legitimate form of knowledge. Other knowledge is mere belief, becoming legitimate only when verified by algorithmic methods.

Fourth is unlimited wants. It is human nature that we always want more than we have and that there is, consequently, never enough. The possibilities of abundance are always one step beyond our reach. Despite the enormous growth in production and consumption, we are as much in thrall to the economy as our parents, grandparents, and great-grandparents. Most US families find one income inadequate for their needs, not only at the bottom of the distribution—where falling real wages have eroded the standard of living over the past 25 years—but also in the middle and upper ranges of the distribution. Economics, which encapsulates in stark form the assumptions of the modern West, is frequently defined as the study of the allocation of limited resources among unlimited wants.

Finally, the assumption of modern Western culture is that the nation-state is the preeminent social grouping and moral authority. Worn out by fratricidal wars of religion, early mod-

ern Europe moved firmly in the direction of making one's relationship to God a private matter—a taste or preference among many. Language, shared commitments, and a defined territory would, it was hoped, be a less divisive basis for social identity than religion had proven to be.

An Economical Society

Each of these dimensions of modern Western culture is in tension with its opposite. Organic or holistic conceptions of society exist side by side with individualism. Altruism and fairness are opposed to self interest. Experiential knowledge exists, whether we recognize it or not, alongside algorithmic knowledge. Measuring who we are by what we have has been continually resisted by the small voice within that calls us to be our better selves. The modern nation-state claims, but does not receive, unconditional loyalty.

So the sway of modern Western culture is partial and incomplete even within the geographical boundaries of the West. And a good thing too, since no society organized on the principles outlined above could last five minutes, much less the 400 years that modernity has been in the ascendant. But make no mistake—modernity is the dominant culture in the West and increasingly so throughout the world. One has only to examine the assumptions that underlie contemporary economic thought—both stated and unstated—to confirm this assessment. Economics is simply the formalization of the assumptions of modern Western culture. That both teachers and students of economics accept these assumptions uncritically speaks volumes about the extent to which they hold sway.

It is not surprising then that a culture characterized in this way is a culture in which the market is the organizing principle of social life. Note my choice of words, "the market" and "social life," not markets and economic life. Markets have been with us since time out of mind, but the market, the idea of markets as a system for organizing production and exchange, is a distinctly modern invention, which grew in tandem with the cultural assumption of the self-interested, algorithmic individual who pursues wants without limit, an individual who owes allegiance only to the nation-state.

There is no sense in trying to resolve the chicken-egg problem of which came first. Suffice it to say that we can hardly have the market without the assumptions that justify a market system—and the market system can function acceptably only when the assumptions of the modern West are widely shared. Conversely, once these assumptions are prevalent, markets appear to be a "natural" way to organize life.

Markets and Communities

If people and society were as the culture of the modern West assumes, then market and community would occupy separate ideological spaces, and would co-exist or not as people chose. However, contrary to the assumptions of individualism, the individual does not encounter society as a fully formed human being. We are constantly being shaped by our experiences, and in a society organized in terms of markets, we are formed by our experiences in the market. Markets organize not only the production and distribution of things; they also organize the production of people.

The rise of the market system is thus bound up with the loss of community. Economists do not deny this, but rather put a market friendly spin on the destruction of community: impersonal markets accomplish more efficiently what the connections of social solidarity, reciprocity, and other redistributive institutions do in the absence of markets. Take fire insurance, for example. I pay a premium of, say, US$200 per year, and if my barn burns down, the insurance company pays me US$60,000 to rebuild it. A simple market transaction replaces the more cumbersome method of gathering my neighbors for a barn-raising, as rural US communities used to do. For the economist, it is a virtue that the more efficient institution drives out the less efficient. In terms of building barns with a minimal expenditure of resources, insurance may indeed be more efficient than gathering the community each time somebody's barn burns down. But in terms of maintaining the community, insurance is woefully lacking. Barn-raisings foster mutual interdependence: I rely on my neighbors economically—as well as in other ways—and they rely on me. Markets substitute impersonal relationships mediated by goods and services for the personal relationships of reciprocity and the like.

Why does community suffer if it is not reinforced by mutual economic dependence? Does not the relaxation of economic ties rather free up energy for other ways of connecting, as the English economist Dennis Robertson once suggested early in the 20th century? In a reflective mood toward the end of his life, Sir Dennis asked, "What does the economist economize?" His answer: "[T]hat scarce resource Love, which we know, just as well as anybody else, to be the most precious thing in the world." By using the impersonal relationships of markets to do the work of fulfilling our material needs, we economize on our higher faculties of affection, our capacity for reciprocity and personal obligation—love, in Robertsonian shorthand—which can then be devoted to higher ends.

In the end, his protests to the contrary notwithstanding, Sir Dennis knew more about banking than about love. Robertson made the mistake of thinking that love, like a loaf of bread, gets used up as it is used. Not all goods are "private" goods like bread. There are also "public" or "collective" goods which are not consumed when used by one person. A lighthouse is the canonical example: my use of the light does not diminish its availability to you. Love is a *hyper* public good: it actually increases by being used and indeed may shrink to nothing if left unused for any length of time.

Economics is simply the formalization of the assumptions of modern Western culture. That both teachers and students of economics accept these assumptions uncritically speaks volumes about the extent to which they hold sway.

If love is not scarce in the way that bread is, it is not sensible to design social institutions to economize on it. On the contrary, it makes sense to design social institutions to draw out and develop the community's stock of love. It is only when we focus on barns rather than on the people raising barns that insurance appears to be a more effective way of coping with disaster than is a community-wide barn-raising. The Amish, who are descendants of 18th century immigrants to the United States, are perhaps unique in the United States for their attention to fostering community; they forbid insurance precisely because they understand that the market relationship between an individual and the insurance company undermines the mutual dependence of the individuals that forms the basis of the community. For the Amish, barn-raisings are not exercises in nostalgia, but the cement which holds the community together.

Indeed, community cannot be viewed as just another good subject to the dynamics of market supply and demand that people can choose or not as they please, according to the same market test that applies to brands of soda or flavors of ice cream. Rather, the maintenance of community must be a collective responsibility for two reasons. The first is the so-called "free rider" problem. To return to the insurance example, my decision to purchase fire insurance rather than participate in the give and take of barn raising with my neighbors has the side effect—the "externality" in economics jargon—of lessening my involvement with the community. If I am the only one to act this way, this effect may be small with no harm done. But when all of us opt for insurance and leave caring for the community to others, there will be no others to care, and the community will disintegrate. In the case of insurance, I buy insurance because it is more convenient, and—acting in isolation—I can reasonably say to myself that my action hardly undermines the community. But when we all do so, the cement of mutual obligation is weakened to the point that it no longer supports the community.

The free rider problem is well understood by economists, and the assumption that such problems are absent is part of the standard fine print in the warranty that economists provide for the market. A second, deeper, problem cannot so easily be translated into the language of economics. The market creates more subtle externalities that include effects on beliefs, values, and behaviors—a class of externalities which are ignored in the standard framework of economics in which individual "preferences" are assumed to be unchanging. An Amishman's decision to insure his barn undermines the mutual dependence of the Amish not only by making him less dependent on the community, but also by subverting the beliefs that sustain this dependence. For once interdependence is undermined, the community is no longer valued; the process of undermining interdependence is self-validating.

Thus, the existence of such externalities means that community survival cannot be left to the spontaneous initiatives of its members acting in accord with the individual maximizing model. Furthermore, this problem is magnified when the externalities involve feedback from actions to values, beliefs, and then to behavior. If a community is to survive, it must structure the interactions of its members to strengthen ways of being and knowing which support community. It will have to constrain the market when the market undermines community.

A Different Development

There are two lessons here. The first is that there should be mechanisms for local communities to decide, as the Amish routinely do, which innovations in organization and technology are compatible with the core values the community wishes to preserve. This does not mean the blind preservation of whatever has been sanctioned by time and the existing distribution of power. Nor does it mean an idyllic, conflict-free path to the future. But recognizing the value as well as the fragility of community would be a giant step forward in giving people a real opportunity to make their portions less meager and avoiding the poison.

The second lesson is for practitioners and theorists of development. What many Westerners see simply as liberating people from superstition, ignorance, and the oppression of tradition, is fostering values, behaviors, and beliefs that are highly problematic for our own culture. Only arrogance and a supreme failure of the imagination cause us to see them as universal rather than as the product of a particular history. Again, this is not to argue that "anything goes." It is instead a call for sensitivity, for entering into a dialogue that involves listening instead of dictating—not so that we can better implement our own agenda, but so that we can genuinely learn that which modernity has made us forget.

STEPHEN A. MARGLIN is Walter S. Barker Professor of Economics at Harvard University.

Why God Is Winning

Religion was supposed to fade away as globalization and freedom spread. Instead, it's booming around the world, often deciding who gets elected. And the divine intervention is just beginning. Democracy is giving people a voice, and more and more, they want to talk about God.

TIMOTHY SAMUEL SHAH AND MONICA DUFFY TOFT

After Hamas won a decisive victory in January's Palestinian elections, one of its supporters replaced the national flag that flew over parliament with its emerald-green banner heralding, "There is no God but God, and Muhammad is His Prophet." In Washington, few expected the religious party to take power. "I don't know anyone who wasn't caught off guard," said U.S. Secretary of State Condoleezza Rice. More surprises followed. Days after the Prophet's banner was unfurled in Ramallah, thousands of Muslims mounted a vigorous, sometimes violent, defense of the Prophet's honor in cities as far flung as Beirut, Jakarta, London, and New Delhi. Outraged by cartoons of Muhammad originally published in Denmark, Islamic groups, governments, and individuals staged demonstrations, boycotts, and embassy attacks.

On their own, these events appeared to be sudden eruptions of "Muslim rage." In fact, they were only the most recent outbreaks of a deep undercurrent that has been gathering force for decades and extends far beyond the Muslim world. Global politics is increasingly marked by what could be called "prophetic politics." Voices claiming transcendent authority are filling public spaces and winning key political contests. These movements come in very different forms and employ widely varying tools. But whether the field of battle is democratic elections or the more inchoate struggle for global public opinion, religious groups are increasingly competitive. In contest after contest, when people are given a choice between the sacred and the secular, faith prevails.

God is on a winning streak. It was reflected in the 1979 Iranian Revolution, the rise of the Taliban in Afghanistan, the Shia revival and religious strife in postwar Iraq, and Hamas's recent victory in Palestine. But not all the thunderbolts have been hurled by Allah. The struggle against apartheid in South Africa in the 1980s and early 1990s was strengthened by prominent Christian leaders such as Archbishop Desmond Tutu. Hindu nationalists in India stunned the international community when they unseated India's ruling party in 1998 and then tested

nuclear weapons. American evangelicals continue to surprise the U.S. foreign-policy establishment with their activism and influence on issues such as religious freedom, sex trafficking, Sudan, and AIDS in Africa. Indeed, evangelicals have emerged as such a powerful force that religion was a stronger predictor of vote choice in the 2004 U.S. presidential election than was gender, age, or class.

The spread of democracy, far from checking the power of militant religious activists, will probably only enhance the reach of prophetic political movements, many of which will emerge from democratic processes more organized, more popular, and more legitimate than before—but quite possibly no less violent. Democracy is giving the world's peoples their voice, and they want to talk about God.

Divine Intervention

It did not always seem this way. In April 1966, *Time* ran a cover story that asked, "Is God Dead?" It was a fair question. Secularism dominated world politics in the mid-1960s. The conventional wisdom shared by many intellectual and political elites was that modernization would inevitably extinguish religion's vitality. But if 1966 was the zenith of secularism's self-confidence, the next year marked the beginning of the end of its global hegemony. In 1967, the leader of secular Arab nationalism, Gamal Abdel Nasser, suffered a humiliating defeat at the hands of the Israeli Army. By the end of the 1970s, Iran's Ayatollah Khomeini, avowedly "born-again" U.S. President Jimmy Carter, television evangelist Jerry Falwell, and Pope John Paul II were all walking the world stage. A decade later, rosary-wielding Solidarity members in Poland and Kalashnikov-toting mujahedin in Afghanistan helped defeat atheistic Soviet Communism. A dozen years later, 19 hijackers screaming "God is great" transformed world politics. Today, the secular pan-Arabism of Nasser has given way to the millenarian pan-Islamism of Iranian President Mahmoud Ahmadinejad, whose religious harangues against America and Israel resonate with millions of Muslims, Sunni and Shia alike. "We increasingly see that people around the world are flocking towards a main focal point—that is the Almighty God," Ahmadinejad declared in his recent letter to President Bush.

The modern world has in fact proven hospitable to religious belief. The world is indeed more modern: It enjoys more political freedom, more democracy, and more education than perhaps at any time in history. According to Freedom House, the number of "free" and "partly free" countries jumped from 93 in 1975 to 147 in 2005. UNESCO estimates that adult literacy rates doubled in sub-Saharan Africa, Arab countries, and South and West Asia between 1970 and 2000. The average share of people in developing countries living on less than a dollar a day fell from 28 percent to 22 percent between 1990 and 2002, according to World Bank estimates.

If people are wealthier, more educated, and enjoy greater political freedom, one might assume they would also have become more secular. They haven't. In fact, the period in which economic and political modernization has been most intense—the last 30 to 40 years—has witnessed a jump in religious vitality around the world. The world's largest religions have expanded at a rate that exceeds global population growth. Consider the two largest Christian faiths, Catholicism and Protestantism, and the two largest non-Christian religions, Islam and Hinduism. According to the *World Christian Encyclopedia,* a greater proportion of the world's population adhered to these religious systems in 2000 than a century earlier. At the beginning of the 20th century, a bare majority of the world's people, precisely 50 percent, were Catholic, Protestant, Muslim, or Hindu. At the beginning of the 21st century, nearly 64 percent belonged to these four religious groupings, and the proportion may be close to 70 percent by 2025. The World Values Survey, which covers 85 percent of the world's population, confirms religion's growing vitality. According to scholars Ronald Inglehart and Pippa Norris, "the world as a whole now has more people with traditional religious views than ever before—and they constitute a growing proportion of the world's population."

Not only is religious observance spreading, it is becoming more devout. The most populous and fastest-growing countries in the world, including the United States, are witnessing marked increases in religiosity. In Brazil, China, Nigeria, Russia, South Africa, and the United States, religiosity became more vigorous between 1990 and 2001. Between 1987 and 1997, surveys by the Times Mirror Center and the Pew Research Center registered increases of 10 percent or more in the proportions of Americans surveyed who "strongly agreed" that God existed, that they would have to answer for their sins before God, that God performs miracles, and that prayer was an important part of their daily life. Even in Europe, a secular stronghold, there have been surprising upticks in religiosity.

God's comeback is in no small part due to the global expansion of freedom. Thanks to the "third wave" of democratization between the mid-1970s and early 1990s, as well as smaller waves of freedom since, people in dozens of countries have been empowered to shape their public lives in ways that were inconceivable in the 1950s and 1960s. A pattern emerged as they

exercised their new political freedoms. In country after country, politically empowered groups began to challenge the secular constraints imposed by the first generation of modernizing, postindependence leaders. Often, as in communist countries, secular straitjackets had been imposed by sheer coercion; in other cases, as in Atatürk's Turkey, Nehru's India, and Nasser's Egypt, secularism retained legitimacy because elites considered it essential to national integration and modernization—and because of the sheer charisma of these countries' founding fathers. In Latin America, right-wing dictatorships, sometimes in cahoots with the Catholic Church, imposed restrictions that severely limited grassroots religious influences, particularly from "liberation theology" and Protestant "sects."

As politics liberalized in countries like India, Mexico, Nigeria, Turkey, and Indonesia in the late 1990s, religion's influence on political life increased dramatically. Even in the United States, evangelicals exercised a growing influence on the Republican Party in the 1980s and 1990s, partly because the presidential nomination process depended more on popular primaries and less on the decisions of traditional party leaders. Where political systems reflect people's values, they usually reflect people's strong religious beliefs.

Many observers are quick to dismiss religion's advance into the political sphere as the product of elites manipulating sacred symbols to mobilize the masses. In fact, the marriage of religion with politics is often welcomed, if not demanded, by people around the world. In a 2002 Pew Global Attitudes survey, 91 percent of Nigerians and 76 percent of Bangladeshis surveyed agreed that religious leaders should be more involved in politics. A June 2004 six-nation survey reported that "most Arabs polled said that they wanted the clergy to play a bigger role in politics." In the same survey, majorities or pluralities in Morocco, Saudi Arabia, Jordan, and the United Arab Emirates cited Islam as their primary identity, trumping nationality. The collapse of the quasi-secular Baathist dictatorship in Iraq released religious and ethnic allegiances and has helped Islam play a dominant role in the country's political life, including in its recently adopted constitution. As right- and left-wing dictatorships have declined in Latin America and democratization has deepened, evangelicals have become an influential voting bloc in numerous countries, including Brazil, Guatemala, and Nicaragua.

The New Orthodoxies

Far from stamping out religion, modernization has spawned a new generation of savvy and technologically adept religious movements, including Evangelical Protestantism in America, "Hindutva" in India, Salafist and Wahhabi Islam in the Middle East, Pentecostalism in Africa and Latin America, and Opus Dei and the charismatic movement in the Catholic Church. The most dynamic religiosity today is not so much "old-time religion" as it is radical, modern, and conservative. Today's religious upsurge is less a return of religious orthodoxy than an explosion of "neo-orthodoxies."

A common denominator of these neo-orthodoxies is the deployment of sophisticated and politically capable organizations. These modern organizations effectively marshal specialized institutions as well as the latest technologies to recruit new members, strengthen connections with old ones, deliver social services, and press their agenda in the public sphere. The Vishwa Hindu Parishad, founded in 1964, "saffronized" large swaths of India through its religious and social activism and laid the groundwork for the Bharatiya Janata Party's electoral successes in the 1990s. Similar groups in the Islamic world include the Muslim Brotherhood in Egypt and Jordan, Hamas in the Palestinian territories, Hezbollah in Lebanon, and the Nahdlatul Ulama in Indonesia. In Brazil, Pentecostals have organized their own legislative caucus, representing 10 percent of congresspeople. Religious communities are also developing remarkable transnational capabilities, appealing to foreign governments and international bodies deemed sympathetic to their cause.

Today's neo-orthodoxies may effectively use the tools of the modern world, but how compatible are they with modern democracy? Religious radicals, after all, can quickly short-circuit democracy by winning power and then excluding non-believers. Just as dangerous, politicized religion can spark civil conflict. Since 2000, 43 percent of civil wars have been religious (only a quarter were religiously inspired in the 1940s and 50s). Extreme religious ideology is, of course, a leading motivation for most transnational terrorist attacks.

The scorecard isn't all negative, however. Religion has mobilized millions of people to oppose authoritarian regimes, inaugurate democratic transitions, support human rights, and relieve human suffering. In the 20th century, religious movements helped end colonial rule and usher in democracy in Latin America, Eastern Europe, sub-Saharan Africa, and Asia. The post-Vatican II Catholic Church played a crucial role by opposing authoritarian regimes and legitimating the democratic aspirations of the masses.

Today's religious movements, however, may not have as much success in promoting sustainable freedom. Catholicism's highly centralized and organized character made it an effective competitor with the state, and its institutional tradition helped it adapt to democratic politics. Islam and Pentecostalism, by contrast, are not centralized under a single leadership or doctrine that can respond coherently to fast-moving social or political events. Local religious authorities are often tempted to radicalize in order to compensate for their weakness vis-à-vis the state or to challenge more established figures. The trajectory of the young cleric Moqtada al-Sadr in postwar Iraq is not unusual. The lack of a higher authority for religious elites might explain why most religious civil wars since 1940—34 of 42—have involved Islam, with 9 of these being Muslim versus Muslim. We need look no further than Iraq today to see religious authorities successfully challenging the forces of secularism—but also violently competing with each other. Even in a long-standing democracy like India, the political trajectory of Hindu nationalism has demonstrated that democratic institutions do not necessarily moderate these instincts: Where radical Hindu nationalists have had the right mix of opportunities and incentives, they have used religious violence to win elections, most dramatically in the state of Gujarat.

The belief that outbreaks of politicized religion are temporary detours on the road to secularization was plausible in 1976, 1986, or even 1996. Today, the argument is untenable. As a framework for explaining and predicting the course of global politics, secularism is increasingly unsound. God is winning in global politics. And modernization, democratization, and globalization have only made him stronger.

TIMOTHY SAMUEL SHAH is senior fellow in religion and world affairs at the Pew Forum on Religion & Public Life. **MONICA DUFFY TOFT** is associate professor of public policy at the John F. Kennedy School of Government and assistant director of the John M. Olin Institute for Strategic Studies at Harvard University.

UNIT 2

Political Economy and the Developing World

Unit Selections

Key Points to Consider

- In what ways are emerging markets playing a growing role in the global economy?

- What are the challenges of the Doha Round of world trade talks?

- How are the developing countries disadvantaged by international trade?

- How have cotton subsidies affected the poor cotton-producing countries?

- Have industrialized countries delivered on their promise to increase aid to poor countries?

- Why has aid to Africa failed to make a bigger contribution to development?

- What are "vulture funds" and why have they come under major criticism?

- What are the causes and effects of the global food crisis?

- What are the criticisms of microcredit?

- What is the reason behind the optismistic belief that there will be a dramatic increase in Africa's agricultural production?

Student Web Site
www.mhcls.com/online

Internet References

Center for Third World Organizing
http://www.ctwo.org/
ENTERWeb
http://www.enterweb.org
International Monetary Fund (IMF)
http://www.imf.org
TWN (Third World Network)
http://www.twnside.org.sg/
U.S. Agency for International Development (USAID)
http://www.usaid.gov
The World Bank
http://www.worldbank.org

Economic issues are one of the most pressing concerns of the developing world. Economic growth and stability are essential to tackle the various problems confronting developing countries. Though the developing world is beginning to play a larger role in the global economy, many countries still continue to struggle to achieve consistent economic growth. Although there is some indication that the number of people below the poverty line is decreasing worldwide, over a billion people still live on less than a dollar a day. Economic inequality between the industrial countries and much of the developing world still exists. This is especially true of the poorest countries that have become further marginalized due to their limited participation in the global economy. Inequality within a developing countries is also obvious, where the elite's access to education, capital, and technology has significantly widened the gap between the rich and the poor. Since their incorporation into the international economic system during colonialism, the majority of developing countries have been primary suppliers of raw materials, agricultural products, and inexpensive labor. Dependence on commodity exports means that developing countries have had to deal with fluctuating, and frequently declining, prices for their exports. At the same time, prices for imports have remained constant or have increased. At best, this decline in terms of trade has made development planning difficult; at worst, it has led to economic stagnation and decline. Although industrialization in China and India has boosted demand for primary products, dependence on export of raw materials and agricultural goods is not an ideal long-term strategy for economic success.

With a few exceptions, most of the developing nations have had limited success in breaking out of this dilemma through the process of diversifying their economies. Efforts at industrialization and export of light manufactured goods have led to competition with the less efficient industries of the industrialized world. The response of industrialized countries has often been that of protectionism and includes demands for trade reciprocity, which can overwhelm the markets of the developing countries. The World Trade Organization (WTO) was established to standardize trade regulations and increase international trade, but critics charge that the WTO continues to be dominated by the wealthy industrial countries. The developing world also asserts that they are often shut out of trade negotiations, must accept deals dictated by the wealthy countries, and that they lack sufficient resources to effectively participate in the wide range of forums and negotiations that take place around the world. Moreover, developing countries charge that the industrialized countries are selective in their efforts to dismantle trade barriers and emphasize only those trade issues that reflect their interests. Delegates from economically poor countries walked out of the 2003 WTO ministerial meeting in Cancún, Mexico protesting the rich countries' reluctance to eliminate agricultural subsidies and their efforts to dominate the agenda. Neither the 2005 Hong Kong WTO ministerial meeting nor the 2006 talks in Geneva made much progress on a forming a comprehensive international trade agreement. In yet another effort to conclude

© Arabian Eye/PunchStock

an agreement, trade ministers agreed in 2007 to reopen negotiations. A successful conclusion to the Doha Round requires the willingness of both industrialized and developing countries to make concessions, the prospects of which are not likely. The economic situation in the developing world, however, is not entirely attributable to colonial legacy and protectionism on the part of industrialized countries. Developing countries have sometimes constructed their own trade barriers and have relied on preferential trade relationships. Evidence suggests that developing countries would benefit from dismantling their trade barriers even if the industrialized countries do not reciprocate. This may become even more important as preferential trade arrangements are phased out. Industrialization schemes involving heavy government direction were often ill-conceived or have resulted in corruption and mismanagement. Industrialized countries frequently point to these inefficiencies in calling for market-oriented reforms, but the emphasis on privatization does not adequately recognize the role of the state in developing countries' economies; and privatization may result in foreign control of important sectors of the economy, as well as a loss of jobs. Debt has further compounded economic problems for many developing countries. During the 1970s, developing countries' prior economic performance and the availability of petrodollars encouraged extensive commercial lending. Developing countries sought these loans to fill the gap between revenues from exports and foreign aid, and development expenditures. The second oil price hike in the late 1970s, the declining export earnings, and the worldwide recession in the early 1980s left many developing countries unable to meet their debt obligations. The commercial banks weathered the crisis, and some actually showed a profit. Commercial lending declined as an aftermath of the debt crisis, and international financial institutions became the lenders of last resort for many developing countries. Access to the World Bank and International Monetary Fund became conditional on the adoption of structural adjustment programs that involved steps such as reduced public expenditures, devaluation of currencies, and export promotion, all geared to debt reduction. The consequences of these programs have been painful for developing countries resulting in declining public services, higher prices, and greater reliance on the exploitation of resources. The poorest countries in particular have struggled with heavy debt burdens, and the IMF and World Bank have come under increasing criticism for their programs in these countries. Though these institutions have made efforts to shift the emphasis to poverty reduction, some critics charge that the reforms are superficial, that the international financial institutions lack accountability, and that the developing countries do not have adequate influence in decisionmaking. Eliminating the debt of the world's poorest countries was a major focus of the G-8 summit in July 2005 but whether the promised debt relief will have the desired effect remains to be seen. The emergence of so-called "vulture funds" that specialize in collecting unpaid debt has re-opened the controversy over Third World debt.

Globalization has produced differing views regarding the benefits and costs of this trend for the developing world. Advocates claim that closer economic integration, especially through trade and financial liberalization, increases economic prosperity in developing countries and encourages good governance, transparency, and accountability. Critics respond that globalization favors the powerful nations and through the international financial institutions, imposes difficult and perhaps counterproductive policies on the struggling economies. They also charge that globalization undermines workers' rights and causes environmental degradation. Moreover, most of the benefits of globalization have gone to those countries that are already growing—leaving the poorest even further behind. Partly due to the realization that the poverty in the developing world contributes to the despair and resentment that leads some to terrorism, there has been increased focus on foreign aid. The Commitment to Development Index tracks rich countries' contributions and ranks countries across several dimensions including foreign aid. The renewed emphasis on aid has also focused attention on how it can be used more effectively. While aid has often been criticized, it does produce benefits. Those benefits, however, could be enhanced by more effective implementation.

Industrial Revolution 2.0

In the corner offices of New York and Tokyo, business leaders cling to the notion that their designs, technologies, and brands are cutting edge. Increasingly, however, that just isn't so. In industries ranging from steel and cement to automobiles and electronics, "Third World companies" are poised to overtake their Western rivals. Get ready for the biggest firms you've never heard of to become household names.

ANTOINE VAN AGTMAEL

For a few minutes, I held the future in my hand. The third-generation cell phone in my palm made a BlackBerry look like a Model T Ford. Looking down at the color video screen, I could see the person on the other end of the line. The gadget, which fit easily into my pocket, could check local traffic, broadcast breaking television news, and play interactive computer games across continents. Internet and e-mail access were a foregone conclusion. So were downloading music and watching video clips.

None of this would be all that surprising were it not for where I was standing. I wasn't visiting Apple Computers in Cupertino, California, or Nokia headquarters outside Helsinki. It was January 2005, and I was in Taiwan, standing in the research lab of High Tech Computer Corporation (HTC). The innovative Taiwanese company employs 1,100 research engineers, invented the iPAQ pocket organizer (which it sold to Hewlett-Packard), and developed a series of advanced handheld phones for companies such as Palm, Verizon, and Vodafone. All around me were young, smart, ambitious engineers. They represented the cream of the crop of Taiwanese universities with, in some cases, years of experience in international firms. They were hard at work testing everything from sound quality in a sophisticated acoustics studio to the scratch resistance of newly developed synthetic materials.

I was being shown not just the prototype of a new smart phone but the prototype of a new kind of company—savvy, global, and, most important, well ahead of its nearest competitors in the United States and Europe. My experience in Taiwan is not that unusual. From Asia to Latin America, companies that many still regard as "Third World" makers of cheap Electronics or producers of raw materials are emerging as competitive firms capable of attaining world-class status. Only a decade ago, the attention of the international business community was focused on a new economy backed by hot tech firms in California and

Tokyo. But the reality of the current global dynamic is that, more likely than not, the next Microsoft or General Electric will come from the "new economies" of Asia, Latin America, and Eastern Europe, not the United States, Europe, or Japan.

Today, emerging-market countries account for 85 percent of the world's population but generate just 20 percent of global gross national product. By 2035, however, the combined economies of emerging markets will be larger than (and by the middle of this century, nearly double) the economies of the United States, Western Europe, or Japan. The reality of globalization—which is only slowly and reluctantly sinking in—is that outsourcing means more than having "cheap labor" toil away in mines, factories, and call centers on behalf of Western corporations. Yet in the West, business leaders and government officials cling to the notion that their companies lead the world in technology, design, and marketing prowess.

Just as the Industrial Revolution turned American companies from imitators to innovators, emerging-market multinationals will do the same.

Increasingly, that just isn't so. South Korea's Samsung is now a better recognized brand than is Japan's Sony. Its research and development budget is larger than that of America's Intel. And its 2005 profits exceeded those of Dell, Motorola, Nokia, and Philips, Mexico's CEMEX is now the largest cement company in the United States, the second largest in the United Kingdom, and the third largest in the world. The gas reserves of Russian giant Gazprom are larger than those of all the major oil companies combined, and its market capitalization—or total stock value—is larger than that of Microsoft. South Korean engineers are helping U.S. steel companies modernize their outdated plants. New proprietary drugs are being developed in Indian and Slovenian labs, where researchers are no longer content to turn out high volumes of low-cost generics for sale in the United States and Europe. New inventions in consumer electronics and wireless technology are moving from Asia to the United States and Europe, not just the other way around.

The growth in emerging-market companies has been nothing short of astounding. In 1988, there were just 20 companies in emerging markets' with sales topping $1 billion. Last year, there were 270, including at least 38 with sales exceeding $10 billion. In 1981, the total value of all stocks listed on stock exchanges in emerging markets was $80 billion. That was less than the market capitalization of the largest emerging-market firm, Samsung, in 2005. Over the past quarter century, the total market capitalization of emerging markets as a group has risen to more than $5 trillion. Twenty-five years ago, portfolio investors had invested less than a few hundred-million dollars in emerging-market firms. Today, annual portfolio investment flows of more than $60 billion constitute the leading edge of a trend. Fifty-eight of the Fortune 500 top global corporations are from emerging markets, and many of them are more profitable than their peers in the West. The era of emerging-market companies being nothing more than unsophisticated makers of low-cost, low-tech products has ended.

Lifting the Veil

Most people are blissfully unaware that companies from emerging markets already play a major part in their lives by making much of what they eat, drink, and wear. One reason that these new multinationals have flown below the radar of so many executives, as well as the general public, is that companies such as Taiwan-based Yue Yuen and Hon Hai remain deliberately hidden in the shadows. Even though Yue Yuen produces the actual shoes for Nike and Hon Hai makes much of what can be found inside Dell computers, Apple iPods, and Sony PlayStations, the bigger brands continue to control the distribution and marketing. When will they remove their veil? These firms' prevailing invisibility—a conscious stealth strategy in some cases—does not mean that they are powerless, less profitable, or that they will be content to have a low profile forever. It won't be long before the biggest companies you have never heard of become household names.

Companies like Samsung, LG, and Hyundai, all based in South Korea, began by making products efficiently and cheaply. Now, they have recognized brand names, a high-quality image, world-class technology, and appealing designs. China's Haier, the country's leading producer of household appliances, is following in their footsteps. In fact, it is already better known than GE, Sony, or Toyota by hundreds of millions of consumers in China, India, and other emerging markets. Firms such as Haier have not relied on big brand names to reach consumers in the United States and Europe. Instead, they used niche products such as small refrigerators and wine coolers to get their lines into big-box stores such as Walmart. And as time goes on, more

emerging-market firms will overtake the long-established Western companies that they now supply.

That has already happened in a number of industries ranging from semiconductors to beer. Samsung now holds the No. 1 global market position not only in semiconductors used in hard disks and flash memory cards but also in flat-screen monitors used for computers and televisions. In 2004, China's Lenovo purchased IBM's ThinkPad brand. In a wholly different industry, Brazilian investment bankers merged domestic beer companies in 1999 and then swapped shares with Europe's largest beer giant, Interbrew, to form a new entity that is now managed by a Brazilian CEO. Meanwhile, Corona beer, produced by Mexico's Modelo, is now the leading imported beer brand in the United States. Elsewhere, the global supply chain is turning upside-down, with Western companies selling components and services to multinationals from emerging markets. GE, for instance, sells jet engines to Brazilian plane manufacturer Embraer. Other smart firms will soon follow suit. Just as the rise of the United States after the Industrial Revolution turned American companies from imitators into innovators, emerging-market multinationals will increasingly do the same.

For many of these firms, the road to success included weathering global financial crises. These economic shocks squeezed out many emerging-market companies. The ensuing Darwinian struggle for survival left only battle-hardened firms still standing. As newcomers, emerging multinationals had to fight for shelf space against preconceived notions of inferior product quality (a bias that wasn't always without justification). When the financial crises were over, a few world-class companies had carved out leading roles. Today, more than 25 emerging-market multinationals have attained a leading global market share in their respective industries. Fifteen command the No. 1 market share—and they are no longer limited to a narrow slice of low-tech industries. The truth is, emerging multinationals now maintain dominant market positions in some of the world's fastest-growing industries. Consider Samsung, which is the global market leader in flash memory cards used in iPods, cameras, and mobile phones. The memory card market was worth $370 million in 2000. This year, it is valued at $13 billion. In fact, more than half of all emerging-market companies of world-class status operate in capital-intensive or technology-oriented industries, where high rates of spending on research and development are required to remain competitive.

Nothing to Lose

But the road to success has not been easy. Emerging-market multinationals did not succeed simply by following textbook practices and solutions. Contrary to popular belief, it is unconventional thinking, adaptability, a global mind-set, and disciplined ambition—not natural resources or the advantage of lowcost labor—that have been the crucial ingredients for their success. As newcomers, emerging-market firms could only wrestle away market share from deeply entrenched incumbents through audacious solutions. Their success hinged upon novel thinking that was widely ridiculed by competitors from the rich world. In many cases, emerging multinationals became

From Small-Time to Prime-Time

A growing number of companies in emerging markets now enjoy the No. 1 global market share for their products. Here's a look at some of the industries they dominate.

Company	Industry	Country
Samsung Electronics	Flat-screen televisions	South Korea
Aracruz Celulose	Market pulp for paper products	Brazil
Sasol	Synthetic fuels	South Africa
TSMC	Logic semiconductors	Taiwan
Yue Yuen	Athletic and casual shoes	Hong Kong
MISC	Liquified natural gas shipping	Malaysia
Embraer	Regional jet aircraft	Brazil
Gazprom	Natural gas	Russia
Hon Hai	Electronics manufacturing by contract	Taiwan
Tenaris	Oil pipes	Argentina

successful only by following the opposite of tried and true textbook policies. Two of the best examples are Taiwan's HTC and Argentina's Tenaris.

By the 1990s, Taiwanese companies had carved out a leading position in notebook computers and various PC accessories. But they were way behind on smaller, more cutting-edge personal digital assistants (PDAs) and smart phones. Until 1997, that is, when a group of Taiwanese engineers got together and decided that the future was elsewhere. Instead of making knockoff organizers or cheap cell phones, the engineers at HTC designed the stylish iPAQ, the first PDA to challenge Palm's unrivaled position. The iPAQ had elements that Palm and other manufacturers had studiously avoided—a Microsoft operating system, an Intel chip, and a Sony screen, all technologies that mobile companies had hitherto considered inferior. But HTC recognized that wireless technology would soon turn PDAs into pocket PCs, combining cell phones with e-mail and Internet access. That insight helped them land a contract to become the primary manufacturer of the Treo PDA and inspired them to embark on a leapfrogging Effort by designing a whole series of versatile handhelds and smart phones that eventually became the chief Windows-based competitors of BlackBerry.

A similarly innovative approach was taken in Argentina by oil-pipe manufacturer Siderca. Realizing that government protection had led to technological mediocrity and a poor global image, Siderca CEO Paolo Rocca decided that global oil giants wanted more than top-quality pipes. They wanted suppliers that could react quickly to their needs anywhere in the world, able to deliver a pipe to a remote oil well in the middle of Nigeria on short notice. Siderca already had loose alliances with companies in Brazil, Italy, Japan, Mexico, and Romania. Rocca transformed this ad hoc group of companies into a well-oiled machine that was able to integrate researchers from far-flung subsidiaries to invent sophisticated pipes that were increasingly in demand for deep-ocean and arctic drilling operations. He also introduced high-tech systems that enabled the company to deliver its pipes "just in time" to the major oil companies, a feat that took leading, rich-world players such as Mannesmann several years to match. When Rocca was finished, the small "club" of traditional Western oil-pipe makers had lost its stranglehold on the market.

Emerging markets now control the bulk of the world's foreign exchange reserves and energy resources.

Other examples abound. Take Aracruz, in Brazil. The company used eucalyptus trees to make market pulp, even though it had generally been looked down upon before as "filler pulp" while the "real" pulp was made from slow-growing pine trees. In Mexico, CEMEX began a global acquisition spree by taking over two Spanish cement producers after it was locked out of the U.S. market by anti-dumping laws. The company's CEO, Lorenzo Zambrano, says, "For Spaniards, the idea of a Mexican company coming to Spain and changing top management was unthinkable."

Superior execution and an obsession with quality are now hallmarks of virtually all of the world-class companies based in emerging markets. That has helped feed a mind-set in which emerging multi-nationals are no longer content with being viewed as leading Chinese, Korean, Mexican, or Taiwanese companies. They aspire to be global, and this aspiration is rapidly becoming a reality.

Back to the Future?

Those who recall the Cold War may be forgiven for entertaining a sense of déjà vu. The launch of Sputnik in 1957 prompted anxieties that the West was falling behind. Two decades later, the overwhelming success of Japanese firms Toyota and Sony resulted in alarmed cries that "the Japanese are winning." Similar calls, proclaiming that the Chinese and the Indians are winning, can be heard today. But those who speak of winners and losers are regarding the global economy as a zero-sum game. There is ample reason to believe that is not the case—not based on naive internationalism, but on the well-justified belief that, in the current global economic order, both sides can come out ahead.

Many emerging multinationals are already owned by shareholders from all over the world. Foreign shareholders own 52 percent of Samsung, 71 percent of CEMEX, 57 percent of Hon Hai, and 54 percent of India-based Infosys. As a group, emerging multinationals can claim about 50 percent of their ownership as being foreign. Emerging multinationals are also becoming significant employers in the United States and Europe, as well as attractive prospective employers for business school graduates and scientists. More than 30,000 people in the United States and Europe work for CEMEX, many more than the company employs in Mexico. Its management meetings are conducted in English, because more than half of the firm's employees do not speak Spanish. Hyundai just opened a plant in Alabama, creating 2,000 American jobs; its regional suppliers employ an additional 5,500 workers. Haier makes most of its refrigerators for the U.S. market at a plant in North Carolina.

Of course, the road ahead for these emerging-market winners will not be without setbacks. Motorola's Razr cell phone has already helped the firm recover much of the ground it lost to Samsung. CEMEX's aggressive acquisition strategy may have worked, but the takeover bids of other emerging multinationals have failed, including Haier's bid to buy Maytag. Others have fallen flat, such as the Taiwanese company BenQ's failure to turn around Germany's Siemens Mobile. The very fact that the Latin and Asian financial crises are receding in memory and that new public offerings by Chinese and Russian companies are often oversubscribed could tempt these emerging competitors to rest on their laurels. An unexpected crisis or decline in China's growth could deliver a blow to the economy that many con-

sider the anchor of the developing world. And a growing list of innovative companies—such as Amazon, Apple, Google, Qualcomm, and Toyota, with its new hybrid car in Japan— reveals that the rich world's creativity is far from dead.

Still, the larger trends are clear. In recent years, it has become apparent that the dominance of the United States as a superpower is resulting in its deepening dependence on foreign money, foreign resources, foreign professionals, and, increasingly, foreign technology. Only 25 years ago, most sophisticated investors scoffed at the notion of investing even a tiny portion of respectable retirement funds or endowments in developing-world companies. Just as the conventional wisdom then wrongly depicted emerging markets as "Third World," today it is all too common to underestimate the leading companies from these markets. Emerging markets now control the bulk of the world's foreign exchange reserves and energy resources. They are growing faster than the United States and many European countries (and have been for decades). Most have budget and trade surpluses, and a few are even recognized as major economic powers.

Standing inside a research lab in China, South Korea, or Taiwan, it is painfully clear just how stymieing Western protectionism has been for Western companies. Such measures led to a false sense of security, a reluctance to streamline, and a lack of innovative thinking in industries ranging from steel and automobiles, to electronics and cement. As Western firms spent the 1980s and 90s protecting themselves from foreign exports, emerging multinationals built campuses of bright, young software engineers in India and incredibly efficient mining operations in Brazil and Chile. Instead of denying the new reality, the West must formulate a creative response to this global shift of power. That task is now the central economic challenge of our time.

ANTOINE VAN AGTMAEL, known for coining the term "emerging markets," is founder and chief investment officer of Emerging Markets Management L.L.C. He is the author of *The Emerging Markets Century: How a New Breed of World Class Companies is Taking over the World* (New York: Free Press, 2007).

Governing Global Trade

The multilateral system that has underpinned world trade for over 50 years is facing serious challenges.

URI DADUSH AND JULIA NIELSON

With the Doha Round negotiations of the World trade Organization (WTO) proving to be drawn out and difficult, WTO ministerial conferences plagued by discord inside negotiating rooms and violent protests outside, and preferential trade agreements growing at an unprecedented rate, has the multilateral system of rules that has governed international trade in the postwar era outlived its usefulness?

Our answer is no. But, as for much of the postwar international architecture, the strength of the multilateral trading system cannot be taken for granted. The system is facing significant challenges, and two issues lie at their core: the increased role of developing countries and the sensitivity of the unfinished liberalization agenda. The picture is further complicated by the proliferation of preferential trade agreements. How these challenges are met will determine whether international trade will continue to be governed by multilateral disciplines or characterized by competing trade blocs and escalating disputes.

Underpinnings of Trade Growth

Measured by actual trade flows, the multilateral trading system would appear to have been very successful. Today, WTO members account for more than 90 percent of world trade in goods (including oil). Trade grew, on average, almost twice as fast as GDP between 1990 and 2005 (World Bank, World Development indicators). Global trade is expected to hit about $16 trillion in 2007, equal to 31 percent of world GDP.

At the same time, stocks of foreign direct investment grew almost five times as fast as world GDP. The domestic sales of foreign affiliates are larger than world exports and rely critically on trade in intermediate goods, further underscoring the importance of trade integration in modern economic activity.

Falling transportation costs and other technological innovations have been key drivers of trade growth, but declining barriers to trade have also contributed. Between 1983 and 2003, average applied tariffs on manufacturing in developing countries dropped from slightly less than 30 percent to about 9 percent (World Bank, 2007). Some two-thirds of this liberalization was undertaken unilaterally, and about one-fourth through multilateral agreements.

The trading system embodied in the General Agreement on tariffs and trade (the GATT, the WTO's predecessor) and now in the WTO has underpinned this liberalization in five important ways.

First, it has ensured that progress is locked in, guarding against backsliding, even as circumstances change. China's growing clout in the global economy has prompted calls for tariff increases in importing countries, but WTO rules have held increases in check. Lock-in matters: if Japan had bound its rice tariff in 1955 (bound tariffs, duty rates that countries commit to under the WTO, are difficult to raise), that tariff would still be 46 percent rather than more than 500 percent.

Second, the principle of nondiscrimination (most favored nation, MFN), which lies at the heart of the system, has helped ensure that new trade opportunities arising from tariff reductions under the GATT/WTO have been available to *all* countries participating in the system and not just to a favored few.

Third, the system's predictability and transparency have encouraged reform because countries know the parameters within which their trading partners operate and because of demonstration effects. Multilateral negotiations center on bound and not applied tariffs (the duty actually levied on an imported good, generally lower than the bound tariff), allowing countries to liberalize at their own pace, knowing that they would not waste negotiating chips as they reduced their applied tariffs.

Fourth, WTO accession has permitted countries to negotiate MFN treatment in exchange for liberalization commitments. China's accession in 2001 underpinned far-reaching domestic reforms and helped China become the world's third largest exporter. Accession of such countries as Vietnam, Saudi Arabia, and, prospectively, Russia may imply less far-reaching commitments but has brought, or is expected to bring, almost 250 million people into the mainstream of world trade.

Fifth, the WTO's dispute-settlement mechanism has enabled smaller, poorer countries to achieve changes to trade policies in much larger and more powerful countries. More than 300 disputes have been resolved, about one-third of them brought by developing countries (Messerlin, Zedillo, and Nielson, 2005). Moreover, a number of disputes never make it to court because of the mechanisms the WTO provides for countries to negotiate solutions.

Developing Countries are Key Players

A key question now is how to take account of the increasing role of developing countries. These countries have become major participants in world trade: their share of global exports rose from 22 percent in 1980 to 32 percent in 2005 and is expected to reach 45 percent by 2030 (see Chart 1) (World Bank, 2006). About two-thirds of the WTO's members are developing countries.

Reaching agreements. The strength of the WTO is that it is based on a contract among its members, and its core function is to provide a forum for governments to negotiate with each other. But consensus decision making in the WTO, with 151 members, can be long and arduous. The frank, back-room exchanges that led to deals in the past have become increasingly unwieldy as the membership and expectations of inclusiveness have grown. If the United States and the European Union can no longer present deals to other members as a fait accompli, reaching agreement essentially remains a process of concentric circles: tentative agreements among a small circle of major players and/or small countries for which the issue is critical (in what is known as the "Green Room" process) are gradually extended to others, with additional concessions or adjustments along the way.

A debate has arisen about the inclusiveness of this process, in part because some of the poorest members are not represented at the WTO in Geneva, and other developing countries attempt to cover the broad agenda with small delegations. The solution has been an informal system of like-minded countries—whose leaders are represented in the Green Room process—coming together on particular issues.

Reaping the benefits. Although representative groups of countries are essential, one of the strengths of the negotiating process in the WTO is the fluidity of the alliances that

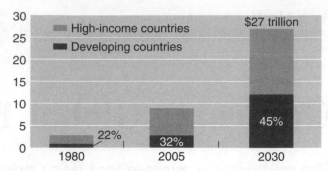

Chart 1 Major Traders. Developing countries are playing an active role in world trade. (total exports, trillion 2001 dollars)
Source: World Bank simulations with Linkage model.

comprise them. Countries can be allies on one issue and opponents on another. This fluidity is a healthy sign of the seriousness with which obligations are taken.

Central to the WTO's success has been the fact that countries have multiple interests that they are constantly balancing against each other. A suboptimal outcome in one area can be accepted in the context of gains in other areas. These trade-offs make consensus possible.

But many of the poorest WTO members may not see a balance of gains across the system. Their immediate gains may be limited to a handful of products, reflecting the lack of diversification in their exports. For them, it may be worth blocking consensus on a broader deal over the outcome on a single issue.

Even developing countries with broader trade interests may feel they cannot benefit from the system. The WTO can reinforce domestic reforms, but reforms are not without adjustment costs, and some developing countries may struggle to provide safety nets. Others may be unable to invest in the machinery necessary to reap the benefits from some WTO agreements (for example, related to standards). Critically, they may be unable to take advantage of new market access.

High costs and delays from inefficient customs, ports, and transportation constrain exports from developing countries. the location of labor-intensive apparel production, traditionally an important export for poor countries, is increasingly determined by lead time and reliability requirements. Costs per operator hour in Kenya may be more than 10 percent lower than in coastal China, but lower productivity and less efficient supply chains eliminate that advantage (Werner international; World Bank, 2007). Shifts into higher-value-added products are also constrained by weak infrastructure.

Some of the poorest countries fear that the system may even harm their interests. Those that have received unilateral preferences for particular products fear that liberalization by trading partners will erode the value of these preferences. They oppose not only their own liberalization, but also liberalization *by others* because of the adjustment costs,

More aid for trade. Additional aid to address these constraints—aid for trade—will be an essential complement to any multilateral trade deal. Paradoxically, part of the solution to helping poor countries feel that they have a stake in the trading system lies in the broader development community, with donors supporting countries that highlight trade as a priority in their development strategies. But donors will need to honor their commitments to increase overall aid if trade needs are to be better addressed without competing for resources with existing development priorities.

Differentiation. Developing countries have formed influential coalitions and are playing a more active role in the Doha Round negotiations. For example, the Group of 20, led by Brazil and India, argues for agricultural reform in developed countries.

This greater activism has occurred in parallel with the decision to make development the focus of the current negotiations. But negotiations under the Doha Development Agenda have struggled, in part because of differences over what a "development round" means. There is general agreement that rich countries should reduce trade barriers, but some think the development round means a focus on developing countries' own reforms, and others feel that development is best served by additional flexibility *not* to reform. Considerable debate has focused on how much flexibility should be extended and to whom.

WTO rules grant "special and differential treatment" to developing countries, with additional flexibility for the least developed countries. But there is no further generalized differentiation by income level among developing countries. The 18 low-income countries that are not classified as least developed receive no additional special treatment beyond that extended to all developing countries. Developing countries also self-designate in the WTO and include some high-income (Singapore) countries. This has complicated negotiations because developed countries are reluctant to extend to China the special treatment they may grant to Cameroon.

There is pressure for greater differentiation among developing countries, both from some developing countries—such as small economies—that want their special problems recognized and from developed countries that want to limit flexibility for more advanced developing countries. However, most developing countries resist greater differentiation, in part because, despite their diverse interests, it undermines their power as a group. For the system to remain relevant beyond the Doha Round, it is likely that reforms will need to be considered to increase the speed and flexibility of the negotiating apparatus.

The Unfinished Agenda

Challenges also remain on the substance of the regotiating agenda.

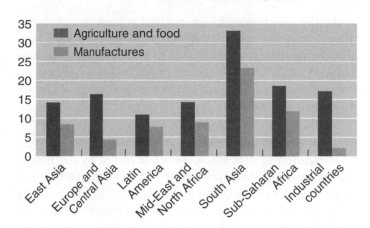

Chart 2 Protection For Agriculture. Barriers are much higher in agriculture than in manufacturing. (average tariffs, percent)

Source: World Bank calculations based on Purdue University, Global Trade Analysis Project, version 6.03.

Agricultural protection. Fifty years of the multilateral trading system has seen limited progress in reining in agricultural protection. In all regions, tariffs remain significantly higher in agriculture than in manufactures (see Chart 2), and trade-distorting subsidies, banned in manufacturing, continue to be a feature of the agricultural sector. According to the Organization for Economic Cooperation and Development, rich-country taxpayers (in the form of subsidies) and consumers (in the form of higher prices because of trade barriers) pay about $268 billion a year to support agriculture, with the European Union ($134 billion), Japan ($47 billion), and the United States ($43 billion) leading the pack.

Meanwhile, in developing countries, 73 percent of the poor live in rural areas, and agriculture and agroprocessing account for 30–60 percent of GDP and an even larger share of employment. But agricultural protection is also high in developing countries, to the detriment of their own poor consumers, exporters, and other poor countries, which are increasingly their trading partners.

Bringing agriculture into line with trade rules for other sectors is an important test of the WTO's ability to deliver for development—all the more because the multilateral system is the only forum in which agricultural subsidies (which cannot be reduced on a preferential basis) can be tackled.

Protection on manufactures. Although the remaining high tariffs in developed countries tend to be concentrated in areas of developing country export interest (labor-intensive manufactures, such as clothing), protection in developing countries is some four times higher than in high-income countries. The price of high tariffs in developing countries is, again, paid by their own consumers, exporters (whose competitiveness in world markets and participation in global production chains are harmed by more expensive inputs), and their developing country trading partners (which account for one-fourth of developing country exports).

As the counterpart to agricultural reform in rich countries, developing countries should be prepared to lower and bind their tariffs on manufactures in the current negotiations. There is considerable scope to do so: bound tariffs are, on average, some two and a half times higher than applied tariffs in developing countries.

Protection on services. But the gains from further liberalization in manufactures are dwarfed by the potential gains from liberalization in services: the increase in real income from halving protection on services would be five times larger than that from comparable liberalization in goods trade. Global trade in services accounts for $2.8 trillion, or not quite one-fifth of world trade (World Bank, World Development indicators). Access to quality and cost-effective services, such as finance, transport, and telecommunications, plays a key role in determining competitiveness.

But market opening in services is complex because new regulations or institutions may be needed to ensure that liberalization strengthens competition and that important public policy goals—such as universal service—are met. Aid for trade may be needed for the design of regulations and financing of new institutions in developing countries. Regulatory and political challenges are also entailed in an area of key offensive interest for developing countries in the Doha Round: the temporary movement of people to supply services. Greater coordination between trade and migration authorities will be required to realize the potential for win-win outcomes for both developed countries with aging populations and developing countries with large numbers of young job seekers.

Current WTO commitments on services are significantly less liberal than the regimes being applied, and narrowing this gap will be an important objective of the current negotiations. Progress in binding services liberalization is a further quid pro quo for the industrial countries in return for their politically difficult reforms in agriculture.

Pressure to include new issues. Notwithstanding this unfinished agenda, some of the most advanced WTO members are seeking rules in new areas, reflecting the sophistication of their economies. Many of these areas (such as competition policy) require investments in domestic institutions, investments that may not represent development priorities for resource-strapped countries.

The system is also under increasing pressure to address such issues as human rights, migration, labor, and environmental concerns. Part of the reason is the effectiveness of the WTO's dispute-settlement system, but the absence of similar mechanisms in the other organizations that exist to address such issues suggests that the problem is one not of forum but of political will.

The PTA Debate

Whether PTAs enhance welfare depends on their design. Although deep integration agreements and open regionalism may benefit the parties and assist MFN liberalization, not all PTAs are high quality, some are net trade diverting, and still others are paper agreements. Such PTAs are creating a web of different requirements, posing problems for small traders in poor countries. Simplified and nonrestrictive rules of origin are critical if PTAs are to promote participation in global production chains, as are parallel reductions in MFN tariffs to limit the scope for trade diversion.

But PTAs, which have been around for centuries, often reflect geopolitical objectives or the desire for more and faster liberalization than can be achieved multilaterally. Few would challenge the notion that PTAs are here to stay. But the WTO can help minimize possible harm. it can promote greater transparency and opportunities for learning and help reduce their trade-diverting effects. And the WTO remains the only place where agricultural subsidies can realistically be tackled and is the key channel for the major trading powers to manage their trade relationships with each other.

This pressure also reflects the fact that globalization has seen large trends in the global economy (often understood as trade) affecting people's lives more directly than ever before. While the system may find it difficult to resist the pressure to address new issues, WTO members' energies would be better spent addressing those outstanding trade issues, such as egregiously high protection on agriculture, that lie at the core of what the system can deliver for development.

Managing these challenges is further complicated by the proliferation in recent years of reciprocal preferential trade agreements (PTAs): more than 200 PTAs are in force, a sixfold increase over the past two decades (see box). By 2010, close to 400 PTAs are due to be implemented.

The challenges facing the multilateral trading system are difficult, and we offer no blueprint for their resolution beyond general observations. the system is a global public good of enormous importance, and its importance grows along with the share of trade in world economic activity. We must continue to build on the existing foundations that have served the global economy well to date. A successful conclusion to the Doha Round will be critical, and a Doha deal along the lines currently being negotiated is possible and would bring significant benefits. Not least, it would demonstrate that the WTO remains capable of making inroads into the large unfinished agenda we have outlined.

References

Messerlin, Patrick, Ernesto Zedillo, and Julia Nielson, 2005, trade for Development, Report of the UN Millennium task Force on trade (London: Earthscan for the UN Millennium Project).

Newfarmer, Richard, ed., 2006, Trade, Doha and Development: A Window into the issues *(Washington: World Bank).*

Werner International; information supplied to authors in 2006.

World Bank, World Development Indicators database.

_____, *2004,* Global Economic Prospects 2005: Trade, Regionalism and Development *(Washington).*

_____, *2006,* Global Economic Prospects 2007: Managing the Next Wave of Globalization *(Washington).*

_____, *2007, "Aid for Trade: Harnessing the Global Economy for Economic Development," paper prepared for the Development Committee, World Bank Annual Meetings, 2007.*

URI DADUSH is Director of the World Bank's International Trade Department, in which Julia Nielson is a Senior Trade Specialist.

Social Justice and Global Trade

Joseph Stiglitz

The history of recent trade meetings—from Seattle to Daha to Cancun to Hong Kong—shows that something is wrong with the global trading system. Behind the discontent are some facts and theories.

The facts: Current economic arrangements disadvantage the poor. Tariff levels by the advanced industrial countries against the developing countries are four times higher than against the developed countries. The last round of trade negotiations, the Uruguay Round, actually left the poorest countries worse off. While the developing countries were forced to open up their markets and eliminate subsidies, the advanced developed countries continued to subsidize agriculture and kept trade barriers against those products which are central to the economies of the developing world.

Indeed, the tariff structures are designed to make it more difficult for developing countries to move up the value-added chain—to transition, for instance, from producing raw agricultural produce to processed foods. As tariffs have come down, America has increasingly resorted to the use of nontariff barriers as the new forms of protectionism. Trade agreements do not eliminate protectionist sentiments or the willingness of governments to attempt to protect producer and worker interests.

The theories: Trade liberalization leads to economic growth, benefiting all. This is the prevalent mantra. Political leaders champion liberalization. Those who oppose it are cast as behind the times, trying to roll back history.

Yet the fact that so many seem to have been hurt so much by globalization seems to belie their claims. Or more accurately, it has shown that the process of "liberalization"—the details of the trade agreements—make a great deal of difference.

That Mexico has done so poorly under NAFTA has not helped the case for liberalization. If there ever was a free trade agreement that should have promoted growth, that was it, for it opened up to Mexico the largest market of the world. But growth in the decade since has been slower than in the decades before 1980, and the poorest in the country, the corn farmers, have been particularly hurt by subsidized American corn.

The fact of the matter is that the economics of trade liberalization are far more complicated than political leaders have portrayed them. There are some circumstances in which trade liberalization brings enormous benefits—when there are good risk markets, when there is full employment, when an economy is mature. But none of these conditions are satisfied in developing countries. With full employment, a worker who loses his job to new imports quickly finds another; and the movement from low-productivity protected sectors to high-productivity export sectors leads to growth and increased wages. But if there is high unemployment, a worker who loses his job may remain unemployed. A move from a low-productivity, protected sector to the unemployment pool does not increase growth, but it does increase poverty. Liberalization can expose countries to enormous risks, and poor countries—and especially the poor people in those countries—are ill equipped to cope with those risks.

Perhaps most importantly, successful development means going stagnant traditional sectors with low productivity to more modern sectors with faster increases in productivity. But without protection, developing countries cannot compete in the modern sector. They are condemned to remain in the low growth part of the global economy. South Korea understood this. Thirty-five years ago, those who advocated free trade essentially told Korea to stick with rice farming. But Korea knew that even if it were successful in improving productivity in rice farming, it would be a poor country. It had to industrialize.

What are we to make of the oft-quoted studies that show that countries that have liberalized more have grown faster? Put aside the numerous statistical problems that plague almost all such "cross-country" studies. Most of the studies that claim that liberalization leads to growth do no such thing. They show that countries that have traded more have grown more. Studies that focus directly on liberalization—that is, what happens when countries take away trade barriers—present a less convincing picture that liberalization is good for growth.

But we know which countries around the world have grown the fastest: they are the countries of East Asia, and their growth was based on export-driven trade. They did not pursue policies of unfettered liberalization. Indeed, they actively intervened in markets to encourage exports, and only took away trade barriers as their exports grew. They avoided the pitfall described earlier of individuals moving from low-productivity sectors into zero productivity unemployment by maintaining their economies at close to full employment.

The point is that no country approaches liberalization as an abstract concept that it might or might not buy in to for the good of the world. Every country wants to know: For a country with its unemployment rate, with its characteristics, with its financial markets, will liberalization lead to faster growth?

If the economics are nuanced, the politics are simple. Trade negotiations provide a field day for special interests. Their agenda is also straightforward: Exporters want others' markets opened up; those threatened by competition do not. Trade negotiators pay little attention to principles (though they work hard to clothe their position under the guise of principle). They pay attention to campaign contributions and votes.

In the most recent trade talks, for example, enormous attention has been focused on developed countries' protection of their agricultural sectors—protections that exist because of the power of vested agricultural interests there. Such protectionism has become emblematic of the hypocrisy of the West in preaching free trade yet practicing something quite different. Some 25,000 rich American cotton farmers, reliant on government subsidies for cotton, divide among themselves some $3 billion to $4 billion a year, leading to higher production and lower prices. The damage that these subsidies wreak on some 10 million cotton farmers eking out a subsistence living in sub-Saharan Africa is enormous. Yet the United States seems willing to put the interests of 25,000 American cotton farmers above that of the global trading system and the well-being of millions in the developing world. It is understandable if those in the developing world respond with anger.

The anger is increased by America's almost cynical attitude in "marketing" its offers. For instance, at the Hong Kong meeting, U.S. trade officials reportedly offered to eliminate import restrictions on cotton but refused to do anything about subsidies. The cotton subsidies actually allow the U.S. to export cotton. When a country can export a particular commodity, it does little good to allow imports of that commodity. America, to great fanfare, has made an offer worth essentially zero to the developing countries and berated them for not taking it up on its "generous" offer.

At home, the Bush administration might be working harder to provide greater access to low-cost drugs. In trade negotiations, though, it takes the side of drug companies, arguing for stronger intellectual property protection, even if the protection of pharmaceutical-company patents means unnecessary deaths for hundreds of thousands of people who cannot afford the monopoly prices but could be treated if generic medicines were made available.

The international community has announced its commitment to helping the developing countries reduce poverty by half by 2015. There have been enormous efforts at increasing aid and debt relief. But developing countries do not want just a hand out; they want a hand up. They need and want enhanced opportunities for earning a living. That is what a true development round would provide.

In short, trade liberalization should be "asymmetric," but it needs to be asymmetric in a precisely opposite way to its present configuration. Today, liberalization discriminates against developing countries. It needs to discriminate in their favor. Europe has shown the way by opening up its economy to the poorest countries of the world in an initiative called Everything But Arms. Partly because of complicated regulations ("rules of origin"), however, the amount of increased trade that this policy has led to has been very disappointing thus far. Because agriculture is still highly subsidized and restricted, some call the policy "Everything But Farms." There is a need for this initiative to be broadened. Doing this would help the poor enormously and cost the rich little. In fact, the advanced industrial countries as a whole would be better off, and special interests in these countries would suffer.

There is, in fact, abroad agenda of trade liberalization (going well beyond agriculture) that would help the developing countries. But trade is too important to be left to trade ministers. If the global trade regime is to reflect common shared values, then negotiations over the terms of that trade regime cannot be left to ministers who, at least in most countries, are more beholden to corporate and special interests than almost any other ministry. In the last round, trade ministers negotiated over the terms of the intellectual property agreement. This is a subject of enormous concern to almost everyone in today's society. With excessively strong intellectual property rights, one can have monopolies raising prices and Stirling innovation. Poor countries will not have access to life-saving medicines. That was why both the Office of Science and Technology Policy and the Council of Economic Advisers opposed the TRIPS (intellectual property) provisions of the Uruguay Round. It reflected the interests of America's drug and entertainment industries, not the most important producers of knowledge, those in academia. And it certainly did not reflect the interests of users, either in the developed or less-developed countries. But the negotiations were conducted in secret, in Geneva. The U.S. trade representative (like most other trade ministers) was not an expert in intellectual property; he received his short course from the drug companies, and he quickly learned how to espouse their views. The agreement reflected this one-sided perspective.

Several reforms in the structure of trade talks are likely to lead to better outcomes. The first is that the basic way in which trade talks are approached should be changed. Now, it is a clear negotiation. Each country seeks to get the best deal for its firms. This stands in marked contrast to how legislation in all other arenas of public policy is approached. Typically, we ask what our objectives are, and how we can best achieve them. Around those themes, of course, there are negotiations. There are often large differences in views both about what should be the objectives and how best to achieve them. If we began trade talks from this position of debate and inquiry, we could arrive at a picture of what a true development round look like.

Thinking of the task of the WTO as creating a legal framework reflecting principles of fairness, social justice and efficiency—akin to how we think about domestic rules and regulations governing economic behavior—helps us think about what other reforms are needed. We simply need to think about how we attempt to improve the quality of domestic democratic processes and legislation by increasing, for instance, transparency and other governance reforms.

Transparency is essential so there can be more open debate about the merits of various proposals and a chance to put a check on the abuses special interests. Clearly, had there been more transparency and open debate, the excesses in intellectual property protection of the Uruguay Round might have been avoided.

As more and more countries have demanded a voice in trade negotiations, there is often nostalgia for the old system in which four partners (the U.S., EU, Canada and Japan) could hammer out a deal. There are complaints that the current system with so many members is simply unworkable. We have learned how to deal with this problem in other contexts, however, using the principles of representation. We must form a governing council with representatives of various "groups"—a group of the least developed countries, of the agricultural exporting countries, etc. Each representative makes sure that the concerns of his or her constituency are heard. Such a system would be far better than the current "green room" procedures wherein certain countries are put together (in the green room) to negotiate a whole or part of the deal.

Finally, trade talks need to have more focus. Issues like intellectual property should never heven have been part of the Uruguay Round. There already was an international institution dealing with matters of intellectual property. It is not only that trade ministers are ill-equipped to understand what is at issue, and they are therefore subject to undue influence from the special interests that have long held sway over trade ministries. Broadening the agenda also puts developing countries at a particular disadvantage, because they do not have the resources to engage on a broad front of issues.

The most important changes are, however, not institutional changes, but changes in mindset. There should be an effort on the part of each of the countries to think about what kind of international rules and regulations would contribute to a global trading system that would be fair and efficient, and that would promote development.

Fifteen years ago, there was a great deal of optimism about the benefits which globalization and trade would bring to all countries. It has brought enormous benefits to some countries; but not to all. Some have even been made worse off. Development is hard enough. An unfair trade regime makes it even more difficult. Reforming the WTO would not guarantee that we would get a fair and efficient global trade regime, but it would enhance the chances that trade and globalization come closer to living up to their potential for enhancing the welfare of everyone.

MR. STIGLITZ is a professor of economics at Columbia University. In 2001, he was awarded the Nobel Prize in economics.

From *Far Eastern Economic Review,* March 2006, pp. 18–21. Copyright © 2006 by Far Eastern Economic Review. Reprinted by permission of Far Eastern Economic Review via the Copyright Clearance Center.

Cotton: The Huge Moral Issue

World cotton prices have dropped to an historic low: the reason being the immoral continuation of EU and US trade subsidies that allow non-competitive and inefficient farming to continue. While the recent WTO meeting in Hong Kong failed to resolve the issue, the livelihoods of West Africa's 12 million cotton farmers will soon be destroyed if subsidies are not slashed. This is a huge moral issue.

KATE ESHELBY

Seydou, dressed in a ripped T-shirt that hangs off his shoulders, looked at me blankly as I questioned him about the effects of US subsidies on his only source of income, cotton farming. "I don't know about cotton in the US but I know cotton prices have fallen here in Burkina Faso," he lamented.

The farmers working in the cotton fields of Burkina Faso, often in remote locations, have little knowledge of the intricacies of world markets. What they do know is that the price they receive for their cotton harvests—essential for basic necessities such as medicines and school fees—is dropping fast.

The end of cotton farming in Burkina Faso and other cotton producing West African countries is rapidly approaching. World cotton prices have dropped to an historic low: the reason being the immoral continuation of EU and US trade subsidies that allow non-competitive and inefficient farming to continue.

Cotton subsidies in richer countries cause over production, artificially distorting world markets. And who suffers? The poor countries, whose economies are wholly dependent on the cotton trade.

In Burkina Faso, a former French colony in West Africa, cotton is the country's main cash crop. It is the primary source of foreign income, making up one-third of export earnings, and the lifeblood for the majority of farmers. Here cotton is grown on small, family-owned farms, seldom bigger than five hectares. One farmer, called Yacouba, explains: "I also grow maize and groundnuts on the farm, to feed my family, but cotton is my only source of cash."

In contrast, US cotton operations are enormous and yet, unlike Burkina Faso, cotton is a minimal proportion of its GDP. Ironically, the US subsidies are concentrated on the biggest, and richest, farms. One such farm based in Arkansas has 40,000 acres of cotton and receives subsidies equivalent to the average income of 25,000 people in Burkina Faso.

The benefits of subsidies only reach a small number of people in the US and other Western countries, whereas two million people in Burkina Faso, one of the world's poorest countries with few other natural resources, depend on cotton for survival.

The farms in Burkina Faso are very productive, it is cheaper and more economical to grow cotton there than in the US. "I have to take out loans each year to buy enough insecticides and fertilisers for my cotton," says Yacouba. "They are very expensive so we have to work hard to ensure we get a good harvest. Each year I worry whether I will earn enough to pay back the loans." Burkinabe farmers are forced to be efficient, also prevailing against climatic uncertainties and limited infrastructure—all this, with no support from subsidies.

Fields are prepared by plough and both seed planting and picking are done by hand, which explains why cotton is also vital for providing jobs—being very labour intensive. Yacouba explains: "My family works on the farm throughout the year, but during harvesting we bring in extra help." Pickers are dotted around the fields surrounding him, plucking the cotton balls from the shoulder-high plants. Some of the women have children tied to their backs and the sacks of cotton are steadily placed under the shade of a giant baobab tree. This scene is in stark contrast to the US where huge, computerised harvesters pick the cotton and aerial spraying administers the chemicals required.

The meeting (in mid-December 2005) of the World Trade Organisation (WTO) in Hong Kong was to address this farcical situation as part of the Doha "development" talks. But nothing much came out of it. Burkina Faso is still resting its hopes on cotton subsidies being eliminated, or at least reduced, in order to save its fundamental crop from demise. The Doha negotiations, launched in 2001, are intended to show that trade could benefit the world's poor. But subsidies are a global injustice, and create major imbalances in world trade—it is argued they should only be available for products that are not exported, and targeted towards family and small-scale farmers.

The US gives approximately $3.4bn a year in subsidies to its 25,000 cotton farmers; this is more than the entire GDP of Burkina Faso. Subsidies dramatically increased in the US after the 2002 Farm Act and as a result US cotton production has recently reached historic highs. It is now the world's second largest cotton producer, after China, and the biggest exporter—an easy achievement because US cotton prices no longer bear any relation to production costs.

Current world cotton prices are in decline due to global over-production, fuelled by agricultural subsidies. EU and US taxpayers and consumers pay farmers billions of dollars to over-produce for a stagnant market. These surpluses are then dumped overseas, often in developing countries, destroying their markets and driving down world prices.

The livelihoods of West Africa's 12 million cotton farmers will soon be destroyed if subsidies are not slashed. This is a huge moral issue. It is simple—Burkina Faso cannot compete against heavily subsidised exports.

In March 2004, a WTO panel ruled that the majority of US cotton subsidies were illegal. The WTO agreements state that "domestic support should have no, or at most minimal trade-distorting effects on production." The US tried to appeal against this decision but it was overruled.

If Africa took just 1% more in world trade, it would earn $70bn more annually—three times what it now receives in aid. In 2003, Burkina Faso received $10m in US aid, but lost $13.7m in cotton export earnings, as a result of US subsidies. No country ever grew rich on charity, it is trade that holds the key to generating wealth. Fair trade would give the Burkinabe cotton farmers a decent opportunity to make a living by selling their produce, at a decent price, to the richer world; enabling them to work their way out of poverty.

The US was legally required to eliminate all trade-distorting subsidies by 21 September 2005, according to a WTO ruling. President George Bush keeps saying he will cut subsidies, but actions are louder than words. The delay is partly due to a long-standing arm wrestle between the US and the EU, neither of whom will budge. The British prime minister, Tony Blair, does seem to want to abolish EU subsidies, but the French argue that subsidies are not even negotiable. Despite four years of haggling, negotiators are still at loggerheads. Numerous reports have been compiled, many meetings held and yet scant progress has been made—and things are only getting worse for the Burkinabe cotton farmers.

"Both the US and EU brag about their boldness, but the actual reform they propose is minuscule, tiny fractions of their massive farm support. The negotiations have recently moved into the finger-pointing phase in which rich countries criticise the inadequacy of each other's proposals. Meanwhile, poor countries await something real," says Issaka Ouandago, from Oxfam's office in Burkina Faso.

Oxfam has been supporting the struggle of African cotton farmers in their campaign known as the "Big Noise", and are hoping to gather a petition of one million signatures against cotton subsidies. "We can only hope the US reform their subsidy programmes and stop dumping cheap cotton onto the world market," Ouandago continues. "Despite their WTO commitments to reduce trade-distorting subsidies, the EU and US have used loopholes and creative accounting to continue. Such practices are undermining the fragile national economics of countries that depend on cotton."

The rich countries have to come forward with more, otherwise the Doha Round will achieve nothing, as the meeting in Hong Kong proved—although developing countries have less political power, they are still capable of blocking the negotiations if they don't get what they want. In the last WTO meeting, held in Geneva, July 2004, negotiations on US cotton subsidies were supposed to be kept separate from broader agricultural negotiations—this did not happen. It was a blow for Burkina Faso and other West Africa countries who produce mainly cotton and are less interested in other commodities. A subcommittee on cotton was set up to "review" the situation, but the EU and US have not taken this committee seriously.

With the emergence of the G20 alliance, some developing countries, such as India and Brazil, are now powerful enough to resist pressures, but African countries have previously never been centre stage. West African cotton producers are, however, becoming far stronger as a group. "We have become more united to make our voice heard. Our aim is to gather all African cotton producers together," explains Yao, a member of the National Union of Cotton Producers in Burkina Faso.

The only reason Burkinabe cotton farmers are still surviving is that producer prices have been maintained at a minimum level-175 CFA per kg of cotton seed is the minimum price the farmers need to break even, prices never go below this, despite being above current world prices.

In recent years, the Burkinabe cotton companies used their profits from previous harvests to support the farmers; these savings are now depleted. The full effects of world prices have, therefore, not yet been felt by the farmers, the worst is to come—once the prices are forced to drop below this minimum, the farmers can no longer survive.

Leaving the house of Seydou, I wonder about his fate. A pile of bright-white cotton sits drying in the glaring sun, in front of his mud house. Inside the walls are bare, except for a single cross; a bundle of clothes hang from a rope and a pile of maize is stacked in the corner. "I cannot afford to buy things because cotton prices keep fluctuating," he says. "I know cotton grows well here but prices are down so I cannot send my youngest son to school. This makes me sad. I know his only chance of a good future is school."

In Burkina Faso, cotton is the country's biggest interest and essential to its economy, so it prays that cotton is addressed more seriously and given the attention it deserves. As the sun sets, the workers leave the fields, holding sacks of cotton above their heads. A donkey cart trundles by, carrying a mound of cotton—kicking up a trail of red earth. Their livelihoods depend on the decisions made at the WTO.

Ranking the Rich

Poverty is blamed for everything from terrorism to bird flu. Rich nations have never sounded more committed to stamping it out. Is it all just hot air? The fourth annual CGD/FP Commitment to Development Index ranks 21 rich nations on whether they're working to end global poverty—or just making it worse.

Last year was dubbed the "Year of Development." Leaders of the world's richest nations made impassioned pleas to help the poor at a summit in Gleneagles, Scotland. At the World Economic Forum in Davos, French President Jacques Chirac proposed an airline ticket tax to fund foreign aid. At a world trade summit in Hong Kong in December, rich countries offered to phase out subsidies for their agricultural exports. U2 rocker-activist Bono jetted everywhere from Nigeria to the National Prayer Breakfast in Washington, touting The One Campaign to end global poverty, and movie stars donned insignia bracelets in support of his cause. "There can be no excuse, no defense, no justification for the plight of millions of our fellow human beings," British Prime Minister Tony Blair said in March. "There should be nothing that stands in the way of our changing it."

But are the world's richest countries actually making things better for those most in need? Each year the Center for Global Development and FOREIGN POLICY look past the rhetoric to measure how rich country governments are helping or hurting poor countries. How much aid are they giving? How high are their trade barriers against imports such as cotton from Mali or sugar from Brazil? Are they working to slow global warming? Are they making the world's sea lanes safe for global trade? To find out, the index ranks 21 nations by assessing their policies and practices across seven areas of government action: foreign aid, trade, investment, migration, environment, security, and technology.

In large part, the deeds of the last year did not live up to the talk. In most policy areas that matter for poor countries, a majority of rich-country governments either failed to follow words with meaningful action—or they simply remained silent. At Gleneagles, British and American negotiators pushed through an agreement to "drop the debt" for up to 40 poor, mostly African countries. It may sound extraordinarily generous, but this debt relief package equals a mere 1 percent increase in aid. The Group of Eight (G-8) industrialized nations also "committed" themselves to "substantially reducing" subsidies and tariffs that protect their farmers at the expense of farmers in poor countries. Again, it may have sounded good, but the G-8's offer, spelled out later in the year, was only equivalent to cutting the European Union's import barriers by 1 percent. The feebleness of the offer is one reason why world trade

negotiations remain hopelessly deadlocked. No development news of the past year commanded more headlines than immigration. In the United States, millions of Latin American migrants marched in the streets and boycotted their jobs in an effort to draw attention to the positive contributions they make to America's economy. In France, demonstrations in the Paris suburbs turned violent as the country's interior minister, Nicolas Sarkozy, announced he might deport tens of thousands of immigrants back to their home countries. Yet this hotly debated issue was followed by precious little action. Prime Minister Blair convened a Commission for Africa, but it studiously avoided talking about how Britain could make it easier for someone from Kenya or Ghana to immigrate, get a job, develop skills, and send money home. In the United States, immigration legislation brewed in the U.S. Congress, but then stalled. And the subject was equally taboo for French politicians.

A less publicized event of 2005 was the notable growth in total foreign aid given by rich countries. It shot to a record $106.5 billion, thanks largely to reconstruction efforts in Iraq. But some $19 billion of that aid came in the form of the cancellation of old loans to Iraq and Nigeria. These write-offs, though long overdue, put little new money in the hands of Iraqis and Nigerians. These aid figures should also be kept in perspective. Consider that India and China added some $400 billion to their combined economic output last year alone. That's proof that internal, not external, forces more often drive economic development. China's export of goods and India's export of services to rich countries have helped produce economic growth and poverty reduction so rapid that the Millennium Development Goal of a 50 percent cut in the number of people living on $1 a day has probably already been met on a global level.

Internal factors may drive development, but external ones can facilitate it—or stand in the way. That point was made by Andrew Natsios, the former head of the U.S. Agency for International Development, when he challenged America's longstanding food aid program before stepping down in January. Natsios criticized a law that requires the U.S. government to buy food from U.S. farmers, ship it on American boats, and deliver it to famine-stricken regions via U.S.-based organizations. The U.S. government must deliver food aid this way even when it depresses local food prices, pushing more farmers into poverty, and even when it

And the Winner Is . . .

This year, the Netherlands beat Denmark to take the No. 1 ranking in the index. A new policy to limit imports of illegally cut timber from tropical nations and its support for an international effort to control bribery helped land the country in the winner's circle this year.

But the main reason the Netherlands came out on top is because others stumbled. The Danes, who have historically been among the index's best performers, registered the largest overall drop. Copenhagen was hurt by a shrinking of its foreign aid spending by 14 percent between 2001 and 2004, while its economy grew by 9 percent. New Zealand also fell, as the number of immigrants it admitted from developing countries plunged from 48,000 in 2001 to 29,000 last year.

One country that made strides this year is Japan, which has finished dead last every year since the index was launched in 2003. It reportedly put an end to a long-held practice of lobbying poor-country governments against enforcing labor, human rights, and environmental standards for Japanese-owned factories. The United States improved its score, due in part to falling farm subsidies and rising foreign aid. Spain posted the most spectacular gains, thanks to a migration policy that makes it easier for immigrants to enter and work legally.

For the 21 rich countries as a whole, the overall trend continues to be one of little change. The average score for all the index countries climbed modestly from 5.0 in 2003 to 5.3 in 2005, then fell slightly to 5.2 this year. Still, twice as many countries have seen their score improve as have seen their score decline in the past four years. That's an encouraging trend, because development is about more than just giving money; it's about the rich and powerful taking responsibility for policies that affect the poor and powerless.

CDI Performance over Time

Country	2003	2004	2005	2006	Change 2003 2006	Rank by Improvement
Spain	3.9	4.4	4.7	4.8	+0.9	1
United Kingdom	4.6	4.8	5.3	5.1	+0.5	2
United States	4.5	4.9	5.0	5.0	+0.5	2
Japan	2.7	2.9	2.8	3.1	+0.4	4
Portugal	4.4	4.9	4.9	4.8	+0.4	4
Sweden	5.9	6.5	6.6	6.3	+0.4	4
Canada	4.9	5.1	5.3	5.2	+0.3	7
Greece	3.7	3.9	4.1	4.0	+0.3	7
Ireland	4.7	4.8	4.9	5.0	+0.3	7
Italy	4.0	4.2	4.5	4.3	+0.3	7
Norway	5.9	6.1	6.2	6.2	+0.3	7
Finland	5.2	5.4	5.6	5.4	+0.2	12
Austria	5.3	5.4	5.4	5.4	+0.1	13
Belgium	4.8	4.6	4.9	4.9	+0.1	13
Switzerland	5.3	5.0	5.1	5.2	0.1	15
France	4.7	4.8	4.8	4.6	0.1	15
Germany	5.4	5.3	5.5	5.3	0.1	15
Netherlands	6.7	6.7	6.8	6.6	0.1	15
Australia	5.8	5.7	5.7	5.5	0.3	19
New Zealand	5.9	5.6	5.6	5.6	0.3	19
Denmark	7.0	6.9	6.7	6.4	0.6	21
Average	5.0	5.1	5.3	5.2	+0.3	

could buy food from farmers just outside a famine zone for much less. Some nongovernmental organizations that get a large fraction of their funding from the program defended the status quo, arguing that dropping the "made in America" requirement would undermine the program's support among American farmers and shippers. Congress quickly axed Natsios's proposal for reform. That the U.S. government must pay off American interests to feed the starving is a sad commentary on how low the commitment to development may still be.

It also helps explain why the United States finishes 13th in this year's index. The Netherlands, meanwhile, ranks first on the strength of its generous aid-giving, falling greenhouse gas emissions, and support for investment in developing countries. Japan improved, but remains in last place as the rich country least committed to helping the poor. It might seem strange that small nations such as the Netherlands beat out large economies such as Japan and the United States. But the index measures how well countries are living up to their potential. In truth, even the Dutch could do better. They are party, for instance, to Europe's Common Agricultural Policy, which effectively levies a 40 percent tax on farm imports from poor countries. That certainly doesn't help world's poorest countries, no matter what anyone says.

Commitment to Development Index 2006

2006 rank	Country	Aid	Trade	Investment	Migration	Environment	Security	Technology	Average
1	Netherlands	8.5	6.2	7.8	4.8	7.5	6.1	5.3	6.6
2	Denmark	10.0	5.9	5.3	5.0	6.1	6.9	5.5	6.4
3	Sweden	9.8	6.1	6.2	4.8	7.0	4.9	5.4	6.3
4	Norway	9.3	1.2	8.0	4.6	6.1	8.1	5.9	6.2
5	New Zealand	2.2	7.6	3.7	6.9	6.4	7.4	4.9	5.6
6	Australia	2.5	6.4	6.9	6.4	3.9	8.1	4.6	5.5
7	Finland	3.9	6.1	6.2	2.7	6.7	6.3	6.3	5.4
7	Austria	2.7	5.9	3.3	10.5	6.2	4.5	4.5	5.4
9	Germany	3.3	5.9	6.8	6.2	6.7	3.7	4.3	5.3
10	Canada	3.3	6.8	7.7	4.7	4.5	3.0	6.6	5.2
10	Switzerland	4.8	3.1	7.2	9.5	5.3	1.6	5.1	5.2
12	United Kingdom	4.6	5.9	8.6	2.6	7.8	1.6	4.5	5.1
13	United States	2.2	7.4	6.9	4.6	3.2	5.9	5.0	5.0
13	Ireland	5.9	5.7	2.5	4.6	7.5	5.9	3.0	5.0
15	Belgium	5.1	5.9	6.5	2.6	6.6	3.4	4.5	4.9
16	Portugal	2.3	6.1	6.2	1.4	6.4	6.2	5.1	4.8
16	Spain	2.5	6.0	6.7	5.2	3.8	3.5	6.1	4.8
18	France	4.1	6.0	5.9	2.6	6.1	0.5	6.9	4.6
19	Italy	1.6	6.1	5.5	3.2	4.8	3.9	5.1	4.3
20	Greece	2.7	5.9	4.0	1.7	5.2	5.6	3.0	4.0
21	Japan	1.1	−0.4	5.6	1.7	4.3	2.8	6.3	3.1

Wasting Aid in Iraq

Last year was a record-smasher for foreign aid. Total aid given by index countries climbed 31.4 percent in 2005, to $106.5 billion. Not surprisingly, flows to Iraq accounted for most of this increase. This sharp rise in generosity, however, is not as much a cause for celebration as it might appear. Rarely has so much been given, and so little received.

Some $6.3 billion of the 2005 aid total was U.S. aid to Iraq, probably the largest single-year transfer between two countries since the Marshall Plan. But the index counts aid to Iraq at just 10 cents on the dollar, because the World Bank puts the country ahead of only Somalia when it comes to combating corruption and enforcing the rule of law. Sadly, events in 2005 confirmed fears about the country's rampant graft and violence. Senior Iraqi government officials estimate that as much as 30 percent of the country's budget is lost to corruption—ranging from bribery to padded contracts and influence peddling. It isn't just the Iraqis who are poor administrators. Even the U.S. government estimates that $8.8 billion disappeared during the first 14 months that the Coalition Provisional Authority ran Iraq. As of early 2005, at least 40 percent of U.S. reconstruction aid was spent on security. "I'd say that 60, maybe even 70 percent [of what] we see as reconstruction aid goes into nonproductive expenditures," says Ali Allawi, Iraq's minister of finance.

Nor are donors as generous as they would have us believe. Of the reported aid to Iraq, $14 billion came in the form of debt relief. Back in the 1980s when Saddam Hussein had warmer ties with the United States, France, and other Western governments, he borrowed heavily from them. The loans went bad after the 1991 Gulf War. But, on paper, interest and penalties piled up until the formal write-off of the debts in late 2004. Although long overdue, in reality this debt relief put almost no additional cash into the coffers of the new Iraqi government, because most of the debts would never have been repaid anyway. Commitment? Yes. Development? Hardly.

The Government Trough

Rich countries spend $84 billion a year subsidizing their farmers. That's nearly as much as they spend on foreign aid, which is about $29 a year for each of the world's 2.7 billion people who live on less than $2 a day. Poor people often get less assistance than the rich world's farm animals. The European Union, for example, doles out almost $30 per year for each sheep living there. In Norway and Switzerland, each cow gets nearly $1,000 of the government's money a year. These subsidies push down global agricultural prices and undermine farmers in poorer countries. Bellying up to the government's trough has never been so costly.

Subsidies per Head per Year (in U.S. $)

Country	Cattle	Chickens	Pigs	Sheep	Aid per poor person in developing world
EU 15	$179.28	1¢	$9.24	$28.93	$16.11
Australia	$17.12	39¢	$6.49	94¢	54¢
Canada	$68.59	15¢	$18.99	0¢	95¢
Japan	$163.23	21¢	$3.92	0¢	$2.38
New Zealand	$2.66	13¢	$2.14	19¢	8¢
Norway	$965.72	$1.48	$39.98	$94.06	83¢
Switzerland	$987.58	$7.83	$139.62	$16.11	61¢
United States	$29.06	58¢	$9.03	$4.12	$7.67
All	$92.59	38¢	$10.58	$12.85	$29.17

Hooray for High Gas Prices

The price of oil has tripled since 2002. That has rich people in the developed world complaining. But for poor countries, it's good news when the rich world pays high prices at the pump. That's because higher gas prices encourage more fuel-efficient cars, less driving, and, ultimately, slower global warming. Poor countries are the most vulnerable to the consequences of climate change, including rising sea levels, floods, and the spread of infectious diseases. The United Nations, for instance, estimates that a mere 1.5-foot rise in sea level could flood more than 6,000 square miles of Bangladesh, displacing 12 million people.

Because taxes on gasoline are one factor that drives up prices, the higher a country's gas taxes, the better it does in the index. The United States, Canada, and Australia have the cheapest gas among the 21 index countries, mainly due to low government taxes. Their citizens also consume the most fuel. For instance, U.S. gasoline taxes average just 39 cents per gallon, whereas in Europe they range between $2.56 and $4.18 a gallon. When gas taxes are low, it is the poor in developing countries who pay the heaviest price.

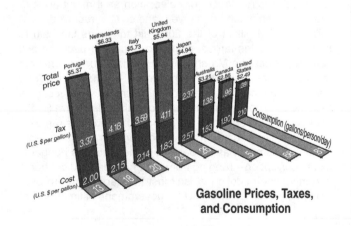

Gasoline Prices, Taxes, and Consumption

Development Begins at the Ballot Box

Democracy has its virtues. Democratic nations, for instance, rarely go to war against each other. Nobel laureate economist Amartya Sen has noted that democracies tend to avoid famines. In the 1960s, while China's Great Leap Forward killed 30 million people, democratic India found ways to feed its growing population. To this list of democratic virtues, the index can add one more: A commitment to democracy at home means a greater commitment to development abroad.

At the World Bank, researchers have built a measure of the quality of democracy, which they call "Voice and Accountability." It is a mathematical synthesis of expert judgments gathered by groups including Freedom House and the Economist Intelligence Unit, which measures elements of democracy such as free and fair elections and how much the government represses dissent. Governments in wealthy countries haven't been shy about using these scores to make favorable comparisons between themselves and developing countries.

But the mirror is equally revealing when turned the other way. When the World Bank's data are compared to the index, it is clear that the more accountable a government is to its own people, the more it does for those to whom it is not accountable. It's not just that a handful of Nordic nations give lots of foreign aid. In fact, as Jörg Faust of the German Development Institute has found, the pattern persists when aid is dropped from the index. The Netherlands, for instance, not only gives aid generously, but is reducing its greenhouse emissions, has put in place policies that support investment in developing countries, and actively contributes to peacekeeping operations around the globe. At the opposite extreme, Japan, which has the second-least accountable government after Greece, has a small aid program and high barriers to workers and agricultural imports from poor countries.

This pattern likely stems from the fact that in wealthy democracies with less accountable governments, special interests hold more sway. They divert government spending away from foreign aid, force aid to be "tied" to spending on donor-country companies, and promote self-interested trade barriers. Development may take place abroad, but the index shows that it often begins at home.

Democracy at Home, Development Abroad
More democracy means a greater commitment to development.

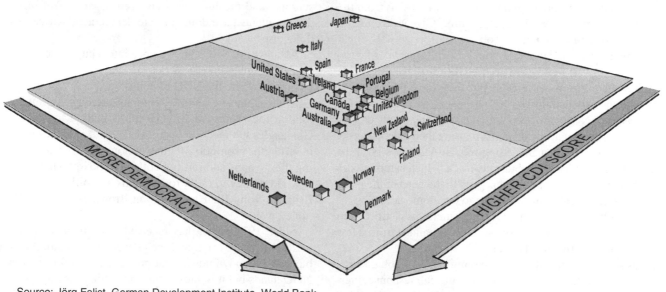

Source: Jörg Falist, German Development Institute, World Bank

Foreign Aid II

This Kind of 'Help' Is Just No Help at All

Aid agencies are not living up to their responsibilities. The new age missionaries seem to have become more of a contributor than a solution to Africa's crises

MICHAEL HOLMAN

The multi-billion dollar aid industry has largely failed in Africa. Not only have they failed along with others in the aid industry, most nongovernmental organisations (NGOs) have become part of the problem. Not that they will admit their failure. They refuse to share the blame for the grim record. Instead they have closed ranks—along with UN development agencies and bilateral agencies—and all sing from the same hymn sheet: 'Aid works', they claim. 'Give us even more money and we will complete the job . . .'

They would say that, wouldn't they? The alternative is far too uncomfortable. The rapid growth of NGOs dealing with Africa has given them enormous power, but they have been slow to adapt to their responsibilities.

Increasingly, NGOs are becoming the spending agents of government development agencies, and are losing their independence. One consequence of their increasing role in Africa has been the atrophy of the muscles of the State in Africa, which in turn erodes loyalty to the State—and I think this goes to the heart of the problems that beset Africa, from corruption to low domestic savings.

The growth of the foreign NGO movement (as distinct from local NGOs) began in the 1970s, and has expanded from a few hundred to tens of thousands today.

It was a response to Africa's deepening crisis—debt, disease, war and disaster. Initially it was a humanitarian response, literally 'first aid'. It soon widened to broad development assistance: from helping to run railways to supplying health clinics, and staffing policy-making teams in government.

But the type of NGO aid, and the attitudes attached to it, reflected ideological battles—socialism versus capitalism, to put it crudely—that NGOs had lost at home and instead fought abroad in states such as Tanzania and Zambia.

As crisis deepened, the number of agencies rose.

Today they still fight these battles over water privatization, for example. NGOs are outraged that water should be sold for a profit, overlooking the fact that from Lagos to Luanda, the poor already pay for their water.

The NGOs' role in telecommunications and deregulation—which led to the growth in mobile phones, independent radio stations, and the Internet—has been negative. Yet these three developments have done more to democratise Africa than anything else.

Meanwhile, NGOs have tapped into a huge reservoir of support and compassion for Africa, and persuaded the public to put its money where the NGO mouth is.

Their domestic public relations strategy is outstanding: look at the professional NGO lobby behind the pop stars at Gleneagles G8 meeting last year. The aid agencies were there in strength, promoting their solutions for Africa's ills, rallying their troops and rattling collection boxes. There is a lot of new aid money to rattle for: billions and billions of dollars, if Britain's Tony Blair and Gordon Brown get their well-intentioned way.

Since 1971 Africa has received more than $350bn in aid; in 2004 it was $15bn, and the Gleneagles' intention is to double this. Nobody knows what proportion of aid passes through NGO hands but it is substantial and getting bigger.

While Africa's crisis has deepened and its problems have multiplied, so the number of foreign NGOs has risen. The more NGOs around, the steeper a country's economic decline. And the NGO staff don't come cheap.

An estimated $4bn is spent annually on recruiting some 100,000 expatriates in Africa, many of them for jobs with NGOs. The result is that there are more foreigners working in Africa than there were at independence five decades ago. They are helping to run everything from ministries to mines, working as policy-makers and performing heroics on the front line against poverty.

Yet Africa's management capacity is weaker today, according to the World Bank, than in the 1960s. The greatest danger to Africa is that it lacks the skills that are needed to manage its own recovery.

As foreigners arrive to take up short-term contracts, each year about 70,000 skilled Africans—doctors, engineers, nurses—leave to work abroad. Western governments should ask whether the growth of NGOs is not only a symptom of Africa's crisis, but perhaps part of the cause. Why are there so many NGOs? How do they coordinate? Where do they get their money? Do they train their staff, and if so what are they taught? What proportions of funds comes from official aid agencies, which increasingly use the NGOs as a conduit?

Some tough questions for the west.

How effectively do the NGOs spend it? Who monitors the spending? Are they adept at spinning the aid story at home, while lacking professionalism in the field? In short, do the NGOs have power and influence without responsibility?

Of course, no one can feel anything but admiration for emergency humanitarian missions, such as the International Red Cross or Oxfam's front-line troops. Today the NGO role usually goes well beyond first aid assistance to people in dire distress. They are important to the development of the region where they are based. However, neither the NGOs nor the official agencies are prepared to accept a share of the blame for Africa's development disaster.

Kenya is a case in point. Forty years after independence and billions of dollars of aid and countless hours of NGO work, the country is miserably worse off. The government itself acknowledges that nearly six in every ten people subsist on less than two dollars a day, and the figure is rising.

It is easy to forget that Kenya is a poor country: it has no mineral resources; two-thirds of the land is arid or semi arid. In a good year of rain, it can feed itself. But good years are the exception and that is not going to change.

Meanwhile the population has doubled in 25 years. There are more mouths to feed and the shambas (farms) are becoming

---

10 Ways of Prospering Without Aid

ENCOURAGE IDEAS The high cost of books in Africa is a de facto tax on ideas. Publishers in rich countries should allow African publishers to print a limited run of their books. If the authors forgo royalties and publishers co-operate, locally printed versions could sell at a fifth of the foreign price.

MAKE FOREIGN NGOS COMPETE NGOs should work more with the private sector: much of their development work should be open to tender. Companies running large projects should include a social component (primary education or healthcare) that the voluntary agencies would tender for and operate.

THE PRIVATE SECTOR SHOULD BUILD INFRASTURCTURE In Kenya, the potholed Nairobi-Mombasa road should be rebuilt under a build-operate-transfer scheme. The construction company operates the project for an agreed period before handling it to the state.

CHARGE FOR PROFESSIONALS' VISAS Professionals who emigrate from Africa, whether doctors or dentists, engineers or lawyers, should have to pay a market rate for the privilege of a visa which allows them to work abroad. The money raised should be used in the emigrants' countries of origin to train replacements.

CHOCOLATE MUST CONTAIN MORE COCOA Double the minimum amount of cocoa required to make chocolate under current trade rules. Cocoa prices will rise and chocolate will taste better.

PROMOTE AFRICAN MUSIC Africa needs a Nashville-style centre to promote its music and attract more commercial backing. It would be a centre for the production of great music and would train managers and musicians.

MAKE AID CONDITIONAL ON IMPROVING THE BUSINESS CLIMATE The latest International Finance Corporation's report on impediments to business shows that registering a company in Kenya takes ten times longer than in Hong Kong and requires five stages, compared to two. This is repeated across Africa, whether registering a business, selling property or recovering a debt.

ABOLISH TAXES ON COMPUTERS EXPORTED TO AFRICA Privatisation, deregulation and the emergence of democracy go hand in hand. Computers are critical to this development. In return, African governments would end import levies on computers.

FAIR TAXES ON COFFEE AND FAIR RETURNS FOR FARMERS Imported raw coffee is taxed at a third of the rate of processed beans, the first stage in a trading system that ensures that less than 0.2% of the value of processed coffee is retained by the growers themselves. Reforming this tax will benefit Africa's growers and their families, some 60m people. There should also be better marketing and packaging for Africa's products. East Africa's coffee producers now use attractive vacuum-sealed, foil packets but in Congo a fine soap made from pure palm oil is sold wrapped in newspaper and in northern Uganda, mangoes rot on the ground because no one can dry and package them to international standards. Foreign retailers should share their expertise with African traders.

10. **GIVE POWER TO AFRICA'S WOMEN** Disenfranchise African men for 5 years.

—Michael Holman and Andrew Rugasira

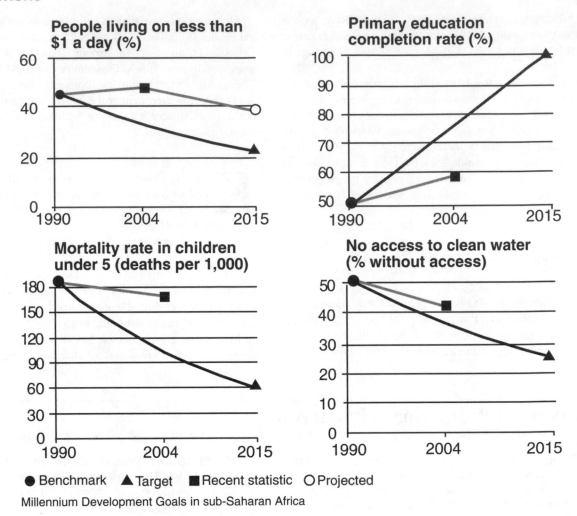

People living on less than $1 a day (%)

Primary education completion rate (%)

Mortality rate in children under 5 (deaths per 1,000)

No access to clean water (% without access)

● Benchmark ▲ Target ■ Recent statistic ○ Projected

Millennium Development Goals in sub-Saharan Africa

smaller and less viable as they get sub-divided. North-east Kenya is worst hit, and much of the food aid is going there.

Have the donors, by providing food over the past four decades, effectively subsidised the people living there, or encouraged families to move there from other parts of Kenya and so helped create the very problem they now seek funds to alleviate? We all know what food aid can do to local agriculture.

Also, by providing food, medicine and shelter, the NGOs may be ensuring that the government of Kenya doesn't have to bear the consequences of its incompetent, corrupt mismanagement. This undermines the relationship between the State and the citizen, with profound consequences.

There is an unwritten contract between the State and the citizen. The State should provide security, the rule of law, and basic services—in return, the citizen has a loyalty to the State and pays taxes. But if the State does not deliver, why should citizens be loyal? Instead the loyalty goes to the clan, the tribe, the region.

What is the role of aid workers in all this? By going beyond first aid and taking over services (the World Food Programme, for example, assists in the management of Kenya railways) the NGOs ensure that the State is cushioned from the consequences of its incompetence.

The NGOs also assist in weakening the State, and contribute to its decline under a system of tribal barons who call themselves cabinet ministers. Yet the belief that NGOs can circumvent corrupt governments, which they helped create, is at the heart of the argument of those who defend increases in British aid to Kenya.

Britain's Development Minister Hilary Benn argues: "Just because poor people live in a country where corruption is a serious problem, does that mean they do not deserve our assistance if it can be effective? . . .Our support to Kenya will mean textbooks in its primary schools and 11m treated bed-nets, saving lives." Minister Benn not only fails to understand the root causes of corruption but he also fails to understand how corruption works, day after day, in Kenya. Textbooks or bed-nets, they cannot avoid being tainted.

The process begins when the consignments arrive at Kenyatta airport and the first pay-off comes when they have to be cleared through customs. It continues when they pass through the numerous police road-blocks en route to their destination. And when they arrive, they are used as patronage or leverage.

Far from challenging conventional wisdom, many NGOs have become little more than an arm of official donor policy.

Why Statistics Are Damn Lies and Dangerous Too

There are just a handful of African countries which maintain reliable statistics. Yet the World Bank and UNDP report, with great precision, about levels of literacy across the continent, or the number of children at school, or radios per head, or maternal death rates.

Official accounts tell us that Africa's GDP has been measured, more or less accurately, and it has fallen or risen by remarkably precise percentages, over or below another remarkably precise percentage—the rate of population increase.

The truth is we really do not know very much about the state of the continent. None of us—Afro-pessimists or Afro-optimists—know how many Africans have access to secure shelter, or clean water, or indeed how many Africans live on the continent, or the rate at which the overall number increases.

We do know that Africa's most populous nation is Nigeria. But we do not know whether there are 100m or 150m Nigerians. The last reliable census was conducted before independence, more than 40 years ago, and more recent efforts are distorted by religious allegiances and financial demands.

We have no idea how many people live in Congo—the last census was in the 1950s. We do know that many people have died, directly or indirectly, in the war there. But when an aid agency says over 3m have died, it is sucking its thumb. There is no way of testing whether the claim is accurate. All it means is that a great many people have perished.

We just don't know. But we pretend to know, or are fooled by bogus statistics.

Aiding and abetting this deception is a cocoon of comfort for visitors, especially journalists, diplomats, businessmen and aid workers. An insulated environment created by business-class travel, five-star hotels, four-wheel drive vehicles, mobile phones, and laptop computers. Living and working in this cocoon creates an illusion of progress, but only for this elite.

The reality on the ground is very different. Conditions for most Africans have got worse over the years due to war, neglect and mismanagement.

Do statistics and assumptions based on guesswork make any difference?

Yes, because Western policy on Africa is built on these false assumptions, using these blunt tools, Ever since the World Bank rang the alarm bell I the early 1980s, warning of Africa's deepening crisis', these non-words, flawed concepts and spurious statistics have been at the heart of Western policy analysis.

Western politicians are reluctant to concede that the policies they have been implementing, costing voters billions of aid dollars, may not work. Indeed, the policies may be part of the problem, and not part of the solution.

Far from admitting defeat, the politicians declare victory. They use a shaky set of so-called 'facts' to reach the conclusion that aid is working, that Africa is recovering—slowly, erratically, perhaps—but recovering nonetheless.

One of Africa's most encouraging developments in recent years has been the growth in civil society, but foreign NGOs have played only a modest part.

Two policy shifts, reluctantly made by African governments, have boosted local democracy: state-controlled television and radio was deregulated, and the telecommunications sector is being privatised. More information became available, mobile phone ownership soared, and the Internet took off.

But many NGOs are still rooted in an ideological past, fighting battles on African soil which have been long lost at home, in which privatisation, profit and the private sector are all treated with deep suspicion.

Aid isn't working, but the aid lobby pretends it is. They do so by treating Africa as one vast Potemkin village. The term goes back to Catherine the Great. One of her generals, Gregori Potemkin, had elaborate fake villages constructed in advance of her tours of the Ukraine and the Crimea.

The term—Potemkin village—today means something that appears elaborate to impressive but in fact lacks substance. In Africa, realities on the continent are concealed by a Potemkin like structure.

Africa's Potemkin village has been erected by well-meaning outsiders. Reality is either distorted or hidden behind false assumptions, phoney statistics, and misleading language.

Schools without books, airports without runways

So when we read about the post-independence developments in Africa—in health, or education, or the damage wrought by war or famine—we use and read words involving concepts that seem familiar. But these words have a substance, a meaning, or an implication that is inappropriate in Africa, however suitable they are in Europe. So we'll read or send reports that refer to villages, clinics, schools, universities, and airports and we will refer to rises or falls in GDP, or the number of Africans subsisting on a dollar or less a day. Yet all too often we are talking about non-villages or un-schools or ex-airports.

What we don't have are words for an airport without a runway, or schools without classrooms, universities without books. Or prime ministers without power, or presidents without a civil service. Or central bank governors without banking systems, and finance ministers without finance.

Yet the assumption is that in Africa these institutions exist and function, roughly in accordance with their counterparts in Europe. We might acknowledge that the "hospital" may be short of medicine. But we assume that it is there, just as we assume that the finance minister has powers he can exercise.

We erect fantastical superstructures, for example, called development plans, using statistics that are no more than extrapolations, built on assumptions, which in turn are based on information from the colonial era. Reality across Africa is different.

We should be worried by the accuracy and quality of reporting on Africa.

When reality is not an objective appraisal, when it becomes what we, who work in or on Africa—journalists, diplomats, aid workers—think it is, or think it should be, we are doomed to make mistakes.

Sometimes, through ignorance, or because the agents of Western policy are out of their depth, a dangerous new reality is created. The NGOs did this in Congo in the mid-1990s, when their warnings of refugees heading for the eastern border became a self-fulfilling prophecy. Refugees gathered by the scores of thousands on the eastern border, having walked there because they knew from their radios that food from donors awaited them.

Although most governments and commentators accept the importance of the private sector in development, NGOs remain suspicious if not downright hostile. A functional partnership between business and the NGOs seems far away.

It's not just that Africa has gone backwards, it is the way the rest of the world has gone forwards which is not understood. The international flow of goods, services, capital and labour dwarfs our imaginings. There's a good reason why Britain is no longer a manufacturer (more efficient producers in Asia), why services are becoming tradable (more productive workers in India), why the huge US current account deficit doesn't matter (inward capital flows), and why developed countries want Malawian doctors and nurses (losing their own elsewhere, or not producing them in the first place).

These developments—like corruption and capital flight—have big implications for Africa. NGO people still don't get this. Not many people do.

From *The Africa Report,* October 2006, pp. 26–30. Copyright © 2006 by The Africa Report. Reprinted by permission.

The Debt Frenzy

From Argentina to Zambia, investment firms are snatching up the poor world's debt. To turn a buck, they sue, harass, and otherwise claw their way into making debtor states pay. Poverty activists say these so–called vulture funds are preying on the impoverished. But they're only doing what the international financial system can't—holding corrupt and irresponsible regimes to account.

DAVID BOSCO

President Denis Sassou Nguesso of the Republic of the Congo likes to live large. In New York City for a series of U.N. meetings last year, he and his entourage holed up at the Waldorf Astoria hotel, where the president prefers to stay. When his party checked out six days later, their tab came to more than $100,000. Sassou Nguesso racked up more than $20,000 in room service charges alone for items including Cristal champagne. It was just the latest indulgence for the president of the impoverished central African nation, which has a per capita gross domestic product of around $1,700 and an average life expectancy of 54 years. In 2005, the president's Manhattan hotel bills exceeded $300,000.

Sassou Nguesso may not have anticipated that his profligate habits would be splashed across the pages of major Western newspapers, as they were earlier this year. But he shouldn't have been surprised. The president has acquired some resourceful adversaries, with good connections and a desire to expose official excess. Their motive? Congo owes them tens of millions of dollars.

Like most governments, Congo has at various times borrowed large sums of money from Western banks and investors. The transactions make sense in theory. The government gets cash it needs, and investors get a legally binding promise of regular interest payments. But like many other poor and mismanaged countries, Congo soon found that it couldn't keep up with the payments. Prodded by activist-rock stars like Bono, many Western governments and multilateral institutions have forgiven billions in debt owed by poor countries. But even so, it is only a fraction of what poor governments like Congo owe. These governments must also pay billions to private investors and businesses, who are often far less charitable.

In the case of Congo, money is owed to Elliott Associates, a hedge fund whose specialties include collecting debts owed by governments. From its offices in Manhattan, Elliott has emerged as the chief debt collector to a host of governments. Colloqui-ally, if somewhat invidiously, referred to as "vulture funds," Elliott and several similar hedge funds fight governments to ensure they pay what they owe. The countries that vulture funds chase down are usually poor and frequently corrupt—Liberia, Nicaragua, Peru, Sierra Leone, Uganda, and Zambia, to name a few. Most vulture funds are based offshore and keep a low profile. One of the most aggressive fund managers is Kenneth Dart. He is heir to a Styrofoam cup fortune, lives in the Cayman Islands and rarely speaks to the media. Firms like his buy up the sovereign bonds and other debts of struggling countries, often at bargain basement prices. Then they do what most Western banks aren't inclined to do and what individual investors don't know how to do: They sue, harass, and shame debtor governments into paying at least a chunk of what they owe. And they do well. In 1998, Peru paid Elliott more than $58 million for a debt the fund had bought for much less. Nicaragua has been ordered to pay more than $200 million. Just this year, Zambia was ordered to pay a British Virgin Islands-based vulture fund more than $15 million. In all, it is estimated that private creditors hold judgments in excess of $1 billion against some of the world's poorest countries.

Claiming the High Ground

Unsurprisingly, vulture funds have become the favorite punching bags of the debt forgiveness movement. "These people are trading in human misery," spits one debt relief campaigner. Congo's Sassou Nguesso calls the vulture funds "snakes in the ocean" and "thug gangsters." The disdain for these debt collectors is shared in Western capitals, too. "By depleting the resources of developing countries' governments, these companies reduce the funds available for schooling and hospital treatment," declares a spokesman for Britain's treasury. Caroline Pearce of the Jubilee Debt Campaign believes that the vulture funds are misguided, even when their targets are middle-income countries that are better positioned to pay. "The way that vulture funds buy out very bad debt and seek to recover as much as possible is not helpful," she says.

Sitting in his understated office in midtown Manhattan, Jay Newman doesn't come across as socially irresponsible. A portfolio manager at Elliott Associates, he is slight and soft-spoken. But if Newman lacks Bono's volume, he can almost match him in righteous fervor. His contempt for governments that refuse to pay what they owe runs deep, as does his belief that vulture funds are a critical check on the "moral hazard" of debt default. Where the debt forgiveness activists see poor countries in need of relief, Newman sees corrupt, deadbeat countries "dragging our legal system down by disregarding the rule of law." Newman and his colleagues simply reject the idea that vulture funds are extracting money from the coffers of the poor. "Debt relief advocates should recognize that the beneficiaries of debt relief are often corrupt or incompetent regimes that squander their nations' assets and then cry poverty to avoid legitimate debts," says an Elliott spokesperson. "This cycle must be broken for countries to achieve economic development."

There will always be countries that cannot pay their bills. Somehow, they and their creditors have to renegotiate the debt—and history suggests that most investors are willing to compromise. In this atmosphere, vulture funds, which usually demand full payment on their bonds, can get in the way. Creditors that might otherwise be willing to accept 60 cents on the dollar may reconsider if a vulture fund can get full value. "It's like surrendering your seat on a crowded bus in favor of an elderly woman only to watch a teenager wearing a varsity wrestling jacket jump into it," notes Lee Buchheit, an attorney at Cleary Gottlieb, a law firm that represents many governments.

'Debt relief advocates should recognize that the beneficiaries of debt relief are corrupt or incompetent regimes.'

Such is the case with the vultures' biggest target yet—Argentina. Hardly one of the world's poorest countries, Argentina is a self-confident Latin powerhouse with a booming economy. Its heated struggle with the vultures is being watched by investors around the world. The outcome will reverberate in global capital and financial markets and influence the behavior of dozens of other governments. Debt forgiveness may have captured the imagination of Hollywood activists, but debt collecting is still a critical part of how the world's financial system works, and Argentina is putting that part of the system to the test.

Argentina's Close Shave

In December 2001, the financial and political crisis that had been consuming Argentina for months came to a head. Capital was fleeing the country and the government was drowning in debt. Argentina's leaders decided to stop interest payments to tens of thousands of individual investors, pension funds, and financial institutions that held the government's bonds. It was the biggest sovereign debt default in history, and it rattled the world's already jittery financial markets, which were still reeling from the Asian financial crisis and Russia's economic meltdown.

In Buenos Aires, the government's decision to default was greeted as a declaration of financial independence. The parliament gave then President Adolfo Rodríguez Saá a standing ovation when he announced the plan. But some officials conceded it was an act of desperation. "We are in a collapse," said one senior Argentine official. "We are broke." In all, Argentina ceased payments on bonds worth more than $80 billion. Thousands of bondholders watched nervously. Many were large financial institutions with diversified portfolios. For them, the Argentine default was an annoyance, not a catastrophe. Others were less fortunate. Thousands of Italian pensioners had bought Argentine bonds in the late 1990s, lured by high interest rates and a blissful ignorance of the country's brewing financial crisis.

As it became clear that Argentina was in a financial free fall, many investors wanted out, and fast. They were desperate to find buyers for what might soon be worthless sheets of paper. For funds such as Elliott Associates, Argentina's chaos was a smorgasbord. Economic crises might be startling events for unseasoned investors, but they are a vulture fund's natural environment. Elliott Associates bought millions of dollars' worth of Argentine bonds, sometimes for as little as 15 cents on the dollar, even before the country defaulted. Meanwhile, Argentina's leaders huddled with financial and legal advisors. They came up with a stark choice for their investors: Trade your existing bonds for new ones worth about one third of the original value, or keep the old bonds and get nothing. In bond-market parlance, Argentina's investors were about to get a "haircut." But this was more than a trim. In most previous restructurings, governments had offered investors new bonds worth 50 to 75 percent of their original value. Argentina, however, was offering only a third of the original value. It was a buzz cut.

Most investors gritted their teeth and took the deal. Suing governments is time consuming, expensive, and uncertain. Moreover, some of the largest holders of bonds were major banks that do repeat business with governments such as Argentina. They had no incentive to anger a customer from whom they might be seeking business in a few months. "Morgan Stanley doesn't want to spend a dollar of its money hiring lawyers," says one New York hedge fund manager. "Most of these money managers have repeat business with sovereigns [governments]. If they come off as an obstreperous or difficult creditor, they may not get the call from the finance minister to issue the next round of bonds." By 2005, more than 70 percent of bondholders had signed on to the draconian restructuring.

Vulture funds are adept at seizing government assets. A Swiss businessman owed money by Russia tried to impound Vladimir Putin's private jet.

But several hedge funds, together with groups of angry individual investors, mainly from Italy and Germany, decided to stand firm. They held on to their existing bonds and filed a series of lawsuits in the United States. As the legal battle escalated, so did the rhetoric. "If we pay more, as we did in the 1990s, it would be a new genocide," declared Argentina's President Néstor Kirchner. "It's time for the world to put a brake on the vulture funds and insatiable banks that want to keep profiting from a broken and wounded Argentina." When Rodrigo de Rato, managing director of the International Monetary Fund (IMF), suggested that Argentina treat its creditors with respect, Kirchner scoffed, "It's pathetic to listen to [the IMF] sometimes." To the frustrated bondholders, Argentina's behavior has been arrogant and reckless. "Argentina is just trying to bully people into accepting an unacceptable offer," says Hans Humes, an asset manager who represents investors holding about $40 billion worth of defaulted debt. As the vulture funds and the Argentines exchange barbs, squadrons of lawyers are fighting the battle in U.S. courts.

Paying the Piper

In May 2006, a New York federal court ruled that Argentina owed an arm of Elliott Associates more than $100 million. Other bondholders, including the mysterious Kenneth Dart, won even larger judgments. In most financial disputes, this ruling would have been a decisive victory. But in the unique arena of litigation against governments, the court's ruling was just the beginning. Somehow, the vulture funds now had to find a way to force Argentina to pay up. The legal rules that govern companies and individuals have always struggled to control the behavior of sovereign states—even in purely financial matters. For centuries, most Western legal systems treated foreign countries as essentially untouchable in the courtroom. Foreign governments could lend and borrow money, but any disputes about those transactions had to be settled politically, not legally. Frustrated investors could only try to persuade their governments to take up their cause. Usually, such pleas fell on deaf ears. Governments don't want the private debts of their citizens or companies to complicate diplomatic relationships.

Occasionally, creditors have pushed their governments to act. In 1902, European gunboats sailed into Venezuela's ports, established a blockade, and sank several ships in an effort to make the country pay on defaulted bonds. Venezuela capitulated. But using gunboat diplomacy to settle debt issues was always rare. And in the 1950s, the United States and Britain decided that better rules were needed. With governments engaging in increasingly complex financial transactions, the notion that they should be immune from the rules that applied to corporations and individuals was untenable. Governments acting for commercial purposes could be sued just like private businesses. The days of total sovereign immunity were over. Then, in the 1980s, another important change occurred. Foreign governments—particularly Latin American governments—shifted their borrowing patterns. Where they had once borrowed mainly from major Western banks, governments began issuing bonds that anyone could buy. The result of these two changes was a

new, diverse, and scattered class of creditors that was harder to coordinate and control.

Despite these changes, being a sovereign government still has its privileges. Their funds are usually hidden away or protected by strict rules. A nervous government can stash its reserves in the Bank for International Settlements in Basel, Switzerland, which is legally protected from creditors. As Elliott's Jay Newman puts it, Argentina's lawyers are fighting a successful rearguard action. The same New York courts that have said that Argentina owes its bondholders vast sums of money have frustrated all attempts to make the country pay.

In this hostile legal landscape, vulture funds have become adept at sniffing out and seizing government assets. In 2000, Elliott Associates convinced a Brussels court to seize money flowing through a European financial clearinghouse and compelled a startled Peruvian government to settle. Some creditors have been even more inventive. A Swiss businessman owed money by Russia has tried to impound President Vladimir Putin's private jet, several valuable works of art, Russian planes at an air show, and a historic Russian ship at a regatta. All of these efforts ultimately failed, but creditors remain vigilant. They are now widening their legal assault to include banks and companies that help debtor governments shelter their assets. In its fight with Congo, an Elliott affiliate filed suit against French banking giant BNP Paribas, alleging that it conspired with Congo's government to shelter oil revenues from creditors. These lawsuits threaten to expose connections with corrupt governments that banks would prefer to keep under wraps.

But for all the fear they inspire, even determined debt collectors are struggling to sustain their efforts. Every time vulture funds find assets to seize, governments close loopholes. Argentina, with the help of Buchheit and other lawyers at Cleary Gottlieb, has proven particularly adept at dodging the vultures. In January, a U.S. appeals court ruled that Argentina's creditors could not seize funds from the country's central bank, a major blow to Elliott Associates. A triumphal note has even appeared in Kirchner's statements. He recently referred to the default as a "finished" matter and the country's parliament has passed a law forbidding the government from reopening negotiations with hold-out creditors. But this smugness may be premature. Frustrated with the legal process, vulture funds are taking to the political arena. Like generations of frustrated creditors before them, they are lobbying for government intervention. That lobbying effort goes by the name "American Task Force Argentina," and it has enlisted Harvard Law School Professor Hal Scott and several Clinton-era officials—including former Under Secretary of Commerce Robert Shapiro and former National Security Council official Nancy Soderberg—to help persuade the Bush administration and Congress to pressure Argentina.

"No one else has behaved this way on the international sovereign debt market," says Shapiro, who takes pains to emphasize that his work is not a simple lobbying exercise, but a major policy effort to restrain Argentina's dangerous behavior. "Countries much poorer, countries with terrible, corrupt regimes—nobody else has tried this." If Argentina gets away with stiffing its investors, Shapiro insists, other countries may follow suit. He might be right. Ecuador recently sought Argentina's advice on how to default on its bonds.

A Debt to Society

These moves would be unnecessary if today's sovereign debt market had a structure for orderly negotiation when a country can't pay what it owes. Despite the IMF's best efforts, no equivalent to bankruptcy court has emerged for governments in distress. The World Bank does what it can to help the poorest countries that face aggressive private creditors. Occasionally, it buys claims from debt holders and clears them from the books, though it is only willing to pay about 8 cents on the dollar, not enough to satisfy most private creditors. Debt relief activists provide poor countries with legal advice and mount name-and-shame campaigns to pressure creditors into forgiving debt. But for the most part, the system remains a free-for-all.

The vulture funds often cast themselves as surprised victims of corrupt and untrustworthy governments. In fact, they actively seek out environments where, by dint of aggressive litigation, they can do much better than the ordinary investor. But they also play an important role in the ecosystem of international capital. They create secondary markets for less aggressive investors who want to unload their holdings and, perhaps more important, they inflict pain on countries that default, which most large institutional investors aren't willing to do. They are, in a sense, the avenging angels of the debt market. "Vulture funds add value," says Mitu Gulati, a professor at Duke University's law school. "The market would not work effectively if they were not there."

That argument carries little weight with debt relief activists. They point to the ongoing case against Zambia as evidence of the hardship that vulture funds can inflict. The debt at issue was born innocuously enough in 1979, when the Romanian government lent Zambia money to buy tractors. It stayed on the books for nearly 20 years, through the fall of communism in Eastern Europe and innumerable changes of government in Zambia. Then, in 1999, a vulture fund convinced the Romanian government to sell its claim for just a few million dollars. Now, more than two decades after Zambia incurred the debt—at a time when it is struggling with wrenching poverty and a runaway AIDS epidemic—it may end up paying many times the amount it borrowed.

For every Zambia, however, there is an Argentina, which has the means to pay and which has treated its creditors, including elderly Italian and German pensioners, with contempt. Sadly, the international legal system can't distinguish between the two. In its eyes, an enforceable debt is an enforceable debt. What is sorely needed is something different, a legal mechanism that can inject some equity into the process. A system that will cry for Zambia but punish Argentina. Until then, the vultures will continue to circle.

DAVID BOSCO is a contributing writer at Foreign Policy.

Across Globe, Empty Bellies Bring Rising Anger

Marc Lacey

Hunger bashed in the front gate of Haiti's presidential palace. Hunger poured onto the streets, burning tires and taking on soldiers and the police. Hunger sent the country's prime minister packing.

Haiti's hunger, that burn in the belly that so many here feel, has become fiercer than ever in recent days as global food prices spiral out of reach, spiking as much as 45 percent since the end of 2006 and turning Haitian staples like beans, corn and rice into closely guarded treasures.

Saint Louis Meriska's children ate two spoonfuls of rice apiece as their only meal recently and then went without any food the following day. His eyes downcast, his own stomach empty, the unemployed father said forlornly, "They look at me and say, 'Papa, I'm hungry,' and I have to look away. It's humiliating and it makes you angry."

That anger is palpable across the globe. The food crisis is not only being felt among the poor but is also eroding the gains of the working and middle classes, sowing volatile levels of discontent and putting new pressures on fragile governments.

In Cairo, the military is being put to work baking bread as rising food prices threaten to become the spark that ignites wider anger at a repressive government. In Burkina Faso and other parts of sub-Saharan Africa, food riots are breaking out as never before. In reasonably prosperous Malaysia, the ruling coalition was nearly ousted by voters who cited food and fuel price increases as their main concerns.

"It's the worst crisis of its kind in more than 30 years," said Jeffrey D. Sachs, the economist and special adviser to the United Nations secretary general, Ban Ki-moon. "It's a big deal and it's obviously threatening a lot of governments. There are a number of governments on the ropes, and I think there's more political fallout to come."

Indeed, as it roils developing nations, the spike in commodity prices—the biggest since the Nixon administration—has pitted the globe's poorer south against the relatively wealthy north, adding to demands for reform of rich nations' farm and environmental policies. But experts say there are few quick fixes to a crisis tied to so many factors, from strong demand for food from emerging economies like China's to rising oil prices to the diversion of food resources to make biofuels.

There are no scripts on how to handle the crisis, either. In Asia, governments are putting in place measures to limit hoarding of rice after some shoppers panicked at price increases and bought up everything they could.

Even in Thailand, which produces 10 million more tons of rice than it consumes and is the world's largest rice exporter, supermarkets have placed signs limiting the amount of rice shoppers are allowed to purchase.

But there is also plenty of nervousness and confusion about how best to proceed and just how bad the impact may ultimately be, particularly as already strapped governments struggle to keep up their food subsidies.

'Scandalous Storm'

"This is a perfect storm," President Elías Antonio Saca of El Salvador said Wednesday at the World Economic Forum on Latin America in Cancún, Mexico. "How long can we withstand the situation? We have to feed our people, and commodities are becoming scarce. This scandalous storm might become a hurricane that could upset not only our economies but also the stability of our countries."

In Asia, if Prime Minister Abdullah Ahmad Badawi of Malaysia steps down, which is looking increasingly likely amid postelection turmoil within his party, he may be that region's first high-profile political casualty of fuel and food price inflation.

In Indonesia, fearing protests, the government recently revised its 2008 budget, increasing the amount it will spend on food subsidies by about $280 million.

"The biggest concern is food riots," said H.S. Dillon, a former adviser to Indonesia's Ministry of Agriculture. Referring to small but widespread protests touched off by a rise in soybean prices in January, he said, "It has happened in the past and can happen again."

Last month in Senegal, one of Africa's oldest and most stable democracies, police in riot gear beat and used tear gas against people protesting high food prices and later raided a television station that broadcast images of the event. Many Senegalese have expressed anger at President Abdoulaye Wade for spending lavishly on roads and five-star hotels for an Islamic summit meeting last month while many people are unable to afford rice or fish.

"Why are these riots happening?" asked Arif Husain, senior food security analyst at the World Food Program, which has issued urgent appeals for donations. "The human instinct is to survive, and people are going to do no matter what to survive. And if you're hungry you get angry quicker."

Leaders who ignore the rage do so at their own risk. President René Préval of Haiti appeared to taunt the populace as the chorus of complaints about la vie chère—the expensive life—grew. He said if Haitians could afford cellphones, which many do carry, they should be able to feed their families. "If there is a protest against the rising prices," he said, "come get me at the palace and I will demonstrate with you."

When they came, filled with rage and by the thousands, he huddled inside and his presidential guards, with United Nations peacekeeping troops, rebuffed them. Within days, opposition lawmakers had voted out Mr. Préval's prime minister, Jacques-Édouard Alexis, forcing him to reconstitute his government. Fragile in even the best of times, Haiti's population and politics are now both simmering.

"Why were we surprised?" asked Patrick Élie, a Haitian political activist who followed the food riots in Africa earlier in the year and feared they might come to Haiti. "When something is coming your way all the way from Burkina Faso you should see it coming. What we had was like a can of gasoline that the government left for someone to light a match to it."

Dwindling Menus

The rising prices are altering menus, and not for the better. In India, people are scrimping on milk for their children. Daily bowls of dal are getting thinner, as a bag of lentils is stretched across a few more meals.

Maninder Chand, an auto-rickshaw driver in New Delhi, said his family had given up eating meat altogether for the last several weeks.

Another rickshaw driver, Ravinder Kumar Gupta, said his wife had stopped seasoning their daily lentils, their chief source of protein, with the usual onion and spices because the price of cooking oil was now out of reach. These days, they eat bowls of watery, tasteless dal, seasoned only with salt.

Down Cairo's Hafziyah Street, peddlers selling food from behind wood carts bark out their prices. But few customers can afford their fish or chicken, which bake in the hot sun. Food prices have doubled in two months.

Ahmed Abul Gheit, 25, sat on a cheap, stained wooden chair by his own pile of rotting tomatoes. "We can't even find food," he said, looking over at his friend Sobhy Abdullah, 50. Then raising his hands toward the sky, as if in prayer, he said, "May God take the guy I have in mind."

Mr. Abdullah nodded, knowing full well that the "guy" was President Hosni Mubarak.

The government's ability to address the crisis is limited, however. It already spends more on subsidies, including gasoline and bread, than on education and health combined.

"If all the people rise, then the government will resolve this," said Raisa Fikry, 50, whose husband receives a pension equal to about $83 a month, as she shopped for vegetables. "But everyone has to rise together. People get scared. But we will all have to rise together."

It is the kind of talk that has prompted the government to treat its economic woes as a security threat, dispatching riot forces with a strict warning that anyone who takes to the streets will be dealt with harshly.

Niger does not need to be reminded that hungry citizens overthrow governments. The country's first postcolonial president, Hamani Diori, was toppled amid allegations of rampant corruption in 1974 as millions starved during a drought.

More recently, in 2005, it was mass protests in Niamey, the Nigerien capital, that made the government sit up and take notice of that year's food crisis, which was caused by a complex mix of poor rains, locust infestation and market manipulation by traders.

"As a result of that experience the government created a cabinet-level ministry to deal with the high cost of living," said Moustapha Kadi, an activist who helped organize marches in 2005. "So when prices went up this year the government acted quickly to remove tariffs on rice, which everyone eats. That quick action has kept people from taking to the streets."

The Poor Eat Mud

In Haiti, where three-quarters of the population earns less than $2 a day and one in five children is chronically malnourished, the one business booming amid all the gloom is the selling of patties made of mud, oil and sugar, typically consumed only by the most destitute.

"It's salty and it has butter and you don't know you're eating dirt," said Olwich Louis Jeune, 24, who has taken to eating them more often in recent months. "It makes your stomach quiet down."

But the grumbling in Haiti these days is no longer confined to the stomach. It is now spray-painted on walls of the capital and shouted by demonstrators.

In recent days, Mr. Préval has patched together a response, using international aid money and price reductions by importers to cut the price of a sack of rice by about 15 percent. He has also trimmed the salaries of some top officials. But those are considered temporary measures.

Real solutions will take years. Haiti, its agriculture industry in shambles, needs to better feed itself. Outside investment is the key, although that requires stability, not the sort of widespread looting and violence that the Haitian food riots have fostered.

Meanwhile, most of the poorest of the poor suffer silently, too weak for activism or too busy raising the next generation of hungry. In the sprawling slum of Haiti's Cité Soleil, Placide Simone, 29, offered one of her five offspring to a stranger. "Take one," she said, cradling a listless baby and motioning toward four rail-thin toddlers, none of whom had eaten that day. "You pick. Just feed them."

Reporting was contributed by Lydia Polgreen from Niamey, Niger, Michael Slackman from Cairo, Somini Sengupta from New Delhi, Thomas Fuller from Bangkok and Peter Gelling from Jakarta, Indonesia.

The Micromagic of Microcredit

Karol Boudreaux and Tyler Cowen

Microcredit has star power. In 2006, the Nobel Committee called it "an important liberating force" and awarded the Nobel Peace Prize to Muhammad Yunus, the "godfather of microcredit." The actress Natalie Portman is a believer too; she advocates support for the Village Banking Campaign on its MySpace page. The end of poverty is "just a mouse click away," she promises. A button on the site swiftly redirects you to paypal.com, where you can make a contribution to microcredit initiatives.

After decades of failure, the world's aid organizations seem to think they have at last found a winning idea. The United Nations declared 2005 the "International Year of Microcredit." Secretary-General Kofi Annan declared that providing micro-loans to help poor people launch small businesses recognizes that they "are the solution, not the problem. It is a way to build on their ideas, energy, and vision. It is a way to grow productive enterprises, and so allow communities to prosper."

Many investors agree. Hundreds of millions of dollars are flowing into microfinance from international financial institutions, foundations, governments, and, most important, private investors—who increasingly see microfinance as a potentially profitable business venture. Private investment through special "microfinance investment vehicles" alone nearly doubled in 2005, from $513 million to $981 million.

On the charitable side, part of microcredit's appeal lies in the fact that the lending institutions can fund themselves once they are launched. Pierre Omidyar, the founder of eBay, explains that you can begin by investing $60 billion in the world's poorest people, "and then you're done!"

But can microcredit achieve the massive changes its proponents claim? Is it the solution to poverty in the developing world, or something more modest—a way to empower the poor, particularly poor women, with some control over their lives and their assets?

On trips to Africa and India we have talked to lenders, borrowers, and other poor people to try to understand the role microcredit plays in their lives. We met people like Stadile Menthe in Botswana. Menthe is, in many ways, the classic borrower. A single mother with little formal education, she borrowed money to expand the small grocery store she runs on a dusty road on the outskirts of Botswana's capital city, Gaborone. Menthe's store has done well, and she has expanded into the lucrative business of selling phone cards. In fact, she's been successful enough

that she has built two rental homes next to her store. She has diversified her income and made a better life for herself and her daughter. But how many borrowers are like Menthe? In our judgment, she is the exception, not the norm. Yes, microcredit is mostly a good thing. Very often it helps keep borrowers from even greater catastrophes, but only rarely does it enable them to climb out of poverty.

The modern story of microcredit began 30 years ago, when Yunus—then an economics professor at Chittagong University in southeastern Bangladesh—set out to apply his theories to improving the lives of the poor in the nearby village of Jobra. He began in 1976 by lending $27 to a group of 42 villagers, who used the money to develop informal businesses, such as making soap or weaving baskets to sell at the local market. After the success of the first experiment, Yunus founded Grameen Bank. Today, the bank claims more than five million "members" and a loan repayment rate of 98 percent. It has lent out some $6.5 billion.

At the outset, Yunus set a goal that half of the borrowers would be women. He explained, "The banking system not only rejects poor people, it rejects women. . . . Not even one percent of their borrowers are women." He soon discovered that women were good credit risks, and good at managing family finances. Today, more than 95 percent of Grameen Bank's borrowers are women. The UN estimates that women make up 76 percent of microcredit customers around the world, varying from nearly 90 percent in Asia to less than a third in the Middle East.

While 70 percent of microcredit borrowers are in Asia, the institution has spread around the world; Latin America and sub-Saharan Africa account for 14 and 10 percent of the number of borrowers, respectively. Some of the biggest microfinance institutions include Grameen Bank, ACCION International, and Pro Mujer of Bolivia.

The average loan size varies, usually in proportion to the income level of the home country. In Rwanda, a typical loan might be $50 to $200; in Romania, it is more likely to be $2,500 to $5,000. Often there is no explicit collateral. Instead, the banks lend to small groups of about five people, relying on peer pressure for repayment. At mandatory weekly meetings, if one borrower cannot make her payment, the rest of the group must come up with the cash.

The achievements of microcredit, however, are not quite what they seem. There is, for example, a puzzling fact at the heart of the enterprise. Most microcredit banks charge interest rates of 50 to 100 percent on an annualized basis (loans, typically, must be paid off within weeks or months). That's not as scandalous as it sounds—local moneylenders demand much higher rates. The puzzle is a matter of basic economics: How can people in new businesses growing at perhaps 20 percent annually afford to pay interest at rates as high as 100 percent?

The answer is that, for the most part, they can't. By and large, the loans serve more modest ends—laudable, but not world changing.

Microcredit does not always lead to the creation of small businesses. Many microlenders refuse to lend money for start-ups; they insist that a business already be in place. This suggests that the business was sustainable to begin with, without a micro-loan. Sometimes lenders help businesses to grow, but often what they really finance is spending and consumption.

That is not to say that the poor are out shopping for jewelry and fancy clothes. In Hyderabad, India, as in many other places, we saw that loans are often used to pay for a child's doctor visit. In the Tanzanian capital of Dar es Salaam, Joel Mwakitalu, who runs the Small Enterprise Foundation, a local microlender, told us that 60 percent of his loans are used to send kids to school; 40 percent are for investments. A study of microcredit in Indonesia found that 30 percent of the borrowed money was spent on some form of consumption.

Sometimes consumption and investment are one and the same, such as when parents send their children to school. Indian borrowers often buy mopeds and motorbikes—they are fun to ride but also a way of getting to work. Cell phones are used to call friends but also to run businesses.

For better or worse, microborrowing often entails a kind of bait and switch. The borrower claims that the money is for a business, but uses it for other purposes. In effect, the cash allows a poor entrepreneur to maintain her business without having to sacrifice the life or education of her child. In that sense, the money is for the business, but most of all it is for the child. Such lifesaving uses for the funds are obviously desirable, but it is also a sad reality that many microcredit loans help borrowers to survive or tread water more than they help them get ahead. This sounds unglamorous and even disappointing, but the alternative—such as no doctor's visit for a child or no school for a year—is much worse.

Commentators often seem to assume that the experience of borrowing and lending is completely new for the poor. But moneylenders have offered money to the world's poor for millennia, albeit at extortionate rates of interest. A typical money-lender is a single individual, well-known in his neighborhood or village, who borrows money from his wealthier connections and in turn lends those funds to individuals in need, typically people he knows personally. But that personal connection is rarely good for a break; a moneylender may charge 200 to 400 percent interest on an annualized basis. He will insist on col-lateral (a television, for instance), and resort to intimidation and sometimes violence if he is not repaid on time. The money-lender operates informally, off the books, and usually outside the law.

So compared to the alternative, microcredit is often a very good deal indeed. Microcredit critics often miss this point. For instance, Aneel Karnani, who teaches at the University of Michigan's business school, argues that microfinance "misses its mark." Karnani says that in some cases microcredit can make life for the planet's bottom billion even worse by reducing their cash flow. Karnani cites the high interest rates that microlenders charge and points out that "if poor clients cannot earn a greater return on their investment than the interest they must pay, they will become poorer as a result of microcredit, not wealthier." But the real question has never been credit vs. no credit; rather, it is moneylender vs. modern microcredit. Credit can bring some problems, but microcredit is easing debt burdens more than it is increasing them.

At microlender SERO Lease and Finance in Tanzania, bor-rower Margaret Makingi Marwa told us that she prefers working with a microfinance institution to working with a moneylender. Moneylenders demand quick repayment at high interest rates. At SERO, Marwa can take six months or a year to pay off her lease contract. Given that her income can vary and that she may not have money at hand every month, she prefers to have a longer-term loan.

Moneylenders do offer some advantages, especially in rural areas. Most important, they come up with cash on the spot. If your child needs to go to the doctor right now, the moneylender is usually only a short walk away. Even under the best of cir-cumstances, a microcredit loan can take several days to process, and the recipient will be required to deal with many documents, not to mention weekly meetings.

There is, however, an upside to this "bureaucracy." In reality, it is the moneylender who is the "micro" operator. Microcredit is a more formal, institutionalized business relationship. It represents a move up toward a larger scale of trade and busi-ness organization. Microcredit borrowers gain valuable expe-rience in working within a formal institution. They learn what to expect from lenders and fellow borrowers, and they learn what is expected of themselves. This experience will be a help should they ever graduate to commercial credit or have other dealings with the formal financial world.

The comparison to moneylending brings up another impor-tant feature of microcredit. Though its users avoid the kind of intimidation employed by moneylenders, microcredit could not work without similar incentives. The lender does not demand collateral, but if you can't pay your share of the group loan, your fellow borrowers will come and take your TV. That enforcement process can lead to abuses, but it is a gentler form of intimida-tion than is exercised by the moneylender. If nothing else, the group members know that at the next meeting any one of them might be the one unable to repay her share of the loan.

If borrowers are using microcredit for consumption and not only to improve a small business, how do they repay? Most borrowers are self-employed and work in the informal sector of the economy. Their incomes are often erratic; small, unexpected expenses can make repayment impossible in any given week or month. In the countryside, farmers have seasonal incomes and little cash for long periods of time.

Borrowers manage, at least in part, by relying on family members and friends to help out. In some cases, the help comes in the form of remittances from abroad. Remittances that cross national borders now total more than $300 billion yearly. A recent study in Tanzania found that microcredit borrowers get 34 percent of their income from friends and family, some of whom live abroad, but others of whom live in the city and have jobs in the formal sector. That's the most effective kind of foreign aid, targeted directly at the poor and provided by those who understand their needs.

Here again, microcredit does something that traditional banks do not. A commercial bank typically will not lend to people who work in the informal sector, precisely because their erratic incomes make them risky bets. The loan officer at a commercial bank does not care that your brother in Doha is sending money each month to help you out. But a microcredit institution cares only that you come to your weekly meeting with a small sum in hand for repayment. Because of microcredit, families can leverage one person's ability to find work elsewhere to benefit the entire group.

Sometimes microcredit leads to more savings rather than more debt. That sounds paradoxical, but borrowing in one asset can be a path toward (more efficient) saving in other assets.

To better understand this puzzle, we must set aside some of our preconceptions about how saving operates in poor countries, most of all in rural areas. Westerners typically save in the form of money or money-denominated assets such as stocks and bonds. But in poor communities, money is often an ineffective medium for savings; if you want to know how much net saving is going on, don't look at money. Banks may be a daylong bus ride away or may be plagued, as in Ghana, by fraud. A cash hoard kept at home can be lost, stolen, taken by the taxman, damaged by floods, or even eaten by rats. It creates other kinds of problems as well. Needy friends and relatives knock on the door and ask for aid. In small communities it is often very hard, even impossible, to say no, especially if you have the cash on hand.

People who have even extremely modest wealth are also asked to perform more community service, or to pay more to finance community rituals and festivals. In rural Guerrero State, in Mexico, for example, one of us (Cowen) found that most people who saved cash did not manage to hold on to it for more than a few weeks or even days. A dollar saved translates into perhaps a quarter of that wealth kept. It is as if cash savings faces an implicit "tax rate" of 75 percent.

Under these kinds of conditions, a cow (or a goat or pig) is a much better medium for saving. It is sturdier than paper money. Friends and relatives can't ask for small pieces of it. If you own a cow, it yields milk, it can plow the fields, it produces dung that can be used as fuel or fertilizer, and in a pinch it can be slaughtered and turned into saleable meat or simply eaten. With a small loan, people in rural areas can buy that cow and use cash that might otherwise be diverted to less useful purposes to pay back the microcredit institution. So even when microcredit looks like indebtedness, savings are going up rather than down.

Microcredit *is* making people's lives better around the world. But for the most part, it is not pulling them out of poverty. It is hard to find entrepreneurs who start with these tiny loans and graduate to run commercial empires. Bangladesh, where Grameen Bank was born, is still a desperately poor country. The more modest truth is that microcredit may help some people, perhaps earning $2 a day, to earn something like $2.50 a day. That may not sound dramatic, but when you are earning $2 a day it is a big step forward. And progress is not the natural state of humankind; microcredit is important even when it does nothing more than stave off decline.

With microcredit, life becomes more bearable and easier to manage. The improvements may not show up as an explicit return on investment, but the benefits are very real. If a poor family is able to keep a child in school, send someone to a clinic, or build up more secure savings, its well-being improves, if only marginally. This is a big part of the reason why poor people are demanding greater access to microcredit loans. And microcredit, unlike many charitable services, is capable of paying for itself—which explains why the private sector is increasingly involved. The future of microcredit lies in the commercial sector, not in unsustainable aid programs. Count this as another benefit.

If this portrait sounds a little underwhelming, don't blame microcredit. The real issue is that we so often underestimate the severity and inertia of global poverty. Natalie Portman may not be right when she says that an end to poverty is "just a mouse click away," but she's right to be supportive of a tool that helps soften some of poverty's worst blows for many millions of desperate people

---

KAROL BOUDREAUX is a senior research fellow at the Mercatus Center at George Mason University. TYLER COWEN is a professor of economics at George Mason University and author of *Discover Your Inner Economist: Use Incentives to Fall in Love, Survive Your Next Meeting, and Motivate Your Dentist* (2007).

The Coming Revolution in Africa

Even as headlines bring grim news of misery, disease, and death in Africa, an agricultural transformation is lifting tens of millions of people out of poverty. A rising generation of small farmers promises not only to put food on the African table but to fundamentally change the continent's economic and political life.

G. PASCAL ZACHARY

The heat is deadening. After a morning picking cotton on the side of a hill, Souley Madi, wearing a knock-off Nike T-shirt and thongs made from discarded tires, staggers down a steep slope, a heavy bag of cotton bolls on his back. Reaching his small compound 10 minutes later, he greets his two wives. The older one nurses a baby while preparing a lunch of maize and cassava. The second wife, visibly pregnant, rises from a seat under a shade tree, responding to Madi's instructions. He wants to impress his foreign visitor, so he prepares to introduce his latest agro-business brainstorm.

Ducks.

A few words from Madi, and wife number two dashes out of sight. When she reappears, some three dozen baby ducks waddle behind her. Madi beams, scoops up a duck, then hands it to me. He asks me to guess how much it will sell for at maturity.

I guess too low. Three dollars, Madi says. He is the first to raise ducks in the parched village of Badjengo, in the far north of Cameroon, about 45 minutes from the provincial capital of Garoua. Madi is a shrewd risk taker. Despite the challenging climate of Africa's rain-sparse savanna belt, Madi's ducks thrive, thanks partly to the diligent care provided by his new wife.

Madi, who is 41, sells nearly all of the ducks he raises, saving only a few for his family to eat. The birds are big sellers around local holidays, when Cameroonians in Europe and the United States send cash to relatives back home. Madi uses part of his duck money—about $100—to buy inventory for a small grocery store he maintains on the side of a main road. The store, a shack really, is secured by a heavy Chinese-made padlock. When people want to shop, they must first find Madi and coax him to open (he's got too few customers to justify an employee). From the sale of cotton, dry goods, and the ducks, Madi has accumulated a cash hoard he hides in his sleeping hut.

Having finished high school, Madi is better educated than most of his fellow farmers, and he embodies an important rule in rural Africa: The more educated the farmer, the more effective his practices and the higher his income. Madi won't allow his two school-age children to skip class in favor of fieldwork. "They should study instead," he says.

Short and stocky, Madi sits down on a low wooden bench and begins to eat roasted corn. He tells me through a translator how he—a Muslim—took a second wife, not for status or love, but to help him take advantage of the farm boom. He complains that prices, especially for cotton, should be higher. Yet he says he's never had more money saved.

To Americans, bombarded with dire images of Africa—starving Africans, diseased Africans, Africans fleeing disasters or fleeing other Africans trying to kill them—Madi may seem like a character from a novel. But he is no fiction. Despite the horrors of Darfur, the persistence of HIV/AIDS, and the failure to end famines and civil wars in a handful of countries, the vast majority of sub-Saharan Africans neither live in war zones nor struggle with an active disease or famine. Extreme poverty is relatively rare in rural Africa, and there is a growing entrepreneurial spirit among farmers that defies the usual image of Africans as passive victims. They are foot soldiers in an agrarian revolution that never makes the news. In 25 visits to the region since 2000, I have met many Souley Madis, and have come to believe that they are the key to understanding Africa's present and reshaping its future.

After decades of mistreatment, abuse, and exploitation, African farmers—still overwhelmingly smallholders working family-tilled plots of land—are awakening from a long slumber. Because farmers are the majority (about 60 percent) of all sub-Saharan Africans, farming holds the key to reducing poverty and helping to spread prosperity. Over the longer term, prosperous African farmers could become the backbone of a social and political transformation. They are the sort of canny and independent tillers of the land Thomas Jefferson envisioned as the foundation for American democracy. In a region where elites often seem more committed to enjoying the trappings of success abroad than creating success at home, farmers have a real stake in improving their turf. Life will still be hard for them, but in the years ahead they can be expected to demand better government policies and more effective services. As their incomes and aspirations rise, they could someday even form their own political parties, in much the way that farmers in the American Midwest and Western Europe did in the past. At a minimum, African governments seem likely to increasingly promote trade and development policies that advance rural interests.

Improved livelihoods for farmers alone won't reverse Africa's marginalization in the global economy or solve the region's many vexing problems. But among people concerned about Africa—and certainly among those in multinational organizations who must grapple with humanitarian disasters on the continent—the unfolding rural revival holds out new hope. Having once dismissed agriculture as an obstacle or an irrelevance, African leaders and officials in multinational organizations recently have come around to a new view, nicely summarized by Stephen Lewis, a former United Nations official who concentrated on African affairs. "Agricultural productivity," Lewis declared in 2005, "is indispensable to progress on all other fronts."

The potential for advances through agriculture is large. African farmers today are creating wealth on a scale unimagined a decade ago. They are likely to continue prospering into the foreseeable future. Helped by low costs of land and labor and by rising prices for farm products, African farmers are defying pessimists by increasing their output. They are cultivating land once abandoned or neglected; forging profitable links with local, regional, and international buyers; and reviving crops that flourished in the pre-1960 colonial era, when Africa provided a remarkable 10 percent of the world's tradable food. Today, that share is less than one percent.

"The boom in African agriculture is the most important, neglected development in the region, and it has years to run," says Andrew Mwenda, a leading commentator on African political economy.

The evidence of a farm boom is widespread. In southern Uganda, hundreds of farmers have begun growing apples for the first time, displacing imports and earning an astonishing 35 cents each. Brokers ferry the fruit from the countryside to the capital, Kampala, where it fetches almost twice as much. Cotton production in Zambia has increased 10-fold in 10 years, bringing new income to 120,000 farmers and their families, nearly one million people in all. Floral exports from Ethiopia are growing so rapidly that flowers threaten to surpass coffee as the country's leading cash earner. In Kenya, tens of thousands of small farmers who live within an hour of the Nairobi airport grow French beans and other vegetables, which are packaged, bar-coded, and air-shipped to Europe's grocers. Exports of vegetables, fruits, and flowers, largely from eastern and southern Africa, now exceed $2 billion a year, up from virtually zero a quarter-century ago.

Skeptics still insist that farmers in the region will be badly handicapped, in the long run, by climate change, overpopulation, new pandemics, and the vagaries of global commodity prices. Corruption, poor governance, and civil strife are all added to the list of supposedly insurmountable obstacles. But similar challenges haven't stopped Asian and Latin American farmers from advancing. Even people who see future gains for African farmers agree, however, that food shortages and famines will persist, at least within isolated or war-torn areas.

But while Malthusian nightmares dominate international discussions of Africa, food production in the most heavily peopled areas is outstripping population growth. In Nigeria, with the largest population of any African country, food production has grown faster than population for 20 years. In other West African countries, including Ghana, Niger, Mali, Burkina Faso, and Benin, crop output has risen by more than four percent annually, far exceeding the rate of population growth. Farm labor productivity in these countries is now so high that in some cases it matches the levels in parts of Asia.

"The driver of agriculture is primarily urbanization," observes Steve Wiggins, a farm expert at London's Overseas Development Institute. As more people leave the African countryside, there is more land for remaining farmers, and more paying customers in the city. The growth in food production is so impressive, Wiggins argues, that a "green revolution" is already under way in densely populated West Africa.

The growing international demand for food is also helping Africa's small farmers. The global ethanol boom has raised corn prices, and coffee is selling at a 10-year high, for instance. Multinational corporations are becoming more closely involved in African agriculture, moving away from plantation-based cultivation and opting instead to enter into contracts with thousands, even hundreds of thousands, of individual farmers. China and India, hungry to satisfy the appetites of expanding middle classes, view Africa as a potential breadbasket. Finally, African governments are generally more supportive of farmers than in the past. Even African elites, long disdainful of village life, are embracing farming, trying to profit from the boom—and raising the status of this once-scorned activity.

While Malthusian nightmares dominate international discussions of Africa, food production in the most heavily peopled areas is outstripping population growth.

No one model explains the surge in African agriculture. Diverse sources of success befit an Africa that, across the board, defies easy generalizations. One recent study finds 15 different farming "systems" in sub-Saharan Africa. At the level of the single African farm, diversity abounds too. Most individual farmers juggle as many as 10 crops. Outcomes among small farmers also vary. The top 25 percent of smallholders are believed to produce four to five times as much food as the bottom 25 percent. Just as in America not everyone is rich, in Africa not everyone is poor.

African farmers do share much in common. "A man with a hoe" remains an accurate description of nearly all who till the soil. Mechanization is rare. Less than one percent of land is worked by tractors. Only 10 percent is worked by draft animals. Nearly 90 percent is worked by hand, from initial plowing to planting, weeding, and harvesting. Irrigation is also rare; only one percent of sub-Saharan cropland receives irrigation water. Unpredictable weather, often drought and sometimes too much rain, bedevils farmers in many areas. Relatively little fertilizer is used; globally, farmers apply nine times as much per acre as Africans do. "Much of the food produced in Africa is lost" after harvest, according to one estimate, because of inaccessible markets, poor storage methods, and an absence of processing facilities. Finally, use of improved seed varieties is very limited by global standards.

But these sobering characteristics feature a silver lining: The potential for gains is large. Some ways farmers can move ahead are simple. One is to plant crops in straight lines. In Uganda, for instance, it was long the practice of many farmers to sow seeds haphazardly; they have been taught in recent years to plant in regularly spaced rows that vastly improve yields. When so simple a change delivers such great benefits, the importance of human choice is clear. In discussions of African affairs, the central role of the power of the individual and the desire of ordinary people to do better is often lost in a haze of dubious statistics, gloomy futuristic scenarios, and impossible calls for improved ethics, leadership, and institutions.

To glimpse a different picture of Africa, imagine traveling on a journey, not to Joseph Conrad's "heart of darkness," but to an uncharted, elusive, almost mythical part of the world's poorest region, where hope, personal responsibility, and new incentives are reshaping the lives of ordinary people, turning Conradian imagery on its head.

T he first stop on our journey is the village of Bukhulu in eastern Uganda. From Kampala, I take an old van jammed with 15 people and rumble along dirt roads so pockmarked that pieces of the vehicle fly off during the journey without eliciting any reaction from the driver. The next morning, from the provincial center of Mbale, I hitch a ride through the foothills of towering Mount Elgon with an agricultural extension officer who works for a South African company that pays Ugandan farmers to grow cotton for export. On the final leg of the journey, I switch to a bicycle taxi. Balanced precariously on a makeshift rear seat, the man in front cycling leisurely, I pass cornfields brimming with ripening ears nearly ready to harvest. The ride costs a dime.

I am here to visit one of my favorite farmers, Ken Sakwa, who is in the forefront of a significant yet little-noticed back-to-the-land trend. The movement is powered by city dwellers who either can't earn enough money in the cities or are earning so much that they want to plow their savings into agro-businesses. Doomsayers constantly point to Africa's urbanization as a relentless scourge, stripping the countryside of talent, but quie-

tly, some Africans are going back to "the bush." Sakwa, 37, is one of them. He spent a decade in Uganda's mushrooming capital, doing odd jobs for cash. He enjoyed the excitement of city life but survived only because of the goodwill of relatives. Ultimately, he exhausted that goodwill. "I was a parasite," he admits.

Five years ago, Sakwa decided to claim the vacant farm of his deceased father in Bukhulu, the village of his birth. None of his brothers and sisters wanted the land, so he got it all. His wife in Kampala refused to join him. He divorced her and went back alone.

"I knew I'd achieve if I went back to my father's land," he recalls. "I felt ambition inside me."

Farmers in Bukhulu mainly grow cotton, corn, peanuts, and beans. Even the largest farms encompass no more than a dozen acres. In his first year back, Sakwa grew corn and beans on one acre, opening the ground alone, with a small hand hoe. "I worked like an animal," he recalls. Even before his first harvest, he looked for a wife. A few months after his return, he met Jessica in a nearby village. He decided to court her when he learned her parents were farmers.

"I wanted a wife who could help on the farm and would be happy doing so," Sakwa says. He married Jessica and, with her considerable help, he prospered. In his second year in Bukhulu, he tilled two acres of land, hiring a tractor to assist in plowing. From an American aid project, he and some neighbors learned to plant crops in straight lines. By the third year Sakwa mastered basic farming, "doing much, much better." When his old Kampala friends visit him, they ask, "How is this poor village man getting all this money?"

Accumulation is only part of Sakwa's story. How he spends his profits is significant. One early purchase was a mobile phone, which allows him to keep abreast of local markets and negotiate better prices for his crops. That a farmer who lives without electricity or running water should be able to receive phone calls from anywhere in the world is perhaps the most radical change in African material life in decades. Though wireless service came late to the region, nearly one in five sub-Saharan Africans now owns a cell phone, and the World Bank estimates that the region's wireless phone market is the "fastest-growing in the world." One morning, after he plants cottonseeds in a small field, Sakwa receives a call from the headmaster at his daughter's boarding school (yes, he can afford that too!). The headmaster asks for 500 pounds of beans. Sakwa, who has the beans bagged for sale, wants 15 cents a pound. "Will you accept?" he asks.

The headmaster wants to pay less. Sakwa refuses. "I can hold my beans until I get a fair price," he says.

A few days later, the headmaster calls back and agrees to the price.

O ne day, I walk with the Sakwas to one of their fields. The ground is wet from recent rains. We cut through a path separating the land of different farmers and soon meet a family harvesting beans. A husband and wife and their two children are haphazardly tossing uprooted beans on a

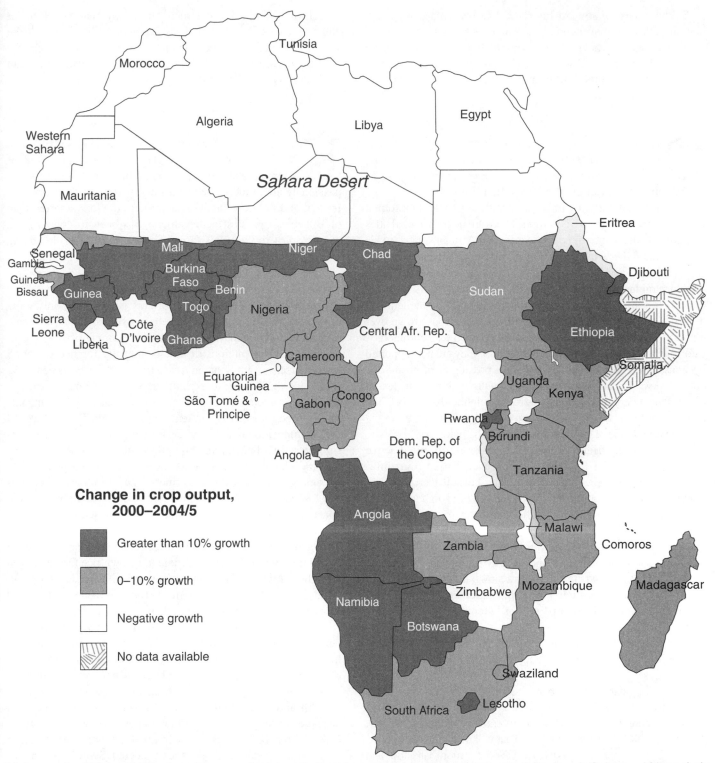

Change in crop output, 2000–2004/5

- Greater than 10% growth
- 0–10% growth
- Negative growth
- No data available

Violence, drought, and other disruptions can deal devastating blows to farmers, but in many countries in sub-Saharan African their output is expanding. The World Bank reports that many African economies "appear to have turned the corner and moved to a path of faster and steadier economic growth."

wooden cart. Sakwa greets them and stops to explain that they will fit more on the cart if they make neat piles. The man acts as if he's received a revelation. Sakwa starts rearranging the beans to make sure the man grasps his advice. The man begins to shift the beans around, and his wife flashes Sakwa a big smile, thanking him.

We turn off the path, slice through another field, and come upon a patch of peanuts. Ever the innovator, Sakwa is experimenting with different types in order to see which grow best. He pulls a few samples from the ground to show me. Just as I begin to chew on a peanut, Jessica screams in the distance.

Sakwa races off toward his wife. I follow. When we reach her, she cries out, "Someone has stolen the beans!"

The plants have been ripped from the field. "They must have come in the night," Sakwa says. He has been forced to hire a neighbor to guard this field in the daytime. He tells the man he will harvest the corn soon.

One of Sakwa's innovations isn't agricultural but commercial. In order to expand output and raise his income, he leases land from his neighbors and hires them as casual laborers, enriching them as well as himself.

Land sales are virtually impossible in rural Africa, but informal leases are becoming more common. There are no formal land titles in Sakwa's village, nor in nearly every other African village, so his claim to his father's land is grounded in the community's knowledge of Sakwa and his lineage. Until recently, no one ever bought or sold rural land in Uganda, but with the rise of small-scale commercial farming the value of farmland can now be "monetized," in rough terms, by estimating profit from cash crops grown over a period of years. Land is coming to be viewed as a commodity. Informal land deals are flexible, but because they are not supported by unassailable titles, there is always a possibility of costly disputes. Sakwa recently experienced such a problem when he leased a half-acre of very productive land from a neighbor for nearly $800. But one of the man's brothers, who didn't get any money in the deal, has sued Sakwa in court. He wants to be paid.

Sakwa and his friend Francis Nakiwuza are the most active acquirers of land in Bukhulu, having each leased four different plots over the past three years. The lawsuit worries them. One day Nakiwuza and I sit in Sakwa's living room as he sifts through his business records, which he stores in a worn leather briefcase stowed under his bed. He keeps records on each of his "gardens," listing the costs and income.

One reason for disputes: poorly drawn contracts. The lease for his newest plot, written in Sakwa's own hand, boils down to a single sentence in which a neighbor agrees to permit Sakwa to use "my swampy land of 61 strides in length and 32 strides in width" for about $200.

The contract lacks any surveyor information and isn't registered with any government agency or court. "We trust people," Sakwa says.

The rudimentary contract partly reflects the inexperience of the parties involved. Desiring land is new to Sakwa, and he dreams of obtaining more. He wants to double his current holding of 10 acres. "I want to make 20 acres," he says. "That will make my life good."

Across the table sits Nakiwuza. He wants more land too, and brings news of a neighbor who needs to raise money. The man was caught in a sex act with a young girl. In years past, there would have been no legal consequences. But today men caught abusing underage women can go to prison or pay a large fine. For this man, the only way to avoid prison is to raise money by leasing land.

Ken Sakwa's friends in Kampala ask, "How is this poor village man getting all this money?"

Sakwa is sorry for the man but happy that either he or Nakiwuza will get to expand his acreage. "Why shouldn't the stronger farmers have more land?" Nakiwuza asks. Often, the land they lease had been sitting idle. "We are using the land well," he says. "Others did nothing with it. Now they have our money, and we have crops to sell."

Ken Sakwa is Africa's future writ small. Gilbert Bukenya is the future writ large. He is the vice president of Uganda and a rarity among African politicians: He is passionate about the value of farming, is himself an innovative farmer, and publicly encourages farmers to work smarter. One of Bukenya's greatest achievements has been to encourage a can-do spirit in Uganda's farmers and a sense of pride among other Ugandans in what their farming compatriots produce.

I met Bukenya one balmy afternoon at his home on the shores of Lake Victoria, where he experiments with fruits, vegetables, and dairy cattle. "By farming smarter, Ugandans not only grow more, they earn more money," he tells me. Bukenya is an advocate of food self-sufficiency, pointing to the example of rice. Ugandans pay tens of millions of dollars annually for rice imported from overseas—sub-Saharan Africa as a whole imports nearly $2 billion worth. In order to expand the output of homegrown rice, Bukenya promoted a new African variety that grows in uplands (as opposed to paddies) and requires less water. Then he argued for the imposition of a 75 percent duty on foreign rice. The measure passed Parliament and brought rapid benefits: A few of the country's largest rice importers invested in milling plants, thus becoming customers of local farmers. The new mills created jobs and lowered the cost of bringing domestic rice to market, so that consumers now pay more or less the same for rice as always.

Since foreign rice exporters—notably the United States, Thailand, and Pakistan—subsidize their growers, Bukenya thinks it only fair that Uganda defend its own rice farmers, even though he realizes that some import-substitution schemes fail. (And rice is only one of the African crops hampered by U.S. and European farm subsidies and trade barriers.)

Fresh from his rice success, Bukenya is now promoting the benefits of raising livestock. One September morning I find him lecturing before a classroom full of ordinary farmers, about 50 of them, gathered in a school about an hour from Kampala. Wearing a loose-fitting shirt and sandals, Bukenya jokes easily with his audience, speaking in a local language. The classroom has no electricity, a concrete floor, and exposed wooden rafters. Bukenya recalls how his mother earned the money to send him to school from sales of a beer she concocted. Switching to a prepared talk, he preaches a simple lesson: "Make money daily." One way they can do that, he tells the small crowd, is by keeping a milk cow or egg-laying chickens. Only a few of the farmers do anything like this now, and Bukenya spends a good deal of time explaining how they can get started.

Then he criticizes the country's traditional big-horned Ankole cattle. These animals are beautiful and beloved but provide very little milk, he says, "no matter how hard you squeeze." He prefers European Friesian cows. "Five of them will produce the same as 50 Ankoles," he says.

Bukenya asks one of the women in the audience to stand up. He praises the bananas she grows and notes the high output of her Friesian cows. "You are a model for the others," he says. The woman smiles. Then, spreading out his arms and looking across the room, he says, "Everybody must be a model."

That kind of exhortation might seem hokey to Americans, but in an African context Bukenya's words are incendiary. It is the mental attitude of African farmers, as much as their lack of money, that holds them back, Bukenya argues. For ordinary farmers to be called heroes, or even recognized at all, by a senior political leader is unprecedented. And Bukenya's message makes perfect sense. Surprisingly, few farmers in Uganda or other parts of Africa keep livestock. In some locales, that's because of the extreme heat; disease is another limitation. Yet many farmers don't raise animals (at least productive ones) even when conditions for doing so are favorable, because of the irrational pull of tradition and a lack of knowledge. But teaching skills to farmers isn't enough, Bukenya says. "You have to instill confidence in them that by working harder, they will benefit."

The potential for breeding (as Souley Madi knows) is large. Two government ministers in Uganda have recently launched poultry operations. Uganda's farm output is soaring, having helped push total exports in 2006 to nearly $1 billion, double the value of 2002. Much of the growth came in agriculture: Exports of coffee, cotton, fish, fruits, and tea doubled. Corn exports nearly tripled. Cocoa quadrupled. Sesame seed exports are up nearly 10-fold. Says Bukenya, "We are doing very well, but we can run even faster."

The beginnings of a profarmer political movement represents a watershed in African history. During the 1960s and '70s, in the first decades after independence from European colonial rule, African political leaders blatantly exploited farmers as part of a calculated effort to speed economic development and make food cheaper for Africa's then-tiny urban elite. They essentially nationalized cash crops, such as cotton and coffee, forcing farmers to sell everything they grew to government "marketing boards" at fixed prices, often well below the going rate. That destroyed the incentive to produce. Worse, the boards were corrupt and inefficient, and they did little or nothing to introduce farmers to new growing techniques, crop varieties, or customers. Meanwhile, the industrial schemes financed by the agricultural "surplus" virtually all flopped.

It is the mental attitude of African farmers, as much as their lack of money, that holds them back.

By the 1990s, African countries were importing large amounts of food, at great cost and sometimes under absurd circumstances. Fresh tomatoes rotted in Ghana's fields, while canned tomatoes from Italy dominated grocery sales. The story was similar elsewhere, with the exception of South Africa. A lack of canneries and other means of preserving fresh fruit and vegetables meant that a third or more of African output spoiled.

The reliance on imported food, and the demoralization of farmers, drove many Africans from the bush to the city. But the situation also spawned a backlash. Change came in two forms. First, international aid agencies, which during the 1980s and '90s had essentially abandoned support for agriculture and encouraged Africans to develop light industry and services, began to realize the folly of their approach. As the World Bank admitted in late 2007, "Agriculture has been vastly underused for development."

African leaders also reversed course, albeit by fits and starts, liberalizing agriculture and permitting multinational corporations to begin buying cash crops such as coffee and cotton directly from smallholders, who were eager to sell to these private buyers after being underpaid or even stiffed by government agencies. In Uganda, once called the "pearl of Africa" by Winston Churchill because of its enormous agricultural output and excellent climate, thriving colonial-era agro-businesses were destroyed by the predations of government after independence in 1962. When a rebel leader named Yoweri Museveni assumed power in the mid-1980s, he took steps to reverse course, including a gradual dismantling of the socialized structure that made every farmer a de facto employee of the state. But the farmers, having been burned, did not respond quickly. They remembered the worthless IOUs dispensed by the government.

Besides, telling farmers to grow more is not enough; even giving them the freedom to sell to whomever they wish is not enough. Farmers need cash buyers. Without willing customers, paradoxically, growing more food can grievously hurt farmers—it raises costs and saddles them with worthless surpluses.

Incredibly, this commonplace escaped farm experts in Africa for half a century. They have learned the hard way that food shortages and famines often result not from a scarcity of food but from too much food. When farmers can't convert their surplus into cash, they stop growing extra. No less a farm expert than Norman Borlaug, celebrated for launching the "green revolution" in Latin America and Asia, made a sobering error in Ethiopia five years ago (for which he later apologized). Having helped introduce higher-yielding grains to Ethiopian farmers, he witnessed a huge growth in output. But because no one thought about who would purchase the expanded supplies of grain, in a bumper harvest the surplus rotted and the farmers, who had borrowed money to obtain seed and other "inputs," suffered badly.

Now farm experts are beginning to change their views, putting the customer ahead of production. In 2004, the U.S. Agency for International Development (USAID) became the first aid donor to pledge to organize its spending around the principle that the end customer is the prime mover in African agriculture. Given a ready buyer who is offering a fair price, African farmers will defy stereotypes of their inherent conservatism and backwardness. "They move like lightning when money is on the table," says David Barry, a British coffee buyer based in Kampala. "Cash is king."

USAID realized that expanding farm output only makes sense when farmers respond to the right signals from buyers about which products are in demand. Part of the answer was for the agency to pay the costs of training farmers to grow those crops, and in higher-quality forms and greater volumes, that the private buyers sought. It also directly assisted private agro-firms, paying part of their costs for training farmers.

A method known as "contract farming" has become a crucial instrument of African empowerment. Buyers agree to purchase everything a farmer grows—coffee, cotton, even fish—freeing him from the specter of rotting crops and allowing him to pro-duce as much as possible. And because the buyers—some of them domestic companies, others multinationals—profit, they have a stake in farmer productivity and an incentive to provide such things as training and discounted seed.

A wonderful example of this virtuous circle has unfolded in Uganda. The country's largest provider of cooking oil, Muk-wano, had long sold only palm oil imported from Southeast Asia. As an experiment, the company hired Ugandan farm-ers to grow sunflower seeds, which were then crushed into oil locally. In two years, Mukwano enlisted 100,000 farmers, hiring an experienced trainer from India, C. P. Chowdry, to organize farmers into groups, train leaders, distribute seeds, and collect the harvest.

Even though Mukwano is the only seller of the particular seed variety needed, and so sets the price, sunflowers are attractive to farmers because they require little tending or water, can be "intercropped" with corn or cotton, and are harvested three times a year. During the planting season, the company broadcasts a weekly radio program that gives advice on how to manage the crop. The effort is wildly popular among farmers. When I visited Uganda's sunflower belt on the eve of planting season, I witnessed one farmer, Isaac Aggrey, ask Chowdry for seeds. In the previous season, Aggrey had earned a whopping $300 from three acres of sunflowers, putting enough cash in his pocket to buy a motorbike. When Chowdry told him, "The seeds are gone," Aggrey became distraught. Chowdry reminded him that he had warned that this could happen. "Next time, set aside the money and buy as soon as we put the seeds on sale," he said sternly.

About the same time aid donors recognized the necessity of helping farmers grow more of what buyers want, the mentality of agricultural experts underwent a sea change. For nearly half a century, starting in the 1960s, there seemed to be an inverse correlation between the application of agricultural expertise by national and international aid agencies and the productivity of African farming: the greater the number of experts, the worse Africa's agricultural performance.

Disdainful of the market, these agricultural specialists pre-ferred to obsess over arcane questions about soil quality, seed varieties, and some mythical ideal of crop diversity. In classic butt-covering mode, they blamed "market failures" and Africa's geography for farmer's low incomes and their vulnerability to famine and food shortages.

Then, about five years ago, a few brave specialists suddenly realized that under their very noses some of Africa's most sig-nificant farm sectors were booming—and booming without any help from the legions of agricultural scientists and bureaucrats in Africa. In West Africa, corn production doubled between 1980 and 2000. Harvests of the lowly cassava—a starchy root that provides food insurance for many people—steadily expanded. In East Africa, sales of fresh flowers soared. Once-moribund cash crops, such as cotton, saw a large expansion, first in West Africa and then in Tanzania, Uganda, and Zambia. The list of improbable winners went on and on.

Even as a steady diet of stories about "urgent" food crises in Africa dominated public discussion, these successes became impossible to ignore. In 2004, the International Food and Policy Research Institute (IFPRI) published a series of papers titled "Successes in African Agriculture." The papers both reflected and provoked a revolution in thinking about African farming. They also ended a long conspiracy of silence among aid agencies and professional Africanists. For decades the "food mafia," led by the World Food Program and the UN's Food and Agriculture Organization, had refused to acknowledge any good news about African farming out of fear that evidence of bright spots would reduce the flow of charitable donations to the UN's massive "famine" bureaucracy, designed to feed the hungry.

The IFPRI report shattered the convenient consensus among experts, donors, and African governments that farmers south of the Sahara were doomed, perpetual victims who could never feed themselves and hence must permanently proffer the beg-ging bowl. Now, because of IFPRI (itself a junior member of the "mafia"), some African agricultural successes could not be denied. That raised a logical question: If some African farmers can succeed, why can't even more?

The sea change in serious thinking about African farming is now of more than academic interest. In nation after nation, farming is commercially viable, expanding, diversifying, and generating profits at all levels of society. Though doomsayers continue to see a bleak outlook for African farmers (the new specter is climate change), even elites are catching farm fever, recognizing that record prices for many foodstuffs, along with growing domestic markets and the possibility of expanding farm acreage in most African countries, means a brightening future.

Not coincidentally, the World Bank devotes its newest *World Development Report* to the status of agriculture globally, and the authors highlight Africa's recent gains and future potential. What a turnaround. As recently as five years ago, economists at the World Bank were telling me that farm production mat-tered little since Africans could always import the food they needed. They would explain that Africans should exploit their "comparative advantage" in labor costs by building world-class manufacturing or service industries and allow others, "low-cost producers" elsewhere in the world, to deliver the necessary foodstuffs to African cities.

Today, Africans have a much greater appreciation of the value of food self-sufficiency. Africa never spawned the indus-tries the World Bank favored, and in the face of the withering onslaught from rapidly industrializing China and India, it isn't likely to. Yet Africans are some of the world's lowest-cost pro-ducers of food. And the absence of large plantations (except in parts of Kenya, Ivory Coast, and southern Africa) is beneficial. International buyers of major African crops from Europe, Asia, and the United States have told me repeatedly that small farmers

A Wish List for Africa's Farmers

Bigger Cities: Often presented as a bane of African life, urbanization increases the demand for food and helps farmers and local agro-businesses strengthen their links to world markets.

Land and Legal Reform: Vast amounts of African farmland lie fallow or underused. In some countries, such as Kenya, Malawi, and Zambia, land locked up in large plantations created by colonial-era land grabs could be more productively employed if put in the hands of small farmers. But poor people also control a great deal of fallow land. Legal reforms are needed to allow efficient farmers to buy or lease land more easily.

More Technology and Infrastructure: Sub-Saharan Africa has the world's lowest utilization rates for irrigation, fertilizer, and genetically modified crops (which are illegal everywhere except South Africa). The continent lacks canneries, mills, and other ordinary food-processing facilities; even storage facilities are rare. Small improvements could make a big difference.

Better Farm Policy: Even successful agricultural country in the world—from the United States and France to Brazil and China—has relied on government intervention and incentives to assist farmers. Poor though they are, African governments can do much more to help growers—for example, by imposing tariffs on imported food and offering modest subsidies for fertilizer and other farm productivity enhancers.

Agricultural Airpower: For decades, poor or non-existent roads have crippled African farmers. Reformers should be bold. Think planes, not roads. Impossible? Just a dozen years ago, there were virtually no mobile phones in Africa. Today, nearly one in five Africans owns one. Just as the mobile phone by passed the vastly expensive challenge of upgrading dysfunctional African land-line systems, a big push into rural-based aviation, aimed at moving crops from the bush to African cities and beyond, would leapfrog the problem of bad roads.

Globalization: African farm exports have increased, along with farm prices, but the continent's farmers mostly serve local markets. They are still hampered by the trade barriers and farm subsidies in wealthy countries that hurt growers throughout the developing world. Such obstacles should be reduced. Over the longer term, rising worldwide demand for crop-based fuels such as ethanol and Asia's growing appetite for food will benefit African farmers. Because the continent has the world's lowerst growing costs, some food production is likely to migrate there from India and China.

—G. Pascal Zachary

The marriage of capitalism and agriculture is not a panacea for rural Africans. Uganda and Cameroon boast some of the best land in the sub-Saharan region. Many other African countries are doing well enough in farming that they can continue to raise output and incomes rapidly by working smarter, notwithstanding the challenges of climate change and poor soil. Yet a few parts of Africa live up to the nightmarish visions of the pessimists.

Malawi is one of those places. In this poor southern African country, Lorence Nyaka, a postal worker turned farmer, is fighting a losing battle.

On less than an acre of dry and dusty land, Nyaka, who is 51, tries to support his wife, Jesse, and 10 children, growing corn and cassava with only a hoe. Without fertilizers or irrigation, his yields are poor and he's totally dependent on uncertain rains.

Not long before I visited Nyaka, he lost a third of his land to his wife's brother, who had become old enough to collect his share of the family's inherited property. As he explained the situation, Nyaka slashed at a patch behind his house that was barely larger than a pool table. He was preparing furrows for corn seeds that he would plant at the onset of the rains, still months away.

Worse, thanks to disease, Nyaka has more mouths to feed. AIDS took the lives of Jesse's brother and his wife, so their four children now live with the Nyakas. That means less food for their own six children, but to Nyaka his obligation is clear. "If I don't help these children," he says, "they probably die."

In these parts, people are so crowded that there's little space for cattle or other domesticated animals. Nyaka does have six chickens, one of which stays, for safekeeping, in his bedroom.

"Our problem in Malawi is we do work hard, but we don't get enough food," Nyaka says. He and his family subsist on a diet of cassava and a fluffy corn dish called *nsima;* both provide calories but scant protein. There is nothing he can do, he says, to alter his routine except wait for the rains—and pray. His fatalism, however frustrating, is typical of poor farmers in these parts.

In truth, Nyaka's options are limited. Thomas Malthus, the English economist and demographer, is getting his revenge on Lorence Nyaka and hundreds of thousands others in Malawi, the most densely populated country in Africa, where 13 million people jam into a narrow strip of land. Two hundred years ago, Malthus described a world undone by too many people and too little food—a world much like Malawi today, where life expectancy is less than 40 years and food shortages are chronic. With about half its population under the age of 15, Malawi is expected to approach a population of 20 million by 2020.

While much of the world now worries about the effects of plunging birthrates and declining populations, in Africa overpopulation remains the most serious threat to well-being, and perhaps nowhere is the problem worse than in Malawi, a 550-mile-long wedge between much larger Zambia and Mozambique. "The challenge here is to enable the population to survive," says Stephen Carr, a specialist on rural development who has worked in Africa for 50 years.

Few Malawians use birth control, and any coercive action to cap family size is unthinkable. Nyaka says that whether he

in Africa, relying on their own land and family labor and using few costly inputs such as chemical fertilizers, are more efficient producers than plantations. Counterintuitively, Africa's attractiveness to global food buyers is growing precisely because its agriculture is dominated by small farmers. And there are plenty of them.

and his wife have more children "depends on God." Even in the midst of the AIDS pandemic—one in five Malawian adults is HIV positive—condom use is infrequent. Only one in two Malawians can read. The government seems confused, at best, over how to help farmers. "The distribution of the spoils of office takes precedence over the formal functions of the state, severely limiting the ability of public officials to make policies in the general interest," according to a 2006 study from a British think tank.

Carr, who advises the World Bank, says that migration "may be the only way to prevent a Malthusian meltdown." With aid from the World Bank, the Malawian government has started a resettlement scheme, bringing people from the country's overcrowded south to the north, but the effort helps relatively few. Another possibility is to encourage people to leave the country, just as migrants left Germany and Ireland during times of economic hardship. Land is plentiful in neighboring Mozambique, for example, and many people in both countries speak the same indigenous language and share customs. Zambia, another neighbor, needs more farm workers for its fertile land. Mobile Malawians could benefit both countries.

Time and again, of course, human ingenuity has provided an escape hatch, giving the lie to Malthus's central claim that population growth invariably outstrips food production. In Malawi, however, the chances are growing that his grim forecast is right on target.

While much of the world worries about declining birthrates, overpopulation is the most serious threat to Africa's well-being.

Even here, though, there is reason for hope, if only farmers can be roused to do more. Nyaka, for instance, lives within 200 yards of a working well. Water flows all day long. If he carried water to his land, he could bucket-irrigate vegetables during the long dry season. When I ask him why he won't irrigate in this manner, he creases his brow and shakes his head. The possibility is inconceivable.

Yet 30 miles away, outside the old colonial town of Zomba, nestled in the central highlands of Malawi, Philere Nkhoma, an inspired trainer in one of the Millennium Villages demonstration projects masterminded by Columbia University economist Jeffrey Sachs, is showing farmers the benefits of hand-irrigation. On the morning I visit, dozens of men are dripping water on row after row of vegetables in a "garden" the size of a football field. This method of babying high-value crops goes beyond watering. While Nkhoma chews on a piece of sugar cane, men feed spoonfuls of fertilizer to a row of cabbage plants. Nkhoma shouts encouragement to one farmer, addressing him as "brother" and complimenting him on his effort. "One secret of this thing," she says later, "you need to know how to speak to the people. You should make sure you're part of them."

Nkhoma's close involvement with hundreds of small farmers in central Malawi won't grab headlines, but it represents a radical new beginning for farmers, long ignored by the very people paid to help them. Malawi's "agricultural extension service has collapsed," according to a confidential British report. The gap is partly filled by aid projects such as the one that employs Nkhoma, whose own life story mirrors the shift in the status of farming in Africa. She's part of a new generation of urban Africans unafraid of getting their hands dirty. After more than 10 mostly frustrating years as a government farm adviser, she was chosen by a foreign donor to earn a bachelor's degree in agriculture. After graduation she joined the Sachs project, where she has wide latitude to innovate and the resources to carry out plans. "If you have an energetic extension worker, you only need to change the mindset of the people," she says. "When that happens, change can occur very quickly."

Indeed, last fall Malawi posted a record corn crop, far exceeding expectations and eliminating, at least for now, any threat of general famine in the country.

Men and women do not live by bread alone. I am reminded of this cliché on a cool September afternoon in Kampala, where I meet Ken Sakwa inside a fast-food restaurant called Nando's. Sakwa is in the capital alone, having traveled from his village in eastern Uganda in a rickety van. He looks fit, if a bit thinner than I recall him.

As we munch on grilled chicken and french fries, he recounts his latest achievements. In February he leased another piece of land, bringing his total acreage to 12, and he now regularly employs six of his neighbors to help him work his fields. In a sign of his standing in his community, village elders brokered a favorable settlement of his vexing dispute with the brother of a neighbor from whom he had leased land. Managing the resentments of less prosperous farmers in the village remains a burden. Sakwa tells me that lately he has been finding small bottles, stuffed with curious contents, near his house. He ignores them, though he knows they are meant as a form of juju, intended by his neighbors to put a hex on him. To smooth relations, Sakwa now lends money to people in need, but he admits, "I usually don't get paid back."

Sakwa's success is indeed striking. He has saved more than $10,000 out of his farm profits over the prior five years, and he's now constructing a large commercial building along the main road near his village. He plans to rent out about a dozen shops, then sell the building and bank his profits.

While we talk, one of Sakwa's cousins, a younger man who lives in the city, joins us. "My relatives in Kampala think I am rich now," Sakwa says. "But I feel I overwork myself." He normally works from dawn until dusk, and unlike many farmers he never drinks alcohol, sparing himself the expense of buying the local brew from the makeshift village pub.

I ask Sakwa whether he might make an exception today and share a Club beer with me. We have something to celebrate. His wife, Jessica, gave birth to twin daughters a few months before, and I imagine he must be proud. He says nothing. When his cousin steps away to the toilet, Sakwa whispers to me, "The children are sick."

He adds, "I am here to get medicine for them." Oh, no. Earlier, I told a friend of mine that Sakwa was traveling to Kampala for no apparent reason. She is from the same region and ethnic group as Sakwa and guessed that he must need "special" medicine that he is afraid to obtain near his village. I scoffed at her suggestion. I lean toward Sakwa and say softly, "Your newborn babies have AIDS."

Sakwa purses his lips and nods. Suddenly, his loss of weight seems ominous. His eyes look gaunt. "And you?" I ask.

"I tested positive. Jessica also."

I ask Sakwa if I can telephone my friend. She counsels people with the disease, helping them to get services and anti-retroviral drugs, often provided at no charge by foreign donors and the government. The ARVs are indeed remarkable, bringing many years of health to most who take them properly.

An hour later, I sit in an outdoor café with Sakwa and my friend. They immediately begin speaking in Gisu, the language of their ethnic group. "You can still be a successful farmer, even more successful," she tells Sakwa. "So long as you get treatment, you can still farm as well as you do now."

I wonder whether he believes her. She looks him in the eyes and says, this time in English, "Don't let the disease take away your success."

The woman, who is a few years younger than Sakwa, realizes that her sister attended school with him. She promises to help him and Jessica get treatment quickly.

Sakwa thanks us when he leaves. It is night in Kampala now, and I sit in the darkness. The electricity is out, and I clutch my Club beer, sipping at the bottle even though it is empty.

My friend orders me another beer, and a soda for herself. "It is good we can deal with what is," she says.

G. PASCAL ZACHARY teaches journalism at Stanford University and is finishing a book on Africa for Scribner.

UNIT 3
Conflict and Instability

Unit Selections

Key Points to Consider

- What factors account for the worldwide decline in conflict?

- What are the regional implications of the Iraq war?

- What factors have contributed to the Taliban's resurgence in Afghanistan?

- What prompted the post-election violence in Kenya?

- What are the causes of the crisis in Zimbabwe?

- What are the causes of the continuing crisis in Somalia? How has Colombia's rebel insurgency changed over time?

- What are the ways to enhance international peacekeeping?

Student Web Site

www.mhcls.com/online

Internet References

The Carter Center
http://www.cartercenter.org

Center for Strategic and International Studies (CSIS)
http://www.csis.org/

Conflict Research Consortium
http://conflict.colorado.edu/

Institute for Security Studies
http://www.iss.co.za

PeaceNet
http://www.igc.org/peacenet/

Refugees International
http://www.refintl.org

While evidence points to a decline in conflict worldwide, conflict and instability in the developing world remain major threats to international peace and security. Conflict stems from a combination of sources including ethnic and religious diversity, nationalism, the struggle for state control, and competition for resources. In some cases, colonial boundaries either encompass diverse groups or separate people from their ethnic kin. A state's diversity can increase tension among groups competing for scarce resources and opportunities. When some groups benefit or are perceived as enjoying privileges at the expense of others, ethnicity can offer a convenient vehicle for mobilization. Moreover, ethnic politics lends itself to manipulation both by regimes that are seeking to protect privileges, maintain order, or retain power and those that are challenging existing governments. In an atmosphere charged with ethnic and political tension, conflict and instability often arise as groups vie to gain control of a state apparatus to extract resources and gain a hand in allocating benefits. While ethnicity has played a role in many conflicts, competition over power and resources may be mistaken as ethnic warfare. Ethnic diversity and competition for resources combined with other factors, which resulted in the war that raged in the Democratic Republic of Congo between 1998 and 2004, is a prime example of the complexity of the root causes of conflicts. The war generated economic disruption, population migration, massive casualties, environmental degradation, and drew several other countries into the fighting. Failing states are also potential places for conflict. Failed states not only encourage warlord behavior but may also offer a haven for terrorists and criminals. The spill-over from the conflict in these states can cause further instability.

Early literature on modernization and development speculated that as developing societies progressed from being traditional to modern, primary attachments such as ethnicity and religious affiliation would fade and be replaced by new forms of identification. Clearly, however, ethnicity and religion continue to remain as potent forces. Ethnic politics and the emergence of religious radicalism demonstrate that such attachments have survived modernization. Inspired and encouraged initially by the establishment of the theocratic regime in Iran, radical Muslims have not only pushed for the establishment of governments based on Islamic law but have also engaged in a wider struggle with what they regard as the threat of western cultural dominance. Radical Islamic groups that advocate a more rigid and violent interpretation of Islam have increasingly challenged the mainstream Islamic thought. These radicals are driven by hatred toward the West and the United States in particular. They were behind the 1993 New York City World Trade Center bombing, the United States embassy bombings in Kenya and Tanzania in 1998, the devastating attacks that destroyed the World Trade Center and damaged the Pentagon in September 11, 2001, as well as the 2004 Madrid bombings and the 2005 London attacks. While these incidents encourage the tendency to equate Islam

U.S. Navy

with terrorism, it is a mistake to link the two. A deeper understanding of the various strands of Islamic thought is required to separate the legitimate efforts that challenge repressive regimes and forge an alternative to western forms of political organization from the actions of radicals who pervert Islam and resort to terrorism.

There is no shortage of conflict around the world, though the causes may differ according to the regions. The war in Iraq drags on, attacks against both the U.S. and the Iraqi government forces persist, and the civilian death toll continues to rise. There is also the concern that the Iraq war will inspire greater sectarian violence in the region. Meanwhile, the Taliban poses a renewed security threat in Afghanistan, where ethnic tensions are rising as well. The nuclear weapons programs of Iran and North Korea have heightened tensions in the United States, and illustrate the growing problem of nuclear proliferation. Parts of Africa continue to be conflict-prone. Somalia remains the world's most prominent example of a failed state, and the chaos in the region has escalated once again. The tenuous peace in the Democratic Republic of Congo has been marred by sporadic fighting in the eastern part of the country. Disputed elections in Kenya unleashed ethnic violence that had been simmering just below the surface. Zimbabwe continues its slide toward economic disaster, while President Mugabe's supporters have stepped up a campaign of intimidation to try and ensure his victory in run-off elections. The killing in Darfur continues despite the deployment of a UN peacekeeping operation, highlighting the difficulties of effective international intervention. Colombian rebels have branched out into kidnapping and drug running. Accusations of connections between the FARC and Venezuelan president Hugo Chavez have heightened tensions in the region.

Although the number of conflicts may have declined worldwide, the threat to peace and stability in the developing world remains complicated, dangerous and clearly has the potential to threaten international security.

The End of War?

Explaining 15 years of diminishing violence.

GREGG EASTERBROOK

Daily explosions in Iraq, massacres in Sudan, the Koreas staring at each other through artillery barrels, a Hobbesian war of all against all in eastern Congo—combat plagues human society as it has, perhaps, since our distant forebears realized that a tree limb could be used as a club. But here is something you would never guess from watching the news: War has entered a cycle of decline. Combat in Iraq and in a few other places is an exception to a significant global trend that has gone nearly unnoticed—namely that, for about 15 years, there have been steadily fewer armed conflicts worldwide. In fact, it is possible that a person's chance of dying because of war has, in the last decade or more, become the lowest in human history.

Five years ago, two academics—Monty Marshall, research director at the Center for Global Policy at George Mason University, and Ted Robert Gurr, a professor of government at the University of Maryland—spent months compiling all available data on the frequency and death toll of twentieth-century combat, expecting to find an ever-worsening ledger of blood and destruction. Instead, they found, after the terrible years of World Wars I and II, a global increase in war from the 1960s through the mid-'80s. But this was followed by a steady, nearly uninterrupted decline beginning in 1991. They also found a steady global rise since the mid-'80s in factors that reduce armed conflict—economic prosperity, free elections, stable central governments, better communication, more "peacemaking institutions," and increased international engagement. Marshall and Gurr, along with Deepa Khosla, published their results as a 2001 report, *Peace and Conflict,* for the Center for International Development and Conflict Management at the University of Maryland. At the time, I remember reading that report and thinking, "Wow, this is one of the hottest things I have ever held in my hands." I expected that evidence of a decline in war would trigger a sensation. Instead it received almost no notice.

"After the first report came out, we wanted to brief some United Nations officials, but everyone at the United Nations just laughed at us. They could not believe war was declining, because this went against political expectations," Marshall says. Of course, 2001 was the year of September 11. But, despite the battles in Afghanistan, the Philippines, and elsewhere that were ignited by Islamist terrorism and the West's response, a second edition of *Peace and Conflict,* published in 2003, showed the total number of wars and armed conflicts continued to decline. A third edition of the study, published last week, shows that, despite the invasion of Iraq and other outbreaks of fighting, the overall decline of war continues. This even as the global population keeps rising, which might be expected to lead to more war, not less.

In his prescient 1989 book, *Retreat from Doomsday,* Ohio State University political scientist John Mueller, in addition to predicting that the Soviet Union was about to collapse—the Berlin Wall fell just after the book was published—declared that great-nation war had become "obsolete" and might never occur again. One reason the Soviet Union was about to collapse, Mueller wrote, was that its leaders had structured Soviet society around the eighteenth-century assumption of endless great-power fighting, but great-power war had become archaic, and no society with war as its organizing principle can endure any longer. So far, this theory has been right on the money. It is worth noting that the first emerging great power of the new century, China, though prone to making threatening statements about Taiwan, spends relatively little on its military.

Last year Mueller published a follow-up book, *The Remnants of War,* which argues that fighting below the level of great-power conflict—small-state wars, civil wars, ethnic combat, and clashes among private armies—is also waning. *Retreat from Doomsday* and *The Remnants of War* are brilliantly original and urgent books. Combat is not an inevitable result of international discord and human malevolence, Mueller believes. War, rather, is "merely an idea"—and a really bad idea, like dueling or slavery. This bad idea "has been grafted onto human existence" and can be excised. Yes, the end of war has been predicted before, prominently by H.G. Wells in 1915, and horrible bloodshed followed. But could the predictions be right this time?

First, the numbers. The University of Maryland studies find the number of wars and armed conflicts worldwide peaked in 1991 at 51, which may represent the most wars happening simultaneously at any point in history. Since 1991, the number has fallen steadily. There were 26 armed conflicts in 2000 and 25 in 2002, even after the Al Qaeda attack on the United States and the U.S. counterattack against Afghanistan. By 2004, Marshall and Gurr's latest study shows, the number of armed conflicts in the world had declined to 20, even after the invasion of Iraq. All told, there were less than half as many wars in 2004 as there were in 1991.

Marshall and Gurr also have a second ranking, gauging the magnitude of fighting. This section of the report is more subjective. Everyone agrees that the worst moment for human conflict was World War II; but how to rank, say, the current separatist fighting in Indonesia versus, say, the Algerian war of independence is more speculative. Nevertheless, the *Peace and Conflict* studies name 1991 as the peak post-World War II year for totality of global fighting, giving that year a ranking of 179 on a scale that rates the extent and destructiveness of combat. By 2000, in spite of war in the Balkans and genocide in Rwanda, the number had fallen to 97; by 2002 to 81; and, at the end of 2004, it stood at 65. This suggests the extent and intensity of global combat is now less than half what it was 15 years ago.

How can war be in such decline when evening newscasts are filled with images of carnage? One reason fighting seems to be everywhere is that, with the ubiquity of 24-hour cable news and the Internet, we see many more images of conflict than before. A mere decade ago, the rebellion in Eritrea occurred with almost no world notice; the tirelessly globe-trotting Robert Kaplan wrote of meeting with Eritrean rebels who told him they hoped that at least spy satellites were trained on their region so that someone, somewhere, would know of their struggle. Today, fighting in Iraq, Sudan, and other places is elaborately reported on, with a wealth of visual details supplied by minicams and even camera-enabled cell phones. News organizations must prominently report fighting, of course. But the fact that we now see so many visuals of combat and conflict creates the impression that these problems are increasing: Actually, it is the reporting of the problems that is increasing, while the problems themselves are in decline. Television, especially, likes to emphasize war because pictures of fighting, soldiers, and military hardware are inherently more compelling to viewers than images of, say, water-purification projects. Reports of violence and destruction are rarely balanced with reports about the overwhelming majority of the Earth's population not being harmed.

Mueller calculates that about 200 million people were killed in the twentieth century by warfare, other violent conflicts, and government actions associated with war, such as the Holocaust. About twelve billion people lived during that century, meaning that a person of the twentieth century

had a 1 to 2 percent chance of dying as the result of international war, ethnic fighting, or government-run genocide. A 1 to 2 percent chance, Mueller notes, is also an American's lifetime chance of dying in an automobile accident. The risk varies depending on where you live and who you are, of course; Mueller notes that, during the twentieth century, Armenians, Cambodians, Jews, kulaks, and some others had a far higher chance of death by war or government persecution than the global average. Yet, with war now in decline, for the moment men and women worldwide stand in more danger from cars and highways than from war and combat. World Health Organization statistics back this: In 2000, for example, 300,000 people died in combat or for war-related reasons (such as disease or malnutrition caused by war), while 1.2 million worldwide died in traffic accidents. That 300,000 people perished because of war in 2000 is a terrible toll, but it represents just .005 percent of those alive in that year.

This low global risk of death from war probably differs greatly from most of the world's past. In prehistory, tribal and small-group violence may have been endemic. Steven LeBlanc, a Harvard University archeologist, asserts in his 2003 book about the human past, *Constant Battles,* that warfare was a steady feature of primordial society. LeBlanc notes that, when the aboriginal societies of New Guinea were first observed by Europeans in the 1930s, one male in four died by violence; traditional New Guinean society was organized around endless tribal combat. Unremitting warfare characterized much of the history of Europe, the Middle East, and other regions; perhaps one-fifth of the German population died during the Thirty Years War, for instance. Now the world is in a period in which less than one ten-thousandth of its population dies from fighting in a year. The sheer number of people who are *not* being harmed by warfare is without precedent.

Next consider a wonderful fact: Global military spending is also in decline. Stated in current dollars, annual global military spending peaked in 1985, at $1.3 trillion, and has been falling since, to slightly over $1 trillion in 2004, according to the Center for Defense Information, a nonpartisan Washington research organization. Since the global population has risen by one-fifth during this period, military spending might have been expected to rise. Instead, relative to population growth, military spending has declined by a full third. In current dollars, the world spent $260 per capita on arms in 1985 and $167 in 2004.

The striking decline in global military spending has also received no attention from the press, which continues to promote the notion of a world staggering under the weight of instruments of destruction. Only a few nations, most prominently the United States, have increased their defense spending in the last decade. Today, the United States accounts for 44 percent of world military spending; if current trends continue, with many nations reducing defense spending while the United States continues to increase such spending as its military is restructured for new global anti-terrorism and peacekeeping roles, it is not out of the question that, in the future, the United States will spend more on arms and soldiers than the rest of the world combined.

Declining global military spending is exactly what one would expect to find if war itself were in decline. The peak year in global military spending came only shortly before the peak year for wars, 1991. There's an obvious chicken-or-egg question, whether military spending has fallen because wars are rarer or whether wars are rarer because military spending has fallen. Either way, both trend lines point in the right direction. This is an extremely favorable development, particularly for the world's poor—the less developing nations squander on arms, the more they can invest in improving daily lives of their citizens.

What is causing war to decline? The most powerful factor must be the end of the cold war, which has both lowered international tensions and withdrawn U.S. and Soviet support from proxy armies in the developing world. Fighting in poor nations is sustained by outside supplies of arms. To be sure, there remain significant stocks of small arms in the developing world—particularly millions of assault rifles. But, with international arms shipments waning and heavy weapons, such as artillery, becoming harder to obtain in many developing nations, factions in developing-world conflicts are more likely to sue for peace. For example, the long, violent conflict in Angola was sustained by a weird mix of Soviet, American, Cuban, and South African arms shipments to a potpourri of factions. When all these nations stopped supplying arms to the Angolan combatants, the leaders of the factions grudgingly came to the conference table.

During the cold war, Marshall notes, it was common for Westerners to say there was peace because no fighting affected the West. Actually, global conflict rose steadily during the cold war, but could be observed only in the developing world. After the cold war ended, many in the West wrung their hands about a supposed outbreak of "disorder" and ethnic hostilities. Actually, both problems went into decline following the cold war, but only then began to be noticed in the West, with confrontation with the Soviet empire no longer an issue.

Another reason for less war is the rise of peacekeeping. The world spends more every year on peacekeeping, and peacekeeping is turning out to be an excellent investment. Many thousands of U.N., NATO, American, and other soldiers and peacekeeping units now walk the streets in troubled parts of the world, at a cost of at least $3 billion annually. Peacekeeping has not been without its problems; peacekeepers have been accused of paying very young girls for sex in Bosnia and Africa, and NATO bears collective shame for refusing

support to the Dutch peacekeeping unit that might have prevented the Srebrenica massacre of 1995. But, overall, peacekeeping is working. Dollar for dollar, it is far more effective at preventing fighting than purchasing complex weapons systems. A recent study from the notoriously gloomy RAND Corporation found that most U.N. peacekeeping efforts have been successful.

Peacekeeping is just one way in which the United Nations has made a significant contribution to the decline of war. American commentators love to disparage the organization in that big cereal-box building on the East River, and, of course, the United Nations has manifold faults. Yet we should not lose track of the fact that the global security system envisioned by the U.N. charter appears to be taking effect. Great-power military tensions are at the lowest level in centuries; wealthy nations are increasingly pressured by international diplomacy not to encourage war by client states; and much of the world respects U.N. guidance. Related to this, the rise in "international engagement," or the involvement of the world community in local disputes, increasingly mitigates against war.

The spread of democracy has made another significant contribution to the decline of war. In 1975, only one-third of the world's nations held true multiparty elections; today two-thirds do, and the proportion continues to rise. In the last two decades, some 80 countries have joined the democratic column, while hardly any moved in the opposite direction. Increasingly, developing-world leaders observe the simple fact that the free nations are the strongest and richest ones, and this creates a powerful argument for the expansion of freedom. Theorists at least as far back as Immanuel Kant have posited that democratic societies would be much less likely to make war than other kinds of states. So far, this has proved true: Democracy-against-democracy fighting has been extremely rare. Prosperity and democracy tend to be mutually reinforcing. Now prosperity is rising in most of the world, amplifying the trend toward freedom. As ever-more nations become democracies, ever-less war can be expected, which is exactly what is being observed.

For the great-power nations, the arrival of nuclear deterrence is an obvious factor in the decline of war. The atomic bomb debuted in 1945, and the last great-power fighting, between the United States and China, concluded not long after, in 1953. From 1871 to 1914, Europe enjoyed nearly half a century without war; the current 52-year great-power peace is the longest period without great-power war since the modern state system emerged. Of course, it is possible that nuclear deterrence will backfire and lead to a conflagration beyond imagination in its horrors. But, even at the height of the cold war, the United States and the Soviet Union never seriously contemplated a nuclear exchange. If it didn't happen then, it seems unlikely for the future.

In turn, lack of war among great nations sets an example for the developing world. When the leading nations routinely attacked neighbors or rivals, governments of emerging states dreamed of the day when they, too, could issue orders to armies of conquest. Now that the leading nations rarely use military force—and instead emphasize economic competition—developing countries imitate that model. This makes the global economy more turbulent, but reduces war.

In *The Remnants of War,* Mueller argues that most fighting in the world today happens because many developing nations lack "capable government" that can contain ethnic conflict or prevent terrorist groups, militias, and criminal gangs from operating. Through around 1500, he reminds us, Europe, too, lacked capable government: Criminal gangs and private armies roamed the countryside. As European governments became competent, and as police and courts grew more respected, legitimate government gradually vanquished thug elements from most of European life. Mueller thinks this same progression of events is beginning in much of the developing world. Government and civil institutions in India, for example, are becoming more professional and less corrupt—one reason why that highly populous nation is not falling apart, as so many predicted it would. Interstate war is in substantial decline; if civil wars, ethnic strife, and private army fighting also go into decline, war may be ungrafted from the human experience.

Is it possible to believe that war is declining, owing to the spread of enlightenment? This seems the riskiest claim. Human nature has let us down many times before. Some have argued that militarism as a philosophy was destroyed in World War II, when the states that were utterly dedicated to martial organization and violent conquest were not only beaten but reduced to rubble by free nations that initially wanted no part of the fight. World War II did represent the triumph of freedom over militarism. But memories are short: It is unrealistic to suppose that no nation will ever be seduced by militarism again.

Yet the last half-century has seen an increase in great nations acting in an enlightened manner toward one another. Prior to this period, the losing sides in wars were usually punished; consider the Versailles Treaty, whose punitive terms helped set in motion the Nazi takeover of Germany. After World War II, the victors did not punish Germany and Japan, which made reasonably smooth returns to prosperity and acceptance by the family of nations. Following the end of the cold war, the losers—the former Soviet Union and China—have seen their national conditions improve, if fitfully; their reentry into the family of nations has gone reasonably well and has been encouraged, if not actively aided, by their former adversaries. Not punishing the vanquished should diminish the odds of future war, since there are no generations who suffer from the victor's terms, become bitter, and want vengeance.

Antiwar sentiment is only about a century old in Western culture, and Mueller thinks its rise has not been given sufficient due. As recently as the Civil War in the United States and World War I in Europe, it was common to view war as inevitable and to be fatalistic about the power of government to order men to march to their deaths. A spooky number of thinkers even adulated war as a desirable condition. Kant, who loved democracy, nevertheless wrote that war is "sublime" and that "prolonged peace favors the predominance of a mere commercial spirit, and with it a debasing self-interest, cowardice and effeminacy." Alexis De Tocqueville said that war "enlarges the mind of a people." Igor Stravinsky called war "necessary for human progress." In 1895, Oliver Wendell Holmes Jr. told the graduating class of Harvard that one of the highest expressions of honor was "the faith . . . which leads a soldier to throw away his life in obedience to a blindly accepted duty."

Around the turn of the twentieth century, a counterview arose—that war is usually absurd. One of the bestselling books of late-nineteenth-century Europe, *Lay Down Your Arms!,* was an antiwar novel. Organized draft resistance in the United Kingdom during World War I was a new force in European politics. England slept during the '30s in part because public antiwar sentiment was intense. By the time the U.S. government abolished the draft at the end of the Vietnam War, there was strong feeling in the United States that families would no longer tolerate being compelled to give up their children for war. Today, that feeling has spread even to Russia, such a short time ago a totalitarian, militaristic state. As average family size has decreased across the Western world, families have invested more in each child; this should discourage militarism. Family size has started to decrease in the developing world, too, so the same dynamic may take effect in poor nations.

There is even a chance that the ascent of economics to its pinnacle position in modern life reduces war. Nations interconnected by trade may be less willing to fight each other: If China and the United States ever fought, both nations might see their economies collapse. It is true that, in the decades leading up to World War I, some thought rising trade would prevent war. But today's circumstances are very different from those of the fin de siècle. Before World War I, great powers still maintained the grand illusion that there could be war without general devastation; World Wars I and II were started by governments that thought they could come out ahead by fighting. Today, no major government appears to believe that war is the best path to nationalistic or monetary profit; trade seems much more promising.

The late economist Julian Simon proposed that, in a knowledge-based economy, people and their brainpower are more important than physical resources, and thus the lives of a country's citizens are worth more than any object that might be seized in war. Simon's was a highly optimistic view—he assumed governments are grounded in reason—and yet there is a chance this vision will be realized. Already, most Western nations have achieved a condition in which citizens' lives possess greater economic value than any place or thing an army might gain by combat. As knowledge-based economics spreads throughout the world, physical resources may mean steadily less, while life means steadily more. That's, well, enlightenment.

In his 1993 book, *A History of Warfare,* the military historian John Keegan recognized the early signs that combat and armed conflict had entered a cycle of decline. War "may well be ceasing to commend itself to human beings as a desirable or productive, let alone rational, means of reconciling their discontents," Keegan wrote. Now there are 15 years of positive developments supporting the idea. Fifteen years is not all that long. Many things could still go badly wrong; there could be ghastly surprises in store. But, for the moment, the trends have never been more auspicious: Swords really are being beaten into plowshares and spears into pruning hooks. The world ought to take notice.

From *The New Republic,* May 30, 2005, pp. 18–21. Copyright © 2005 by The New Republic, LLC. Reprinted by permission of The New Republic.

The Shiite "Threat" Revisited

"Reverberations from the 2003 invasion of Iraq may last for decades. But an inexorable spread of Sunni-Shiite conflict is only the worst case, and frankly it is not very likely."

Augustus Richard Norton

I n the early 1980s, when the shock of the revolution in Iran was still reverberating in North American and European capitals, there was a worry that Iran's revolution would spread like a cancer in the Persian Gulf. The shah of Iran, toppled in January 1979, had been viewed as a surrogate and bulwark of American security in the Gulf. After the shah's fall, concerned US officials would unfold maps showing swaths of green ink marking the countries threatened by Iran. Special note was taken of places where local Shiite communities—presumed allies of Iran—were located. In fact, the fears proved misplaced. While Iran was able to make inroads in Lebanon, especially thanks to the Israeli invasion of 1982, each of the other Gulf governments survived intact.

Now, a quarter century later, the old maps are unfolding once again, and talk of a "Shiite crescent" has resumed. Jordan's King Abdullah, whose kingdom is now host to 700,000 Iraqi refugees, was the first to sound the call in December 2004, but the tune has been picked up by other Arab leaders, the Western press, and some in the Bush administration. Just as before, however, there is much exaggeration in the warnings. None of the Gulf governments is at real risk of being toppled by a Shiite uprising.

US Secretary of State Condoleezza Rice has worked strenuously to construct an alliance of "moderate" Sunni Muslim Arab states, particularly Egypt, Jordan, and Saudi Arabia, to counter the "Shiite threat." These governments are motivated by a combination of justified apprehension about the consequences of the disastrous Iraq War, and by opportunism. Aside from the questionable moderation of the governments in Cairo, Amman, and Riyadh, which neither promote free political life in their own societies nor fully embrace US goals in the region, the wisdom of playing the sectarian card is dubious because it deepens anti-American sentiments among both Shiites and Sunnis.

Sunni Muslims are well aware that the Baghdad government, which enjoys massive support from the Americans, has been implicated in death squad activities and ethnic cleansing operations targeting Sunni Iraqis. Meanwhile, people across the Middle East—in Lebanon, Bahrain, Kuwait, Saudi Arabia, Syria, and certainly in Iraq—see the United States trying to play both sides of the sectarian divide and become only more suspicious of Washington's motives.

"I Thought They Were All Muslims"

The basic problem facing the United States stems from its invasion of Iraq. By crushing the regime led by Saddam Hussein, the Americans gave a huge geopolitical gift to Iran, which is now the most powerful opponent of US hegemony in the Gulf. As American forces struggle to bring order to Iraq, the keenest concern is that the community they have empowered, the Iraqi Shiites, will spurn US influence and ally with Iran. This fear was expressed candidly in late October by US Ambassador Ryan Crocker in Baghdad. He was voicing concern about the strength of Moktada alSadr, whose *Jaysh al-Mahdi* (army of the divinely guided one) is growing in power and support, particularly among the large Shiite underclass. Sadr has been a fierce opponent of the US occupation, and now challenges other Shiite groups in Iraq that are more favorably disposed to cooperating with the Americans.

Ambassador Crocker worried aloud about "Hezbollahization." He was referring to the Shiite Islamists' building of social networks through self-help groups, businesses, service agencies, and community offices, just as Hezbollah ("party of God") had done in Lebanon. Indeed, most of the successful Islamist groups in today's Middle East have built networks of interlinked units that not only help their constituents but also reflect values such as empowerment, self-help, and resistance to oppression. In addition, like Lebanon's Hezbollah, Sadr's Mahdi Army has benefited from Iran's largesse.

It is no exaggeration to say that US leaders were completely surprised by some of the challenges that have emerged from the Iraq War. In a remarkable encounter in January 2003, two months before the Anglo-American invasion, members of the Iraqi opposition were meeting in the Oval Office with President

George W. Bush. Kanan Makiya, an Iraqi-American academic, began speaking about Sunnis and Shiites in Iraq, but Bush interrupted him, puzzled: "I thought they were all Muslims."

Bush would not make the same mistake today. Nonetheless, considerable confusion about the two major sects of Islam persists. Senior US Homeland Security officials, for instance, have been documented identifying Al Qaeda as a Shiite group; it is in fact dogmatically anti-Shiite. In Capitol Hill hearings, congressmen are on record using "Palestinian" as a synonym for Shiite, though there are almost no Palestinian Shiites.

The Heirs of Ali

In all, there are thought to be about 1.3 billion Muslims in the world, and as many as 15 percent of them are members of some branch of Shiism. There are three major Shiite sects, but they all share a special regard for the House of the Prophet Muhammad and the belief that the Prophet's spiritual guidance was transmitted by divine ordination through his descendents, especially through his son-in-law and cousin Ali. (The Sunnis believed caliphs did not need to be descended from the Prophet.) For Shiite Muslims, the holy day Ashura commemorates the martyrdom of one Imam Hussein—the grandson of the Prophet and son of Ali—whose demise in the seventh century, near the city of Karbala in modern-day Iraq, has become a lodestone of modern identity for Shiites, much as the crucifixion of Jesus is central to Christian identity.

The two smaller Shiite sects are the Ismailis, found in small numbers in Syria and Iran, and the Zaydis, who account for a quarter of Yemen's population of 22 million. In the thirteenth century the Ismailis were known as the "Assassins," but today they are respected, prosperous, and deeply involved in education and ecumenical aesthetic pursuits. Their leader is known as the Aga Khan; they number only a couple of million adherents worldwide. (The Druze, an offshoot of the Ismailis, number less than a million and are found in Israel, Syria, and Lebanon. The Alawites, who rule Syria and comprise 11 percent of its population, are often considered to be a Shiite faction as well.) The Zaydis, who ruled Yemen until 1962, embrace a firm moral code in this life but they reject the mystical religious beliefs usually associated with Shiism.

Hezbollah's rivals fear that its ultimate aim is to transform Lebanon into an Islamic state.

Almost all Shiites believe in the eventual return of an imam who will lead the community up to the day of judgment. The largest Shiite sect, the Twelvers, traces the descendents of Muhammad to the Twelfth Imam, who disappeared when he went into occultation more than a millennium ago. In the absence of the Hidden Imam, these believers seek guidance from respected and specially educated clerics, such as Ayatollah Muhammad Hussein Fadlallah of Lebanon, or Ayatollah Ali Sistani in Najaf, Iraq—by far the world's most influential Shiite cleric. In contrast, religious authority in the majority Sunni sect is much more diffuse.

While Iraq and Iran may come quickly to mind when the topic of Shiism is introduced, Shiites are found in significant numbers in six other Middle Eastern countries, as well as outside the region. By far, the largest concentration of Shiites is in Iran, where they comprise 90 percent of the country's 70 million inhabitants; followed by Iraq, where 60 percent of the population of 27 million are Shiites. There are about 1.3 million in Lebanon. Not counting guest workers, about 2 million Shiite citizens are distributed among Bahrain, Kuwait, Qatar, Saudi Arabia, and the United Arab Emirates.

Except for Bahrain, where they account for 70 percent of the half-million citizens (another 250,000 expatriate workers live on the island), in the other Gulf states the Shiites represent only a small fraction of the total population (ranging from 5 to 8 percent in Saudi Arabia to 25 percent in Kuwait). In fact, some of the largest populations of Shiites are found outside the Gulf and the Middle East. There are locally significant populations in Indonesia, perhaps 6 million in Azerbaijan, approximately 10 million in India, and at least 30 million in Pakistan.

The Fluidity of Identity

Popular authors such as the historian Bernard Lewis promote the view that sectarian identity is a permanent, historically rooted quality that lies at the heart of Middle Eastern politics. Lewis has also popularized the view that a longing for the lost glory of the past lies at the heart of Muslim hostility to the West and to the United States in particular. These can be very self-satisfying perspectives for Western readers because they offer a simple formula for understanding Middle East politics, and they absolve external powers from responsibility for political problems in the region.

A mere century or so ago, sectarian affiliation was neither a particularly important marker of faith nor an important basis for political action. In recent decades, before the present fever of sectarianism infected the region, there were actually several initiatives toward *taqarub* (rapprochement) between Sunnis and Shiites. While these ecumenical impulses were not successful, they hint that assuming an unbridgeable gulf between the sects is a contemporary prejudice.

Although the differentiation of the Shiite and Sunni sects dates to the earliest days of Islam, the political salience of sectarian identity has varied dramatically over the course of history, not to mention in recent decades. For instance, in Iraq and Lebanon well into the 1960s, Shiite Muslims were politically mobilized very successfully by the Communist party. Arab Sunnis and Shiites alike were widely attracted to the ideology of Nasserism in the 1950s and 1960s. In Bahrain, where the sparks of Sunni-Shiite tension have ignited several recent clashes, the Shiites were fervent admirers of Egyptian President Gamal Abdel Nasser just a few decades ago.

By the 1970s in the Arab world, heretofore dominant secular-nationalist ideologies began to be energetically challenged by Sunni Islamist groups, which offered both a critique of the secular state and a call for activism informed by a renewal of piety. In some instances, these groups were overtly hostile to Shiism. Yet it was the self-styled "Islamic Revolution" in predominantly Shiite Iran that offered the most profound critique of the secular state in the Middle East.

If Ayatollah Ruhollah Khomeini and his co-revolutionaries were disappointed by the Sunnis' reluctance to embrace their revolution and its idiosyncratic religio-political structure, the exemplar of a state informed by Islam was still powerful. In Egypt, a few Sunnis were so inspired by the revolution that they converted to Shiism, but their very small numbers underline the limited appeal of Iran's model to Sunnis. The most enthusiastic Sunni embrace of the "Islamic Revolution" came in Lebanon, where Iran founded Hezbollah in the early 1980s, taking advantage of the opportunity created by Israel's 1982 invasion and the long Israeli occupation of southern Lebanon, which ended only in 2000.

People across the Middle East see the United States trying to play both sides of the sectarian divide.

There were a few half-hearted attempts to imitate the Iranian example. In Bahrain, an amateurish coup was thwarted in 1981. In the same period, Kuwait suffered several acts of terrorism emanating from its Shiite community. Bursts of militancy erupted among minority Shiites in Saudi Arabia's Eastern province, but these did not last long. Since then, particularly in the past decade, the Saudi government has taken some steps to lift controls on the public practice of Shiism and has afforded the Shiite community modest levels of representation at the national level. Considering that the dominant Saudi religious group is the puritan Wahhabis, who consider Shiism to be anathema, it was a milestone when Saudi Arabia's King Abdullah received Sadr, the Iraqi Shiite cleric, near the holy city of Mecca.

In Iraq, the Baathist regime turned the screws of repression on Shiites and, in 1980, opportunistically launched what would be an eight-year war to contain the Iranian revolution (with clear support from the United States as well as Sunni-dominated countries, including Saudi Arabia and Kuwait). When that war finally ended in 1988 it was Iran that tasted defeat. Iraq's immense Shiite population, which comprised much of the rank and file in the army, had proved deaf to Iran's clarion.

Nonetheless, hints of the sectarian passions that would later brutally affect Iraqi politics were visible in the spring of 1991. Heeding President George H. W. Bush's call for an uprising to topple Hussein, whose army had just been expelled from Kuwait, many of Iraq's Shiite Muslims joined an intifada against the regime. Iraq's army unleashed a furious and pitiless response.

Iraqi Shiites begged at the Kuwait border for sanctuary, where the US military stood watch. American soldiers might as well have been spectators in Rome's Coliseum. The supplicants were rebuffed and turned back to their wretched fates. No state in the region lifted a finger to help the victims, except

Iran, and Iran did nothing to stanch the bloodshed. An estimated 100,000 Iraqi Shiites were killed. Incredibly, this horrendous moment made so little impression on American war planners in 2003 that the invading US forces did not anticipate the lingering suspicion and contempt that often greeted them among the Iraqi Shiites.

Academic experts in some cases only added to the public's ignorance by pandering to or promoting stereotypes. Johns Hopkins University's Fouad Ajami, who was then testifying before Congress on Islamic radicalism, offered the now famous aphorism: "The Sunnis are homicidal and the Shiites are suicidal." Suicide, he said, "is definitely a Shiite phenomenon because of the ethic of martyrdom and martyrology which is exalted in the Shiite experience and which knows no equivalent in Sunni life." As quotidian examples from Palestine and Israel, Iraq, Afghanistan, Chechnya, and a handful of other locales demonstrate, Ajami's insight does not stand up to the evidence. Sunni Muslims have proved adept at transforming themselves into human bombs at great cost to innocent victims, not least on September 11, 2001.

Religious sect, just as any other form of ascriptive identity, such as race or ethnicity, may be used to rationalize a horrifying variety of outrages against those who are different. Abu Musab al-Zarqawi, the late and savage leader of Al Qaeda in Iraq, certainly understood the divisive potential of sectarian affinity. In 2004 he wrote: "If we succeed in dragging [the Shiites] into the arena of sectarian war, it will become possible to awaken the inattentive Sunnis as they feel imminent danger." Before he died at US hands, Zarqawi ordered numerous suicide attacks against Shiite targets, thereby helping to push Iraq's Sunnis and Shiites into a civil war.

The Case of Lebanon

Lebanon already has fought a civil war along sectarian lines, a war that lasted 15 years, ending only in 1990. Today that country is locked in a tense stalemate that Lebanese fear might end with the eruption of a new civil war. Sectarian passions are inflamed for several reasons: the assassination of former Prime Minister Rafik Hariri in 2005; the 34-day war with Israel in 2006 that brought ruin to Lebanon's economy and destruction to many parts of the country; and the manipulations and encouragement of numerous outside players, including the United States, a variety of European states, Iran, Syria, Israel, Saudi Arabia, and some other Middle Eastern nations. Lebanon has also been cursed with a weak central government and a set of self-interested sectarian leaders who often treat the state as a feeding trough.

The 2006 war started when Hezbollah's paramilitary wing provoked Israel by capturing two Israeli soldiers from Israeli territory, thereby breaking the "rules of the game" that defined the security system in southern Lebanon. The United States encouraged and supported Israel's summer war to disable if not destroy Iran-supported Hezbollah. Israel failed and Hezbollah emerged from the war more or less intact, but surrounded by ruins in southern Lebanon and in the Beirut suburbs where many Shiite supporters of Hezbollah live. The US-backed government in Beirut is now in a fierce test of wills with an opposition that includes not only Shiites, but also many Christians and a number of other Lebanese supporting Hezbollah.

While the wider Arab world celebrated Hezbollah's "victory" in the war, closer to home many questioned the party's motives and the war's consequences, which included an estimated $4 billion to $5 billion in reconstruction costs and a heavy toll in lives and personal property.

Politically, the war divided Lebanon in two. One Lebanon is a coalition of mainly Sunnis, Druze, and Christians who came together after Hariri's assassination. This group, demanding the truth about Hariri's killers and a withdrawal of Syrian forces from Lebanon, mobilized as many as a million protesters in downtown Beirut. After winning the parliamentary elections in May 2005, this coalition was in power during the 2006 war. It accuses Hezbollah of instigating the disastrous war with Israel, and of being an agent of Syria and Iran.

The second Lebanon is also a coalition, consisting mostly of the southern Lebanese Shiite community and large elements of the Christian community—especially the followers of the magnetic Maronite Christian politician and former general Michel Aoun. The "Aounists" and Shiites share a profound sense of victimization in the face of what they see as a corrupt and unresponsive political system.

None of the Gulf governments is at real risk of being toppled by a Shiite uprising.

The slow pace of government payments to those who lost their homes thanks to Israel's relentless bombing is widely viewed as an example of official ineffectiveness, much in contrast to Hezbollah's speedy distribution of $12,000 payments to each family made homeless by the war. The opposition alliance has proved remarkably durable. Most basically, it is trying to expand its share of power at the expense of the traditional Christian elite and the Sunni Muslims. Indeed, it is the threat of a decline in Sunni prerogatives and power in Lebanon that has prompted Saudi Arabia to become a key backer of the government.

In Western circles, Hezbollah and the Aounists are perceived as trying to protect Syria by stifling efforts to authorize an international tribunal to try those accused of responsibility for the killing of Hariri and his associates. (The Syrian regime is widely suspected of having directed the assassination.) There is some truth in the charge, since a weakening of Syria would no doubt weaken its friends in Lebanon.

Back from the Brink

The fall of 2006 was marked by an escalation of tension and demands, including an ultimatum by Hezbollah leader Hasan Nasrallah on October 31 demanding that the government either agree to a national unity government or face widespread demonstrations and other forms of organized pressure such as

blockades on the route to the national airport. In conjunction with these demands, all five Shiite members of the government resigned in November. The opposition then noted that, under a 1989 agreement, every major sect must be represented in government. President Emile Lahoud asserted that the government was no longer legitimate (vis-à-vis the question of an international tribune, notably).

To block a vote on the tribunal, Speaker Nabih Berri refused to convene parliament. But in an endrun around the opposition, Prime Minister Fouad Siniora requested action by the United Nations Security Council to mandate an international tribunal. While Siniora's request was of doubtful legality, given Lahoud's refusal to agree to it, the tribunal was approved by the Security Council in May 2007. The tribunal now is a sword of Damocles that swings over the heads of the opposition.

Meanwhile, seven prominent figures have been assassinated since 2005. All of the victims are opponents of Syrian influence in Lebanon; the most recent was killed in a car bombing in September 2007. The result is a climate of fear among pro-government politicians. The political stakes were raised on December 1, 2006, when opposition supporters erected 1,000 tents in Beirut's Riyadh alSulh and Martyr's Square, literally at the feet of the government, and announced that they would not budge until the government succumbed. Massive numbers of people assembled on the first day of the demonstration, immobilizing the commercial heart of Beirut.

As tensions continued to rise, fighting erupted in January 2007 between Sunni gunmen and Shiite protesters. Four people were killed. But Hezbollah at this point stepped back from the brink. Appearing on television, Nasrallah declared that "anyone using a firearm against a Lebanese brother is working for Israel." The situation calmed. It helped that the Lebanese army during this period performed with both neutrality and firmness. Since early 2007 neither side has budged much politically from its position.

While the stalemate has been enormously costly to Lebanon's economy, and while the continuing risk of a new civil war is obvious, the demonstrations are now restrained and usually peaceful. Initially tens of thousands of opposition supporters occupied the tents, but today the tents often stand empty, quiet canvas testaments to the frozen political situation. In all, 10 deaths may be attributed to the demonstrations, which have been under way for a year.

At the same time, however, extremist Sunni groups, some inspired by Al Qaeda, have proliferated in Lebanon. These groups are generally hostile to Shiites. In May 2007, clashes broke out in the Nahr al-Bared Palestinian refugee camp in northern Lebanon. It took the lightly equipped Lebanese army four months to defeat the Sunni group, at the cost of more than 160 dead soldiers and the displacement of more than 34,000 civilians. The urgency of the crisis was further demonstrated in June, when six soldiers from Colombia and Spain serving in the UN mission were killed in the south, following calls by Al Qaeda's number two leader, Ayman al-Zawahiri, for Muslims to confront the "Crusaders," meaning the international soldiers. The attacks led to quiet security contacts between UN officials and Hezbollah, prompting Zawahiri to pointedly criticize Hezbollah.

Hezbollah's rivals fear that its ultimate aim is to transform Lebanon into an Islamic state and that the party is only feigning attachment to Lebanon as a pluralist society. But Nasrallah and his colleagues have claimed frequently that the conditions for establishing a state based on Islamic rule will probably never exist in Lebanon, since such a state could only be established on the basis of broad consent, which is highly unlikely. Whatever dreams Hezbollah might entertain, the conclusion that there will never be widespread support for an Islamic state is a sound one.

A Less Fractious Future?

In his commendably lucid book, *The Shia Revival: How Conflicts within Islam Will Shape the Future*, Vali Nasr emphasizes—in my view overstates—enduring Sunni-Shiite tensions in history. But his argument largely turns on the importance of the mayhem in Iraq as a historical watershed. In the past, social and political conventions kept sectarian distrust and enmity hidden from view. With Iraqi society in chaos and the fate of the state uncertain, the veneers are stripped away, exposing the deep-grained realities. But even if this holds for Iraq, which some respected scholars doubt, it is deceptive to generalize from the Iraqi case. The invasion destroyed the already dry-rotted institutions of a dictatorship, imposed an incompetent occupation on Iraq, empowered a disenfranchised majority, and did so in country where civil society had been obliterated for years. Fortunately, this would be a hard case to replicate.

Even so, the invasion and its aftermath effectively lent validation to Al Qaeda's ideology, and have inspired some anti-Shiite Sunnis to open Al Qaeda "franchises" in places far removed from Iraq. There have been other dubious "accomplishments" as a result of the war. When Hussein was hanged at the end of 2006, he won posthumous fame as a Sunni hero. An Egyptian weekly published a commemorative edition that included a poster depicting the late dictator and captioned: "He lived heroically and died a man."

These developments have had variant impacts in societies where Sunnis and Shiites live side by side. In prosperous Kuwait, the Shiites participate in government, and the Shiite community is defined by several distinct orientations, ranging from secularism and quietism to radicalism. Some Kuwaiti Shiites follow the late and moderate Ayatollah Muhammad Shi-

razi; others support the Iranian regime; still others adhere to Arab religious authorities, such as Iraq's Sistani. While relations among the sects in Kuwait are generally good, the Salafis (Sunnis who favor a return to an earlier, "purer" form of Islam) are usually hostile to the Shiites. In March 2007, a Kuwaiti Sunni cleric named Uthman al-Khamis announced plans to launch "Tibah" (disclosure), a new satellite channel to warn Muslims of "the Shiite threat."

In Bahrain, where Shiites comprise 70 percent of the population but have suffered considerable discrimination by the government, Lebanon's Hezbollah is extremely popular. Bahrain, though tiny in population, is strategically important to the United States. The Fifth Fleet is headquartered in Bahrain and many US Navy vessels are replenished and repaired there. A growing number of Bahrainis are expressing opposition to the American role in their country, and one can expect this opposition to grow. In fact, Hezbollah's al-Manar satellite station is the most popular source of news in the monarchy. Bahrain is the poorest of the small Arab Gulf states, and many of its disadvantaged Shiites are a rapt audience for Nasrallah. In Manama, the capital, at least three stores sell a variety of Hezbollah literature, DVDs, tee shirts, and decorations. The Bahraini Shiites, moreover, boast a proud and long history of political and economic protests. The minority regime is firmly in place in Bahrain, but much will depend on how wisely it responds to inevitable calls for reform.

Throughout the Middle East, reverberations from the 2003 invasion of Iraq may last for decades. But an inexorable spread of Sunni-Shiite conflict is only the worst case, and frankly it is not very likely. One hopes imaginative political leaders will pursue enlightened and conciliatory policies. A spirit of conciliation is implied, for instance, in a recent observation by King Abdullah of Saudi Arabia: "If sectarianism deepens and spreads, its destructive effect will reflect on everyone. It will foster division, polarization, and isolationism. Our region will drown in a conflict whose outcome cannot be foreseen." Equally important, if leaders in North America, Europe, and Asia are able to escape the conceptual prisons they have built for themselves, a less fractious future is possible.

AUGUSTUS RICHARD NORTON, a Current History contributing editor, is a professor in the international relations and anthropology departments at Boston University. He is the author of Hezbollah: A Short History (Princeton University Press, 2007).

Letter from Afghanistan

Are the Taliban Winning?

"There is no doubt that Afghanistan has progressed enormously since 9-11, but now even the positive achievements carried out by the international community appear to be unraveling."

AHMED RASHID

I n Kabul today, most Afghans, from illiterate cooks to well-educated civil servants, take it for granted that the Taliban are coming back to power. Afghans speak of yet another American betrayal, trading theories on why the United States and the international community have not been serious about combating the Taliban insurgency, stemming the flow of jihadists out of Pakistan, or devoting money and resources sufficient to rebuild the country.

Many Afghans see President Hamid Karzai as an increasingly forlorn figure, trapped in the presidential palace as events spin out of his control, grasping for political straws to stem the widespread disillusionment with his government, begging the international community for more support.

Public morale has been most affected by the revived Taliban insurgency in southern and eastern Afghanistan, areas covering one-third of the country, and by the gradual withdrawal of US troops from the insurgency-hit areas and their replacement by less well-equipped or less motivated NATO forces. On average five NATO soldiers have died every week since May, three times the casualties taken by US troops in the same period. More than 4,000 Afghans, including Taliban fighters, were killed in 2006. Some 700 have died in more than 80 suicide bombings, which until 12 months ago were almost unknown in the 27 years of conflict since the Soviet Union invaded Afghanistan.

The Taliban have been able to launch attacks involving battalion-size units of more than 1,000 men, and for the first time in their four-year-old insurgency, they now receive considerable local support. The major Al Qaeda and Taliban leaders are still at large. And the critical Pakistan-Afghanistan border zone, inhabited by the Pashtun tribes, has become the world's "terrorism central," a base area where once again terrorist attacks worldwide are planned, and training and funding are coordinated.

Afghans, including aides to Karzai, believe that the hard-line neoconservatives within the US administration never had the intention to stabilize or rebuild Afghanistan after 9-11.

Iraq is not just a major distraction, sucking in eight times more American troops and seven times more money than Afghanistan has received. It is Washington's ideological and foreign policy focus, whereas stabilizing Afghanistan is a sideshow.

While Iraq has bathed in US funding for infrastructure projects (though these projects have rarely been completed), there is less electricity in Kabul now than there was under Soviet occupation in the 1980s. Afghanistan remains one of the poorest countries in the world—even though it provides 92 percent of the world's heroin, which pumps some $3 billion annually into the Afghan economy, or more than 60 percent of gross domestic product. More than five years after 9-11, and after a well-documented explosion in drug production, there is still no international agreement or adequate funding for a major anti-drug campaign that would offer Afghan poppy farmers new jobs or alternative crops to grow.

Most of the depressing developments in Afghanistan are matters of fact. Others may be matters of perception, or even falsehood. But in a largely illiterate society that for three decades has been fed a diet of violence and rumors, as well as real and imagined conspiracies and interference by neighboring countries, perceptions are all-important. For many Afghans, the perception is that the war against the Taliban is already lost.

Two Steps Back

There is no doubt that Afghanistan has progressed enormously since 9-11, but now even the positive achievements carried out by the international community appear to be unraveling. It took at least $300 million for the United Nations to hold presidential and then legislative elections in 2004 and 2005, inaugurate the parliament, and pass a new constitution. Since then parliamentarians have been killed by the Taliban and abused by warlords, and many from the south cannot go home because of the insurgency. The new constitution is in virtual abeyance across the country because implementing it is impossible.

Japan contributed $100 million to a highly successful UN-led program that collected heavy weapons from warlords and disarmed some 62,000 Afghan militiamen. But now a follow-up UN program to disarm more than 1,000 smaller illegal gangs and armed groups is at a standstill. In northern and western Afghanistan the price of weapons has doubled, as warlords and ordinary Afghans rearm to protect themselves against Taliban fighters arriving in their areas.

The rebuilding of a 70,000-man Afghan National Army by the Americans and the training of a 60,000-man police force by the Germans are going far too slowly. The army numbers just 34,000 men and is poorly equipped, lacking armor and helicopters. Now, in order to protect towns and villages in the south, the government has asked tribal chiefs to provide local guards—a return to the kind of local warlordism that the new political order was supposed to replace.

The beacon of the international aid effort in Afghanistan—restoring education and placing 5.1 million children in school—has been badly affected as the Taliban have killed teachers and students and burned down school buildings, causing 300 schools to shut down. Afghans are passionate about education. It has become the most important indicator of progress and change, and it highlights the differences between conditions today and those under the former Taliban regime—which is precisely why the Taliban are targeting schools and in particular girls' schools.

For many Afghans, Taliban bases and sanctuaries in Pakistan are at the heart of the problem. The Bush administration knows these bases and sanctuaries exist but refuses to acknowledge them. Karzai and US and NATO military commanders believe the Taliban leadership is based in Quetta, the capital of Balochistan province, just 80 miles from the Afghan border. From this safe haven the Taliban are able to recruit, organize logistics, import arms and ammunition, and carry out fund-raising.

Since 9-11 the Pakistani military and the Inter-Services Intelligence (ISI) have deliberately allowed "Talibanization" to take place along the 1,600-mile-long Pakistan-Afghanistan border, both sides of which are populated by Pashtun tribes. Tens of thousands of Afghan Taliban retreated into Pakistan after their defeat in 2001. The radical Islamic schools and parties in Pakistan, which had supported their cause since 1994, gave them shelter. And they were joined by Pakistani Taliban, young Pashtun men who had been indoctrinated by the same madrassas. Today, hundreds of Pakistani Taliban join in attacks inside Afghanistan.

Pakistan sees the Taliban as a proxy card to be kept in reserve and used to mount pressure on Karzai, so that Pakistan can regain its dominant position among the Afghan Pashtuns in the south. Islamabad also believes that Talibanization or the Islamization of Pashtun culture and politics will serve as a bulwark against secular and democraticminded Pashtun nationalism, which is reemerging in Kabul, Peshawar, and Quetta.

A Talibanized Pashtun belt will owe first loyalty to Islamabad rather than to Kabul, and will counter growing Indian influence in Afghanistan, which Pakistan sees as a threat to its security. Finally, the Pakistani military, arguing that only it can combat Islamic fundamentalism, believes that the threats posed by Al Qaeda and the Taliban encourage continued international support for General Pervez Musharraf's regime and for military rule.

Angry and Bewildered

Afghans are disillusioned with the United States and the international community because they see them as providing cover for Pakistan's actions. Anti-Pakistan feeling is running at an all-time high among Afghans across the political and ethnic spectrum.

In a US Senate Foreign Relations Committee hearing on September 21, 2006, General James Jones, NATO's supreme commander, testified that the Taliban's headquarters is based in Quetta. Yet President George W. Bush did not even bring up Quetta when he hosted a dinner for Musharraf and Karzai in Washington on September 27. Jones's comments were largely ignored by the US media—infuriating many Afghans.

Tom Koenigs, the UN secretary general's special representative for Afghanistan, reported to the UN Security Council in September that "five distinct leadership centers of the insurgency can be identified." These include a Taliban northern command active in Afghanistan's northeastern provinces, a Taliban eastern command, and a Taliban southern command, as well as separate fronts established by two Taliban allies, the Islamist warlords Gulbuddin Hekmetyar and Jalaluddin Haqqani.

Although Koenigs did not openly allege that all these fronts are based in Pakistan, NATO and US intelligence place all the top leaders of these fronts—Haqqani, Hekmetyar, Taliban leader Mullah Mohammed Omar, and Mullah Dadullah, the chief commander in the south—in Pakistan. "The leadership relies heavily on cross-border fighters, many of whom are Afghans drawn from nearby refugee camps and radical seminaries in Pakistan," said the report to the Security Council. "They are trained and paid to serve as medium-level commanders, leading operations inside Afghanistan and are able to retreat back to safe havens outside the country," the report added.

The UN Security Council declined to debate Koenigs's findings, which again left Afghans angry and bewildered. Afghans were even more infuriated when Musharraf, during his September visit to Washington, waved the UN report at journalists at the White House, saying that it vindicated Pakistan's denials about providing sanctuary to the Taliban. The State Department declined to correct Musharraf's misreading of the report.

However, the ISI is cooperating fully with the United States and Britain in dealing with their domestic terrorism threat, which in Britain largely emanates from young men born in Pakistan or of Pakistani descent who now hold British citizenship. Access to information from Pakistani intelligence about potential terrorist threats has trumped concerns about Afghanistan.

Many Afghans see President Hamid Karzai as an increasingly forlorn figure, trapped in the presidential palace as events spin out of his control.

Meanwhile, the Pakistani military's controversial September 5 deal with Afghan and Pakistani Taliban in the North Waziristan tribal region has allowed Pakistani Taliban to set up a virtual Islamist state. Although Islamabad insisted the deal would prevent attacks against both Pakistani troops in Pakistan and US forces in Afghanistan, Lt. Gen. Karl Eikenberry, the commander of US forces, told me that attacks out of North Waziristan have gone up 300 percent since the deal was signed.

After promising a strategy of peace with the seven tribal agencies that border Afghanistan, the Pakistani military, under US pressure, bombed a religious school in the Bajaur tribal agency on November 1, killing 80 people believed to be extremists. The action inflamed emotions and left Pakistanis baffled by the military's vacillating tactics and apparent lack of strategy.

Pakistan's military has carried out few of the reforms promised by Musharraf after 9-11. There has been no reform of the madrassas, where radicals and militants are trained, and no serious attempt to deal with extremists. In fact, the military remains in alliance with the largest Islamic fundamentalist party that aids the Taliban—the Jamiat-e-Ullema Islam. Next year Musharraf plans to continue his alliance with these radicals when he runs for another five-year term as president.

India, Iran, the Central Asian states, Russia, and even Pakistan's longstanding ally China are looking warily at Pakistan's support of the Taliban. Most of these states have zero tolerance for Sunni Islamic radicalism of the Taliban variety and they expect the United States to contain Pakistan. If America proves unable or unwilling to do so, Washington's clout in the region will diminish substantially. Weaker countries such as those in Central Asia will move closer to China and Russia to protect themselves, instead of relying on the United States.

Failed Commitments

For many Afghans the other part of the crisis is the incompetence and corruption of the regime. President Karzai has failed to carry out tough measures against well-known drug traffickers, including several in his cabinet and parliament. Western nongovernmental organizations say corruption is epidemic, with aid money and profits from reconstruction contracts being siphoned off to senior officials. Key parts of the reform agenda that Karzai promised he would carry out after he was elected president in 2004 remain to be implemented. The lack of developmental activities in the south has resulted in part from Karzai's failure to purge corrupt or drug-trafficking officials from powerful positions. This has fuelled disillusionment among Pashtuns, the dominant ethnic group in southern and eastern Afghanistan, many of whom are now offering to fight for or at least offer sanctuary to the Taliban.

The other part of the blame rests with the international community's failure to rebuild the shattered infrastructure in the south, including roads, electricity, and water supply, and to invest in agriculture to wean farmers from growing poppies. NATO cannot combat the growing insurgency in Afghanistan unless it shows the flexibility and determination to effectively address major problems that stem from the legacy of the American failure in Afghanistan over the past five years. Turning the tide will mean that NATO has to act not just as a military alliance, but also as an economic, political, and diplomatic alliance—something it has never done before.

NATO now commands some 30,000 troops in Afghanistan drawn from 37 countries, including 8,000 American troops, while another 10,000 US troops remain under separate US command. NATO will need to use military victories as a lever to pry more money out of the European Union, the United States, and the Muslim world—money that, along with funds from Western development agencies, could be devoted to expensive infrastructure projects.

NATO also has to play a critical political role in resuscitating the Afghan government and giving it the confidence to perform better and to eliminate public corruption. At the same time, NATO needs to play a more aggressive diplomatic role in convincing Pakistan to stop supporting the Taliban.

However, as a result of the intense fighting in the south, European countries are balking at providing more troops to the NATO forces in Afghanistan. Norway, Denmark, Sweden, and others have refused to send more soldiers. France, Germany, Spain, Turkey, and Italy, which have troops stationed in the more peaceful regions of Afghanistan, are refusing to send them to the south, where British, Canadian, and Dutch forces are facing the bulk of the fighting. NATO members have also been extremely slow to come up with a reserve brigade and the necessary military equipment for their troops, especially much-needed helicopters.

Lieutenant General David Richards, the NATO commander in Afghanistan, says he is trying to persuade all NATO countries to lift the caveats that governments have imposed on their contingents, caveats that prevent troops from taking part in combat or being deployed where commanders want them. Not surprisingly, the publics, parliaments, and media in many NATO countries whose soldiers are dying in Afghanistan are up in arms—demanding that their governments recall their troops. In many European countries, public opinion equates Afghanistan with Bush's misjudged occupation of Iraq, and the dislike for Bush's policies means Afghanistan suffers as a result.

Stiff Resistance

NATO was ill prepared for the Taliban offensive in the south this past summer. When the NATO forces deployed there, they found themselves under heavy attack by the Taliban, who aimed to inflict such heavy casualties that Western publics would demand a recall of their troops. In "Operation Medusa," from September 4 to September 17, 2006, NATO forces in Kandahar's Panjwai district defeated a well-entrenched force of 1,500 Taliban who had planned to attack Kandahar city. NATO commanders say they killed a staggering 1,100 Taliban fighters, including hundreds of Taliban reinforcements who arrived from Quetta in pickup trucks.

A post-battle report compiled by NATO and Afghan intelligence showed that during the battle the Taliban had fired an estimated 400,000 rounds of ammunition, 2,000 rocket-propelled grenades, and 1,000 mortar shells. The Taliban had stocked over 1 million rounds of ammunition, much of it presumably acquired in Pakistan. "Taliban decision-making and its logistics are all inside Pakistan. There are several Taliban shuras [councils] in Quetta, each with a Pakistani ISI officer coordinating it," said Afghan Defense Minister and army chief General Rahim Wardak.

As in their comments about the war in Iraq, senior US officials have downplayed the threat of any imminent collapse of the Afghan government or defeat for NATO forces. They have insisted that all is well and the Taliban violence is only a sporadic response to NATO's wider deployment. But to many Afghans, it seems the Americans are talking about some other country, not Afghanistan.

NATO and US commanders now believe that there will be no winter lull in Taliban attacks as has happened in the past, and that suicide bombings in the cities against soft Afghan targets and concerted Taliban strikes against NATO forces will continue. Since the Panjwai battle there have been major Taliban attacks in the southern provinces of Helmand, Uruzgan, and Zabul, demonstrating that the huge losses they suffered have not demoralized the fighters.

A major problem for the West is its inability or refusal to acknowledge past failures in Afghanistan, or the country's present predicament, and to offer serious future commitments of both money and troops. Until that happens, Afghans will continue to believe that they are losing the war against the Taliban.

AHMED RASHID is a journalist who has written for the *International Herald Tribune, The Washington Post,* and *The New York Review of Books.* He is the author of *Jihad: The Rise of Militant Islam in Central Asia* (Penguin Books, 2002) and *Taliban* (Yale Press, 2001).

Again

Never again? What nonsense. Again and again is more like it. In Darfur, we are witnessing a genocide again, and again we are witnessing ourselves witnessing it and doing nothing to stop it. Even people who wish to know about the problem do not wish to know about the solution. They prefer the raising of consciousnesses to the raising of troops. Just as Rwanda made a bleak mockery of the lessons of Bosnia, Darfur is making a bleak mockery of the lessons of Rwanda. Some lessons, it seems, are gladly and regularly unlearned. Except, of course, by the perpetrators of this evil, who learn the only really enduring lessons about genocide in our time: that the Western response to it is late in coming, or is not coming at all.

Were the 1990s really that long ago? They are remembered now as the halcyon and money-happy interval between the war against Soviet totalitarianism and the war against Islamic totalitarianism, but the truth is that, even in the years immediately following the cold war, history never relented. The '90s were a decade of genocides—unimpeded (Rwanda) and partially impeded (Bosnia) and impeded (Kosovo). The relative success of those genocides was owed generally to the indifference of that chimera known as "the international community," but, more specifically, it was owed to the learning curve of an American president about the moral—and therefore the operational—difference between genocide and other foreign policy crises. The difference is simple. In the response to most foreign policy crises, the use of military force is properly viewed as a last resort. In the response to genocide, the use of military force is properly viewed as a first resort.

The notion of force as a first resort defies the foundations of diplomacy and also of common sense: A willingness to use hard power abroad must not become a willingness to use it wildly. But if you are not willing to use force against genocide immediately, then you do not understand what genocide is. Genocide is not a crisis that escalates into evil. It is evil from its inception. It may change in degree if it is allowed to proceed, but it does not change in kind. It begins with the worst. Nor is its gravity to be measured quantitatively: The intention to destroy an entire group is present in the destruction of even a small number of people from that group. It makes no sense, therefore, to speak of ending genocide later. If you end it later, you will not have ended it. If Hitler had been stopped after the murder of three million Jews, would he be said to have failed? Four hundred thousand Darfuris have already been murdered by the Janjaweed, the Arab *Einsatzgruppen.* If we were to prevent the murder of the 400,001st, will we be said to have succeeded?

This elementary characteristic of genocide—the requirement that the only acceptable response is an immediate and uncompromising response or else we, too, will be complicit in the crime—should have been obvious after the inhumane ditherings, the wrenchingly slow awakenings to conscience, of the '90s; but the discussion of the Darfur genocide in recent years shows that this is not at all obvious. To be sure, there is no silence about Darfur. Quite the contrary. The lamentations about Darfur are everywhere now. There is eloquence, there is protest. Unlikely coalitions are being formed. Movie stars are refusing to be muzzled, and they are standing up and being counted. Even officials and politicians feel that they must have something pained and wrathful to say. These latecomers include the president of the United States.

All of this is to the good, of course. In a democratic and media-maddened society, this right-thinking din is one of the conditions of political action, as domestic pressures are increasingly significant factors in the formulation of US foreign policy. But it makes no sense—and, in this instance, it is a sophisticated form of indecency—to care about a problem without caring about its solution. During the Bosnia crisis, there were many people who cared about the ethnic cleansing and systematic rape of the Bosnian Muslims, but they insisted that it was a European problem with a European solution. They were half right: It was indeed a European problem, classically so. But it was perfectly plain to every honest observer of the genocide that there would be no European solution, and that the insistence upon such a solution amounted to a tender indifference to the problem.

The Darfur variety of the Bosnia hypocrisy is now upon us. We are told that this genocide must be stopped, now, now, never again, all it takes for the triumph of evil is for good men to do nothing, not on our watch, fight the power, we shall overcome—but stopped by us? Of course not. This is an African problem with an African solution. The African solution comes in two versions. There is the view that Darfur will be rescued from the genocide by the successful resolution of the negotiations taking place in Abuja—or, more precisely, that the people who are perpetrating the evil are the ones to whom we must look for the end of its perpetration. (At the rally on the Mall in Washington last week, Russell Simmons jammed excitedly that the Khartoum government had just accepted a draft of a peace accord. Def, indeed.) This version of the African solution does not even acknowledge the requirement of military force to halt the evil. And there is the version of the African solution that looks to the troops of the African Union to do the job. Nancy Pelosi is especially enamored of this remedy. She has boldly proclaimed that AU troops must be "given more mobility" and "freed from the restriction that limits their effectiveness," all in the name of stopping the genocide. It would be nice, wouldn't it? But, so far, the forces of the African Union have had no significant impact on the emergency. To ask them to do the job is to admit that you do not really need the job done.

Then there is the other alibi for Western inaction, the distinguished one: the belief that salvation will come from blue helmets. After the slaughters of the '90s, all of which numbered the fecklessness—and even the cynicism—of the United Nations among their causes, it defies belief that people of goodwill would turn to the United Nations for effective action. The United Nations is not even prepared to call the atrocities in Darfur a genocide. Kofi Annan says all sorts of lofty things, but everybody knows that he is only the humble servant of a notoriously recalcitrant body. Meanwhile the Sudanese regime maneuvers skillfully—what is the Chinese word for oil?—to prevent reprisals of any kind from the Security Council. And even if the United Nations were somehow to recover its ethics and its efficacy, it would take many months—in some estimates, most of a year—before a UN force could be deployed. No, they are not losing any sleep in Khartoum over the UN option.

There is also the view that this is an African problem with a European solution—but let us come to the heart of the matter. All these proposals for ending the genocide in Darfur are really proposals to prevent the United States from ending it. It appears that there is something even more terrible than genocide in this very terrible world, and it is the further use of American military power abroad. And in a Muslim country! Why, it would make us more unpopular. Remember that in the post-September 11,

post-Operation Iraqi Freedom environment, the sensitivities of Muslims—insofar as they can be clearly known and accurately predicted—must not be further offended. Never mind that they themselves give gross offense: This is a genocide committed by Muslims against Muslims that no Muslims are racing to stop. The poor Darfuris: Their plight interferes with the anti-imperialist integrity of liberals in the only country in the world with the power and the authority (yes, still) to help them. The Democrats in Washington are now clamoring for the appointment of a special envoy to Sudan. (No mention so far of Brent Scowcroft.) That is to say, they are searching for reasons to deflect the responsibility of refusing to let crimes against humanity stand. In the matter of genocide, the party of Clinton is still the party of Clinton.

But it is not only, or mainly, the Democrats who impede a US—or a US-led, or a US-NATO—campaign against the killers. This is a Republican era, after all. And the record of the Bush administration on Darfur has been disgraceful (see Marisa Katz, "A Very Long Engagement"). The president has his own uses for all the alibis. He is not inclined to order one more American soldier into action. (But would the camels of the *Janjaweed* pose a tactical challenge to us? Surely all that is required is a little shock and no awe at all.) And there are other disturbing reasons for Bush's tepidity about Darfur. One of them, again, is Sudan's oil, which suddenly confers upon this repulsive state a certain strategic prestige. And there is also the haunting memory of Sudan's previous hospitality to anti-American jihadist terrorism. In the view of the White House, then, an intervention in Darfur may be counter to American interests. So, in this crisis, too, the streets of Washington now run with realism.

All this is grotesque. Sure, interventions are always more complicated than planned (though they are rarely as poorly planned as Iraq, which must not serve as the only model); but not all interventions are quagmires waiting to happen. And the risks to American values if we fail to act against genocide are far greater than the risks to American interests if we act against it. Is Iraq now all that the United States needs to know? Will we allow Abu Ghraib and Guantánamo Bay to disqualify us from our moral and historical role in the world? Is idealism in US foreign policy only for fair weather? What is so unconscionable about nation-building anyway? Why will we never get the question of genocide right, when, in some ways, it is the easiest question of all? The discussion of Darfur, even by many people whose outrage is sincere, has become a festival of bad faith. Everybody wants to do everything but what must be done. It is the season of heartless bleeding hearts.

Will the Kenyan Settlement Hold?

"It is possible that in 10 years' time Kenyans will look back on the current crisis as the turning point at which the country came close to political disintegration, but drew back and established a long-term framework for democratic consolidation."

JOEL D. BARKAN

On the next-to-last day of February, with former UN Secretary General Kofi Annan standing behind them, Kenyan President Mwai Kibaki and opposition leader Raila Odinga signed a historic power sharing agreement, thus ending a nine-week crisis that had threatened to reduce Kenya to another failed or semi-failed African state.

The standoff between the two men and their respective political parties—the Party of National Unity (PNU) and the Orange Democratic Movement (ODM)—followed the flawed presidential election of December 27, 2007. Most domestic and international observers concluded that Odinga had probably won the election with a narrow plurality of the vote, but the Electoral Commission of Kenya (ECK) declared Kibaki the winner two and a half days after the polls closed. The legitimacy of Kibaki's "victory" was further undermined by the fact that the ODM won 99 of 210 seats in the Kenya National Assembly, compared to 43 for the PNU, making the ODM the largest party. Most troubling of all, the elections polarized the country along ethnic lines, as both parties had mobilized ethno-regional constituencies by appealing to voters' sense of identity. Passions ran high on election day as a record 9 million voters—70 percent of the registered electorate—turned out.

Afterwards, a wave of political unrest and inter-ethnic violence not experienced since independence in 1963 was set off by the delay in reporting the outcome, widespread suspicion about the results, and the polarization of the electorate. In the month following, between 1,000 and 1,500 people died as supporters of both sides attacked the other side, burned homes, and so forth. The attacks occurred in urban centers across western Kenya, in areas of the northern Rift Valley with settlements of Kikuyus (the nation's largest ethnic group), and in the slums of Nairobi. About 350,000 Kenyans were displaced from their homes, many permanently. And while some of this violence was spontaneous, most of it was encouraged, albeit indirectly, by political leaders and local elites on both sides of the party divide.

Kenya's economy was deeply affected by the crisis. Tourism, which had been enjoying a boom, evaporated, and the country's horticultural exports to Europe were interrupted. Foreign direct investment ceased overnight and the value of the Kenyan shilling fell by 9 percent. The IMF estimated that the economic losses during the unrest averaged more than $550 million a week, approaching what Kenya receives annually in foreign assistance. The economic effects of the crisis were also felt in Uganda, southern Sudan, Rwanda, and eastern Congo, places whose imports and exports flow through the Kenyan port of Mombasa.

Kenya, moreover, was becoming "zoned." Members of the Kikuyu, who make up 22 percent of the country's population, fled east from towns in western Kenya to the Kikuyu heartland of Central Province. Luos, who make up 13 percent of the population, and Kalenjins, who constitute 14 percent, were chased out of towns such as Naivasha and Nakuru and forced to migrate west to their ancestral homelands.

Progress Interrupted

The national elections in December, which also included voting for the National Assembly and local governments, were the fourth since the reintroduction of multiparty politics in 1992. Each of the previous elections had proceeded better than the one that preceded it, and the hope was that the 2007 poll would also be better than the last.

In 1992, when Kenya held its first multiparty balloting in 24 years, the playing field before the election was not level. Opposition candidates were routinely harassed by the provincial administration and by the police. The electoral commission was neither independent nor neutral. And there was widespread violence in the western Rift Valley, on a scale close to that which occurred this year. The one bright spot in that election was that, for the first time in Kenya's history, roughly 8,000 domestic electoral observers established a toehold in the process, with active diplomatic and financial support from the United States and other like-minded donors.

The 1997 elections were better, but still flawed. They too were marred by ethnic violence in the western Rift Valley and the area south of Mombasa, but the number of domestic observers nearly doubled. Also, the elections were preceded by a series of "mini-constitutional" reforms that, among other things, enlarged the electoral commission to include members nominated by the opposition and eliminated the president's right to unilaterally appoint 12 members of the National Assembly. The 1997 elections resulted in near legislative parity between the government and the opposition. Significantly, from that point on, President Daniel arap Moi, then in his nineteenth year in office, could no longer govern Kenya on his own, and the legislature began to emerge as a meaningful check on executive power.

Kenya's smaller, poorer ethnic groups have been calling for federalism for nearly 50 years.

The 2002 elections were better still. The logistics were improved. Harassment of opposition candidates all but ceased. A cadre of 24,000 domestic monitors covered all polling places. And Kenya experienced, for the first time since independence, a change in government via the ballot box. That election brought Kibaki to power as head of a broad-based pan-ethnic coalition that included not only his own community, the Kikuyu, but also the Luo, Kenya's third-largest ethnic group and the political base of Odinga.

Hopes of a fair and peaceful outcome for the December 2007 elections were therefore high, despite Kenya's polarized political climate. Public opinion polls conducted before the elections indicated that the presidential race was too close to call, and this increased the temptation for both sides to engage in fraud—but most Kenyans, as well as the international community, believed that Kibaki, Odinga, and the ECK would rise to the occasion. After all, democratization arguably had advanced more during Kibaki's presidency than at any time since independence, and the president himself stated that if the voters chose a candidate other than himself, he would "respect the wishes of Kenyans." The election campaign, though marked by isolated incidents of violence, had been largely free and fair. There was widespread confidence in the ECK's preparations for the elections and in the ECK chairman, Samuel Kivuitu. Domestic monitoring efforts, under the umbrella of the Kenya Elections Domestic Observation Forum (KEDOF), were expected to be as robust as they had been in 2002.

The election, it turned out, was arguably the freest and fairest since independence—until its last stages. International observers, including myself, witnessed an election that was reasonably well administered on election day. The polls opened roughly on time; the presiding officers were adequately trained; there were sufficient ballots and other required materials on hand; procedures were largely followed by the presiding officer at each polling station; all or nearly all voters who wished to vote had

done so by the time the polls closed; and though the counting of the paper ballots at the polling stations was slow—in many places continuing until midnight—it was transparent. Agents of the rival candidates signed off on the count and went home thinking that the rest of the process would proceed according to procedures specified by the ECK.

Sadly, they were wrong, as became apparent during the 48 hours following the close of the polls. In upwards of 35 parliamentary constituencies, the tabulation of the vote at constituency headquarters and the reporting of that tally to ECK headquarters in Nairobi were highly flawed. Domestic and international observers found that both sides probably inflated vote totals. They concluded that Kibaki supporters had perpetrated the far greater fraud. The European Union, which mounted the largest international observation effort, involving roughly 130 observers, called for an internationally supervised forensic audit of the tallies—as did the KEDOF.

With the benefit of hindsight, we now see that the international community, including the United States, was too complacent about several aspects of the polling. First, the fact that the register of voters was not fully purged of deceased voters was largely ignored, increasing the likelihood that vote totals could be inflated without (a telltale sign) exceeding the number of voters registered. Second, too much emphasis was placed on the individual leading the ECK, Kivuitu, instead of the ECK as an institution. The international community had lobbied hard for Kivuitu's reappointment as chairman, but paid insufficient attention both to Kibaki's appointment of five new commissioners and to procedures for reporting the vote from the polling stations to the ECK. Third, the international community missed the fact that Kenyan civil society in 2007 had failed to reestablish the robust organization for domestic election observation that it had mounted in 2002. Only 17,000 people observed the elections this time around—7,000 fewer than in 2002—with the result that not all polling stations were covered on election day.

Last but not least, the United States failed to respond quickly to the problems that unfolded during the two days after the election. Indeed, the State Department congratulated the Electoral Commission on its handling of the election on the very day—December 29—when the election came apart at the seams. Washington amended this statement on December 31, the day after Kibaki was hastily sworn in for a second term, but the damage to US credibility had been done.

While it is impossible to argue with certainty that Odinga won the election, it is possible to argue with near certainty that Kibaki did *not* win. Further, an exit poll conducted on election day suggests that the president may have failed to meet the requirement of winning at least 25 percent of the vote in five of Kenya's eight provinces—a test Odinga easily passed.

Fault Lines

The vote, like the opinion surveys that preceded the election, revealed fault lines in Kenyan society—fault lines that threatened to roll back the democratization and economic gains achieved in the five years since Kibaki was elected to succeed President Moi in 2002. Whereas the Moi years were marked by economic stagnation and resistance to democratic reform, Kibaki's administration turned the country around on both fronts. Indeed, the economy in 2007 was growing at nearly 7 percent annually, the highest rate in more than 30 years. A genuine "trickle-down" of benefits, including free universal primary education, and the resurrection of state agencies responsible for the marketing of coffee, tea, meat and milk, had touched the lives of Kenyans in all regions. Investment and tourists were pouring into the country. Civil society, the press, and the parliament had come alive, advancing to unprecedented levels what had been a tortuous quest for democratization. Kenya, it appeared, had been reborn, and President Kibaki should have won reelection handily. Deep schisms, however, existed within the political elite, reflecting the persistent divides in Kenyan society.

Many attribute Kibaki's victory in 2002 to Odinga. Odinga campaigned tirelessly for Kibaki and swung his political allies and followers in Nyanza Province, the heartland of the Luo people, behind Kibaki. A broad multiethnic coalition was formed, the National Rainbow Coalition (NARC), which brought the Kikuyu and Luo together. The formation of NARC was based on a now-controversial memorandum of understanding between Kibaki and Odinga that ostensibly promised Odinga the position of prime minister, which would carry substantial executive power. The coalition, which included other prominent non-Kikuyu leaders from outside Nyanza, was also promised an "equal" number of posts in Kibaki's cabinet should he win the election. After the election, however, Kibaki reneged on the deal—though he did appoint Odinga minister of works and housing. This perceived betrayal planted seeds for the turmoil that erupted five years later.

Kibaki further miscalculated by relying heavily as president on a small group of ministers from his own Kikuyu tribe, as well as from the culturally related Meru and Embu communities. These ministers, dubbed the "Mount Kenya Mafia" because they came from the ethnic groups that inhabit the slopes around Mount Kenya, controlled the key departments of finance, defense, internal security, justice, and information.

Kibaki began his first term in ill health, the result of a debilitating auto accident before the 2002 election and at least one stroke soon after his inauguration. As a consequence, especially during the first half of his presidency, he relied heavily on the "Mafia." This group of mostly older politicians was determined to run Kenya as it had been run during the 1960s and 1970s by the country's first president, Jomo Kenyatta. That is, they meant to pursue sound macroeconomic policies and delegate substantial authority to the civil service and the business community. In marked contrast to Moi, Kibaki and his inner circle did not micromanage either the bureaucracy or the private sector. The result was that individual Kenyans enjoyed more personal freedom, both political and economic, than at any time since independence.

The problem was that many members of other ethnic groups regarded the Mount Kenya Mafia, and thus the Kibaki administration, as favoring the Kikuyu at the expense of their own communities. The Kikuyu, as the largest ethnic group in Kenya, as well as the best educated and most prosperous, have long held a disproportionate number of positions in the civil service and the profes-

sions. Kikuyu are also overrepresented in the business community, which has prospered as the country's economy has regained its dominance in East Africa. As a result, the same perception that had dogged the Kenyatta regime at the end of the 1970s, and that had triggered the ruinous redistribution policies of the Moi era, now confronted Kibaki and his government—that the Kikuyu run the country to serve themselves (even though all regions and ethnic groups have arguably benefited under Kibaki's rule).

Hence, even as Kibaki campaigned for reelection in 2007 on the theme that the country had never had it so good, the opposition, led by Odinga, mobilized the electorate with appeals for change—arguing that a new administration would do a better job of equally distributing the fruits of Kenya's economic and political success across the country's 42 ethnic groups. Odinga and the ODM also called for *majimbo,* the establishment of a federal form of government that would protect the interests of the other ethnic groups. The implicit anti-Kikuyu message was clear.

The Violent Aftermath

This appeal, in addition to a well-organized, well-financed, and colorful campaign by the ODM, enabled Odinga and other prominent non-Kikuyu leaders to rally a majority of Kenyans against Kibaki. Inevitably, the campaign also polarized the country along ethnic lines. While over 90 percent of the Kikuyu and Meru residents around Mount Kenya voted for Kibaki, a similar percentage of Luos in Nyanza voted for Odinga. Odinga also rolled up large majorities of between 55 and 70 percent of the vote in Western Province, the home of the Luhya people; in Rift Valley Province, the homeland of the Kalinjin and a half dozen other small tribes; in Coast Province, which is also inhabited by smaller ethnic groups, as well as most of Kenya's Muslim population; and in North Eastern Province. Odinga obtained a narrow majority in Nairobi, the capital, as well.

As noted previously, Odinga's ODM won many more seats than did Kibaki's PNU. When the seats held by allies of the two parties were added in, the ODM majority became much smaller—roughly 105 to 88, with the balance of the seats not committed to either side. The results, nonetheless, reflected dissatisfaction across Kenya with Kibaki's government. Even within the Kikuyu heartland, more than half the members of Kibaki's cabinet were defeated, as were a substantial number of Kikuyu incumbents, including two members of the old guard—Njenga Karume, the minister of defense, and David Mwiraria, the former minister of finance. The election revealed, in addition to the tensions between the Kikuyu and the other ethnic groups, deep generational divisions within the Kikuyu community. Many younger Kikuyu, especially professionals and members of the business community, believe that Kibaki's "exclusivist" approach to governance has not served their long-term interests nor the interests of the group, because it stokes resentment on the part of the other tribes.

Resentment against the Kikuyu runs particularly deep in the area of the western Rift Valley, in the triangle formed by Nakuru, Eldoret, and Kericho. It is in this area, inhabited by Kenya's white settler community before independence, that most of the killing occurred in the week following the election. In the 1960s and early 1970s, land vacated by the former settlers was purchased by Kikuyu with the assistance of the Kenyan government—then led by Kenyatta, himself a Kikuyu— instead of being returned to the communities from which the land had been taken. This, along with Kikuyu migration into the area as far back as the 1920s, created a domestic Kikuyu diaspora 100 miles west of the Kikuyu's Mount Kenya homeland. It was this group that suffered the most during the post-election violence.

In this context, the election and the violence that followed it made clear that Kibaki and his allies could not govern the country, despite having been sworn in for a second term. Nor could Odinga. Neither Kibaki nor Odinga won more than 46 percent of the vote. Neither was regarded by a majority of Kenyans as their legitimate representative, and it was quickly evident that a negotiated deal between the two principals and their parties was essential for long-term stability and economic wellbeing.

Talks That Nearly Failed

To this end, Kibaki announced on January 7, 2008, that he was prepared to form a government of national unity that presumably would give the ODM a large proportion of seats in the cabinet. Unfortunately, the president and his advisers misunderstood what type of deal would be required to return the country to the peace it had enjoyed before the elections. Moreover, on January 8, Kibaki undermined the prospects for a quick settlement by appointing as vice president Kalonzo Musyoka, the candidate who finished third in the presidential race with roughly 8 percent of the vote. He also appointed 16 people to the cabinet. His spokesperson described the new appointees as only "part" of the cabinet, but the appointments included the most powerful minis tries—finance, internal security, justice, local government, and defense.

The election was arguably the freest and fairest since independence—until its last stages.

These moves may have been meant to signal to Odinga and the ODM that the president was fully in charge. But they were more examples of the self-isolating and ethnically insensitive policies that had already marked the Kibaki presidency. In fact, based on his cabinet appointments, it appeared that Kibaki intended to base his new government on a central-eastern alliance of the Kikuyu, Embu, Meru, and Kamba peoples—versus everybody else.

This was precisely the type of governance that Odinga and his colleagues wanted to end, and they would not settle for mere posts in an expanded cabinet. After making it clear that they did not recognize Kibaki or his hastily appointed government as legitimate, they demanded genuine power sharing between the two sides. This would involve, at a minimum, the creation of a prime minister position—a prime minister who would exer-

cise real executive power and supervise the day-to-day work of government ministries, and who would be accountable to the National Assembly, *not* to the president. The ODM also demanded at least half the positions in the cabinet and, most important, a new constitution that would guarantee the arrangement, grant greater power to the legislature, and possibly establish a federal form of government.

The leaders of Kenya's smaller, poorer ethnic groups—the "have-nots," compared to the Kikuyu—have been calling for federalism for nearly 50 years. As in India in the 1950s, Nigeria in the 1980s, and Ethiopia in the 1990s, the effort to defuse linguistic and ethnic strife may require restructuring the basic rules of the political game by providing every group a homeland—even though this could result in ethnically homogeneous "zones" in which members of other groups have limited rights. Given the realities of Kenya and other plural societies across Africa, democratization must entail more than the expansion of individual rights, both political and economic. Group rights, to address the ethnic factor, must be afforded too, especially when inequities are perceived.

Kibaki and Odinga thus articulate and represent two different visions of Kenya's political future, and it is not surprising that in the aftermath of the election debacle the two sides quickly fell into stalemate—a condition that persisted for two months, despite carnage and heavy economic costs. During January, each side's strategy was simply to outlast the other. Kibaki, having been sworn in as president and in control of the state apparatus, refused, along with the PNU hard-liners around him, to offer the opposition more than a number of unspecified posts in a "government of national unity." They calculated that Odinga and the ODM, out of financial resources and not in office, would soon cave. The government rebuffed mediation efforts by figures such as Nobel laureate Desmond Tutu; Ghanaian President John Kufuor, then in his capacity as the rotating chair of the African Union (AU); and Mark Malloch Brown, Britain's foreign minister for Africa, Asia, and the UN. From the hard-liners' perspective (especially the minister of justice, Martha Karua), these visitors were meddling in Kenya's internal affairs.

Odinga and the ODM, in contrast, called for international mediation, and announced mass demonstrations to protest Kibaki's rule. They also calculated that they could outlast their adversaries because the economic losses borne by the Kikuyu business class would ultimately force Kibaki to address opposition demands. The result, in the near term, was more violence—including the shooting of several protesters in Kisumu and Nairobi, continued evictions of Kikuyu from the western Rift Valley, and mounting damage to the economy.

Three significant constituencies, one internal and two external, became increasingly alarmed about the possibility that what all regarded as the "anchor state" of East Africa and a symbol of political and economic reform for Africa as a whole was moving closer to the political abyss. The first such constituency was the country's civil society and press (both of which are arguably the most robust on the continent, save perhaps for South Africa's). The second constituency consisted of the heads of AU member states, particularly Kufuor, Abdoulaye Wade of Senegal, Yoweri Museveni of Uganda, Paul Kagame of Rwanda, and Jakaya

Kikwete of Tanzania. All of these leaders stated publicly that a negotiated solution to the crisis had to be found. The third constituency was the international community beyond Africa, led by the United States, Britain, and the EU. They stepped up consultations among themselves and agreed that the best approach was to throw their collective weight behind the AU's position of bringing in Annan to mediate the dispute. This proposal was one Kibaki and the hard-liners around him could not refuse, though it became evident in the negotiations that followed that they did not intend to change their positions.

The obvious questions are if the deal will hold and if the government will function. The answers are unclear.

Following Annan's arrival in late January, the two sides sat down to what became four weeks of talks that yielded little progress. The sides were each represented by three senior leaders, but the principals themselves were not involved. Without them, both sides stuck to their basic positions. For the PNU, this meant expanding the cabinet to accommodate the ODM, and creating a non-executive prime minister position that would be filled by and accountable to the president. Most important from the PNU's standpoint was that any deal would have to be arranged within the framework of the country's existing constitution, which assigns most powers to the president. The ODM leaders said no. They, remembering Kibaki's failure to appoint Odinga prime minister after the 2002 elections, insisted that any deal be cemented by an amendment to the constitution.

Although the talks made little progress, the teams did succeed in defining four issues that had to be addressed for Kenya to achieve a lasting peace. These were ending the violence; providing humanitarian assistance to those who need it; addressing the longstanding political issues underlying the conflict, including the country's constitution; and addressing long-term socioeconomic issues such as land tenure rights, poverty, and inequality. But apart from listing these issues, little was achieved. An uneasy calm spread across Kenya while the talks were under way, but few had any illusions about what would happen if the negotiations failed.

They nearly did fail. As the weeks passed, Annan made his frustrations known and stated the obvious—that both sides must make painful concessions if there was to be a settlement. He gained some assistance on February 18 when US Secretary of State Condoleezza Rice, who was in Africa at the time, flew to Nairobi to put pressure on the principals. Rice's visit, plus her blunt talk to both sides (especially Kibaki and the members of his negotiating team) pushed the talks to completion—though not immediately. Annan spoke in generalities about making hard choices, but Rice said explicitly that resolving the crisis required "genuine power sharing, not *pretend* power sharing." Rice reiterated her view five days later upon returning to the United States. At a tarmac press conference in Washington she again called for genuine power sharing, adding that she was

"disappointed" by the lack of progress since her visit to Nairobi, and that the US-Kenya relationship could not be "business as usual" if the two sides failed to reach an agreement. On the other hand, she said, the international community would stand by Kenya through its crisis should a deal be reached.

On February 25, Annan suspended the talks and announced that he would negotiate directly with Kibaki and Odinga to break the impasse. These new talks took place on February 27, with the participation of AU Chair Kikwete. Kikwete twisted Kibaki's arm by arguing that just as Tanzanian presidents had learned to live with a prime minister and a divided government, Kibaki could too—and that this was essential for peace and prosperity in Kenya and in the region. At that point, Kibaki agreed to a power sharing arrangement very much along the lines proposed by the ODM. Not surprisingly, the deal met with jubilation across western Kenya but with tepid acceptance across Central Province, the Kikuyu heartland.

Now the Hard Part

Although the accord resolves the immediate crisis, the obvious questions are if the deal will hold and if the government will function. The answers are unclear, especially when one notes what the agreement does *not* resolve. Apart from creating a prime minister accountable to the National Assembly, the deal is silent on the constitutional issues facing Kenya—particularly the powers of the president, the specific division of labor between the president and the prime minister, the balance of power between the executive and the legislature, and the parameters of any future federal arrangement. Also unmentioned in the accord are the four sets of issues identified during the negotiations as key to lasting peace. In short, implementing the spirit and the letter of the deal depends entirely on establishing trust between Kibaki and Odinga, and between their respective lieutenants.

The two leaders, in an effort to assure both Kenyans and the international community that they were serious about implementing the accord, moved during the first week of the parliamentary session that convened on March 11 to pass the National Accord and Reconciliation Act and the companion Constitutional Amendment Act. They also released four supplementary agreements. The first creates a commission of inquiry to examine the nature and cause of the violence that engulfed Kenya following the elections. The second establishes a Truth and Reconciliation Commission (TRC) to examine the historical grievances, including land issues, that have divided Kenya since independence in 1963. The TRC, which will function for a maximum of two years, is modeled on a similar body that existed in South Africa following apartheid. The third agreement establishes a committee of experts to review all aspects of the electoral process to ensure that the flaws evident in the 2007 elections are corrected before the next elections. (Significantly, the committee is *not* charged with conducting an audit or recount to determine who actually won the election.) Last is an agreement calling on the National Assembly to establish a statutory basis for a review of the nation's constitution and a referendum on any new or revised constitution.

While the basic power sharing deal is solidified by the passage of the National Accord and Reconciliation Act and the supplementary agreements, the hard work has only begun (as Annan rightly noted at the time the agreement was signed). This is particularly true when it comes to negotiating a new constitution, a subject on which even the supplementary agreement is vague. So what are the prospects for overall success?

One of three scenarios is likely to unfold, depending on how well Kibaki and Odinga are able to work together and keep their respective hard-liners in check. The most optimistic scenario is smooth sailing all the way. This is highly unlikely, especially on the issue of constitutional reform. Kenya has tried three times over the past 15 years to amend its constitution and has failed on two of those occasions. Sorting out a permanent structure for the executive, and deciding whether and in what form power will devolve to subnational units of government, will be particularly difficult. Already there is friction between the PNU and the ODM over which party will control which ministries in the new government.

The second and most likely scenario is muddling through. Under this scenario, negotiations for both the formation of a new government and the resolution of other issues will be protracted—but incremental (if not holistic) solutions will be found that avoid a total breakdown of the power sharing process. Power sharing, however, is in any case not an end in itself and cannot be sustained indefinitely. Rather, it is a mechanism to put Kenya back on track.

The third scenario is, within six to eighteen months, a political divorce, a breakdown, and the resumption of violence. This is also unlikely. While the coalition government will probably not last until the next election, neither will there likely be an acrimonious divorce—if for no other reason than that the leadership on both sides, especially Kibaki and Odinga themselves, have been chastened by the recent crisis.

While one must be cautious in assessing the future, it is possible that in 10 years' time Kenyans will look back on the current crisis as the turning point at which the country came close to political disintegration, but drew back and established a long-term framework for democratic consolidation, peace, and prosperity.

JOEL D. BARKAN is a senior associate at the Center for Strategic and International Studies and a professor emeritus of political science at the University of Iowa.

Zimbabwe Goes to the Brink

The "Big Man", last of the independence leaders, never seriously contemplated electoral defeat. But as the results trickled out, it became clear Mugabe's 28-year rule was threatened. He may dig his heels in but the country faces certain change.

ALEC RUSSELL

As starry-eyed supporters of the Zimbabwean opposition Movement for Democratic Change (MDC) queued to vote on Saturday 29 March there were far too many police around for them to dare make their feelings plain. So, instead, a series of irreverent text messages hummed from polling station to polling station across the country.

"Bob 23 verses one to five," started one, a spoof of Psalm 23. "Mugabe is my shepherd I shall not work. He makes me to lie down on park benches. He leads me to be a thief, a prostitute, a liar and an asylum-seeker. He restores my faith in MDC. He guides me in the path of unemployment. Though I walk in the valley of Zim I shall still be hungry!!!"

"Do you know anyone with a pick-up truck?" ran another. "I have a client who I want to move. He is moving this weekend from State House to Kutama [Mugabe's rural retreat]."

For almost 24 hours the same giddy mood prevailed among supporters of the MDC. Few celebrated publicly. Most in Harare walked home from the polls—almost everyone walks in Zimbabwe these days to save the cost of a standard bus fare, Z$40,000 or about US$1, equivalent to a tenth of a standard labourer's monthly wage—keeping their voting preference to themselves and their close friends. But increasingly people dared to dream that, after 28 years in power—and three disputed elections in the past eight years—the "old man" was finally on his way out.

Such optimism reached fever pitch after a pre-dawn press conference on the Sunday morning following voting, when Tendai Biti, the puckish secretary general of the MDC, strode to a podium and informed bleary-eyed diplomats and journalists that his party was comfortably ahead. But, for watchers of state television, it all came to a juddering halt a few minutes before midnight on Sunday night. ZBC was playing an unbelievably bad movie premised on Jim Hawkins running into Long John Silver in the Caribbean 20 years after the *Treasure Island* escapade and falling in love with his daughter.

Suddenly Long John et al vanished off the screen to be replaced by the expressionless features of a correspondent at the state-appointed Zimbabwe Election Commission (ZEC).

Increasingly people dared to dream that Robert Mugabe was finally on his way out.

The presenter quickly introduced Judge George Chiweshe, chairman of the ZEC. He had last been seen that same day as he was chased across the lobby of a Harare hotel by outraged MDC supporters demanding to know why he had not released any results. This time he was on safer ground. He was in the election command centre in central Harare.

People who were complaining about the time it was taking to verify the results should be patient, he told the nation. "It's an involving and laborious process. It takes time for results to filter through." And as for "stakeholders" (read the MDC) who had ventured to release early results: "The commission would like to reiterate that it and it alone is the sole legitimate source of all results."

Innocents in the world of Zimbabwe's ruling Zanu-PF party might have struggled to understand the import of what developed into a 20-minute ramble. To the MDC, however, the message was all too stark. After 24 hours of seemingly being stunned into silence, the authorities had returned to the fray: Mugabe and Zanu-PF were not going to go easily.

Party insiders say that Mugabe was startled by the initial returns from polling stations, which made it clear he was heading for defeat.

For the previous 12 months his senior aides had stacked the odds in his favour. In March last year they gave orders to agricultural equipment companies to have large numbers of rotivators, and rather smaller numbers of tractors, ready for March 2008. These were duly rolled out with great fanfare to small farmers in impoverished rural communities in the weeks leading up to the 29 March vote. Food aid was doled out to party supporters and, according to a dogged Human Rights Watch researcher, Tiseke Kasambala, denied to MDC supporters. The ZBC churned out endless encomia to the president, or the Fist of Empowerment, as he is called on election posters.

Meanwhile, day after day, giant rallies of happy, smiling people greeted him on the campaign trail, presumably reassuring him that the opposition talk of economic implosion had not been accepted by his loyal people.

As the *New Statesman* went to press it was clear that despite Zanu-PF's advantages it was all but impossible for it to deny the MDC had won and also that insiders in the ruling party were realising there was no way to massage the outcome. A projection by an independent survey group underlined the difficulty the ZEC would have in issuing results giving Mugabe victory. The findings gave Morgan Tsvangirai's MDC 49.4 per cent, with Mugabe 41.8 per cent.

This suggested that the MDC leader was below the 50 per cent-plus-one vote mark he needed to avoid a run-off, but the MDC's results suggested he had enough votes to avoid a run-off. In short, Mugabe had been beaten.

He was not going to go without a fight. On Sunday night he met the "securocrats" of the Joint Operations Command, the body of security, intelligence and military chiefs who in recent years have increasingly dominated policymaking. According to some accounts of the meeting, some dared to take a "dovish" stance and suggest that the veteran autocrat should consider reaching an accommodation with the MDC.

The ultra-hawks urging an immediate declaration of a state of emergency were believed to have been talked out of such a drastic response. But what is widely believed to have been the final decision was hardly conciliatory. It was to stall for time, order the ZEC to dribble out results slowly and see if they could not end up "fixing" the election in the counting process, a senior former Zanu-PF official said. Not long afterwards, the ZBC interrupted *Treasure Island 2* or whatever it was and introduced Chiweshe into Zimbabwean living rooms.

The phenomenon of a long-serving independence leader being rejected by his people has been seen before in Southern Africa. Kenneth Kaunda, the veteran Zambian leader with a penchant for waving handkerchiefs, was unceremoniously dumped by the electorate in 1991. Then, in 1994, Hastings Banda, the eccentric Malawian tyrant, suffered a similar ejection from State House. Both ultimately accepted their lot.

In recent weeks both Tsvangirai and Simba Makoni, Mugabe's other challenger, a former finance minister, have tried to tempt Mugabe to bow out gracefully. Both indicated to me in interviews that they would not seek to humiliate the former hero of the independence era if he lost.

Clinging to Power

But while Mugabe was unwilling to follow the lead of these regional predecessors—Harare legend has it that he laughed scornfully when he heard that Kaunda had lost power through the ballot box—increasingly, as the days passed after the elections, MDC optimism grew that a deal would be struck with some of the more conciliatory generals loyal to his regime. They would then, the MDC hoped, aided by support from regional leaders, persuade Mugabe to step down.

Zimbabwe in Numbers

100,000+%
rate of inflation

Z$100,000
= £1.70

Z$6.6m
official cost of a loaf of bread

Z$15m
black-market cost of a loaf of bread

37
average life expectancy

80%
unemployment rate

15.6%
of population is infected with HIV/Aids

75%
of doctors emigrate after earning medical degree

45%
of Zimbabweans are malnourished

5.9m
registered voters

9m
ballots printed by Electoral Commission

Research by Jax Jacobsen

The smart money among diplomats and regional analysts is betting that even if Mugabe does finagle his way back into power and cheat Tsvangirai of his apparent victory, he cannot hope to last long in office. Makoni's defection, while not backed in public by many senior cadres, reflects an increasingly mutinous sentiment within Zanu-PF. While inflation on paper is a "mere" 100,000 per cent, economists expect it may be 500,000 by the end of this month.

Whatever happens, Mugabe's aura of invincibility has been destroyed by the dramatic events of the past week.

An extension of his rule, even by, say, six months, would be a disaster for Zimbabwe. Yet more desperate people would flee across the southern border to join the between one and three million who have already crossed into South Africa. Infant mortality, illiteracy and all those other statistics that made Zimbabwe in Mugabe's early years in power the envy of sub-Saharan Africa would continue to rise.

In short, the spoof Psalm 23 would suddenly seem rather unfunny. At the time of writing it was still possible that Mugabe would try to dig his heels in one last time. But there was a sense that one of the last of Africa's "Big Men" independence leaders was on his way out.

ALEC RUSSELL is Southern Africa correspondent of the *Financial Times*.

The Somali Catastrophe

Bigger than the Horn—and Not Over Yet

"All indications point to the Mogadishu insurgency growing more violent and uncontrolled."

KENNETH J. MENKHAUS

Somalia has now entered its 17th year as a collapsed state, a crisis that in recent years has grown more intractable, violent, radicalized, and internationalized. It is by far the longest-running instance of complete state collapse in the post-colonial era. The unprecedented duration of this crisis raises the question: Why? Is it driven primarily by factors internal to Somalia, or by external forces beyond the control of Somalis? The claim that Somalia's perpetual crisis is engineered by external actors has long been a popular conspiracy theory among some Somalis. By contrast, most analysts explain the impasse as the product of a complex mix of forces and interests both external and internal to Somalia. And yet the tumultuous events of 2006 and 2007 have dramatically internationalized the conflict.

During this time we have seen a four-month war between a US-backed coalition of militia leaders against Islamist militias in Mogadishu, the ascendance of the Council of Islamist Courts (CIC) as the dominant political force in southern Somalia, the presence of foreign Al Qaeda operatives in the capital, an Ethiopian military offensive that routed the CIC in late December 2006, subsequent US air strikes against suspected Al Qaeda operatives, the introduction of Ugandan peacekeeping forces in Mogadishu to replace Ethiopian forces, and the rise of an increasingly violent insurgency against the Transitional Federal Government (TFG) and foreign troops in the capital.

Although a case can be made that the prolonged Somali crisis is mainly a product of domestic constraints—including warlordism, the manipulation of clan loyalties, myopic leadership, and fears of a revived state among some local interests—the role of external actors in the impasse is without doubt more important than at any time since the departure of UN peacekeepers in 1995.

The Long Impasse

In the 10 years that followed the failed UN intervention, Somalia's political scene was characterized by paralysis. Numerous externally mediated efforts to broker a national peace accord and revive a central government were made, but none succeeded. At the local and regional level, Somali communities built a variety of systems of governance designed to improve basic security and rule of law, but these local coping mechanisms did not translate into momentum for a revived central state. Indeed, one could argue that Somali communities adapted too well to state collapse, so much so that portions of the public may have lost a sense of urgency about reviving a central government.

International involvement in Somalia after 1995 was limited, reflecting both a backlash against the negative peacekeeping experience there and the country's very limited strategic and economic importance. As a result, Somalia's factions and clan militias were not very dependent on external patrons in the 1990s. Still, there were several early indicators that the Somali crisis might eventually morph into regional or even global proxy wars.

The first was Al Qaeda's expressed interest in supporting Somali attacks on American and UN peacekeepers in 1993. Al Qaeda's actual role in the clan-based insurgency that culminated in the infamous "Black Hawk Down" firefight was far less significant than has sometimes been portrayed, but its aspirations to derail the US-led peacekeeping mission hinted that Somalia could become a battlefield between radical Islam and the West. In 1996 and 1997, Ethiopia and Egypt sponsored competing peace processes, the first sign that Somalia's crisis was becoming an arena in which regional rivalries were playing themselves out.

By 2000, external sponsors of Somalia's quarreling factions began to reflect a rift between African and Arab states. One Somali coalition, concentrated in Mogadishu and built around the Hawiye clan, enjoyed financial and diplomatic support from Gulf Arab states and Islamist causes. Another coalition, dominated by the Darood clan and led by Abdullahi Yusuf, had the support of Ethiopia and its African allies. An attempt to establish a Transitional National Government in 2000 was undermined in part by this rivalry, with Gulf states backing the transitional government and Ethiopia supporting an opposition coalition known as the Somali Reconciliation and Reconstruction Council.

In 2003, yet another reconciliation process was launched. The Kenyan peace process, as the talks came to be known, was sponsored by a regional organization, the Inter-Governmental Authority for Development. Although this group has long sought to play a lead role in conflict management in the Horn of Africa, its capacity to do so has always been hampered by the fact that most of its seven member states—Sudan, Ethiopia, Eritrea, Djibouti, Somalia, Kenya, and Uganda—are rivals and regularly sponsor proxy wars in each other's hinterlands. Somalia would prove to be no exception.

A new jihadist movement has vowed to attack any peacekeepers deployed in Somalia.

After two years of impasse, the Kenyan peace process enjoyed sudden progress in the fall of 2004. This forward movement resulted in part from a decision by Ethiopia and Djibouti to push the process. They apparently decided it was better to support a state revival project in Somalia in hopes of controlling the outcome than to simply oppose the process altogether and then be blamed for its failure. By pressuring its clients in the Somali Reconciliation and Reconstruction Council to agree to terms, Ethiopia played a decisive role in jump-starting the peace process. This was an important indicator that the next phase of Somali state-building would entail a significantly greater level of external involvement.

In rapid succession, the Somali delegates in Kenya produced an accord on a transitional charter for Somalia and then agreed on the selection of a transitional parliament, which in turn elected Yusuf as president. Yusuf, a former liberation front leader, militia leader, president of the autonomous region of Puntland, and close client of Ethiopia, was a divisive choice. Complaints of vote-buying were later invoked by Somalis challenging the legitimacy of the government.

Yusuf named a prime minister—Ali Mohamed Ghedi, another client of Ethiopia—and an 82-person cabinet was selected, within which power was concentrated in the hands of Yusuf's pro-Ethiopian allies. A split in the parliament developed immediately, between the "Yusuf wing" and the "Mogadishu Group" of the new Transitional Federal Government—a split that closely mirrored the long-running divide between the old opposition coalition, the Somali Reconciliation and Reconstruction Council, and the now-defunct Arab-backed Transitional National Government.

Two issues—the site of the transitional capital and a proposal to introduce foreign peacekeepers, including Ethiopian forces, into Somalia—were especially divisive, leading to a chair-throwing brawl in the parliament in March 2005. Thereafter, the Mogadishu Group left for Mogadishu and insisted that the parliament convene there. This robbed the TFG of the ability to muster a quorum, and the legislature failed to meet for nearly a year. Relations deteriorated to a point that the two factions nearly went to war in September 2005. The TFG itself was paralyzed and weak, barely able to project its authority in the provisional capital of Baidoa. By late 2005, the TFG appeared to be yet another stillborn transitional government, and Somalia seemed condemned to an indeterminate future of continuing state collapse.

The Alliance-Islamist War

The event that triggered the series of dramatic changes in Somalia last year was the formation, in February 2006 in Mogadishu, of the Alliance for the Restoration of Peace and Counter-Terrorism. The assorted Hawiye militia leaders, warlords, and businessmen who comprised the Alliance were rivals whose militias occasionally clashed with one another. Their common link was that all served as local partners with the US government in counter-terrorism operations. In the absence of a Somali government, US defense and intelligence agencies sought out relations with non-state actors in hopes they could monitor, report, and apprehend for rendition foreign terrorists seeking to use Somalia as a safe haven.

Washington was increasingly concerned about both the rising power of Somali Islamists in Mogadishu and the presence of a small number of "high value" foreign Al Qaeda operatives living in the capital under the protection of hardline Somali Islamists. The Al Qaeda figures were accused of planning and executing the 1998 bombing of the US embassy in Nairobi. Efforts by the US government to engage the Somali clans providing haven to the suspects were met with blanket denials that Al Qaeda figures were even present in Mogadishu. Efforts to apprehend the suspects through local partners exposed the limited reach of those allies outside their immediate clan enclaves.

As a result, US intelligence agents encouraged the creation of the Alliance, hoping it would strengthen the collective capacity of their local partners and serve as a counterweight to the growing clout of hard-line Islamists in Mogadishu. It was a huge miscalculation. Far from advancing counterterrorism objectives in Mogadishu, it triggered a disastrous setback for both the United States and its local partners. It accelerated a dramatic expansion of power among the very Islamists that the administration of George W. Bush was hoping to contain.

The announcement of the Alliance's formation provoked alarm and anger within the leadership of the Islamists, who viewed the organization as an American proxy designed to attack them. The "Courts"—an umbrella group of local, clan-based courts of Islamic law that formed the base of the Islamist movement in Mogadishu—was a loose coalition. It included moderate Sufi Muslims and nonviolent Salafists. It also included a small but dangerous collection of jihadists (later known as the *shabaab* militia) who were implicated in a "dirty war" of political assassinations and targeted killings of international aid workers in 2004 and 2005. In addition to the separate court militias, the umbrella Islamic Courts Union (later reorganized under the name Council of Islamic Courts, or CIC) possessed an integrated force of about 400 well-trained, committed fighters. The leadership of the Courts could also count on support from much of Mogadishu's powerful business community.

The Islamic Courts Union wasted no time attacking positions held by Alliance militia, and by March 2006 Mogadishu experienced its heaviest fighting in a decade. The Islamist militias were far better commanded, trained, equipped, and motivated than the young, often unpaid gunmen in the Alliance militias. Many of the Alliance militias simply abandoned their positions rather than fight, or surrendered and joined what they correctly surmised was the winning side. By early June the Courts had completely routed the Alliance, appropriated most of its military hardware and fighters, and assumed control over the entire city of Mogadishu. Defeated Alliance leaders fled to Ethiopia or Kenya. It was the first time in 15 years that the capital had come under a single authority.

Ascent of the Islamic Courts

The extraordinary successes of the Council of Islamic Courts did not stop with its military victory over the Alliance. Within three months it extended its authority across most of south-central Somalia. Most of this expansion occurred in areas inhabited or occupied by the Hawiye, the clan most closely associated with the Islamists, and generally followed negotiations with local authorities and sub-clans. In the few locations, such as Kismayo, where the CIC had to use force to oust resistant local powers, it won with ease. By September 2006, only three pockets of territory lay beyond the CIC's control: the northern autonomous state of Puntland, a clan stronghold of Yusuf; the regions of Bay, Bakool, and Gedo in southern Somalia, which were protected by Ethiopian "advisers" and remained loosely under the authority of the TFG; and the secessionist state of Somaliland in the northwest.

Even in these three holdout areas, the CIC enjoyed support from a network of Islamists and appealed to a broad section of the community. Both the Islamists and external observers believed the CIC was in a position to take both Puntland and the TFG areas without firing a shot; they could simply orchestrate takeovers from within. There was some speculation that even secessionist Somaliland was vulnerable. In a remarkably short time, the ascendant Islamist movement had created a sense of inevitability about its expansion throughout the country.

The CIC not only expanded its authority territorially; it actually sought to govern. This was a novel concept in contemporary Somalia, previously attempted in varying degrees only in Somaliland and Puntland. The CIC sharia (Islamic law) courts and security sector expanded into newly held territories and immediately brought dramatic improvement in public security. Militia roadblocks, criminal gang violence, kidnappings for ransom, and armed robbery—all endemic features of Somali life since 1991—were almost eliminated. In Mogadishu, residents were able to walk freely throughout the city even at night. The CIC administration reopened the main seaport and international airport, began trash collection, and gave citizens a taste of responsive government for the first time in decades. The Islamists, in sum, earned a strong measure of legitimacy based on performance.

For a combination of reasons—including the CIC's successful conflation of an Islamist platform with pan-Somali nationalist rhetoric—the Islamists enjoyed broad and sometimes intense support across most of the Somali population. The CIC appeared to be delivering what Somalis had yearned for: unity, justice, public order, a revived state, a mobilizing ideology, and an end to warlordism, clannism, and years of humiliation. Although its political base was clearly within the Hawiye clan, the CIC made genuine efforts to transform the movement into one that transcended clan and attracted leaders from all Somali communities. The Islamists earned support even from many Somalis who did not share their Salafist tendencies and who had misgivings about some of their social policies.

The large Somali diaspora—now thought to number about 1 million—was especially passionate in its support of the CIC. The Islamists used the diaspora as a source not only of fundraising, but also of skilled labor. Diaspora members counted among many of the top CIC leaders. Hundreds of young Somali men returned from the diaspora to train and serve in the Islamist militias as well. This became a growing source of concern in Western countries, where it was feared that radicalized Somali diaspora members with new skills in explosives might pose a terrorist threat if they returned to their host countries. The fact that many of the Somalis in the TFG parliament and cabinet also hold passports to second countries points to a new and important trend: the diasporization of Somali politics, which further internationalizes Somali conflicts and peace processes.

The CIC was successful, at least in the short run, in winning over an uncertain international community. It issued several well-crafted communiqués saying all the right things—pledging its support for peace, democracy, dialogue with the TFG, and cooperation with external states, and presenting itself as a popular uprising against lawlessness and warlordism. The CIC's charm offensive included placing a known moderate and Sufi figure, Sheik Sharif Ahmed, as head of the Executive Committee of the CIC, rather than the hard-liner Hassan Dahir Aweys, who has been designated by the United States as a terrorist with links to Al Qaeda. This served to reinforce the already well-established view that the CIC was a broad coalition that included moderates as well as hard-liners. Most of the international community, including the US Department of State, embraced a policy of engagement with the moderate Islamists and called for dialogue between the CIC and the TFG with the aim of rendering the TFG a more inclusive government.

The Hard-Liners Prevail

While most other international actors were willing to give the CIC the benefit of the doubt and work with its moderate wing (hoping that the hard-line wing and the *shabaab* militia could be marginalized), Ethiopia was never convinced that coexistence with the Islamists was an option. Like the TFG leadership, Ethiopia was more inclined to view the CIC movement as monolithic, radical, and linked to Al Qaeda.

The fact that some of the top leadership in the CIC, including Sheikh Aweys, were former members of the dissolved Al-Itti had Al-Islamiya, which conducted a series of terrorist bombings and assassination attempts in Ethiopia in the 1990s, reinforced a tendency among Ethiopian decision makers to view the CIC as an unacceptable threat. Though disappointed with the weak performance of their Somali clients leading the TFG, Ethiopia's leaders were committed to protecting the transitional government in Baidoa and preventing an Islamist takeover. Already by July 2006, tensions between Ethiopia and the CIC were growing, leading many to conclude that a war between the two was likely.

Hard-liners in the CIC—particularly Aweys—helped to make war inevitable. They did so by engaging in a series of actions seemingly designed to provoke Ethiopia. Small numbers of Ethiopian troops ("advisers," according to the TFG) had been present around Baidoa and parts of the border region of southern Somalia since the transitional government relocated from Nairobi to Somalia in June 2005. Aweys and the Courts seized on this to demand the withdrawal of Ethiopian "occupation forces" from Somali territory.

Aweys went further. He repeatedly called for jihad against Ethiopia; made irredentist claims on Somali-inhabited territory of eastern Ethiopia; called for the people of Ethiopia to rise up and topple the regime of Prime Minister Meles Zenawi; and allowed two armed Ethiopian insurgencies, the Oromo Liberation Front and the Ogaden National Liberation Front, to use Somalia as a base for training and receipt of weaponry. He also forged close ties with Ethiopia's regional enemy Eritrea, which became a source of weapons and military training. Even without these provocations, Ethiopia may have taken military action against the CIC. But the jihadist, irredentist posturing and the alliance with Eritrea ensured an Ethiopian response.

Some observers believe hard-liners in the CIC were hoping to lure Ethiopia into war in the mistaken belief that an Ethiopian attack would bog Ethiopia down in a quagmire, produce a flood of support from outside Islamist sympathizers, and potentially lead to Muslim insurgencies inside Ethiopia itself. The CIC's sense of its own military prowess was overinflated by the dramatic victory over Alliance forces in Mogadishu, leading it to conclude that it could withstand Ethiopian attacks. According to this interpretation, hubris and clouded judgment drove the Islamists to provoke an unnecessary and disastrous war when their movement could have achieved its remaining political goals without firing another shot.

US officials argue that Ethiopia was committed to a military offensive with or without US support.

Other observers argue that the CIC hard-liners wanted not an actual war with Ethiopia but only the threat of war. That would have allowed them to exploit strong anti-Ethiopian sentiment to mobilize public support, close ranks, and marginalize moderates in the movement. The hard-liners' jihadist rhetoric was, according to this interpretation, warmongering designed to consolidate their power at home, not to take down Ethiopia. According to this line of reasoning, the CIC leaders were convinced that Ethiopia would not launch an attack against them out of fear of a quagmire and domestic unrest.

Playing with Fire

Whatever the explanation—and it is likely that CIC calculations were informed by a messy combination of both lines of reasoning—the CIC leaders badly miscalculated. In their defense, they were not alone in their misreadings. Many external observers were also convinced that Ethiopia would face a barrage of guerrilla attacks and ambushes if it were lured into a war, and that the conflict had the potential to spread into Ethiopia and attract the interest of global jihadists. Memories of the successful urban insurgency led by General Hussein Aideed against a far superior force of US special forces and UN peacekeepers in 1993 may well have distorted both the tactics of the Islamists and the forecasts of many observers.

Eritrea's deep involvement with the CIC—its provision of arms (including surface-to-air missiles to help the Islamists neutralize Ethiopian airpower), ammunition, training, and military advisers—was also premised on the hope and expectation that Ethiopia would take the CIC bait and then get bogged down in Somalia. Eritrea's support for the CIC, as well as for Ethiopian rebel forces based in CIC territory, seemed a straightforward case of using a proxy conflict to weaken and distract a regional nemesis. But the strategy was not without risks. Eritrea's secular, authoritarian regime rules over a population evenly divided between Christianity and Islam. Inflaming and empowering a movement calling for jihad in the region was playing with fire.

The CIC also enjoyed support from a variety of other states and non-state actors. As war clouds built up in the second half of 2006, arms and ammunition flowed into Somalia at unprecedented levels, leading a UN panel of experts to sound an alarm in November 2006.

The fact that hard-liners hijacked the CIC's foreign policy and led the Islamists into a jihad with one of sub-Saharan Africa's largest and most seasoned armies was a monumental mistake. But it was not the only critical error the Islamists made. Another was allowing extremists in the movement to impose a series of increasingly draconian and retrograde social policies in Mogadishu. Morality police began closing cinemas and forbidding parties in which men and women mixed. CIC officials imposed new restrictions on the media, sought to outlaw meetings in which political issues were discussed, and moved to restrict the work of local civic organizations.

Some of these policies were the work of rogue elements in the Islamist fold and were reversed by moderates, who took pains to distance the CIC from the more outrageous restrictions. In fairness to the CIC, it was unprepared to assume governance responsibilities, and both its policies and its chain of command were more chaotic than outsiders knew at the time. Still, the creeping authoritarianism and radical rhetoric of the movement were disquieting to many of its supporters, and began eroding the movement's domestic support and its international goodwill.

The other mistake that appears to have doomed the CIC was its complete unwillingness to address the chief concern of the United States: the alleged presence of three foreign Al Qaeda operatives said to be enjoying safe haven under the protection of Somali hard-liners. Dismissive denials by CIC leaders of any knowledge of foreign Al Qaeda presence in Mogadishu, combined with the movement's jihadist rhetoric against Ethiopia and the creeping radicalization of its social policies, undermined those US officials who had argued for engagement with the moderates in the Courts.

Once it was concluded that the hard-liners were driving policies and the moderates were not in control, US government policy shifted, and American pressure on Ethiopia not to attack the CIC—pressure that may well have prevented a war in the summer of 2006—was dropped. State Department officials began describing the CIC in much more negative ways, as a group essentially controlled by Al Qaeda–affiliated individuals. Many press accounts described the shift in American policy as amounting to a "green light" to Ethiopia, implying that the United States controlled Ethiopian policy and was subcontracting the war on terror to a regional proxy.

The tumultuous events of 2006 and 2007 have dramatically internationalized the Somali conflict.

In private, US officials working on Somalia policy object to that depiction. They argue that Ethiopia was committed to a military offensive with or without US support; that Washington has never been able to exercise much influence on the Ethiopian government; and that the shift in US policy amounted to acquiescing to an attack that American officials believed was both inevitable and justifiable given the CIC's growing radicalism.

The Ethiopian Offensive

On December 24, 2006, the war that had been expected and dreaded for five months finally started. It unfolded in a manner that no one had predicted and that took everyone—the Islamists, the Somali public, regional analysts, and perhaps even the government of Ethiopia itself—by surprise. First, Ethiopian forces routed the CIC militia in three initial battles in open countryside. It was very unclear why the CIC military command chose to expose its forces in a way that gave Ethiopia's military clear advantages. Then, the CIC leaders and militia returned to Mogadishu, where everyone expected them to lure Ethiopia into the kind of conflict the Islamists presumably wanted to fight—an asymmetrical, urban, guerrilla war.

Instead, the CIC leaders announced that they were dissolving the organization. Most of the militia and equipment were returned to clan leaders in Mogadishu. Remnants of the CIC militia, including most of the *shabaab,* and most of the top CIC leaders fled southward to the city of Kismayo, where they pledged to fight the advancing Ethiopian forces. But again they opted to fight in open terrain, near the Juba river. They took heavy losses, and were forced to scatter in the remote coastal areas bordering Kenya. Some tried to cross the Kenyan border and were captured by the Kenyan military, which sealed the border despite protests from humanitarian agencies concerned about the plight of thousands of displaced Somalis unable to reach safety in Kenya.

As remnants of the CIC scattered in the border areas, US military and intelligence agencies believed they had tracked a convoy of vehicles that included one or more of the foreign Al Qaeda operatives they sought. On January 8, an American gunship attacked the targeted convoy, the first of two confirmed air strikes. US government officials later said that eight Somali *shabaab* militia were killed and one of the most notorious Somali jihadists was injured, but that no foreign Al Qaeda operatives were hit in the attack. The US air attacks—and subsequent news stories exposing the presence of American soldiers on the ground in Somalia—took a war driven mainly by regional dynamics and helped to globalize it as an extension of America's war on terror. It also tethered the United States much more closely to the Ethiopian offensive in the eyes of Somalis.

In short, almost every decision taken by the CIC leadership during the short, intense period in the final days of 2006 was counterintuitive and disastrously counterproductive for the movement. The most important puzzle is why the CIC did not do the obvious—hole up in Mogadishu and fight Ethiopian forces on its terms and its terrain. It is not even clear Ethiopian troops would have risked entering Mogadishu, in which case the CIC could simply have waited them out.

CIC supporters claim the leaders sought to spare Mogadishu from destructive warfare, a claim that makes less and less sense in the context of the current insurgency in the capital city. An alternative explanation offered by some Somali observers is that the CIC had been deeply divided over the impending war with Ethiopia, with both Islamic moderates and many supporters in Mogadishu furious with the hard-liners for dragging them into an unwanted and costly war. According to this explanation, the CIC leaders faced sharp criticism in Mogadishu, were made to return the militia units and equipment to the clans, and were told that they could not stay to fight Ethiopia in the capital.

In any case, the unexpected and sudden victory led to Ethiopian forces occupying Mogadishu. They were met by a Mogadishu population that was sullen and shocked. The TFG leadership entered the capital and took over government buildings with the intent to govern and impose a victor's peace. But the victory was earned by Ethiopian forces, not the TFG, and would last only as long as the Ethiopians stayed—which was not long. Ethiopia understood that it would soon face armed resistance in Mogadishu and was keen to withdraw from the capital as quickly as it could to avoid the quagmire scenario so many had predicted for it. On the other hand, a rapid withdrawal would expose the TFG to attack and almost certain defeat.

The solution, as the Ethiopians saw it, was to accelerate the deployment of African Union peacekeepers to replace their own forces. The United States helped launch a campaign to pressure African states to commit peacekeepers to the proposed African Union mission, but only Uganda approved a deployment, of 1,500 troops. Several other states have pledged peacekeepers but face legislative branches that have yet to approve such action. Their hesitancy is understandable: the presence of foreign peacekeepers is fiercely rejected by much of the Mogadishu population, and African Union forces face a mortal danger of attacks in the city. A new jihadist movement has vowed to attack any peacekeepers deployed in Somalia.

Complex Insurgency

The dramatic changes wrought by Ethiopia's victory were viewed in Washington and elsewhere as a window of opportunity for a revived TFG. Vigorous efforts were launched to promote three pillars: political dialogue (with the aim of making the TFG more inclusive), increased governance capacity, and security (provided by the African Union protection force). But none of the pillars has enjoyed much success. Political dialogue has been almost nonexistent. The TFG refuses to negotiate with ex-CIC officials, branding them all terrorists, while the Islamists insist that all foreign forces must leave the country as a condition for talks. The TFG's capacity to govern remains as minimal as ever. Its newly assembled police force is unable and unwilling to patrol effectively. The streets of Mogadishu have quickly reverted to violence and lawlessness.

Within a week of the Ethiopian occupation of Mogadishu, armed resistance began to surface and grow. By late January, mortar, rocket, and small arms fire on Ethiopian and TFG installations rapidly mounted. The attacks and counterattacks have produced high levels of insecurity in the city, with hundreds dead and injured and more than 40,000 displaced. Mogadishu is now in the grips of a "complex insurgency" in which attacks on the TFG and foreign forces are being mounted by several separate groups: clan militias, regrouping Islamist militias, warlord militias, and armed criminal gangs. These groups have little in common except a shared desire to thwart the TFG and drive Ethiopian and Ugandan forces out of the country.

The TFG and its external supporters have tried to portray the rising insurgency as an Al Qaeda operation. While it is true that the Somali crisis has attracted Al Qaeda's attention, reducing the violence in Mogadishu to an externally engineered plot is a fundamental misreading. The insurgency is first and foremost a reflection of clan opposition to the TFG and Ethiopian occupation of the city.

All indications point to the Mogadishu insurgency growing more violent and uncontrolled. An explosion of violence in March produced gruesome scenes of dead TFG and Ethiopian soldiers being dragged through the streets of Mogadishu by angry mobs, eerily reminiscent of the "Black Hawk Down" catastrophe of 1993. Days later a cargo plane serving the fledgling African Union presence was shot down. Prospects for the success of the TFG were never good; now they are increasingly poor. Earlier fears that an Ethiopian offensive to rid Somalia of an Islamist threat would only create a quagmire—and mobilize support for the hard-line Islamists rather than neutralize them—may have been dismissed too soon in the aftermath of the Ethiopian victory.

KENNETH J. MENKHAUS is a professor of political science at Davidson College.

From *Current History*, May 2007. Copyright © 2007 by Current History, Inc. Reprinted by permission.

Dangerous Liaisons

As Farc guerrillas drag Latin America to the brink of war, ratings for Colombia's ultra-right Álvaro Uribe soar. Now the left is determined to divorce itself from the group.

ALICE O'KEEFFE

Orlando Ordoñez no longer looks like a *guerrillero*. He is clean-shaven, with suit, shiny boots and long hair slicked into a neat ponytail. Calloused hands and a worn expression on his broad face are the only clues to his past: Ordoñez spent ten years rising through the ranks of the Revolutionary Armed Forces of Colombia (Farc), Latin America's oldest and most powerful guerrilla army. By the time he left in 2005, he was, as describes himself, a high-ranking *comandante*, managing millions of dollars of the group's profits from extortion and drug trafficking.

Ordoñez experienced the moral decline of the Farc from the inside. He joined as an idealistic 28-year-old, attracted by the organisation's revolutionary agenda. "When I joined, being a *guerrillero* was a source of pride," he says. "We had the respect of the Colombian people." Initially, he looked after a small territory where peasants grew crops including coca, and the Farc charged the drug traffickers a tax for the service. It was only in the late 1990s that he realised the organisation was increasingly producing and trafficking drugs itself. "The ideology was changing."

His disillusionment grew over time. He discovered that other *comandantes* had been abusing, threatening and displacing peasants in the areas they controlled. "Our reputation in those communities suffered very badly." Then he was given a promotion, and moved into a position where he was expected to buy influence with politicians, businessmen and police. "I was unhappy with my life, and with the Farc," he says. He took the potentially life-threatening decision to desert and handed himself in to the army.

Ordoñez is now training at a community television station, and hopes to persuade others to demobilise. "I want all the *guerrilleros* to know that if they want to really make a difference, they should rejoin Colombian society. If they want to work for the left-wing cause, this is a democracy and they are free to do that."

At present, the Colombian left is in a sorry state. Unlike much of the rest of Latin America, where centre-left and left-wing

administrations have become increasingly common, Colombia is governed by a right-wing, militaristic, pro-business president, Álvaro Uribe. After winning two elections by large majorities on the promise that he would smash the guerrillas with a "strong hand", he saw his popularity recently hit 84 per cent. The opposition is floundering. This is even though the country has one of the most unequal societies in the world: its cities are filled with shiny 4x4s, designer beauty queens and chichi shopping malls, but in its slums and rural areas 50 per cent of the population lives in poverty.

No Support

Those on the left in Colombia have one explanation for their lack of popularity: the Farc effect. "It is our greatest problem," says José Sanín Vásquez, director of the trade union research institute Escuela Nacional Sindical. "If being on the left means wanting change, then the Farc has become ultra-right-wing. It is a great obstacle to change in this country." It is a mark of how far the Farc has fallen that, despite great injustices in Colombia, it commands almost no support from any section of society. In a recent Gallup poll, all but 3 per cent of Colombians said they had an unfavourable opinion of the Farc.

Trade unionists, human rights campaigners, community leaders and left-wing politicians all have the same complaint: their credibility is continually damaged by insinuations in politics and the media that they are "guerrilla sympathisers" (Uribe has made a habit of smearing his critics, including Amnesty International and other NGOs, in this way). "It suits the government to describe the Farc as left-wing, as that way it stigmatises the opposition," says Sanín. "It suits the Farc because it gives it a certain legitimacy. Meanwhile, the real left in Colombia is completely squashed between the two."

The Farc was founded in 1964, and headed by a peasant leader and member of the Communist Party known as Manuel Marulanda, or "Tirofijo." Its members came from existing peasant militias, but during the 1960s and 1970s it adopted a Marxist ideology. As other guerrilla groups in Colombia and across Latin America have been defeated or drawn into mainstream politics, the Farc has continued to wage an implacable war against the Colombian state, fuelled increasingly by profits from the drugs trade. It also specialises in kidnapping and extortion, with some of its hostages—most notoriously the former presidential candidate Ingrid Betancourt—kept in jungle hideouts for years.

The impact of the guerrilla movement in Colombia has been particularly devastating because it has given rise to an array of right-wing paramilitary groups, which sprang up around the country during the 1990s. Their aim was to protect the interests of large landowners and they were brutally dismissive of the rights of the civilian population, taking revenge on anyone they considered to be a guerrilla supporter. The armed groups from left and right have contributed to a bloody and seemingly intractable civil war, in which the value of human life has been disregarded by both sides. Tens of thousands of Colombians—usually from the poorest communities—have been killed, and three million more displaced; the country has the world's second-largest internally displaced population, outstripped only by Sudan's.

Harsh Discipline

The highest estimated figure for Farc membership stands at 30,000, though the Colombian government claims that numbers have fallen to around 8,000. Its soldiers are drawn largely from the most deprived social groups, attracted by the offer of a basic wage. "I always liked guns, and what's more I come from a very poor family. The Farc told me they would help me if I joined," says Francisco, a softly spoken 22-year-old from a peasant family in the Antioquian region, who joined the group when he was 17. Like many Farc foot soldiers, he is illiterate. "They taught me all about the ideology and to sing the revolutionary anthems. They taught us that the Farc would bring the Cuban Revolution to Colombia. Once I was trained, they gave me a gun and set me missions, like collecting a certain amount of base [coca paste] from a particular area, and bringing it back to the camp."

The conditions for recruits are harsh: the group operates from bases deep inside Colombia's vast, dense jungles, where disease is rife and resources are scarce. Discipline is brutal; those who break the rules are subjected to trials, or "war councils." "When somebody broke the rules, they would tie them up and present them in front of the group to decide their punishment," says Francisco. "If they had a good record, they might be given a chance. If they had stolen food from the store tent or something, and had done it a number of times, they would be given the maximum penalty. Often they would just tie people up and punish them for nothing."

In Colombia, it has long been widely accepted across the political spectrum that although the Farc continues to use Marxist rhetoric, it has abandoned any claim to political legitimacy. "The foot soldiers are still taught the ideology, and believe it," says Jaime Echevarría, another former member who did not want his real name published. Jaime has a university education, but had lost his job and was destitute when he was recruited to the Farc's urban division. "But to judge by my contact with the higher ranks and the secretariat [the Farc's seven-man governing body], I would say they have left that behind. They are businessmen."

The increasingly public alliance between the Farc and the Venezuelan president, Hugo Chávez, which reared its head last month, has served to bolster Uribe's position and further demoralise the Colombian left. The extent of the collaboration between the two is a matter of debate—the Colombian government claims to have evidence that Chávez has provided the Farc with funds, although he denies this. He has, however, made no secret of his political support (as reported in the *NS* of 11 February). The two countries were brought to the brink of war in March following an illegal raid by Colombian troops into Ecuadorian territory, during which one of the Farc secretariat, Raú Reyes, was killed. Ecuador was understandably furious, but Chávez went further, ordering troops to the border and announcing a minute's silence in Reyes's honour.

> ## "Thankfully, we were spared annihilation because we did not ally ourselves closely with Chávez."

"Venezuela does not support the Farc, but Chávez has made a strategic alliance with them," says Fernando Gerbasi, formerly Venezuela's ambassador in Colombia and now a professor of international relations at the Universidad Metropolitana in Caracas.

Having turned its back on the political arena at home, the Farc has focused on building up international support, effectively playing on tensions between right-wing Colombia and its "21st-century socialist" neighbour. With a huge amount of military aid pouring into Colombia from the United States—around $5bn since 2000—its neighbours, with comparatively scant military resources, understandably fear that the country has become a foothold from which the US can extend its influence in the region.

"The danger is that the US would like Colombia to be its proxy for an anti-Chávez campaign," says Rodrigo Pardo, editor of the Colombian political magazine *Cambio*. "That would be disastrous for regional relations."

Strengthening Uribe

Gustavo Petro, a senator for Colombia's left-wing opposition Polo Democrático Alternativo party, describes himself as a personal friend of Chávez. He believes that the Venezuelan president allowed himself to be persuaded that the Farc offered the only way of challenging the Uribe administration, and protecting himself against American aggression.

"This was a grave error, and if he had consulted us it never would have happened," Petro says. "The relationship between the Farc and the Latin American left represents a mortal danger for the left." He despairs that the crisis has once again boosted the popularity of the already unchallengeable Uribe. "It has affected the left in Colombia profoundly. We have been damaged—thankfully, we were spared annihilation because we did not ally ourselves closely with Chávez."

Meanwhile, the Uribe administration continues to implement controversial policies, virtually unchecked by a serious opposition. Colombia is opened up to business while trade unionists fear for their lives; millions of dollars are poured into the military while the displaced population is abandoned to live in squalid poverty. The government offers cash incentives for the murder of suspected *guerrilleros*—last month, it gave a $2.6m reward to a Farc soldier who killed another member of the secretariat and delivered his hand to the authorities in a plastic bag.

"There is a lot of work for the left to do in this country," says Petro with a weary smile."

Call in the Blue Helmets

Peacekeeping: Can the UN cope with increasing demands for its soldiers?

Call it peacekeeping, peace-enforcement, stabilisation or anything else, but one thing is clear: the world's soldiers are busier than ever operating in the wide grey zone between war and peace.

The United Nations has seen a sixfold increase since 1998 in the number of soldiers and military observers it deploys around the world. About 74,000 military personnel (nearly 100,000 people including police and civilians, and increasing fast) are currently involved in 18 different operations—more than any country apart from the United States. And it is not just the UN that is in high demand. NATO, the European Union and the African Union (AU), as well as other coalitions of the willing, have some 74,000 soldiers trying to restore peace and stability in troubled countries. Added to their number come the more than 160,000 American, British and other troops in Iraq.

The "war on terror" is one cause of this military hyperactivity. But Jean-Marie Guéhenno, the UN's under-secretary for peacekeeping, also sees more hopeful reasons. The growing demand for blue helmets, he says, is a good sign that a number of conflicts are ending.

This is only partly true. In Congo, southern Sudan and Liberia—the UN's three biggest operations—the blue helmets are shoring up peace agreements. But in countries such as Lebanon or Côte d'Ivoire, they are at best holding the line between parties still in conflict.

One reason for the surge in UN peacekeeping is that Africa, the region most in need of peacekeepers, is least able to provide for itself. The AU is trying to improve its peacekeeping capacity, but is desperately short of resources. It has handed over its operation in Burundi to the UN. Now it wants the blue helmets to help relieve its 7,000 hard-pressed AU peacekeepers in Sudan's troubled region of Darfur.

The Sudanese government has long resisted such a deployment, accusing the UN of being an agent of the West. But under sustained international pressure to halt what Washington regards as genocide, it has grudgingly agreed to allow in a "hybrid" UN and AU force. An advance party of 24 police advisers and 43 military officers, wearing blue berets and AU armbands, has started to arrive in Darfur to test Sudan's co-operation. According to a three-phase plan, the force will be built up into a contingent of 17,000 soldiers and 3,000 police officers.

Can the UN take on another onerous peacekeeping operation? Mr Guéhenno says the world already faces two kinds of "overstretch": the military sort, in which many armed forces of many leading countries are badly strained by foreign operations; and "political overstretch", in which the world's political energies are focused on just a few acute problems while the UN is left to deal as best it can with many chronic or less visible conflicts.

Mr Guéhenno is cautious about what he can achieve in Darfur. He says he may get the soldiers, given the right political conditions, but is worried about getting enough "enablers"—the crucial specialised units and equipment that enhance the ability of a force to move and operate. These include army engineers and logisticians, field hospitals and nurses, heavy-lift aircraft and transport helicopters, as well as proper command-and-control and intelligence-gathering: in other words, the wherewithal of modern Western expeditionary forces. These capabilities are in short supply and are expensive; the few countries that have them are using them, and the others can't afford them.

In a region as vast as Darfur, an effective UN force would need to be highly mobile, and make use both of unmanned surveillance drones and special forces. It would need to sustain itself in a harsh environment, some 1,400km (870 miles) from the nearest harbour and with few airfields. Engineers could drill for water, but would be under pressure to share it with local populations and with refugees. And then there is the problem of time. On current plans it would take six to nine months to build up to full strength in Darfur. Having to merge with the AU adds further complications to the command structure.

Finding a Fire Engine

Apart from military capability, or lack of it, there is the question of political will. Who will risk their soldiers' lives, and their valuable military assets, in a faraway conflict? NATO, the world's foremost military alliance, has struggled for months to find a few thousand additional soldiers—and a few extra helicopters—to back up its troops fighting in southern Afghanistan.

By contrast, European countries moved with unusual speed when the UN appealed for its hapless mission in Lebanon to be reinforced last summer in order to end the war between Israel and Hizbullah. Within weeks of a ceasefire being called in August, French and Italian peacekeepers were coming ashore. It was the first time that sizeable Western forces had donned blue helmets since the unhappy days of the war in Bosnia.

But there were particular reasons for this. Lebanon, of course, is more easily accessible than Afghanistan or Darfur. But it is also less dangerous than southern Afghanistan, and European governments regard the Israeli-Arab conflict as much closer to their interests than the effort to pacify rebellious Pashtun tribesmen.

Kofi Annan, the former UN secretary-general, liked to say that the UN is the only fire brigade that must go out and buy a fire engine before it can respond to an emergency. The Security Council must first authorise an operation and pass a budget, and then the secre-

Current UN Peacekeeping Missions

Location	Mission Name	Year of Deployment	Number of Personnel*
Congo	MONUC	1999	22,167
Liberia	UNMIL	2003	18,382
Southern Sudan	UNMIS	2005	13,021
Lebanon	UNIFIL	1978	11,431
Côte d'Ivoire	UNOCI	2004	11,150
Haiti	MINUSTAH	2004	3,142
Kosovo	UNMIK	1999	4,631
Burundi	ONUB	2004	3,142
Ethiopia and Eritrea	UNMEE	2000	2,687
Timor-Leste	UNMIT	2006	1,340
Golan Heights (Israel/Syria)	UNDOF	1974	1,247
Cyprus	UNFICYP	1964	1,069
Afghanistan[a]	UNAMA	2002	850
Western Sahara	MINURSO	1991	459
Georgia	UNOMIG	1993	419
Middle East[b]	UNTSO	1948	374
Sierra Leone[a]	UNIOSIL	2006	298
India and Pakistan	UNMOGIP	1949	113

*Includes military, police and civilians

[a]Political or peace-building missions

[b]Egypt, Jordan, Israel, Lebanon and Syria

Source: United Nations

tariat beseeches governments to contribute forces and arranges the means to transport them. This system has created a two-tier structure: powerful countries decide the missions (and pay for them) while poor countries such as India, Pakistan, Bangladesh, Nepal and Jordan supply the soldiers. They receive a payment for doing so; this becomes for some a subsidy for their own armed forces, while the deployment also provides their troops with training.

Idealists such as Sir Brian Urquhart, a former UN under secretary-general, believe it is high time the UN had its own "fire engine": a permanent force that could deploy quickly to stop conflicts before they spin out of control. The UN's founding fathers envisioned some kind of international army, but all proposals for a standing UN force have foundered—partly because of political objections to giving the UN too much power, partly because of the practical difficulties of recruiting, training and paying for such a force.

After the failure of the UN in the mid-1990s to stop blood-letting in Somalia, Rwanda and the Balkans, many argued it would be better for those who are properly equipped to deal with putting out the fires of conflict. In 1999, it was NATO that stopped the killing of ethnic Albanians in Kosovo, while a force led by Australia halted the conflict in East Timor. A year later, in Sierra Leone, the quick deployment of about 1,000 British soldiers helped save what was then the UN's largest peace-keeping mission from collapsing under attack by rebels of the Revolutionary United Front.

All this seemed to confirm that the UN could take on only soft peacekeeping and "observer" missions with co-operation from the warring sides. But in 2000 a panel headed by Lakhdar Brahimi recommended a complete rethink of UN peacekeeping. The United Nations, it acknowledged, "does not wage war"; but its operations nevertheless had to "project credible force" and be ready to distinguish between victim and aggressor.

Mr Brahimi's central recommendation was the creation of multinational brigades around the world ready to deploy at short notice. This idea of pre-assembling bits of the fire engine has made only fitful progress. But other proposals have been acted on. They include the creation of a more powerful headquarters to oversee the UN effort; stockpiling of equipment; compilation of lists of military officers, police and other experts who will be on *call* to join UN missions; and the meshing of peacekeeping with ordinary policing, government reform and economic development.

New missions are now much more likely to be given robust mandates authorising them to use "all necessary means" under Chapter VII of the UN Charter: in other words, aggressive military force. In places such as Congo and Haiti, the UN has even been accused of using too much force.

Since the world is likely to need large numbers of peacekeepers for the foreseeable future, a further option is being explored: "leasing" the fire engine by hiring private security companies to do more of the work. Don't expect anything to happen quickly, though. The world, and especially the Americans, has moved a long way towards the privatisation of war. But for many, the privatisation of peacekeeping is still a step too far.

UNIT 4

Political Change in the Developing World

Unit Selections

Key Points to Consider

- What are the current trends in democracy in different parts of the world?

- What factors influence Turkey's relations with the West?

- Is Islam compatible with democracy?

- What issues are likely to influence South Africa's 2009 elections?

- What are the reasons for the tenuous conditions of peace in the Democratic Republic of Congo?

- Why have African liberation movements found it difficult to make the transition into political parties?

- What problems does Brazil face in finding a balance between its regional and global roles?

- Why is the success of Venezuela's revolution uncertain?

Student Web Site

www.mhcls.com/online

Internet References

Latin American Network Information Center—LANIC
http://www.lanic.utexas.edu
ReliefWeb
http://www.reliefweb.int/w/rwb.nsf
World Trade Organization (WTO)
http://www.wto.org

A history of authoritarian rule and the lack of a democratic political culture have hampered efforts to extend democracy to many parts of the developing world. Authoritarian colonial rule and the failure to prepare colonies adequately for democracy at independence account for the present situation. Even when there was an attempt to foster parliamentary government, the experiment failed frequently, largely due to the lack of a democratic tradition and a reliance on political expediency. Independence-era leaders frequently resorted to centralization of power and authoritarianism, either to pursue ambitious development programs or more often simply to retain power. In some cases, leaders experimented with socialist development schemes that emphasized ideology and the role of party elites. The promise of rapid, equitable development proved elusive, and the collapse of the Soviet Union discredited this strategy. Other countries had the misfortune to come under the rule of tyrannical leaders who were concerned only with enriching themselves, and who brutally repressed anyone with the temerity to challenge their rule. Although there are a few notable exceptions, the developing world's experiences with democracy since independence have been very limited.

Democracy's "third wave" brought redemocratization to Latin America during the 1980s after a period of authoritarian rule. The trend toward democracy also spread to some Asian countries, such as the Philippines and South Korea, and by 1990 it could be felt in sub-Saharan Africa too. The results of this democratization trend have been mixed so far. While democracy has increased across the world, the pace of democratic change has slowed recently; and in some instances democratic reform has regressed. Latin America has been the developing world's most successful region in establishing democracy, but the widespread dissatisfaction due to corruption, inequitable distribution of wealth, and the threats to civil rights have produced a left wing, populist trend in the region's politics recently. The trend has been most evident in Venezuela, although it exists in several countries of the region at varying degrees. Venezuelan president Hugo Chavez's efforts to change the constitution to eliminate term limits has led some to view this populist trend as drifting towards authoritarian rule.

Africa's experience with democracy has also been varied since the third wave of democratization swept over the continent beginning in 1990. Although early efforts resulted in the ouster of many leaders, some of whom had held power for decades, and international pressure forced several countries to hold multiparty elections, the political system in Africa includes states consolidating democracies and the states still mired in conflict. Some African liberation movements have found the transition to democratic ruling parties difficult to accomplish. South Africa's democracy, the continent's biggest success story, is slated for its fourth round of democratic elections in 2009. Although its democratic consolidation still faces major challenges, the situation within the state is in sharp contrast to the circumstances in other parts of Africa, especially to the one

Department of Defense Photo by Helen C. Stikkel

in Zimbabwe, where President Mugabe continues to cling to power through intimidation and manipulation. Congo's 2006 elections brought a state of tenuous peace to most of the country but failed to bring an end to the sporadic fighting that occur in the eastern part of the country. Nigeria's 2007 elections were flawed and the country continues to face widespread corruption and political unrest in the Niger Delta region.

Political change has begun in the Middle East but it will be a long term challenge. Iraq's government consists of representatives from the Sunni, Shiite, and Kurdish communities and the violence between the Sunnis and the Shiites threatens to escalate. The role of Islam in the region and its compatibility with democracy continues to be a major issue. The struggle of Turkey's secular government with the growing Islamic political influence illustrates the tension between Islam and democracy.

While there has been significant progress toward democratic reform around the world, there is no guarantee that these efforts will be sustained. Although there has been an increase in the percentage of the world's population living under democracy, nondemocratic regimes still exist. Furthermore, some semi-democracies hold elections but citizens lack full civil and political rights. International efforts to promote democracy often tend to focus on elections rather than on the long-term requirements of democratic consolidation. More effective ways of promoting and sustaining democracy must be found in order to expand freedom further in the developing world.

The Democratic Rollback

The Resurgence of the Predatory State

LARRY DIAMOND

Since 1974, more than 90 countries have made transitions to democracy, and by the turn of the century approximately 60 percent of the world's independent states were democratic. The democratization of Mexico and Indonesia in the late 1990s and the more recent "color revolutions" in Georgia and Ukraine formed the crest of a tidal wave of democratic transitions. Even in the Arab world, the trend is visible: in 2005, democratic forces in Lebanon rose up to peacefully drive out Syrian troops and Iraqis voted in multiparty parliamentary elections for the first time in nearly half a century.

But celebrations of democracy's triumph are premature. In a few short years, the democratic wave has been slowed by a powerful authoritarian undertow, and the world has slipped into a democratic recession. Democracy has recently been overthrown or gradually stifled in a number of key states, including Nigeria, Russia, Thailand, Venezuela, and, most recently, Bangladesh and the Philippines. In December 2007, electoral fraud in Kenya delivered another abrupt and violent setback. At the same time, most newcomers to the democratic club (and some long-standing members) have performed poorly. Even in many of the countries seen as success stories, such as Chile, Ghana, Poland, and South Africa, there are serious problems of governance and deep pockets of disaffection. In South Asia, where democracy once predominated, India is now surrounded by politically unstable, undemocratic states. And aspirations for democratic progress have been thwarted everywhere in the Arab world (except Morocco), whether by terrorism and political and religious violence (as in Iraq), externally manipulated societal divisions (as in Lebanon), or authoritarian regimes themselves (as in Egypt, Jordan, and some of the Persian Gulf monarchies, such as Bahrain).

Before democracy can spread further, it must take deeper root where it has already sprouted. It is a basic principle of any military or geopolitical campaign that at some point an advancing force must consolidate its gains before it conquers more territory. Emerging democracies must demonstrate that they can solve their governance problems and meet their citizens' expectations for freedom, justice, a better life, and a fairer society. If democracies do not more effectively contain crime and corruption, generate economic growth, relieve economic inequality, and secure freedom and the rule of law, people will eventually lose faith and turn to authoritarian alternatives. Struggling democracies must be consolidated so that all levels of society become enduringly committed to democracy as the best form of government and to their country's constitutional norms and constraints. Western policymakers can assist in this process by demanding more than superficial electoral democracy. By holding governments accountable and making foreign aid contingent on good governance, donors can help reverse the democratic recession.

Beyond the Façade

Western policymakers and analysts have failed to acknowledge the scope of the democratic recession for several reasons. First, global assessments by the Bush administration and by respected independent organizations such as Freedom House tend to cite the overall number of democracies and aggregate trends while neglecting the size and strategic importance of the countries involved. With some prominent exceptions (such as Indonesia, Mexico, and Ukraine), the democratic gains of the past decade have come primarily in smaller and weaker states. In large, strategically important countries, such as Nigeria and Russia, the expansion of executive power, the intimidation of the opposition, and the rigging of the electoral process have extinguished even the most basic form of electoral democracy. In Venezuela, President Hugo Chávez narrowly lost a December 2 referendum that would have given him virtually unlimited power, but he still does not allow the sort of free and fair political process that could turn him out of office.

Despite two decades of political scientists warning of "the fallacy of electoralism," the United States and many of its democratic allies have remained far too comfortable with this superficial form of democracy. Assessments often fail to apply exacting standards when it comes to defining what constitutes a democracy and what is necessary to sustain it. Western leaders (particularly European ones) have too frequently blessed fraudulent or unfair elections and have been too reluctant to criticize more subtle degradations of democracy. They tend to speak out only when democratic norms are violated by unfriendly governments (as in Russia and Venezuela or in Bolivia) and soft-pedal abuses when allies (such as Ethiopia, Iraq, or Pakistan) are involved.

Before democracy can spread further, it must take deeper root where it has already sprouted.

Elsewhere in the developing and postcommunist worlds, democracy has been a superficial phenomenon, blighted by multiple forms of bad governance: abusive police and security forces, domineering local oligarchies, incompetent and indifferent state bureaucracies, corrupt and inaccessible judiciaries, and venal ruling elites who are contemptuous of the rule of law and accountable to no one but themselves. Many people in these countries—especially the poor—are thus citizens only in name and have few meaningful channels of political participation. There are elections, but they are contests between corrupt, clientelistic parties. There are parliaments and local governments, but they do not represent broad constituencies. There are constitutions, but not constitutionalism.

As a result, disillusioned and disenfranchised voters have embraced authoritarian strongmen (such as Vladimir Putin in Russia) or demagogic populists (such as Chávez in Venezuela). Many observers fear that Evo Morales in Bolivia and Rafael Correa in Ecuador may be headed down the same road as Chávez. In Thailand, voters (especially in the countryside) have turned repeatedly to a softer autocrat by electing Thaksin Shinawatra, whom the military overthrew in September 2006 only to see his party reemerge triumphant in the December 2007 elections. All of these cases of democratic distress reflect a common challenge: for democratic structures to endure—and to be worthy of endurance they must listen to their citizens' voices, engage their participation, tolerate their protests, protect their freedoms, and respond to their needs.

For a country to be a democracy, it must have more than regular, multiparty elections under a civilian constitutional order. Even significant opposition in presidential elections and opposition party members in the legislature are not enough to move beyond electoral authoritarianism. Elections are only democratic if they are truly free and fair. This requires the freedom to advocate, associate, contest, and campaign. It also requires a fair and neutral electoral administration, a widely credible system of dispute resolution, balanced access to mass media, and independent vote monitoring. By a strict application of these standards, a number of countries typically counted as democracies today—including Georgia, Mozambique, the Philippines, and Senegal—may have slipped below the threshold. Alarmingly, a January 2008 Freedom House survey found that for the first time since 1994, freedom around the world had suffered a net decline in two successive years. The ratio of the number of countries whose scores had improved to the number whose scores had declined—a key indicator—was the worst since the fall of the Berlin Wall.

Where democracy survives, it often labors under serious difficulties. In most regions, majorities support democracy as the best form of government in principle, but substantial minorities are willing to entertain an authoritarian option. Furthermore, in much of the democratic world, citizens lack any confidence that politicians, political parties, or government officials are serving anyone other than themselves. According to surveys by Latinobarómetro (a Santiago-based corporation conducting public opinion surveys throughout Latin America), only one-fifth of the Latin American population trusts political parties, one-quarter trusts legislatures, and merely one-third has faith in the judiciary. According to similar surveys conducted by the Scotland-based New Democracies Barometer, the figures are even worse in the new democracies of eastern Europe.

Public confidence in many civilian constitutional regimes has been declining. The Asian Barometer (which conducts public opinion surveys throughout Asia) found that the percentage of Filipinos who believe democracy is always the best form of government dropped from 64 percent to 51 percent between 2001 and 2005. At the same time, satisfaction with democracy fell from 54 percent to 39 percent, and the share of the Filipino population willing to reject the option of an authoritarian "strong leader" declined from 70 percent to 59 percent. The Afrobarometer (which conducts similar surveys in African countries) uncovered even sharper decreases in Nigerians' public confidence in democracy between 2000 and 2005 and also found that the proportion of the Nigerian public that felt the government was working to control corruption dropped from 64 percent to 36 percent. This is no surprise: during this period, President Olusegun Obasanjo saw many of his laudable economic reforms overshadowed or undone by continuing massive corruption, by his obsessive bid to remove a constitutional term limit on his presidency, and by the gross rigging of the 2007 elections on behalf of his ruling party.

Electoral fraud and endemic corruption have once again ravaged a promising democratic experiment. If Nigeria reverts to military rule, descends into political chaos, or collapses, it will deal a harsh blow to democratic hopes across Africa. Indeed, the many African countries that remain blatantly authoritarian will never liberalize if the continent's new and partial democracies cannot make democracy work.

It's the Government, Stupid

It is often assumed that economic growth—or the free-market economy, as Michael Mandelbaum recently argued in these pages—is the key to creating and consolidating democracy. Certainly, the viability of democracy does hinge to some significant degree on economic development and open markets. But in most of the world's poor countries, the "economy first" advocates have the causal chain backward. Without significant improvements in governance, economic growth will not take off or be sustainable. Without legal and political institutions to control corruption, punish cheating, and ensure a level economic and political playing field, pro-growth policies will be ineffective and their economic benefits will be overshadowed or erased.

Kenya is a tragic case in point. In the last five years, under President Mwai Kibaki's leadership, it has made significant economic progress for the first time in many years, achieving a record five percent annual growth rate and establishing free universal primary education. But much of this progress has since unraveled amid the paroxysms of ethnic violence that greeted allegations of fraud following the December 27, 2007, presidential election. President Kibaki did not fail on the economic policy front, nor did his country lack international tourism and development aid (apart from a brief suspension of World Bank assistance in 2006 due to reports of egregious graft). Rather, he failed politically by condoning massive corruption, ethnic favoritism, and electoral malpractice—a poisonous mix that has brought a promising new democracy to the brink of chaos.

Without legal and political institutions that control corruption, pro-growth policies will be ineffective.

In the coming decade, the fate of democracy will be determined not by the scope of its expansion to the remaining dictatorships of the world but rather by the performance of at-risk democracies such as Kenya. A list of such democracies would encompass more than 50 states, including most countries in Latin America and the Caribbean, four of the eight democracies in Asia, all of the post-Soviet democracies that do not belong to the European Union, and virtually all of the democracies in Africa. The most urgent task of the next decade is to shore up democracy in these countries.

At-risk democracies are almost universally plagued by poor governance. Some appear so trapped in patterns of corrupt and abusive rule that it is hard to see how they can survive as democracies without significant reform. The problem in these states is that bad governance is not an aberration or an illness to be cured. It is, as the economists Douglass North, John Wallis, and Barry Weingast have argued, a natural condition. For thousands of years, the natural tendency of elites everywhere has been to monopolize power rather than to restrain it—through the development of transparent laws, strong institutions, and market competition. And once they have succeeded in restricting political access, these elites use their consolidated power to limit economic competition so as to generate profits that benefit them rather than society at large. The result is a predatory state.

In such states, the behavior of elites is cynical and opportunistic. If there are competitive elections, they become a bloody zero-sum struggle in which everything is at stake and no one can afford to lose. Ordinary people are not truly citizens but clients of powerful local bosses, who are themselves the clients of still more powerful patrons. Stark inequalities in power and status create vertical chains of dependency, secured by patronage, coercion, and demagogic electoral appeals to ethnic pride and prejudice. Public policies and programs do not really matter, since rulers have few intentions of delivering on them anyway. Officials feed on the state, and the powerful prey on the weak. The purpose of government is not to generate public goods, such as roads, schools, clinics, and sewer systems. Instead, it is to produce private goods for officials, their families, and their cronies. In such a system, as Robert Putnam wrote in his classic *Making Democracy Work*, "corruption is widely regarded as the norm," political participation is mobilized from above,

civic engagement is meager, compromise is scarce, and "nearly everyone feels powerless, exploited, and unhappy." Predatory states cannot sustain democracy, for sustainable democracy requires constitutionalism, compromise, and a respect for law. Nor can they generate sustainable economic growth, for that requires actors with financial capital to invest in productive activity.

The most egregious predatory states produce predatory societies. People do not get rich through productive activity and honest risk taking; they get rich by manipulating power and privilege, by stealing from the state, extracting from the weak, and shirking the law. Political actors in predatory societies use any means necessary and break any rules possible in their quest for power and wealth. Politicians bribe election officials, attack opposition campaigners, and assassinate rival candidates. Presidents silence dissent with threats, detentions, show trials, and murder. Government ministers worry first about the money they can collect and only second about whether government contracts serve the public good. Military officers buy weapons on the basis of how large a kickback they can pocket. In such societies, the line between the police and the criminals is thin. The police do not enforce the law, judges do not decide the law, customs officials do not inspect goods, manufacturers do not produce, bankers do not invest, and borrowers do not repay. Every transaction is manipulated to someone's immediate advantage.

By contrast, sustainable democracy and development require active "civic communities," in which citizens trust one another and interact as political equals. In sustainable democracies, institutions of good governance—such as impartial judicial systems and vigorous audit agencies—induce, enforce, and reward civic behavior. The tendency toward corrupt governance and the monopoly of power is checked by the rule of law (both culturally and institutionally) and a resourceful civil society. As Putnam argues, people in such societies by and large obey the law, pay their taxes, behave ethically, and serve the public good not simply because they are public-spirited but because they believe others will, too—and because they know that there are penalties for failing to do so.

Escaping the Predators

For democracy to triumph, the natural predatory tendencies of rulers must be restrained by rigorous rules and impartial institutions. Some fundamental innovations are necessary to transform closed, predatory societies into open, democratic ones. Proponents of democracy both within troubled countries and in the international community must understand the problem and pursue the necessary reforms if they hope to restore the forward momentum of democracy in the world. Citizens must build links across ethnic and regional divides to challenge elitist hierarchies and rule by strongmen. This requires dense, vigorous civil societies, with independent organizations, mass media, and think tanks, as well as other networks that can foster civic norms, pursue the public interest, raise citizen consciousness, break the bonds of clientelism, scrutinize government conduct, and lobby for good-governance reforms.

States must also build effective institutions in order to constrain the nearly unlimited discretion that predatory rulers enjoy, subject those rulers' decisions and transactions to public scrutiny, and hold them accountable before the law. This requires both vertical and horizontal accountability. The premier example of vertical accountability is a genuinely democratic election. But ensuring democratic elections requires a truly independent electoral administration capable of conducting all the necessary tasks—from registering voters to counting votes—with strict integrity and neutrality. Other effective forms of vertical accountability include public hearings, citizen audits, the regulation of campaign finance, and a freedom-of-information act.

Horizontal accountability invests some agencies of the state with the power and responsibility to monitor the conduct of their counterparts. No institution is more important than a countercorruption commission, which should collect regular declarations of assets from all significant elected and appointed officials. To be effective, such commissions need legal authority, professional staffs, vigorous leadership, and the resources to check the veracity of financial declarations, probe allegations of wrongdoing, impose civil penalties, and bring criminal charges against violators. Their work must be reinforced by ombudsmen; public audits of all major government agencies and ministries; parliamentary oversight committees to investigate evidence of waste, fraud, and abuse by executive agencies; and competent independent judiciaries capable of penalizing bribery and embezzlement. In at-risk democracies, these institutions often exist but do not function well (or at all)— largely because they are not meant to. Typically, they either limp along, starved of resources and bereft of morale and serious leadership, or become instruments of the ruling party and investigate only its political opponents. Countercorruption agencies cannot make a difference unless they are independent of the government actors they are supposed to monitor, restrain, and punish.

The central purpose of foreign assistance must be real development, not the care and feeding of the massive global aid industry.

Poorly performing democracies need better, stronger, and more democratic institutions—political parties, parliaments, and local governments—linking citizens to one another and to the political process. In shallow democracies, these institutions do not generate much citizen participation (beyond occasional voting) because the political systems are so elite-dominated, corrupt, and unresponsive. Reform requires the internal democratization of political parties through the improvement of their transparency and accessibility and the strengthening of other representative bodies.

It is not only the regulatory and participatory institutions of government that need strengthening. Effective democracy also requires improving the technical skills, resources, professional standards, and organizational efficiency of the state. Such improvements allow the government to maintain security, man-

age the economy, develop infrastructure, settle disputes, and deliver services such as health care, education, and clean water. Just as corruption erodes the basic functions of government, a feeble state drives people toward informal and corrupt networks to get things done.

Finally, reforms must generate a more open market economy in which it is possible to accumulate wealth through honest effort and initiative in the private sector—with the state playing a limited role. The wider the scope of state control over economic life, the greater the possibility of graft by abusive and predatory elites. Reducing administrative barriers to doing business and implementing corporate-responsibility initiatives can address the supply side of the corruption problem. Strong guarantees of property rights, including the ability of owners of small farms and informal-sector workers to obtain titles to their land and business property, can provide the foundation for a broader institutional landscape that limits government corruption.

The most urgent imperative is to restructure and empower the institutions of accountability and bolster the rule of law. Changing the way government works means changing the way politics and society work, and that, in turn, requires sustained attention to how public officials utilize their offices. This is the fundamental challenge that all at-risk democracies face.

Aiding the Democratic Revival

The current situation may seem discouraging, but there is hope. Even in very poor nations drowning in corruption and clientelism, citizens have repeatedly used the democratic process to try to replace predatory governments. Connected by grassroots movements, community radio stations, cell phones, civic organizations, and the Internet, citizens are rising up as never before to challenge corruption, defend the electoral process, and demand better governance. The most important challenge now for the United States and other international actors is to stand with them.

The leverage needed to bring about radical change will never exist unless the politicians and officials who sit atop the structures of predation come to realize that they have no choice but to reform. In the early 1990s, many African regimes moved toward free elections when a combination of internal and external pressure left them no choice: they were running out of money and could not pay their soldiers and civil servants. Now, with the momentum going against democracy, a resurgent and oil-rich Russia flexing its muscles, and China emerging as a major aid donor in the rest of Asia and Africa, it will be more difficult to encourage reforms. Forcing change that leads to better governance will require serious resolve and close coordination among the established bilateral and multilateral donors.

The key is the principle of conditionality (or selectivity), which lies at the core of the Millennium Challenge Account—one of the Bush administration's least heralded but most important foreign policy innovations. Under the program, states qualify for generous new aid payments by competing on the basis of three broad criteria: whether they rule justly, whether they invest in basic health care and education, and whether they promote economic freedom. The instrument of aid selectivity is showing promise as a tool that civil-society actors in predatory states can use to campaign for governance reforms and as an incentive for corrupt governments in need of more aid to reform their ways.

The international donor community's habit of keeping afloat predatory and other troubled states (in some cases covering up to half of their recurrent government expenditures) must end. The overriding purpose of foreign assistance must be genuine development, not the assuaging of Western guilt or the care and feeding of the massive network of career professionals, nonprofit organizations, and private-sector companies that constitute the global aid industry. It is time to start listening to the growing chorus of activists and organizations in developing countries that are imploring the West to please stop "helping" them with indiscriminate aid that only serves to entrench corrupt elites and practices. To be sure, it will be an uphill struggle to get international donors, and especially institutions such as the World Bank, to refocus their aid strategies on good-governance goals. Still, the reality of the link between development and decent governance—in particular the control of corruption—is gradually taking hold in foreign-aid circles, and the civil societies of developing countries are emerging as some of the most compelling and legitimate advocates of this concept.

Now, as democratic setbacks multiply, is the moment for a new strategy. Without a clear understanding of the fundamental problem—bad governance—and the necessary institutional responses, more democratic breakdowns are likely. Without a resolute and relentless international campaign to rein in corruption and improve the quality of governance in at-risk democracies, the current democratic recession could lead to a global democratic depression. Such a development would be enormously costly to human freedom and dangerous for U.S. national security. Public opinion surveys continue to show that majorities in every region of the world believe democracy is the best form of government. The urgent imperative is to demonstrate, through the effective functioning of democracies worldwide, that it really is.

LARRY DIAMOND is a Senior Fellow at the Hoover Institution and Co-Editor of the *Journal of Democracy*. This essay is adapted from his new book, *The Spirit of Democracy: The Struggle to Build Free Societies Throughout the World* (Times Books, 2008).

Turkey Face West

Rebuffed by the European Union, angered by U.S. policies in the Middle East, and governed by an Islamist political party, Turkey seems to have every reason to turn its back on the West. To most Turks, however, that would be inconceivable.

SOLI ÖZEL

In most countries, the news that one of their own has been awarded a Nobel Prize is an occasion for universal pride and self-congratulation. That was not the ease when the renowned Turkish novelist Orhan Pamuk received the Nobel Prize for Literature this past October. Many Turks still angrily remembered Pamuk's controversial assertion in a Swiss newspaper in 2005 that "a million Armenians and thirty thousand Kurds have been killed in this land," which provided fodder for allegations that Ottoman Turkey had committed genocide against Armenians during and after World War I. The Turkish government scandalously put Pamuk on trial for defaming "Turkishness," provoking a public outcry in Turkey and abroad before he won acquittal in 2006. When the news of the Nobel broke, some Turks could barely hide their resentment and spite. For them the prize was simply a function of Pamuk's political views, which, in their view, he had expressed only to curry favor in the West and secure the Nobel.

Those with clearer minds rejoiced in Pamuk's accomplishment. By honoring him, the Swedish Academy had acknowledged the Western part of modern Turkey's identity. It cited his literary achievements as a master novelist who transformed the literary form and in the process helped to make East and West more intelligible to each other. Still, the unhealthy reaction by a sizable portion of the Turkish public spoke volumes about the country's current state of mind toward the West.

The West certainly has given Turks a great deal to think about. Indeed, less than two hours before the Academy notified Pamuk of the great honor he had received, the French National Assembly staged its own crude attack on freedom of expression by passing a resolution making it a crime to deny that Ottoman Turkey was guilty of genocide against the Armenians. In September came Pope Benedict XVI's infamous lecture at the University of Regensburg, in which he infuriated Muslims around the world by quoting a Byzantine emperor: "Show me just what Muhammad brought that was new, and there you will find things only evil and inhuman, such as his command to spread by the sword the faith he preached." Then, in mid-December, came the cruelest cut of all. The European Union announced the suspension of negotiations on eight of 35 policy issues that must be addressed before Turkey can complete the long EU accession process begun in 2004, bringing accession to a virtual halt. Even worse from the Turkish perspective was the intensity with which some European states suddenly objected to Turkey's membership, a matter that presumably had been settled in 2004. Many Turks saw the decision as yet another example of the EU's double standard in its dealings with its Muslim applicant.

In the past when the Turks were upset with Europe, they turned to the United States. Ankara and Washington have a history of close relations dating to the Cold War, when the Soviet Union loomed menacingly over its southern neighbor. Turkish troops fought alongside the Americans during the Korean War, and Turkey joined NATO in 1952. In the post-Cold War era, the United States was an enthusiastic supporter of the recently completed Baku-Ceyhan pipeline that carries oil from Azerbaijan to the Turkish port of Ceyhan on the Mediterranean, making Turkey a significant energy player while reducing Western dependence on Russia. When Turkey faced a severe economic crisis in 2001, the United States used its clout to convince the International Monetary Fund to assist Ankara.

But the Iraq war opened a rift. The Bush administration was embittered by Turkey's refusal to allow the deployment of U.S. troops in the country to open a northern front against Iraq. Ankara was angered by Washington's hard-nosed policies and alarmed by the potential for upheaval among its own traditionally restive Kurdish population created by events in the Kurdish areas of Iraq. And many Turks believe, along with other Muslims, that the United States is leading a crusade against Muslims. Anti-Americanism has begun to consume the Turkish public. The latest German Marshall Fund survey of transatlantic trends found that only seven percent of Turks approve of President George W. Bush's policies.

Turkey's unique experiment in Westernization was already under intense scrutiny in the post-9/11 world, and these latest blows have led many to question whether that experiment will continue. Will the Turks drift away from the path of Westernizing modernization? The answer to this question, if it implies that Turkey may take a U-turn from its chosen path, is empathically no.

The Turkish experiment, after all, is two centuries old, having begun with the decision of Sultan Mahmud II (1784–1839) to meet the challenge of a rising Europe with a thorough reform of the Ottoman Empire. Under Mahmud and his successors, the reforms included legal equality for all subjects of the empire, extension of private property rights, reform of the educational system, and the restructuring of the military and the notoriously ponderous Ottoman bureaucracy. With the determined leadership of Kemal Atatürk, the elite that founded the Turkish Republic on the ashes of the empire in 1923 pursued a more radical modernization, with a staunch secularism as its mainstay. Religion would be subjugated to the state and relegated strictly to the private sphere. Turkey under Atatürk replaced its alphabet and civil law virtually overnight; even the way men and women dressed was reformed.

Turkish democracy traces its practical origins to 1950, when an opposition party defeated the incumbent Republican Party and peacefully assumed power. As politicians became more responsive to popular sentiment, religion returned to the public realm and the Turkish military took it upon itself to serve as the primary custodian of the secular republican order. In its name, the army staged four direct or indirect military interventions; the last of these was the so-called postmodern coup of February 28, 1997, in which it mobilized public opinion and the news media to force the resignation of a coalition government led by the Islamist Welfare Party.

Yet significant political and economic changes were under way by the beginning of the 1990s. In the past decade and a half, the country has progressed in modernizing its economy, liberalizing its political system, and deepening its democratic order. Trade, financial flows, and investment increasingly integrate Turkey into world markets. Office towers are rising over Istanbul, which has recovered the cosmopolitan reputation it enjoyed in Ottoman times. "Cool Istanbul," as the global media sometimes call it, is a center for investment capital from East and West, a gateway to Central Asia, and a magnet for affluent sophisticates drawn by its prosperity, its spectacular nightlife, and its museums and other cultural riches.

Throughout Turkey, the burgeoning market economy is rapidly breaking down traditional economic habits and drawing in ordinary Turks, breeding more individualistic attitudes and spreading middle-class values, even as many embrace religious piety. The results can be paradoxical. In a recent survey by the Turkish Economic and Social Studies Foundation, 45 percent of Turks identified themselves first as Muslims rather than Turks, up from 36 percent in 1999. Yet support for the adoption of sharia—Islamic law—fell from 21 percent to nine percent, and the percentage of women who said they wore an Islamic headscarf declined by more than a quarter, to 11.4 percent. It is no small part of the Turkish paradox that the rush toward reform

and the EU is being led by the Islamist Justice and Development Party (AKP), which won control of parliament in November 2002 and installed the current prime minister, Recep Tayyip Erdoğan, the following March.

All of these changes have been accompanied by a somewhat painful process of self-inspection. International conferences held in Turkey on the tragic fate of the Ottoman Empire's Armenian population, the status of the Kurds (the country's main ethnic minority), and the role of Islam in modern Turkey's social and political life are emblematic of the new openness. Turkish society is increasingly pluralistic. After decades of state control, there are now more than 300 television and 1,000 radio stations on the air, broadcasting everything from hard rock to Turkish folklore, from BBC reports to Islamic and Kurdish newscasts. The questioning of established dogmas has generated intense debates. Turkish modernity, long a top-down phenomenon directed by the heirs of Atatürk, is being reshaped and redefined at the societal level. Inevitably, tensions, contradictions, and disagreements over the nation's direction abound.

The Turkish debate over Westernization has never been a winner-take-all contest between supposedly pure Westernizers and retrograde Muslims. The strategic aim of Atatürk and other founding fathers of the Turkish Republic in 1923 was to be part of the European system of states, just as the Ottomans had been. Yet even among committed Westernizers there were lines that could not be transgressed, and suspicions that could not be erased when it came to dealing with the West. After all, the Republic had been founded after a bitter struggle amid the rubble of the empire against occupying Western armies. Its founding myths had an undertone of anti-imperialist cum anti-Western passion.

In his remarkable book of autobiographical essays on his hometown, Istanbul: Memories and the City (2005), Orhan Pamuk observes that "when the empire fell, the new Republic, while certain of its purpose, was unsure of its identity; the only way forward, its founders thought, was to foster a new concept of Turkishness, and this meant a certain cordon sanitaire to shut it off from the rest of the world. It was the end of the grand polyglot multicultural Istanbul of the imperial age. . . . The cosmopolitan Istanbul I knew as a child had disappeared by the time I reached adulthood."

In all his work, Pamuk reflects on the Turkish ordeal of Westernization. In Istanbul, he notes that "with the drive to Westernize and the concurrent rise of Turkish nationalism, the love-hate relationship with the Western gaze became all the more convoluted." The Republic sought to Westernize, be part of the European universe, but kept its guard up against Western encroachments and did not quite trust its partners-to-be. Today, the nationalist reflexes of Atatürk's heirs—the secularist republican elites in the military, the judiciary, the universities, and among the old professional and bureaucratic classes—arguably play as large a role in the blossoming anti-Western sentiment as the Islamist political parties and the more religious segment of the population. These old elites are keenly aware of their ebbing power amid the transformative effects of the market economy and democratization.

Yet it is also easy to overstate the degree of anti-Western animus. Ordinarily, the Turkish public sees itself as a mediator between "civilizations," to use the fashionable term of the day, and believes profoundly in its historical right to such a role. This self-confidence is a function of its long association with the West and the secular-democratic nature of its political order. As if to illustrate this sense of mission, Prime Minister Erdoğan stood on a podium in Istanbul this past November beside his Spanish counterpart, José Luis Rodríguez Zapatero—in symbolic terms, the two heirs to leadership of the contending Muslim and Christian superpowers of the past—along with UN secretary general Kofi Annan, Archbishop Desmond Tutu, and former Iranian president Muhammad Khatami, to launch the idea of an "Alliance of Civilizations."

Pope Benedict's highly publicized visit to Turkey in December offered a more surprising illustration of the limits of Turkish anti-Westernism. Erdoğan, a strong critic of the pope's Regensburg speech who also has a politician's exquisite sensitivity to the public mood, initially decided to stay away from the country while Benedict was there. Once the debate in Turkey intensified, however, those who believed that the prime minister had to meet with this important visitor gained the upper hand. Erdoğan rescheduled his departure for a NATO summit in Latvia and, in a gesture that took everyone by surprise, greeted the pope on the tarmac.

The visit itself went exceedingly well (except for the residents of Ankara and Istanbul, who suffered the torturous inconveniences of maximum security for the pope). Protest rallies organized by fundamentalist political parties failed to draw the predicted multitudes, and widely feared disruptions by radical groups did not materialize. Benedict met with Turkey's highest official religious leader, Professor Ali Erdoğan, and removed his shoes and faced Mecca to pray alongside Istanbul's most senior religious official at the famed Blue Mosque. Most remarkably, the pope, who spoke in Turkish on several occasions, reportedly told the prime minister that he looked favorably upon Turkey's accession to the EU—an extraordinary turnabout for a man who had vehemently objected to such an eventuality when he was a cardinal. His earlier vision of the EU, shared by many Europeans, was of a Christian union rather than one in which membership is obtained when objective and secular criteria are fulfilled.

It was a supreme irony that just as the pope was giving such warm messages, the EU was preparing to deliver its blow, virtually slamming the door on what has been Turkey's great national object—a project that has enjoyed the steady support of some 70 percent of the population.

Ostensibly, the break is a result of Turkey's refusal to open its seaports and airports to traffic from the Greek part of Cyprus, because of the still-unresolved conflict between it and the Turkish north. But most EU insiders acknowledge that this is a fig leaf behind which France, the Netherlands, Denmark, and other countries are trying to conceal their desire to keep Muslim Turkey out of the Union.

For many Turks (as others), entry into the EU is not just the final destination of a journey they undertook a long time ago. It is also a test of Europe's own universalist and multicultural-ist claims, a symbol of the prospects for harmonious relations between different faiths. A snubbing of Turkey that is perceived as religiously based will have repercussions throughout the Muslim world, including Europe's own Muslim immigrant communities. In the words of the Newsweek correspondent in Istanbul, "Not so long ago, it seemed that Europe would overcome prejudice and define itself as an ideology rather than a geography, a way of being in the world rather than a mere agglomeration of nation-states. But that chance is now lost."

Yet it is hardly the case that all is lost for Turkey, or that it must now turn its back on the West. The transformations of recent decades have put the country firmly on a modernizing path, as the example of the governing AKP itself illustrates. Founded by current prime minister Erdoğan, Abdullah Gül (his foreign minister), and others, the AKP grew out of a split in the Islamist movement in the 1990s. Erdoğan and his allies in the younger generation broke away from the more conservative and ideological (and anti-EU) group. The AKP retained a great deal of support from the traditional constituencies of the Islamist parties. But there was now a new and dynamic constituency that made a bid for increased power in the economic and political system. Turkey's market reforms had propelled a new generation of provincial entrepreneurs who had prospered in the newly competitive and open economy. They were part of a globalizing economy, and were eager to get a bigger share of the economic pie and to pursue EU membership. Also attracted to the AKP were the recent arrivals from the countryside, who lived and worked on the periphery of the major cities and suddenly found themselves with new and different interests.

The AKP won an overwhelming majority in the 2002 parliamentary elections. The exhaustion of the established elites—in particular, their failure to manage the Turkish economy and reform the political system to make it more responsive to the demands of a fast-modernizing society—along with the electorate's desire to punish the incumbents, played a prominent role in the AKP'S success. The promise the party's rise to power held for a better, more inclusive, less corrupt future, rather than the appeal of an ideological call for an Islamic order, won the elections for the AKP. Post-election data showed that half of its support came from voters who had backed secular parties in previous elections. And in its market-oriented economic policies and acceptance of some liberal political principles, the AKP represented a break from the traditional Islamist parties of earlier decades.

Despite its numerous shortcomings (such as its habit of appointing ideological kin rather than qualified personnel to top jobs), the AKP mostly has remained true to its electoral platform, to the surprise of many abroad. Seeking to accelerate Turkey's progress through the EU accession process, it has taken big steps toward political liberalization, civilian control of the military, and consolidation of the rule of law. The example it sets therefore stands as the antithesis of the Islamic order in Al Qaeda's imagination. Still, in the eyes of many the AKP remains suspect because of its origins, its cliquish and ideologically motivated appointments, and the decidedly faith-based cultural preferences of its leading figures—whose wives, for example, wear the Islamic headscarf. Some critics even detect a dangerous tilt in Ankara's foreign policy. Particularly controversial was the visit by Khalid Meshal, a leader of Hamas, after the Palestinian elections, just when the West was trying to isolate Hamas and force it to renounce terrorism and recognize Israel's right to exist. And Turkey has drawn the ire of some in Washington for remaining on good terms with its Syrian and Iranian neighbors—a choice that may look different now that the Iraq Study Group has recommended dialogue with those two countries.

Some of the AKP's critics charge that one more term under the party will leave Turkey less secular, somewhat less democratic, and decidedly non-Western. This is unfair and untrue. Whatever its failings, the party represents something new in Turkish life. Indeed, if one were to speak of fundamentalism with respect to the AKP and its constituents, "market fundamentalism" would have to hold pride of place. The "creative destruction" of Turkey's vibrant capitalism has transformed sleepy provincial towns such as Kayseri, Denizli, Malatya, and Konya, and integrated them into the global markets. Producing consumer goods, machinery, textiles, furniture, and ceramics for export to Europe, the United States, the Middle East, and Central Asia, they have been enriched and exposed to the wider world. The new social mobility has made the conservative weft of the country's cultural fabric more visible and poignant. Partly because Turkish institutions did little to ease the transition, mobility reinforced communitarian tendencies. An ineffective state and a sluggish banking sector that was slow to reach out to credit-starved businesspeople left many Turks with nowhere to turn but to networks based on kin, faith, and community.

At the same time, the newly acquired wealth created demands for the rewards of consumer society. Women in the conservative Muslim middle classes dressed modestly and wore headscarves but eagerly shopped for the latest look at Islamic fashion shows. Seaside hotels with facilities allowing the separation of the sexes at the beach sprang up to accommodate the newly affluent. The children of the new middle classes, both sons and daughters, registered in the best of schools and often went abroad, mostly to Western countries (preferably the United States), to get their college degrees or their MBAs.

Despite the EU's crude rebuff, Turkey's multifaceted modernization will continue. The impact of global integration and ongoing economic and political reforms will still ripple through Turkish society, and the transformation will also strain Turkey's social fault lines. A widening sphere of freedom and democratic engagement brings forth demands from long-suppressed groups—from Kurds to environmentalists—and, as in all such cases, triggers a reaction. Yet these are all the birth pangs of a more modern Turkey that will remain European while redefining itself, even if Europe cannot yet grasp this process and its significance. If it manages its transformations wisely, Turkey will indeed become, as Presidents Bill Clinton and George W. Bush have both predicted, one of the key countries shaping the 21st century.

In awarding the Nobel Prize to Pamuk, the Swedish Academy cited his rendering of Istanbul's melancholy in his work. The Turkish word for this is hüzün. "The hüzün of Istanbul," Pamuk writes, "is not just the mood evoked by its music and its poetry, it is a way of looking at life that implicates us all, not only a spiritual state but a state of mind that is ultimately as life-affirming as it is negating." This hüzün, he says later, "suggests nothing of an individual standing against society: on the contrary, it suggests an erosion of the will to stand against the values and mores of the community and encourages us to be content with little, honoring the virtues of harmony, uniformity, humility."

Arguably the hüzün of Istanbul is no more. At best, it is on its way out. The cosmopolitan city of different ethnicities and religious affiliations and many languages that Pamuk knew is indeed long gone. A new cosmopolitanism, that of financial services and multinational corporations, advertisers and artists, oil men and real estate agents, is rapidly filling the gap. Individuals of all colors who partake of it exude self-confidence and are unlikely to be "content with little." They will want to take on the world.

SOLI ÖZEL, a Southeast Europe Project policy scholar at the Wilson Center in 2006, is a professor of international relations at Istanbul Bilgi University and a columnist for the newspaper Sabah.

The Practice—and the Theory

Can rule by the people be reconciled with the sovereignty of Allah?

"Turkey sets a fantastic example for nations around the world to see where it's possible to have a democracy coexist with a great religion like Islam." Those were George Bush's words of welcome, this week, to Turkey's President Abdullah Gul.

In decades past, a Turkish leader might have been received at the White House with cordial remarks about his country's growing prosperity or its contribution to NATO. But it would have been strange, perhaps, not to mention religion when hosting a head of state who had just set a precedent that was watched with fascination by politically active Muslims in many parts of the world. When he became president, Mr Gul proved that it was possible for a pious Muslim with a headscarved wife to be made head of state, by a perfectly democratic procedure, in a country where the army is an ever-vigilant guardian against theocracy. For those who insist (whether their arguments are theological, or empirical, or both) that Islam and liberal democracy are quite compatible, Mr Gul's election (and Mr Bush's exuberant reaction to it) was a badly needed nugget of hope in a year when that cause has seen quite a lot of setbacks.

Among American officialdom, confidence in the prospects for democracy in Muslim (and in particular, Arab) lands has fluctuated under the Bush administration. It reached a high point, arguably, in mid-2005, when Condoleezza Rice, the secretary of state, declared in Cairo that the bad old days of favouring stability over democracy were over—and then it plunged again the following January when the Islamist Hamas movement swept to victory in Palestine.

For political scientists, especially those who have studied the phenomenon of "Muslim Democracy" in the belief that the Turkish case could be a precedent for others, the recent turmoil in Pakistan and the assassination of Benazir Bhutto have been a great tragedy in a pivotal country that had the potential to develop a new concordat between Islam and open politics.

Vali Nasr, a professor at America's Tufts University, terms "Muslim Democracy" a newish and potentially decisive force in the non-Arab parts of the Muslim world. In his view, the recent experience of Turkey, Pakistan, Bangladesh, Malaysia and Indonesia all points to a single truth: wherever they are given the chance, Muslim Democratic parties (which are responsive to public opinion and thrive in an open political contest) can prevail over harder-line and more violent varieties of political Islam.

Among the parties Mr Nasr identifies as Muslim Democratic are the faction of the Pakistani Muslim League that held sway until the military takeover in 1999; the Bangladesh Nationalist Party (in power till last year's coup); Malaysia's ruling UMNO party; and a cluster of mildly Islamic parties that share power in Indonesia. Exhibit A for Muslim Democracy is Turkey's Justice and Development (AK) party, which won its democratic spurs after several decades of sparring between generals and pious politicians. As with several other Muslim Democratic parties, the AK's rise reflected economic growth and the advent of a devout but non-fanatical middle class which resents the older elites of bureaucrats and generals.

But what if any is the intellectual ground for Muslim Democracy? Roman Catholic thinking had to tread a long path before it reconciled its belief in human sinfulness with popular sovereignty; Christian Democracy, an important force in post-1945 Europe, was the result.

Abdal-Hakim Murad, a British Muslim scholar, argues that Muslim Democrats have an easier road to travel because Islam's view of human nature is a less pessimistic one. But several factors have helped to make the Muslim debate about democracy difficult and inconclusive. Most of the schools of Muslim thought that have emerged over the past century have been intensely interested in political theory, and also intensely concerned with precedents set at the dawn of Muslim era. But the precedents are not clear: some caliphs took power by inheritance, others through consensus, others by force.

Khaled Abou El Fadl, an Egyptian-born law professor, has pointed to a passage from the Koran which seems to endow human beings with a special mandate to look after their own affairs. When your Lord said to the angels: "I have to place a vice-regent on earth," they said: "Will you place one there who will create disorder and shed blood, while we intone Your litanies and sanctify Your name?" And God said: "I know what you do not know."

That verse, Mr Fadl has argued, seems to imply that far from sitting back and letting God to do everything, human beings must organise their own society.

Another relevant text is the story of Ali, the fourth Muslim caliph, whose leadership was challenged by a rival. To the fury of his zealous supporters, Ali agreed that conflicting claims should be submitted to arbitration. Posterity found Ali right and his critics wrong: human institutions do have a place in settling issues of state.

From Cairo to California

For anyone who looks to Islam's foundational texts as the ultimate arbiter of truth, these are resonant allusions. But arguments in favour of Islam's compatibility with democracy are in perpetual danger of being drowned out by a mixture of depressing news from Muslim lands and zealous ideologues on both sides of a looming civilisational divide.

Whether or not they condone violence, many of the most strident advocates of "political Islam" still take their cue from Sayyid Qutb, an Egyptian thinker, executed in 1966, who regarded secular democracy (and all other secular forms of government, including socialism) as blasphemy pure and simple. In places ranging from British campuses to the jails and torture chambers of Uzbekistan, there are zealous ideologues who follow the Qutbist line that all human agencies of power are a violation of the sovereignty of God. Neatly converging with the anti-democratic zeal of these of these malcontents is an increasingly respectable argument, among sceptical Western observers of Islam, which holds that the Muslim faith, by its very nature, cannot be other than theocratic. If that is true, then encouraging moderate—in the sense of apolitical—versions of Islam can only be a waste of time.

In the United States, in particular, an "essentialist" mistrust of Islam in all its forms has been gaining ground. One recent sign of this mood: when Keith Ellison from Minnesota became the first Muslim congressman, he was challenged, during his first television interview, to prove that he was not "working for our enemies".

But in America's free-ranging debates, where the spectrum of views on Islam is probably wider than in any Muslim land or even in Europe, there are also many voices on the other side. Mr Fadl makes his case for the compatibility of democracy and Islam from the University of California at Los Angeles, probably a more secure setting than his native Cairo.

Meanwhile Firas Ahmad, a columnist who co-edits a glossy Muslim monthly from his home in Boston, maintains that a lot of Islamic history—as well as the dilemmas of modern times—should be reconsidered in the light of the robust separation between religion and state which (on his reading, at least), Muslims have quite frequently, and cheerfully, maintained. In modern America, Muslims can make a big contribution to debates about greed and social justice, while fully respecting the country's secular constitution. And his favourite passages in history are the bits where believers (often courageous Sufi mystics) spoke truth to power, not the instances when pliant greybeards did favours to the sultan.

There are, in short, many interesting things to say about Islam and democracy. The pity is that they are mostly being said in the West, not in Islam's heartland.

South Africa After the Age of Heroes

"The silver lining accompanying the ANC's premature display of elite instability is that the country's democracy, just 14 years old, is itself demonstrating new maturity."

JEFFREY HERBST

South Africa's democracy took a new turn in December 2007 when the ruling, dominant African National Congress (ANC), at its party congress in Polokwane, rejected President Thabo Mbeki's attempt to serve another term as party leader. Instead the ANC elected as its leader former Vice President Jacob Zuma—making him also the presumptive next South African president, following 2009 elections that Mbeki cannot contest because of constitutional term limits. This was nothing less than a political rebirth for Zuma, who had been "redeployed" from the vice presidency (that is, fired) in June 2005 after a close business associate was convicted of fraud. Zuma had also been brought to trial in 2006 (though he was eventually acquitted) on rape charges, and he has been ridiculed for his view that a shower can help prevent the transmission of HIV. A few days after taking control of the ANC, he was indicted on fraud charges.

Zuma's rallies, where his supporters sing his theme song, "Get Me My Machine Gun," make him seem very distant from former South African President Nelson Mandela and Archbishop Desmond Tutu, both Nobel Peace Prize laureates. Zuma's well-known populism is also at odds with the neo-liberal economic policies administered by Mandela and Mbeki. Indeed, one of Zuma's first steps as ANC leader was to start using the socialist salutation "comrade" to refer to fellow party members.

The ANC's repudiation of Mbeki's effort to continue leading the party even after he leaves the presidency was extraordinarily public and transparent. Indeed, it was probably the first time in the history of Africa—a continent whose countries give remarkable deference to even the most dysfunctional leaders—that a sitting president was publicly defeated in an attempt to continue managing his party. As such, the Zuma transition represented an iconic democratic moment for South Africa, as well as a traumatic moment for the ANC. Nonetheless, Zuma's actions and views are problematic in many ways. They threaten, under the worst scenarios, to disrupt the hard-earned gains that the South African economy has achieved in recent years.

This complicated, contradictory array of events—an outburst of democracy leading to the nomination of an extremely problematic leader—shows that in many ways South Africa has moved beyond the heroic era of Mandela to one in which leaders are democratically selected but all too human. What this means for South Africa's future is, inevitably, complicated as well.

The ANC's Loss of Discipline

The ANC was not always a very successful national liberation movement. Indeed, for many years it bragged that it was the world's oldest national liberation movement, seemingly unaware that this was not necessarily a positive attribute. The ANC continually misunderstood the strategic situation in South Africa, was often penetrated by apartheid spies, and did not have particularly good links with opposition groups inside the country.

However, the ANC was good at maintaining internal discipline. Overwhelmingly, it prevented its adherents from engaging in the kind of undisciplined terror against the white population that would have been emotionally satisfying but counterproductive to the movement's long-term interests. As stated in a critical strategy and tactics document adopted by the ANC in 1969:

> The riot, the street fight, the outburst of unorganized violence, individual terrorism: These were symptoms of the militant spirit but not pointers to revolutionary technique. The winning of our freedom by armed struggle—the only method left open to us—demands more than passion. It demands an understanding and an implementation of revolutionary theory and techniques in the actual conditions facing us. It demands a sober assessment of the obstacles in our way and an appreciation that such a struggle is bitter and protracted. It demands, too, the dominance in our thinking of achievement over drama.

Very few revolutionary movements would have been able to control their followers the way the ANC did. The feat is especially impressive considering that much of the ANC's leadership spent years in prison or in faraway London, and that so many opportunities for terror existed.

Similarly, although the ANC certainly contained cliques and factions, it generally managed to present a united front; leadership competitions of the type that routinely tear apart revolutionary groups did not unduly hamper it. When Mandela was finally released from prison in 1990 after more than a quarter-century of confinement, among the first things he said in public was: "I am a loyal and disciplined member of the African National Congress. I am therefore in full agreement with all of its objectives, strategies, and tactics."

Over the next four years, the ANC would continue to exhibit an extraordinary degree of discipline. Mandela made numerous concessions to the white population that had never been conceived of during the struggle—concessions that included assuring members of the civil service and military that their jobs would be protected, extending promises to respect property rights, and abandoning the idea of trials for crimes against humanity. Despite all of this, the party and the majority of the black population followed Mandela and voted the ANC into office. And in 1999, when Mandela decided to relinquish the presidency, he was able to transfer power to his chosen successor Mbeki, then vice president, even though it was not at all clear that Mbeki was the most popular choice among the rank and file.

Zuma's victory over Mbeki for the ANC leadership—putting aside how big a mistake Mbeki made by trying to retain control of the party—represents a new development for the ANC, given its ability in the past to manage leadership transitions. Indeed, Mbeki's having "redeployed" Zuma makes the latter's victory an especially acute public rebuke of the sitting South African president. And the results from the party congress at Polokwane were not only a defeat for Mbeki but also a stunning blow to his cabinet and the party's leadership. Winnie Mandela, from whom the ANC had sought to distance itself for many years because of her criminal activities (including kidnapping and fraud), was actually the top vote-getter for the ANC's National Executive Committee at the party conference.

It is hardly surprising to see a breakdown of revolutionary discipline in a party that has achieved power and no longer has a clear, hated opponent. But the ANC's elite instability has occurred a little earlier than might have been predicted, given that South Africa's new, nonracial order only came into existence in April 1994 and that, before then, the ANC was an unusually well-ordered revolutionary movement.

While Zuma may not be a particularly good choice to run the ANC, the party's repudiation of Mbeki represents a remarkable development for South African democratic culture. A new ANC leader was chosen in a very public and transparent manner and without violence. Despite the traumatic breakdown of elite discipline, the party's leaders, starting with Mbeki, handled Zuma's accession to the leadership well—even with some grace. Indeed, the silver lining accompanying the ANC's premature display of elite instability is that the country's democracy, just 14 years old, is itself demonstrating new maturity.

Why Zuma?

Even if Zuma's resurgence was a signal moment for South Africa's democracy, it still raises real questions about the country's political order. To outsiders, Zuma's appeal is hard to fathom. While he was acquitted of the rape charges, his defense was that his Zulu heritage demanded he have intercourse with the woman in question because she, wearing a skirt and displaying her legs, was obviously looking for sex and must not be disappointed. Further, Zuma seems a particularly poor choice to lead the country with the world's largest number of AIDS sufferers, considering that he claims to have warded off infection with a shower after he was exposed to the HIV-positive rape accuser.

Zuma has four wives. He speaks excellent English but during his rape trial insisted on speaking only Zulu. Thus, he is not exactly a role model for South Africa, a country that has worked hard to empower women and to put aside ethnic conflict. Zuma's chief financial adviser has been convicted of fraud; the new party

leader himself has had substantial involvement in transactions that have attracted fraud charges; and he may soon stand trial again. Even if Zuma is not brought to trial, he will operate under a permanent cloud. And Zuma was not the best of a bad lot. He arguably was the reverse. The party can claim a number of exceptional figures—starting with Cyril Ramaphosa, the chief negotiator during the democratic transition—whom it could have chosen as leader instead.

Still, the internal logic of Zuma's victory was powerful. First, as the saying goes, Zuma had a much better war than Mbeki. Mbeki certainly faced hardships during his long exile in the apartheid era, but these involved cold rooms in London and trying to mobilize the world against the apartheid system. Zuma, on the other hand, was imprisoned on Robben Island for a decade. He served after his imprisonment as the ANC's intelligence chief in southern Africa, and was constantly at risk of being assassinated by the efficient, brutal forces of the white South African government. When Zuma's supporters sing "Get Me My Machine Gun," they are not only implicitly threatening whites; they are also comparing Zuma's record as a fighter to Mbeki's as a diplomat. How one fought during the struggle against apartheid still matters a great deal in South Africa. It helps explain, in particular, the suspicions harbored by many ANC stalwarts toward those who did not carry guns, or who after the transition moved too quickly into the camp of big business.

Many black South Africans believed that by now their country would be—after almost 15 years of transformation—more transformed than it is.

Zuma's victory also reflects Mbeki's ideological incoherence during his nearly 10 years as president. After decades of apartheid—which amounted to a kind of racial socialism in which the entire market was rigged against blacks—the post-apartheid governments of Mandela and Mbeki developed the most free-market policies in South Africa's history. The elimination of formalized discrimination represented at least a start at leveling the economic field for all South Africans (though much more still has to be done). In addition, the country's macroeconomic management has been outstanding, as judged by the World Bank and the International Monetary Fund. Government spending has been conservative despite legitimate demands for greater social expenditures; an autonomous central bank has oriented monetary policy toward curbing inflation; and rules regarding both capital and trade have been liberalized considerably. Partially as a result, South Africa is now enjoying its strongest economic growth in decades—growth accompanied by a strong rand and, until recently, low inflation.

Mbeki, however, does not celebrate the market or South Africa's successful globalization. In weekly, widely distributed e-mails that he wrote when he was the ANC leader—e-mails that provided extraordinary insight into his thinking—he never argued that South Africa has adopted and benefited from capitalism, but instead quoted Marx and discussed enslavement as an aspect of the international economy. A particularly telling example of this occurred after confidence in the government was shaken by the release of a draft report in 2004 contemplating significant ownership changes in the mining sector. When Tony Trahar, the chief executive officer of the giant natural resource conglomerate Anglo-American, said that political risk in South Africa, though it was starting to diminish, was not yet eliminated, Mbeki did not accept that the glass was half full. Rather, in a September 2004 message that he e-mailed across the world, he went fully on the attack:

> The poor and the despised . . . have chosen reconciliation rather than revenge. Rather than reparations, they have asked for an opportunity to do a decent job for a decent wage. Do they deserve to be computed as a political risk, when everything they have done and said has made the unequivocal statement that they are ready to let the past bury the past? Is it moral and fair that these, who daily bear the scars of poverty, should suffer from the guilt of their masters, who are fixated by the nightmare of a risky future for our country, which derives not from what the poor have done and will do, but from what the rich fear those they impoverished will do, imagining what they themselves would have done, if they had been impoverished?

Mbeki did not seem to understand that the (declining) political risk identified by Trahar stemmed from the government itself, not the poor. Mbeki never explained to his constituents that South African prosperity would depend on growth generated by companies like the one Trahar led. ANC officials later had to work to mitigate the damage caused by the president's decision to lambaste one of the most important businessmen in the country.

As a result of this extraordinary disjunction between words and deeds, Mbeki leaves no ideological legacy. As Margaret Thatcher might say, "There is no Mbekiism." Those in South Africa who advocate for socialism—despite the gains that Mbeki's neoliberal economic policies have created—do not have to justify breaking away from the Mbeki presidency because Mbeki himself used radical language even as his policies were going in a very different direction. Indeed, surprisingly little public sympathy exists within the ANC for continuing in the current direction—even as the country celebrates its economic growth—because the president himself has not publicly backed his own policies. Zuma differs from Mbeki in actually believing that South Africa should enact more radical policies, but his rhetoric is not very different from Mbeki's.

The Zimbabwe Fantasy

Despite South Africa's considerable achievements, an unmistakable angst exists regarding what the post-apartheid era has come to mean. The very normality of South Africa today compared to the era of heroic struggle is, of course, a disappointment to some (even if they do not miss for a moment the brutality of the old regime). More importantly, many black South Africans believed that by now their country would be—after almost 15 years of transformation—more transformed than it is. The black-white divide remains obvious to all, almost all of the time. The government has made impressive advances in delivering services to the people and, to a much lesser extent, creating jobs, but the life chances of blacks are still radically different from those of whites, and this fact understandably gnaws at many. Flying over Johannesburg, it is easy to guess who lives in the shacks below (though the owners of the homes with swimming pools have become more diverse).

Discontent in South Africa is affected by people's notions about Zimbabwe, which has become a kind of secret fantasy for some in the ANC. Zimbabwean President Robert Mugabe has destroyed

his country with land seizures and a lunatic economic policy that has provoked hyperinflation; those with skills or money or just a desire to survive have been forced to flee. Mugabe has justified the destruction of Zimbabwe by arguing that he is simply completing the revolution that he promised when the country gained independence in 1980, including the return of land that was stolen from Africans. He therefore stands in stark contrast to the ANC—which once promised seizure of whites' property as well, but which has (wisely) decided to pursue a slow policy of redistribution by other means.

Probably no one in the ANC wishes to duplicate Mugabe's policies in South Africa. However, a great many secretly approve of Mugabe's overturning of white economic power in Zimbabwe. South Africa, as a result, has been profoundly ambivalent for years about how to approach its northern neighbor. Although the Congress of South African Trade Unions—a labor umbrella group that is formally allied with the ANC—has called for active opposition to Zimbabwe, the ANC itself has never resolved to fully oppose its neighbor's self-destruction. This is because Mugabe has wrapped his actions in rhetoric that is easy for former apartheid sufferers to understand.

It remains to be seen whether Zuma will run in the 2009 elections, let alone become president. The government seems to be proceeding with corruption charges against him. Zuma may be forced to resign the ANC presidency, or he might become so problematic that the party will eventually decide to jettison him for another candidate for South Africa's presidency. But it is hard to guess what path Zuma might take in the future: Those who observed his trial for rape would hardly have believed he would become president of the ANC two years later. The record suggests it is dangerous to bet against him.

Economic Discipline at Risk?

Zuma's populism, Mbeki's ideological incoherence, the public's disappointment with the government's ability to deliver, and Mugabe's example across the border—all of these factors reasonably put into question whether South Africa's neoliberal economic policies have, in fact, been locked in. Certainly, while South Africa has enjoyed strong economic growth in recent years, it needs to do more if it is to reduce poverty and become a leader in the developing world (its stated ambition). The South African government, when it reviewed in 2003 the first decade of freedom, correctly called the country's economic growth "mediocre" compared to nations like Malaysia, Thailand, and South Korea, with which it hopes to be compared. The government had to admit that the overall economy displayed a "steady but unspectacular performance compared with most developing countries."

But Mbeki's government is not primarily responsible for the South African economy's disappointing performance. The inheritance from apartheid—including the illiteracy and poor training levels of millions of blacks, and an economy devoted to serving a small racial minority—largely explains the poor growth performance. In fact, the government's macroeconomic management has been far superior to that of its white predecessors. Still, the ANC is the government of the day, and it is the ANC that must deal with the consequences of poor growth.

In the short run, it is unlikely, even if Zuma becomes president, that South Africa will go down a substantially different economic path. For one thing, the government has had such tremendous success collecting income tax (another area in which it has significantly outperformed the governments of the apartheid era) that a substantial public surplus now exists, one that can legitimately be spent on addressing social needs without threatening hard-won economic stability. Such additional spending could, over the next few years, reduce calls for more radical redistribution schemes. In addition, the investments that the government has already made in social services will continue to pay off; more poor South Africans as a result will find their life chances improving in the next few years. Also, a significant portion of the ANC itself benefits from the country's current economic arrangements, and would be loath to endorse major changes.

In all probability South Africa will survive if Zuma comes to power, but it will not reach its potential.

If Zuma does come to power, however, South Africa will need to make the case all over again that its economic policies reward investors, both domestic and foreign. After almost 15 years of excellent macroeconomic management, during which many were calling for radical measures, South Africa might rightly feel that it deserves the benefit of the doubt regarding future economic policies. But Zuma's coming to power would essentially wipe away the goodwill that South Africa has, at some cost, bought. That goodwill could be garnered again, but there would be a lag. And leaders other than Zuma could certainly accomplish more, faster.

At the same time, the fact that South Africa will probably stay on its current economic path is not *all* good news: Keeping to the current course probably means a failure to adopt even more ambitious growth targets that would reduce poverty faster and attract more foreign investment. To aim for higher growth, the country would need to embark on further, dramatic changes in the economy, including significant deregulation. Little evidence suggests that a future South African government could pursue such a politically unpopular track, and a government headed by Zuma would be especially unambitious about economic growth. Indeed, one element of the confused ideological legacy that Mbeki leaves is that the ANC itself is not demanding higher growth rates, even though such a development path is necessary for faster reductions in poverty.

Worrying signs also remain regarding corruption (another concern that Zuma would have trouble addressing, given the accusations against him). It should be noted from the start that the ANC is in significant ways less corrupt than previous white governments, which used the numerous distortions in the economy, as well as a sanctions-busting mentality that coursed through much of the private sector, to engage in continual enrichment. The current corruption problem is also not especially significant by global standards. In Transparency International's most recent corruption perception index, South Africa ranks 43rd, tied with high performers like Malaysia and South Korea. Again, however, the ANC is the government of the day, and it needs to limit corruption if it is to deliver on its ambitious social goals and promote economic growth.

Corruption concerns will persist, especially as the government pursues economic policies that enable well-connected black businessmen to gain significant stakes in industry as part of an economic empowerment program. With Zuma as ANC leader, and possibly destined to play an important role in government, South Africa—whether fairly or not—will have to continue proving its case that corruption is not a problem threatening basic economic performance.

The Disease with No Cure

It is impossible to write about South Africa without discussing HIV/AIDS. South Africa is estimated to have the world's largest number of people living with HIV/AIDS (5.3 million) and the largest number of AIDS-related deaths per year (370,000). Mbeki's extremely problematic approach to HIV/AIDS is well-known: He drew international attention with his attempt to discredit HIV/AIDS science, and he has supported the country's health minister, who insists that a homemade regimen of olive oil, lemon, beetroot, and garlic is a legitimate alternative to antiretrovirals. While parts of the South African government have implemented important policies for prevention and treatment of the disease, the overall impression is that the government has been at war with itself on HIV/AIDS. This has undoubtedly hindered efforts to address the epidemic.

The Joint United Nations Program on HIV and AIDS estimates that government policies in recent years have not managed to lower the number of infections, and that only 15 percent of infected pregnant women receive treatment that could prevent transmission of the HIV virus to their babies. Only about 21 percent of HIV-positive people receive medical treatment, an extremely surprising number given the sophistication of South Africa's health system. No one understands for sure how the deaths to come will ultimately affect South Africa's society and economy, but in HIV/AIDS the country faces a challenge that greatly complicates its already difficult transition from apartheid.

Zuma is not the man to lead South Africa's approach to the disease that threatens to cripple the country's future. His attitude toward casual sex and his "shower" remark only complicate the tasks of the committed professionals, both within and outside of government, who are trying to address the disease. Indeed, no matter what Zuma says or does in the future regarding AIDS, he has already signaled to the country that he does not believe in the one approach to HIV/AIDS that has proved most effective in the rest of the world: prevention.

The path from Mandela—without doubt the greatest statesman of his generation—to Zuma could be viewed as farce. But the simple reality is that the time of heroes has passed in South Africa, and sometimes countries choose problematic leaders. In all probability South Africa will survive if Zuma comes to power, but it will not reach its potential. In the area of AIDS, Zuma may be very bad indeed (though it would be hard to do worse than Mbeki). As a result, many South Africans may remain in poverty unnecessarily, and an extraordinary number will die from the epidemic. Unfortunately, it is all too normal for countries to do well, but not as well as they should, and to falter when faced with this disease that has no cure.

JEFFREY HERBST is provost and executive vice president for academic affairs at Miami University in Ohio.

From *Current History*, April 2008. Copyright © 2008 by Current History, Inc. Reprinted by permission.

Congo's Peace

Miracle or Mirage?

"Impunity has been to some extent the glue of the peace process. This fact could undermine the country's fragile stability."

JASON K. STEARNS

On March 22 this year, the worst fighting that Kinshasa has ever seen broke out between government forces and supporters of the opposition. Hundreds of people lay dead in the streets and opposition leader Jean-Pierre Bemba announced his departure into exile. Yet some diplomats in the capital played down the violence as a hiccup in the peace process. "We think," one of them told me, "these are the death throes of the old war, not the beginning of a new one."

Many in the international community feel the same way: too much has been accomplished in the more than four years since the signing of a comprehensive peace agreement in Pretoria, South Africa, for war to break out again. Indeed, the Democratic Republic of Congo, once divided among half a dozen warring factions, is now united. A national army has been created. The eight foreign nations at one time involved in the conflict have withdrawn their forces.

Most importantly, in 2006, presidential, national, and provincial assembly elections took place in the first multiparty polls since 1965. The logic of guns, so the saying goes in Kinshasa, has been replaced by the logic of ballots. The incumbent Joseph Kabila (who had assumed the presidency after the assassination of his father, Laurent Kabila, in 2001) won the 2006 presidential race, and his coalition now dominates parliament and most of the provincial assemblies. There have been other successes: the country has a new, improved constitution; Congo's administration and army have been largely unified; security in parts of the country has improved dramatically.

The peace process, however, has been only partially successful. The elections did eviscerate some rebel groups, but, as the recent fighting demonstrates, new fault lines have emerged. Many reforms have been cosmetic: the Congolese state is unified but remains deeply corrupt and abusive. The administration provides almost no social services to the population. And the integrated army is the largest human rights abuser in the country, terrorizing the people it is supposed to protect.

Herein lies the paradox of the transition's success: in order to avoid alienating anyone and to keep the shaky political process going, a blind eye has been turned to high levels of corruption and abuse. Impunity has been to some extent the glue of the peace process. This fact could undermine the country's fragile stability.

Peace on Kabila's Terms

The war in Congo has been one of the bloodiest of modern times, leaving an estimated 4 million dead, largely from disease and hunger. The conflict dates back to 1996, when a coalition of regional powers, including Rwanda, Uganda, Angola, and Eritrea, backed an invasion by a rebel group led by Laurent Kabila. They toppled the dying dictator Mobutu Sese Seko, installing Kabila as head of state in May 1997. Fighting resumed in 1998 when Kabila asked his Rwandan patrons to leave the country. The Rwandans reinvaded, creating a proxy rebel group in the east. Five years of conflict drew in eight countries and spawned a dozen different Congolese armed groups.

The 2002 peace deal succeeded where its many predecessors had failed, offering each signatory something better than the status quo. The timing had much to do with this. After years of fighting, Rwanda, Uganda, and Zimbabwe were withdrawing their troops from the country, making a military victory for the remaining belligerents almost impossible. For the Congolese Rally for Democracy (RCD) and the Movement for the Liberation of Congo (MLC), Rwanda and Uganda's respective proxy forces, the deal provided a lifeline and lucrative positions in the transition. The agreement also elevated the smaller, auxiliary parties—political opposition groups, civil society, and three small rebel movements—from minor players to high-ranking positions. Finally, by offering Joseph Kabila the presidency and command of the transition, it presented him with peace on his terms and a good chance of winning the elections.

On the face of it, the deal provided relatively equal terms to the principal belligerents. Kabila had to share power with four vice presidents, and all positions in the executive branch, legislature, and security services were divided among the signatories.

However, since Kabila controlled the central state apparatus and most of the country's revenue—in particular from the mining areas of Katanga and the Kasais—many aspects of the agreement amounted not so much to power-sharing as to an integration of the other parties into Kabila's administration.

While the army command, for example, was given to the RCD, the powerful *maison militaire*—the head of state's cabinet of military advisers—controlled army funds and decision making during the first part of the transition. The 10,000-strong presidential guard was an added asset for Kabila, since it fell under his direct control. Similarly, the political opposition took control of the ministry of mines, but businessmen still had to get presidential approval for major deals. Positions in other institutions—such as the central bank; the supreme court; the two largest state-owned mining companies, MIBA and Gecamines; and the intelligence service—were not shared among the signatories, despite promises in the peace deal. Kabila simply refused.

This, of course, did not go down well with Kabila's rivals. The RCD withdrew from the transition process in August 2004; the MLC threatened to do the same in January 2005. However, in both cases, with the international community's help, Kabila was able to call their bluff. Real retreat would have forced them into the isolation of their rebel strongholds where, without the military backing of their former patrons, their future would have been questionable. They would also have foregone Kinshasa's opulence: each vice president was allocated $250,000 dollars per month for himself and his staff. Both the MLC and the RCD had 7 ministers and 118 parliamentarians each, making $4,000 and $1,500 per month respectively (several times more than judges' or doctors' salaries). Some of the directors of state companies, most of whose jobs were finally shared out by 2005, made as much as $20,000 a month. As a dissident RCD member lamented: "They couldn't get their hand out of the sugar bowl."

The international community, which funds over half of the country's budget, has refrained from criticizing Congolese leaders too harshly.

The weakness of the political parties also favored Kabila. The belligerents had been motivated by self-interest, not by ideology; once in the transition, each leader tried to fend for himself. Indeed, five MLC ministers defected to Kabila's camp, as did Olivier Kamitatu, the party's secretary general. Three RCD ministers left their party. This political advantage helped Kabila during the election campaign. He controlled state radio and television; in violation of electoral law, they broadcast mostly Kabila campaign advertisements and coverage. He deployed his presidential guard to the country's main airports, where they harassed rival candidates as they arrived or departed. Riot police in Kinshasa prevented large demonstrations from taking place; given the anti-Kabila sentiment in the capital, protests would have been favorable to the president's rivals. In perhaps the most heavy-handed incident, authorities arrested the private security guard of presidential hopeful Oscar Kashala in May 2006 for an alleged coup plot that was never substantiated.

On August 20, 2006, the day the results of the first round of the presidential election were announced, events offered a glimpse of what might have happened had the transition not worked out in Kabila's favor. Kabila failed to obtain a clear majority, sending him into a runoff with Bemba, head of the MLC and one of the vice presidents. While the exact chain of events that day is not completely clear, Kabila's presidential guard launched a frontal attack on Bemba's residences in Kinshasa with tanks and hundreds of troops.

The international community, which was spending more than $2 billion a year on the UN peacekeeping mission in Congo and aid to the country, did not want to ruffle any feathers—in particular not those of Kabila, the head of state to whom ambassadors were accredited. The International Committee for Supporting the Transition, a group of donors and countries in the region that backed the peace process, had up to that point avoided discussing the threat posed by the presidential guard. When Kabila's guard did become a problem in August 2006, the committee denounced the violence but refrained from pointing fingers. The bias shown toward Kabila in the transition agreement was problematic in that it assumed he would win the election. In hushed conversations, diplomats wondered what would happen if the incumbent were to lose the runoff. But Kabila did not lose, and the polls themselves were relatively free and fair. The president won by a wide margin, garnering 2.5 million votes more than his rival.

Regional Shifts

One of the most important achievements of the peace process has been a realignment of relations in the region. The two main rebel movements, the RCD and the MLC, were created by Rwanda and Uganda, respectively, and relied heavily on their patrons for military survival. During the 2002 peace talks in the South African luxury resort Sun City, both countries came under increasing pressure from donors that supplied more than half of their budgets. Criticism increased after successive UN investigations revealed high-level involvement by Rwanda and Uganda in the looting of timber and minerals from eastern Congo. Perhaps the most damning indictment of their presence in Congo came when the two countries clashed in Kisangani in 1999 and 2000. The fighting over diamonds, in a town more than 300 miles from their borders, rendered absurd their claim that their intrusion in Congo was strictly for self-defense.

In 2002, the United States abstained for the first time in a vote by the International Monetary Fund on renewing loans for Rwanda. Shortly thereafter, under direct pressure from South African President Thabo Mbeki, Kabila and Rwandan President Paul Kagame signed an agreement for Rwandan troops to leave eastern Congo. Kabila was supposed to demobilize Rwandan rebels, now regrouped as the Democratic Forces for the Liberation of Rwanda, whom he had funded and supported during the war.

Under pressure from donors, and less threatened by a weakened rebel resistance, Rwanda slowly shifted its foreign policy from military confrontation to one of diplomacy and cooperation. High Rwandan and Congolese officials held discreet talks. Meanwhile, Rwanda's relations with Uganda thawed considerably. Even its relations with the former Hutu rebels who had come to power in Burundi in 2005 became cordial.

There is a good chance of antigovernment unrest bubbling up in the capital and other western towns.

The logic expressed by Rwanda's leaders was clear, if somewhat quixotic: they want Rwanda to become the service hub of the region, the "Singapore of Africa," an ambitious aspiration for a desperately poor, landlocked country. As part of this effort, Kagame has courted investors, including the Los Angeles Chamber of Commerce and Wal-Mart. He has also recognized the need to clean up appearances—a Rwanda open for business cannot be seen as stoking conflict in Congo.

The impact this realignment had on the RCD was evident. Without Rwanda, the rebels lost their military backbone. After the withdrawal of the Rwandan Defense Forces in July 2002, the RCD almost collapsed as Mai-Mai militias supported by Kinshasa took large chunks of its territory. After it was forced into the political process, the RCD's organizational weaknesses also became apparent. Rwanda had run the rebels as a proxy movement and had never allowed a strong political organization to emerge, focusing instead on military strength. During the war, Rwanda had replaced the RCD's leader four times in five years. Divisions quickly emerged during the transition as many RCD officials distanced themselves from the hard-line Hutu and Tutsi leadership.

Relations between Kigali and Kinshasa did not improve overnight, and the improvement was endangered by a hefty dose of brinksmanship. At the beginning of the transition, both Rwanda and the rebels wanted to keep their options open. According to several rebel sources, high-ranking RCD officers were encouraged to refuse army integration in order to remain as a reserve force. The leader of these dissidents was Brigadier General Laurent Nkunda, a Congolese Tutsi and former intelligence officer in the Rwandan army. In May 2004, as UN investigations later confirmed, Rwanda was involved in a mutiny by the dissidents that captured the town of Bukavu for several days. When Kabila overreacted by sending thousands of troops, sparking brutal fighting, Rwanda briefly reinvaded in November 2004.

Although relations appear to be on the mend today, the brinksmanship is likely to continue. Kagame says he speaks regularly with Kabila on the phone, and both sides now insist that their former rival no longer poses a threat. But Kabila, accused of being a Rwandan stooge himself during the election campaign, is afraid of being seen as pro-Kigali. Kagame was not invited to Kabila's inauguration ceremony, and many Congolese officers still accuse Rwanda of hegemonic ambitions in their country. The UN has evidence that Nkunda is continuing to recruit in Rwandan refugee camps, probably with government consent.

Buying Peace

At times, Congo seems condemned to eternal negotiations. The state does not have a monopoly on violence. Its army is desperately weak. And the 17,000 UN peacekeepers present in the country will not carry out the messy counterinsurgency operations necessary in the east, since they lack the will to sustain the casualties such operations would entail. Left with no choice, the government is forced to bargain with warlords.

It is not surprising, therefore, that, in the words of a human rights worker in Kinshasa, "impunity greased the gears of the transition." In contrast with peace processes elsewhere, justice and reconciliation have ranked low on the list of priorities in Congo. After some talk of an international tribunal for war crimes, it was left out of the 2002 accord. A truth and reconciliation commission was created, but its leadership, too, was divided among the former belligerents, who have little interest in exposing crimes committed during the war.

The absence of justice has ended up rewarding criminal behavior. Six militia leaders from the Ituri region were promoted to the rank of general in 2005 and thirty-two others were offered ranks of colonel, including some of the most notorious human rights offenders in the country. Following an international outcry, some of these warlords were arrested, including Thomas Lubanga, who was the first person to be tried at the International Criminal Court in The Hague. However, as soon as these leaders were removed, others sprang up to replace them. Even Nkunda, the RCD dissident, is currently engaged in negotiations for positions for himself and dozens of fellow officers.

Government officials tend to blame the impunity problem on a weak army and justice system, but it is also closely linked to members of the political elite. Patronage networks permeate the police and army. During the first two years of the transition, this allowed officers to embezzle, according to some estimates, over half of the payroll, or $3 million each month. Powerful generals and politicians in Kinshasa shield their protégés in the field from accusations. The civilian population has borne the consequences of this impunity. According to UN human rights reports, the Congolese national army is the worst abuser. UN observers documented 344 murders and 349 rapes carried out by members of the police and army in 2006. Since the UN presence is thinly spread across the country, this is just the tip of the iceberg. In addition, mismanagement of the army has allowed 14,000 to 18,000 militiamen to continue terrorizing the population in the east. In 2006, half a million people were displaced because of fighting there.

Turning a Blind Eye

Impunity has also devastated public administration, rendering it incapable of even providing social services. According to a UN estimate, more than $1 billion is embezzled in the customs sector alone each year. Again, these losses can be attributed in part to predatory patronage networks that permeate the state to the highest level. In 2004, a parliamentary audit of state companies revealed the complicity of six ministers and Kabila's chief of staff in embezzlement and graft. The state auditor has compiled evidence of colossal mismanagement that leaves about one-third of the budget improperly accounted for. Despite this evidence, not a single official was tried for corruption during the transition.

Although it is too early to make predictions about how the incoming government will perform, many of the figures in it are familiar. Part of the reason for this is that, in contrast with peace deals in countries such as Liberia, the settlement in Congo has kept power largely in the hands of the former belligerents. The elections only allowed for a limited infusion of new faces into the political elite. With the notable exception of Prime Minister Antoine Gizenga, the leader of the Unified Lumumbist Party, most ministers in the new government were in office during the transition. The most important ministries—interior, defense, foreign affairs, reconstruction, finance, and planning—are all occupied by former belligerents. More important, the president and his powerful entourage have remained the same. This raises doubts about the extent to which the government will be willing or able to crack down on the corruption and abuses that they sanctioned and were at times complicit in during the past three years.

The international community, which funds over half of the country's budget, has refrained from criticizing Congolese leaders too harshly. In contrast to Liberia, the Balkans, and East Timor, where serious efforts were made to exclude human rights abusers from security forces through a vetting process, in Congo there has been little talk of accountability. Good governance has also been shelved since Security Council members refused to mandate the UN mission to form a donors group to crack down on corruption. Some donors saw impunity as a necessary evil, needed to keep the transition together. As one diplomat explained: "If we start bringing people to justice, where do we stop? Some of the worst abusers are at the top."

The elections appear to have accentuated donor frailty. During the transition, donors pressured the interim government through the International Committee for Supporting the Transition. They seem more reluctant to do so today with a new, sovereign government. None of the embassies denounced the massacre of 100 civilians in the far western province of Bas Congo in January 2007. And, despite the condemnation of the fighting in Kinshasa, the French development minister arrived in the capital shortly after it broke out to sign an aid package worth $300 million with Kabila.

Another reason for donors' reticence has to do with economic interests. Congo is enormously rich in copper, tin, diamonds, and gold. With the end of the hostilities, the country is opening up to business again. Two of the world's largest mining companies, BHP Billiton and AngloAshanti, have bought large concessions and begun operations. US-based Phelps Dodge has acquired one of the world's largest copper concessions, Tenke Fungurume. Embassies in Kinshasa have been involved in helping to negotiate deals for companies based in their countries. In the absence of strong domestic lobbies for Congo, this has discouraged donors from speaking out too boldly about abuses.

The Fallout of Elections

If the transition was a mixed bag of successes and failures, where does it leave us now? Congo in 2006 held its first multiparty elections in 40 years. Kabila's coalition, the Alliance for the Presidential Majority, emerged victorious. Besides winning the presidential race, his coalition won around two-thirds of the seats in parliament, allowing Prime Minister Gizenga to form an Alliance government. The coalition replicated its victory in the elections of senators and governors by provincial assemblies—although allegedly with the help of hefty bribes—winning 10 of the 11 governorships and a majority in the upper house of the national legislature.

Yet the elections, for all their success, have created new divisions and risks. Whereas, during the war, the east was the center of conflict, the west is now also becoming a source of concern. In coming years, there is a good chance of antigovernment unrest bubbling up in the capital and other western towns. Discontent with Kabila was evident in the elections, which revealed a divided country. Kabila won over 80 percent of the vote in the east, while Bemba won by similar margins in five western provinces. Anti-Kabila sentiment runs high in these provinces, since his government administered Bas Congo and Kinshasa for six years without successfully addressing poverty and social woes there. Unemployment is close to 80 percent, and many families eat only once a day. These frustrations are accentuated by ethnic bias—Kabila and his close advisers are from the Swahili-speaking east. Kabila himself is perceived as a foreigner, since he grew up in Tanzania and speaks stilted French and poor Lingala, the language of the west.

This is the Congolese paradox: a state that is perceived as crushingly brutal, yet is deeply weak.

Another factor stirring up urban unrest in the west is the political marginalization of the opposition, which is largely based in the west and the center. Although Bemba won 42 percent of the popular vote, his opposition coalition, the Union for the Nation, is too weak in the national assembly to challenge the ruling Alliance. Bemba's coalition has a majority in four provincial assemblies, but many of its members were bought out during gubernatorial elections, limiting his control to one provincial government. The sidelining of the opposition could push its supporters into the streets, provoking unruly protests and riots in western cities.

A first sign of this took place in Bas Congo on January 31, 2007, when opposition supporters demonstrated against corruption in the gubernatorial elections. The spiritual leader of a local religious sect, Bundu dia Kongo, had been a candidate on the losing opposition ticket. A melee broke out between his supporters and the police, and several people on each side were killed. Feeling under siege, the governor brought in the army. In the ensuing bloodshed, policemen and soldiers killed more than a hundred civilians.

The Kinshasa fighting in March 2007 was different. This time the government's opposition was armed; Bemba had a guard of 400 to 500 soldiers in the capital. Both sides had indicated they would be willing to negotiate a solution that would guarantee Bemba's safety while downsizing his militia. Hardliners in both camps won out and forced a confrontation, plunging the capital into brutal fighting. According to one human rights group, 330 people were killed; other estimates go as high as 500. While the security situation is now stable, the government seems less and less tolerant of dissent. Dozens of opposition members have been rounded up in Kinshasa under dubious charges of espionage and treason, and several television stations belonging to the opposition have been shut down.

The opposition, however, may lack the unity and strength to galvanize the population. Bemba will go into exile, and there is no clear leader to replace him. The opposition is full of former followers of the late dictator Mobutu, and none of them have Bemba's stature. The lack of lucrative positions to pass around will also weaken his coalition; some allied parties already have protested the MLC's hoarding of the few senatorial and governor positions the opposition can claim.

A Crushing Weakness

After the elections, the defining feature of the Congolese state remains its weakness. This ailment, the result of decades of misrule, affects public administration, the security services, courts, the parliament, and political parties. While most donors perceive governance to be a technical problem, patronage is deeply political. Weakness has become a strategy of rule, as elites undermine institutional checks and balances in order to continue to profit from procurement contracts, mining deals, and customs fraud. In the meantime, the government provides almost no social services—health care and education are mostly paid for by their users, churches, and nongovernment organizations. Infrastructure rehabilitation is carried out almost exclusively by donors. Of the state's own revenues, the bulk of what is not embezzled is spent on salaries.

The weakness of the state contrasts with its omnipresence. There are about half a million civil servants in the country and another 200,000 policemen and soldiers. Few of them make a living wage—the official monthly salary of a soldier is $22 a month, while a doctor makes less than $100—forcing them to look for other ways to make money. In a 2005 World Bank survey, when asked what they would do to the state if it

were a person, many answered: "Kill him." This is the Congolese paradox: a state that is perceived as crushingly brutal, yet is deeply weak.

This weakness is in many ways the biggest obstacle to peace in the country. It allows small militias, which should constitute a law-and-order problem, to press the government for negotiations, only for other commanders to spring up later with new demands. It turns the security forces and public administration into predators, causing rampant abuse. And it depletes the budget of valuable resources needed to rebuild the country.

While many sub-Saharan states are fragile and corrupt, Congo's situation is particularly bad. There are 100,000 demobilized soldiers in the country, many of whom are about to finish a year-long donor program that provided them with meager earnings. There are still thousands of militiamen in the east, operating as warlords in their fiefdoms, as well as an enormous presidential guard. The ranks of the opposition are packed with former rebels and Mobutists who, deprived of lucrative positions in the state, could use civil unrest to bring the government to its knees.

The international community played a crucial role in making elections happen. But the donors' track record in peacebuilding is not nearly as good as in peacemaking: they lose focus quickly, and the new government is eager to make a show of its sovereignty. In addition, with costly peacekeeping operations moving into gear in Sudan, Lebanon, and Somalia, the temptation to declare victory and go home will be great.

There are no silver bullets for Congo's recovery. It is clear that the country will not be able to rise out of the trap of poverty, corruption, and war unless the Congolese leadership itself wants to. In order for this to happen, the government needs to be held accountable for its actions by the parliament, the courts, and the media. In short, democratic institutions need to work.

The international community needs to help in this process. A first step will be coming to an understanding with the new government on terms for the huge international investment there. The billion-dollar question will be: How do you implement reforms that go against entrenched interests of the ruling elite? After the scandals and failures of the first two post-independence republics, Congo's Third Republic has begun with many questions and few answers.

JASON K. STEARNS, based in Kenya, is a senior analyst with the International Crisis Group. From 2002 to 2004 he served with the UN mission in the Democratic Republic of Congo.

Africa: How We Killed Our Dreams of Freedom

How did it all go so wrong? Across the continent, liberation movements that fought against colonial rule proved unable to sustain democratic governance. We cannot keep blaming the past; we have to examine ourselves.

WILLIAM GUMEDE

Zimbabwe's Zanu-PF has become the symbol of the descent of African liberation movements into brutal dictatorship.

The great Tunisian writer Albert Memmi noted this phenomenon back in 1957. In *The Coloniser and the Colonised,* he wrote of the tendency of liberation movements, once in power, to mimic the brutality and callousness of former rulers. Backsliding liberation movements in Algeria, Angola, Ghana, Kenya, Namibia and other countries have left in their wake the lost hopes and shattered dreams of millions.

In the inner sanctum of South Africa's ruling African National Congress they have coined a word for it: "Zanufication." As Zimbabweans flee across the border to avoid police brutality or the hardships of an economy in free fall (inflation at more than 1,700 per cent and shortages of basic foodstuffs), they whisper it in hushed tones, a warning.

A senior national executive member of the ANC, Blade Nzimande, warned recently: "We must study closely what is happening in Zimbabwe, because if we don't, we may find features in our situation pointing to a similar development."

Unions, sections within civil society and church groups daily inveigh against the South African government's head-in-the-sand policy towards Zimbabwe and President Thabo Mbeki's "quiet" diplomacy. The Congress of South African Trade Unions (Cosatu) has complained to the South African Broadcasting Corporation, the public broadcaster, over its failure to cover the Zimbabwean meltdown. Although the ANC in South Africa and Zanu-PF are light years apart, the spectre of "Zanufication" haunts South Africa, raising the question: "Is there something inherent in the political culture of liberation movements that makes it difficult for them to sustain democratic platforms?"

The problem for liberation struggles was establishing a democratic culture. All governments must be kept on their toes.

The irony is that it is the leaders of former heroic liberation movements who have become stumbling blocks to building a political culture on the African continent based on good governance. The former South African president Nelson Mandela and President Thabo Mbeki enthusiastically proclaimed in 1994 that the end of official apartheid was the dawn of a new era. Yet many liberation movement leaders—Mugabe is a good example—still blame colonialism for the mismanagement and corruption on their watch.

Obviously, the legacy of slavery and colonialism, and now unequal globalisation, are barriers to development. However, to blame the west for Zimbabwe's recent problems is not reasonable. Yet the diplomacy of South Africa, from which most African countries take their cue, is based on this assumption. Initially ANC leaders also bought in to this, but thankfully, on Zimbabwe, Mbeki is increasingly isolated. True to his contrarian and stubborn nature, he still argues that because Zimbabwe was given a raw deal by the British, Mugabe's regime should not be criticised publicly. In terms of land, for example, black Zimbabweans did indeed receive a raw deal, yet that is not the whole story. The Zimbabwean government was idle for at least a decade; when it finally implemented a land reform programme, this consisted of giving fertile land to cronies who subsequently left the land fallow.

The story is similar elsewhere on the continent. As African liberation movements came to power, their supporters were keen to overlook shortcomings. The feeling was that a new, popularly elected democratic government needed to be given an extended chance. Liberation movements were seen as the embodiment of the nation as a whole.

In South Africa, criticism of the ANC by supporters has always been muted. "You cannot criticise yourself," an ANC veteran once admonished me. There has also been a fear that criticising the government gives ammunition to powerful opponents. When a top ANC leader, Chris Nissen, broke rank and publicly criticised a party official's errant behaviour, he was warned: "Do not wash the family's dirty linen in public."

As a journalist—active in the liberation struggle—I, too, gave in to this principle in the heady days after South Africa's first non-racial democratic elections in 1994: "Let's not criticise too much; let's give the new government a fighting chance." But that was a grave mistake. All governments must be kept on their toes. The problem for most liberation movements is how to establish a democratic culture.

During a liberation struggle, decision-making is necessarily left in the hands of a few. Dissent and criticisms are not allowed lest they expose divisions within the movement, which could be exploited by the colonial enemy. But if non-criticism continues during the first crucial years of power, it becomes entrenched, part of a political culture. In the early liberation years, governments often operate as if under siege. Critics are marginalised, making later criticism almost impossible.

Take, for example, the South African government's initial inaction on the Aids pandemic. Mbeki embarked on a fatal policy of denial. Many ANC supporters knew he was wrong but kept quiet, in case they were seen as supporting western governments or big pharmaceutical companies bent on perpetuating Africa's underdevelopment. Many activists preferred to reserve their misgivings about government policy, rather than be placed in the camp of the "neo-colonialists."

In Zimbabwe, Mugabe brutally quashed rebellions in the 1980s, killing thousands in the Matabeleland region. No regional liberation movement said anything about it. The silence of Zanu-PF critics laid the foundations for his reign of terror.

In many African countries—with South Africa the exception—the state is virtually the only employer after liberation. Patronage can be used to reward or sideline critics.

The cold war, during which many African governments started their life, reinforced the siege mentality of "them against us" among African liberation movements. Mugabe continues to blame imperialism. So, when the UK or Australia attacks Zimbabwe, African neighbours will fall silent: they don't want to be seen supporting their former masters.

Similarly, Mbeki's silence on Zimbabwe is partly because he does not want to be associated with the "colonial" powers. South Africa's first strong political statement on Zimbabwe during the current crisis, by the deputy foreign affairs minister Aziz Pahad, one of Mbeki's closest personal friends, was to attack the South African media for giving too much attention to the western perspective on Zimbabwe. This was after Tony Blair had called for sanctions against Zimbabwe and Australian leaders had bemoaned South Africa's silence.

Blair's criticism had the effect of silencing Zanu-PF's opponents in the country. About to launch a final assault against Mugabe, they felt they had to soft-pedal so that the president could not paint them as stooges of the west. One of the main problems of the opposition Movement for Democratic Change (MDC) has been to fight off propaganda coming from Mugabe and the media that they are fronts for the west.

That is why it is so important for Mbeki to stand up and publicly condemn Zanu-PF. It would make it far harder to see the conflict in Zimbabwe through the distorting "Africa *v* the west" prism. Mbeki should follow the lead of Archbishop Desmond Tutu and state clearly that Zimbabwe under Robert Mugabe represents the worst backsliding of African liberation movements.

The Nation by Numbers

100,000
people gathered to watch Bob Marley perform on independence day, 18 April 1980

20%
real growth of economy in first year of independence

20,000
numbers killed during Mugabe's crackdown on Matabeleland in the 1980s

70%
of farmland still owned by white farmers in 2000, 20 years after independence

1 million
dead people on the Zimbabwean electoral role in 2002

18%
proportion of population made homeless by "Operation Murambatsvina" slum clearances, starting 2005

56%
of population earn less than $1 a day

52 years
since average income was as low as today

Research by Sarah O'Connor

There is also a problem with the cult of the leader. Members of liberation movements defer too readily to leaders and many African countries famously retained colonial-era "insult laws" by which criticism of the president (which, in Zimbabwe, includes poking fun at him) can attract a lengthy jail sentence. Thus leaders can remain in power for decades and die in office if they are not violently pushed out of power. That is why Mandela felt it important to leave after only one term. That is also why the grass-roots democracy movements mushrooming on the African continent invariably demand that presidents limit their terms in office.

Colonial-era "insult laws" often meant criticism of the president could earn a jail sentence

The anti-colonial struggle was often violent, and few liberation movements have attempted to restore a culture of non-violence. Thus it is no surprise that Mugabe finds it easy to use violence against his people: the colonial state apparatus was attuned to that purpose. Once violence is used, it is used again. Even the idea of an opposition—internal or external—is a difficult concept for

How Mugabe's Violence Will Free Us

Wilf Mbanga is happy that the world has witnessed the tyranny

When President Robert Mugabe's brutal thugs, in police uniforms, thrashed opposition and civic group leaders a few weeks ago, little did they realise they were actually striking blows for freedom from the old tyrant's rule. Gruesome pictures of the battered leaders flashed around the world on the Internet and were widely used in newspapers and on television.

International condemnation, muted over the past ten years by South Africa's monstrous protection of Mugabe, grew to a crescendo. The violence, perpetrated against defenceless citizens, brought Mugabe's brutality against his own people to wide public attention.

Although all foreign correspondents had been barred from the country and though the efforts of local journalists were severely hampered, the word—and the pictures—got out, galvanising anti-Mugabe feelings even in Africa, where leaders have been reluctant to condemn him because of his liberation credentials.

Mugabe—once the world's blue-eyed African, lauded for his eloquence and statesmanship—has finally been recognised as a dangerous megalomaniac. In the words of the president of the African Union, President John Kufuor of Ghana: "We are embarrassed by what is going on in Zimbabwe."

For the past eight years or so, South Africa has conned the world into believing that it has been working behind the scenes to solve the problems in Zimbabwe. But President Thabo Mbeki's "quiet diplomacy" is now derisively referred to as "pussyfoot diplomacy". The early response from that government to atrocities that all could clearly see was a vague statement from the deputy foreign minister Aziz Pahad about obeying rule of law.

However, other voices within South Africa have been vociferous in their condemnation of Mugabe—notably the leader of the opposition Democratic Alliance, Tony Leon, Archbishop Desmond Tutu, Cardinal Wilfred Napier, the powerful trade-union body Cosatu, and a number of student groups.

Inside Zimbabwe, the beatings have been a significant catalyst. People cowed by years of intimidation and weighed down by economic hardship are now angry. Anger has conquered fear. Within Zanu-PF itself, the two groups shadow-boxing for pole position to succeed Mugabe, led by Joyce Mujuru and Emmerson Mnangagwa, have come into the open, courting media attention.

Both the Mujuru and Mnangagwa factions agree Mugabe should not continue beyond the presidential elections scheduled for 2008, but not because they have suddenly seen the light and want a democratic Zimbabwe. They are motivated by self-interest: the EU's travel restrictions are irksome and the economic meltdown is destroying their business empires.

The two factions hate each other, yet neither is strong enough on its own to win a general election. Both know they will need the support of the opposition MDC, because of its local support base and because it holds the key to international recognition and donorfunded reconstruction of the economy.

Mugabe, meanwhile, wants to continue in power. He is a wily politician and we should not underestimate his machinations.

Despite his failed diplomacy, what Mbeki does will be important. His political and economic muscle will determine the ultimate outcome. Tragically for most Zimbabweans, three million of whom live in squalor and fear in South Africa, Mbeki wants to see Zanu-PF continue to rule Zimbabwe—albeit a reformed Zanu-PF.

He is working on it. The recent meetings in Johannesburg between the two countries' vice-presidents is evidence of that. There will be a role for the MDC in a new Zimbabwe, but it is clear Mbeki will exert his considerable influence to avoid an MDC—dominated government on his northern border. He mistrusts the party and fears its trade-union influence.

Wilf Mbanga was founder of Zimbabwe's Daily News, which was closed down by the government in 2003

many. Mugabe's Zanu coerced the Patriotic Front (PF), the other major liberation movement in Zimbabwe, to merge with it in the 1980s, hence the name Zanu-PF. This eliminated a possible opposition force.

The resurgence of an opposition is due partly to a generational change in the country's politics. Many of the MDC's supporters are young and have experienced Zanu-PF mainly as a party in government that exploits its people. They are not impressed by past liberation credentials.

The articulate MDC spokesman Nelson Chamisa is not yet 30 years old. In South Africa, it is young activists in the Treatment Action Campaign and their leader Zackie Achmat who have been responsible for forcing the government to adopt more responsible Aids policies. Zwelinzima Vavi, leader of Cosatu, says: "We are not prepared to be merely 'yes-leader' workers' desks."

The sad truth, however, is that waiting for another generation before there can be real change is costly, even deadly, for ordinary Africans, not least Zimbabweans.

WILLIAM GUMEDE is a former deputy editor of the Sowetan newspaper. His book, "Thabo Mbeki and the Battle for the Soul of the ANC" will be republished by Zed later this year.

Lula's Brazil

A Rising Power, but Going Where?

"One of the most interesting features of the Lula years has been a pessimistic view of the international system combined with a belief that there is scope for an activist and assertive foreign policy."

ANDREW HURRELL

As the world enters a period of increasing challenges to US hegemony, attention shifts naturally to rising powers, emerging nations, threshold states, and regional powers. Such states obviously will be central to the dynamics of the balance of power in the twenty-first century, as well as to the possible emergence of new concert-style groupings of major powers. But these states will also be crucial to the development of international institutions and global governance. Indeed, the current detachment from—or outright opposition to—existing international organizations on the part of many of these nations represents one of the most important weaknesses in the global institutional order.

Think of the major emerging economies' distancing themselves from the World Bank and International Monetary Fund, or the opposition (led by Brazil and India) to developed countries' preferences in the World Trade Organization (WTO), or the effective breakdown of the global aid regime in the face of the emergence of new aid donors such as China and India. These countries are substantively critical to the management of major global challenges such as climate change and nuclear proliferation. And they are procedurally critical if international institutions are to reestablish legitimacy and a degree of representativeness.

Ranking just after China and India, Brazil figures prominently in almost all lists of emerging states and regional powers. As US Secretary of State Condoleezza Rice put it: "In the twenty-first century, emerging nations like India, China, Brazil, Egypt, Indonesia, and South Africa are increasingly shaping the course of history. . . ." But there are other reasons to focus on Brazilian foreign policy. For many on the left (especially in Europe), for many inside Brazil, and for many in the developing world, the assertive foreign policy of the government of President Luiz Inácio Lula da Silva (Lula) is seen as a progressive force in global affairs.

Lula and the Workers Party government may well have been tainted at home by corruption and an association with old-style Brazilian machine politics. They may have followed an orthodox domestic macroeconomic policy and made little progress on structural reforms in areas such as taxation, land redistribution, or tackling violent crime. Nonetheless, Brazil's foreign policy (along with

its conditional cash-transfer program to reduce poverty) is widely regarded as a great success story, as well as a potential bellwether for the global strategies of other emerging powers.

A Nationalist Worldview

The Lula government that came to power in January 2002 sought to differentiate its own more assertively nationalist foreign policy from that of its predecessor, which it portrayed as insufficiently resolute in the defense of Brazilian interests and too closely tied to the acceptance of the liberalizing and globalizing agenda of the 1990s. The incoming administration brought with it a view of foreign policy that stressed both the instability of the international environment and the growing concentration of political and military power, wealth, and ideological sway on the part of the United States and its developed-country allies.

Reflecting a deep-rooted strand of nationalist thought in Brazil (on both right and left), this approach to foreign affairs regards the global economy as containing more constraints and snares than opportunities. It views globalization as a force working to reinforce the power of the developed world while creating new sources of instability (especially in relation to recurrent financial crises) and promoting politically dangerous and morally unacceptable inequality (both within and across countries).

Political power, according to this view, was used throughout the post–cold war period to incorporate developing economies into the globalized system. Developed nations and the international institutions that they control have exploited developing countries' external financial vulnerability, created new forms of coercion and conditionalities, and imposed new economic norms that have generally reflected and reinforced their own political power and the interests of the core economies.

Even before the presidency of George W. Bush, many in Brazil and in particular many who later were associated with the Lula government suspected that the liberal norms of the 1990s concerning human rights, democracy, and free markets had been used in selective ways to reflect narrow national interests. Since the terrorist attacks of September 11, 2001, many have suspected Washington of exploiting new security threats to mobilize support at home and abroad for the projection and expansion of US power.

Within this harsh and conflict-oriented view of the international system, Brazil is seen as vulnerable—on one hand because of its internal inequalities, social cleavages, and incomplete development and, on the other, because of its continued external weaknesses and its absence from international decision-making structures. Yet the country is not without options. Indeed, one of the most interesting features of the Lula years has been a pessimistic view of the international system combined with a belief that there is scope for an activist and assertive foreign policy. Foreign policy discussions repeatedly invoke the idea that Brazil is not small or insignificant and that it has room to maneuver in a world where, despite all the challenges, unipolarity is more apparent than real.

Facing "hegemonic structures of power," Brazil needs to reassert its national autonomy, according to the currently prevalent line of thinking. It needs to form coalitions with other developing states in order to reduce its external vulnerability and increase its bargaining power, and to work, however modestly, toward a more balanced world order. Brazil should seek "to increase, if only by a margin, the degree of multipolarity in the world," as the foreign minister, Celso Amorim, put it.

Building up technological capacity also matters, as can be seen in Brazil's determination to continue protecting its industrial base. Because the proposed Free Trade Area of the Americas is seen as a threat in this regard, the Lula administration has downplayed and significantly diluted the negotiations. Likewise, the government has placed renewed emphasis on the long-term goal of developing the country's nuclear technological capacity (seeking to preserve industrial secrets while maintaining good relations with the global inspection regime).

The Multilateral Route

The cornerstones of Brazilian foreign policy have followed from this general outlook. The Lula years have witnessed efforts to increase Brazil's presence in international institutions—including a (so far unsuccessful) campaign for permanent membership in the UN Security Council, and a (successful) drive to join the core group of states negotiating in the World Trade Organization's Doha Round of talks. Brazil has sought to expand relations with other major developing countries—especially India, China, and South Africa—while launching a more activist policy toward Africa and, to a lesser extent, the Middle East.

The Lula administration has also intensified relations within South America. It has attempted to deepen and broaden Mercosur, the common market that, in addition to Brazil, includes Argentina, Paraguay, Uruguay, and now Venezuela. Lula's apparent aim is to shift Mercosur's focus from purely economic relations toward the development of a political bloc. And Brazil has launched the Union of South American nations, a fledgling intergovernmental organization that will unite Mercosur with the region's other major free-trade bloc, the Andean Community, as part of a continuing process of South American integration.

Brazilian officials have sought to portray foreign policy as the external face of the Lula govern-ment's domestic social commitment. As Lula put it: "Alongside the theme of security, the international agenda should also privilege those issues which aim at the eradication of asymmetries and injustices, such as the struggle against social and cultural exclusion, the genuine opening of the markets of the rich countries, the construction of a new financial architecture, and the imperative of combating hunger, disease, and poverty."

In keeping with both its perceived identity and its power-related interests, Brazil continues to for-swear a hard-power strategy in favor of a heavy emphasis on multilateralism. The Lula administration is attempting to exploit what one observer has called Brazil's diplomatic GNP: its capacity for effective coalition-building and insider activism within international institutions, as well as its ability to frame its own interests in terms of arguments for greater justice. Thus, mobilizing claims for greater representational fairness (as with membership in the Security Council) and distributional justice (as with the promotion of a global hunger fund) has been a central tool of Brazil's recent foreign policy.

> **Brazil has been viewed in Washington as a potentially moderating force in the region, especially in relation to Chávez in Venezuela and Morales in Bolivia.**

Notwithstanding this concentration on soft power, however, it is worth noting that the past five years have seen the first glimmering of a more focused discussion of links between foreign policy and military strategy. This has few concrete implications for current policy, but it represents a new development that could have a significant impact in the future, especially if security relations in the region deteriorate.

A Return to History?

Where does Lula's foreign policy fit within the broader historical picture? How much does it represent a sharp discontinuity with the past? In fact, assertions that Brazil is destined to play a more influential role in world affairs have a long history inside the country. The intensity of these predictions has varied across time. At times ideas about national greatness have been little more than vague aspirations—hardly tied to practical political action or concrete foreign policies and commonly engendering a good deal of cynicism. At other times they have assumed a much more direct role in the shaping of foreign policy, as in the 1970s when high growth rates seemed to establish Brazil as an upwardly mobile middle power, if not one moving ineluctably toward eventual great power status. In this respect, the claim that Brazil should be seen as a major player speaks to a long tradition of thought, and some critics have interpreted the Lula foreign policy in terms of "nostalgia" for the idea of *Brasil-potência* (Brazil as a power).

The third-worldism (*terceiro-mundismo*) of the Lula years also feeds into another debate with deep historical roots that reflects the complex origins of Brazil's international identity. On one hand, Brazil was formed as part of the process of European colonial settlement, a process that involved subjugation of indigenous peoples. Brazil's elites have seen themselves as part of the West in cultural and religious terms and the country harbors a strong tradition of liberalism, including Western ideas about international law and society. On the other hand, Brazilian society has been shaped by the legacies of colonialism and poverty, the imperatives of economic development, and longstanding connections to Africa, the Middle

East, and Asia—connections created most powerfully by the slave trade but also by other waves of immigration.

This duality has remained an important element of Brazilian discussions about where the country "fits in." The cold war years witnessed a persistent and often highly politically charged debate as to whether Brazil was part of the West in its battle against communism and the Soviet Union or a member of the third world in its struggle for development and a greater role in international affairs.

Embracing the Third World

In general terms, the developmentalist line won out. Brazil came to place great emphasis on the pursuit of national autonomy, the politicization of international economic relations, and complaints against the freezing of the international power structure by the powers that be. By the end of the 1960s the close alignment with the United States that followed a coup in 1964 had given way to a broader and more pragmatic approach. Relations with Washington varied between cool and distant, and Brazil sought to diversify its foreign and economic relations, expanding ties with Western Europe, Japan, the socialist countries, and, increasingly, the third world.

Thus, Brazil played a prominent role in such third world forums as the Group of 77 (a United Nations coalition of developing countries) and was heavily engaged in debates during the 1970s regarding a "New International Economic Order." Brazil's embrace of the third world was not as thoroughgoing as India's—and it certainly did not include calls for global revolution, as China's did before 1978—but it did figure prominently in the country's sense of itself and its place in the world.

The developmentalist-nationalist stance was closely tied to economic policy. Brazil's economic policies for much of the post-1945 period relied on a strategy of import substitution, subsidies to strategic sectors, large-scale direct investment in state-owned enterprises, technological nationalism, and a deeply rooted belief in the imperative of continued growth even at the cost of high inflation. The project of national economic development came to be institutionally embedded within and around the Brazilian state and was backed by a wide array of powerful interest groups and a relatively high degree of elite consensus.

It also gave rise to a set of unspoken assumptions whose influence continues to be apparent in Brazilian foreign policy: the importance of defending economic and political sovereignty; the imperative of developing a more prominent international role for the nation; and the suspicion that the United States is more likely to be a hindrance than a help in securing the country's upward progress.

This pattern of foreign policy was not significantly affected by the return to civilian rule in 1985. It began to change, however, by the early 1990s, as the established economic model came under increasing strain, as Brazil along with other countries in the region moved toward economic liberalization, and as the end of the cold war seemed to force acceptance of the reality of both a unipolar world and economic globalization.

The Cardoso Legacy

How far Brazil actually abandoned its foreign policy traditions and embraced "neoliberal globalization"—especially under the government of Fernando Henrique Cardoso from 1994 to 2002—is a subject bitterly contested inside the country. (One important

trend in recent years has been a politicization of foreign policy, both within the foreign ministry and in Brazilian politics more generally.)

It is certainly true that the central preoccupation of the Cardoso administration was with economic stabilization and economic reform rather than foreign policy. It is also the case that the Cardoso government tended to stress the need for Brazil to accommodate itself to US power and to liberal globalization. Brazil showed a greater willingness to accept many of the dominant norms of the post–cold war period. For example, the country moved during the 1990s toward increased acceptance of international norms controlling missile technology, arms exports, and nuclear proliferation.

Similarly, in relation to the environment, Brazil moved sharply away from its defensiveness of the 1980s toward an acknowledgement of the legitimacy of international concerns about environmental matters. Brazil came to accept the activities of nongovernmental organizations, which before had often been denounced as subversive, and it engaged more positively in international negotiations, especially in the process leading to the 1992 Earth Summit in Rio. A parallel move could be seen in relation to international human rights.

It is true, as well, that Brazilian foreign policy during the 1990s frequently demonstrated national reticence, as captured by Cardoso's view that "to provoke friction with the United States is to lose," or by a comment in his memoirs that Brazil's capacity to influence the region politically remained limited. Thus, while action to help maintain democracy in Paraguay was viable, thoughts of involvement in Colombia were resisted as something Brazil was not "yet" able to contemplate.

Nevertheless, Cardoso's own view of the international system and of Brazilian development was never that of a straightforward neoliberal. And over the course of the decade his foreign policy shifted in a more critical and nationalist direction. Even if his approach had achieved its important initial purpose of reestablishing Brazil's international political and economic credibility, by the late 1990s the Cardoso foreign policy of "autonomy via participation" had come to face increasingly serious challenges. The relative optimism with which policy makers had viewed the post–cold war international environment was giving way to a greater emphasis on Brazil's international economic vulnerability and the difficulty of translating into concrete results the country's adaptation to global liberal norms.

There are important differences between Cardoso and Lula, but they cannot be simplified in terms of a contrast between "pro-Western liberalizer" and "progressive third-worldist." Cardoso believed the changing structures of global capitalism meant that there was little alternative but to adapt to globalization and that the potential political opportunities for successful foreign policy activism were limited. But he combined this pragmatic view of the world with a significant degree of optimism that structural reform at home was both possible and necessary and that democracy had become an overriding value.

The Lula government, by contrast, has been rather modest in its domestic policy ambitions, stressing economic orthodoxy and large-scale targeted social programs. But it has combined this domestic accommodation with a high degree of optimism as to what can be achieved abroad.

Regional Destiny?

How is Lula's foreign policy working out? Let us look first at South America. The Latin-Americanization of Brazil's foreign policy in fact goes back to the late 1970s. By the end of the 1990s it was already common to talk of Mercosur as part of Brazil's "destiny" (as opposed to the Free Trade Area of the Americas, which was seen as an option). Nevertheless, it is clear that the Lula government has worked hard to develop a more prominent role in Latin America. Especially during the first Lula administration, the body language (if you will) of assertive regional leadership was highly visible, however much it was couched in the rhetoric of "non-hegemonic leadership."

Brazil has sought to expand relations with other major developing countries— especially India, China, and South Africa.

The Lula government has committed considerable rhetorical energy and high-level political effort in particular to relaunching Mercosur; to restoring with neighboring states economic ties that had frayed during the Argentinian economic crisis at the start of the millennium; to seeking new areas for cooperation, such as with anti-poverty initiatives; and to indicating in a variety of ways a greater willingness to bear costs and make some concessions in order to help sustain the regionalist project.

Brasilia has also been prepared to assume a more assertive political role in the region—in the sense of an expansion of party-to-party relations and greater involvement in politically contested areas, such as Brazil's leadership of the UN peace mission to Haiti (where it has 1,200 troops on the ground) and its recent expressions of willingness to mediate in Colombia.

Yet it is in relation to the region that the limits of Brazil's foreign policy appear in sharpest light. Mercosur itself is now far more divided than at any time in its history. Its already weak institutional structures have not been strengthened, and it is difficult to believe that Venezuela's 2005 accession will do anything other than weaken them still further. The early activism of the Lula years was too personalist and too voluntarist to have much of an institutional impact, and there has been a yawning gap between the rhetoric of leadership and the concrete political, military, and economic resources made available to sustain substantive achievements.

Lula's foreign policy overestimates the willingness of the region to fall into line behind Brazilian pretensions to a global role as the region's leader. In fact, there have been across Latin America numerous instances of resistance to Brazil's role—in opposition, for example, to its campaign for UN Security Council membership and to Brazilian candidates in international organizations. Brazil's foreign policy has also underestimated the readiness of many in the region to find an accommodation with Washington (a readiness likely to become more noticeable in a post-Bush world). And perhaps most difficult, Brazil's pretensions to regional leadership have encountered Venezuela's Hugo Chávez—both as a leader with his own ideas about hemispheric integration and as a symptom of deep-rooted discontent within Latin America.

If the measure of success for Brazil's regional strategy is the creation of a regional bloc with a significant degree of internal cohesion and a capacity to increase the region's power in the world, then there can be little doubt that the strategy has failed. It is crucial, however, to note the structural factors both shaping Brazil's regional policy and constraining its actions.

Compared to 20 years ago, Brazil is now much more firmly enmeshed in the region, and it has to live with the spillovers and externalities that go with ever greater social, economic, and energy interdependence. In this respect Brazil is living with the consequences of a sustained period of successful regional integration. Not only have economic, infrastructural, and energy ties increased, but the protracted violence and the narco-economy of the Andean region have had profound effects on patterns of violence in Brazil's cities.

Equally important, the political complexion of the region has changed dramatically in ways that make it very difficult for Brazil to steer regional developments or to project its own model. The *chavismo* emanating from Venezuela may not establish itself as a stable counter-narrative to political and economic liberalism, but it is more than a purely local or transitory phenomenon, and it reflects the widely perceived failures of economic liberalism, the narrowness of many accounts of electoral democracy, and a powerful resurgence of economic nationalism.

Brazil has thus become ever more entangled in an unstable and crisis-prone area without its being clear that the country has the economic or military resources to play a leadership role. The regional story of the past five years is in some ways better understood in terms of damage limitation under difficult conditions than in terms of the projection of regional leadership.

Relations with Washington

There is a common but mistaken view that relations between Brazil and the United States have historically been harmonious. It is true that there have been periods of close relations, such as the years following Brazil's entry into the Second World War and following the coup in 1964. Still, for much of the cold war era the relationship was not especially close; on the contrary, it was characterized by real clashes of interest (especially over economic and trade issues), by deep divergences in the two countries' views of the international system, and by a recurrent sense of mutual frustration. More recent policy making in Brazil has aimed at prudent coexistence with the United States, possible collaboration, and minimal collision, but it has shied away from any kind of special relationship. Many Brazilians share the traditional nationalist perception that Washington is a potential obstacle to Brazil's progress.

Lula's foreign policy overestimates the willingness of the region to fall into line behind Brazilian pretensions to a global role as the region's leader.

There is also strong and widespread opposition to US policy in Colombia, which is seen as dangerously militarizing conflicts in the Andean region. US policy has also revived in some quarters the old fear that the United States poses a threat to the sovereignty of the Amazon. (The other element of this fear is that viewing tropical forests as part of the common heritage of humanity will lead to calls for the international administration of the region.) And, of course, the unilateralism and interventionism of the Bush years have fueled anti-Americanism even in a country in which such sentiments have traditionally been weak (compared to, say, Mexico or Argentina).

On the other hand, recent relations with Washington have actually been rather cordial. There has, after all, not been much to quarrel about. us foreign policy has obviously been focused elsewhere. And the integrating impulses of the 1990s had already faded by the end of that decade, as is evident in the absence within the United States of either the foreign policy will or the domestic political support to negotiate a Free Trade Area of the Americas.

Much is made of the unique position of the United States, the degree to which (unlike all other modern great powers) it faces no geopolitical challenge from within its region, and how it has been able to prevent, or more accurately to contain, the influence of extra-regional powers. But the other important regional aspect of us power is that country's ability to avoid deep entanglements and mostly to escape from lower-level conflicts within its backyard that could ensnare and divert it. Washington has been able to take the region for granted and, for long periods, to avoid having a regional policy at all—as has arguably been the case since 2001.

And there has been space for some shared interests with Brazil. New issues such as biofuels have provided a basis for cooperation. After the brief and absurd portrayal of Lula in some neoconservative quarters as part of a South American axis of evil, Brazil has been viewed in Washington as a potentially moderating force in the region, especially in relation to Chávez in Venezuela and Evo Morales in Bolivia. While Brazil's economy has not been growing as fast as China's or India's, foreign investment has been rising fast and economic stability has been maintained. Brazilian diplomats, though formally rejecting any role as "bridge-builders," have sometimes stressed the country's moderating influence and fire-fighting role.

Still, limits to an active or close relationship with Washington remain. Brazil has to maintain a very delicate balancing act that would be upset, both within the region and inside Brazil, by any attempt to act as a provider of regional order on behalf of the United States. Serious differences persist over the two countries' preferred models of regional economic integration: Brazil rejects the us notion of integration along the lines of the North American Free Trade Agreement.

There has been considerable frustration in Washington, as well, over Brazil's determination in trade talks to press for deeper agricultural liberalization in the United States and the European Union while resisting further trade and investment openings in Brazil. And on the issue of climate change, Brazil has firmly maintained its position that the internationally accepted formula of "common but differentiated responsibilities" means that the United States and the developed world have a duty to take the lead in reducing greenhouse gas emissions (including accepting binding targets) and to provide funds and technology to help developing countries reduce their emissions.

Above all, the us-Brazilian relationship features none of the sorts of concrete political, security, or economic interests that have underpinned the strategic realignment that has taken place in the case of us-Indian relations. Brazil is not closely linked to major American geopolitical interests, as India is with China, Pakistan, and the issue of nuclear proliferation. The economic relationship with Brazil is nothing like America's with India. Nor is there a large Brazilian diaspora in the United States pushing for improved ties.

Southern Strategy

If Brazil's aspirations for regional leadership and its relations with the United States have so far produced limited gains, the same might be said of the Lula administration's vaunted South-South diplomacy.

Critics of Brazil's attempted solidarity with emerging economies say the policy has generated more rhetoric than concrete achievement.

In 2003, Brazil, along with India and South Africa, formed within the World Trade Organization a coalition of developing countries—the Group of 20—that decided to block the Doha round of trade talks until their demands were met. For many orthodox economists, the G-20 coalition shackles Brazil's true interests as a major agricultural exporter with powerful stakes in trade liberalization. Although South-South trade has increased, the core of Brazil's external economic relations remains with the developed world.

The critics of South-South diplomacy, both in Brazil and elsewhere, argue that economic engagement with the developed world should be given far higher priority—especially since China appears to be emerging more as a competitor to Brazil than an ally. According to this view, China's failure to support Brazil's bid for a seat on the un Security Council demonstrates that Brazilian talk of "strategic partnerships" with India and China is radically out of line with Brazil's actual status in the foreign policies of those countries. Some observers have also noted that Brazil's efforts to gather support for its Security Council membership and its broader attempts at southern solidarity have at times led the country to compromise on its commitment to human rights.

And yet, although there has indeed been a gap between some of the rhetoric and the concrete achievements in South-South diplomacy, the critics' arguments underestimate the way in which Brazilian foreign policy has contributed to perceptions that global power is more diffuse than had appeared to be the case even five years ago. Brazil's weight as a player in international trade, for example, is limited, but its activism and assertiveness have worked to convince many that Brazil has to be part of any stable global trade regime for reasons of political legitimacy as much as narrow economic logic. In relation to climate change, Brazil has helped to shift the focus of negotiations back toward recognition of global warming as a shared and common problem, and has advanced the notion that the responsibilities and burdens of the developed and developing world need to be differentiated.

In general, Lula's Southern strategy forms a clear contrast to the nearly total disappearance of third world self-identification on the part of China, as well as, in Indian foreign policy, the displacement of nonalignment and the relative downgrading of multilateralism. In part, Brazil's approach reflects its relative power position. Brazil is a threshold state that seeks entry into the ranks of the powerful, but for whom coalitions with other developing countries continue to make political sense.

But Brazil's foreign policy under Lula has also reflected a powerful set of ideas about nationalism, development, and globalization that resonate both in the country and across Latin America. As Brazil seeks to carve out a regional and global position for itself as an emerging power, its foreign policy is likely to continue to be marked by tensions among the different facets of the nation's strategy and identity—as a leader of the South, as a potential bridge between North and South, and as a rising power that uses the rhetoric of South-South solidarity and claims for global justice for its own instrumental purposes.

ANDREW HURRELL is director of the Center for International Studies at Oxford University and a faculty fellow of Nuffield College, Oxford. He is the author of *On Global Order: Power, Values, and the Constitution of International Society* (Oxford University Press, 2007).

An Empty Revolution
The Unfulfilled Promises of Hugo Chávez

FRANCISCO RODRÍGUEZ

On December 2, when Venezuelans delivered President Hugo Chávez his first electoral defeat in nine years, most analysts were taken by surprise. According to official results, 50.7 percent of voters rejected Chávez's proposed constitutional reform, which would have expanded executive power, gotten rid of presidential term limits, and paved the way for the construction of a "socialist" economy. It was a major reversal for a president who just a year earlier had won a second six-year term with 62.8 percent of the vote, and commentators scrambled to piece together an explanation. They pointed to idiosyncratic factors, such as the birth of a new student movement and the defection of powerful groups from Chávez's coalition. But few went so far as to challenge the conventional wisdom about how Chávez has managed to stay in power for so long.

Although opinions differ on whether Chávez's rule should be characterized as authoritarian or democratic, just about everyone appears to agree that, in contrast to his predecessors, Chávez has made the welfare of the Venezuelan poor his top priority. His government, the thinking goes, has provided subsidized food to low-income families, redistributed land and wealth, and poured money from Venezuela's booming oil industry into health and education programs. It should not be surprising, then, that in a country where politics was long dominated by rich elites, he has earned the lasting support of the Venezuelan poor.

That story line may be compelling to many who are rightly outraged by Latin America's deep social and economic inequalities. Unfortunately, it is wrong. Neither official statistics nor independent estimates show any evidence that Chávez has reoriented state priorities to benefit the poor. Most health and human development indicators have shown no significant improvement beyond that which is normal in the midst of an oil boom. Indeed, some have deteriorated worryingly, and official estimates indicate that income inequality has increased. The "Chávez is good for the poor" hypothesis is inconsistent with the facts.

My skepticism of this notion began during my tenure as chief economist of the Venezuelan National Assembly. In September 2000, I left American academia to take over a research team with functions broadly similar to those of the U.S. Congressional Budget Office. I had high expectations for Chávez's government and was excited at the possibility of working in an administration that promised to focus on fighting poverty and inequality. But I quickly discovered how large the gap was between the government's rhetoric and the reality of its political priorities.

Soon after joining the National Assembly, I clashed with the administration over underfunding of the Consolidated Social Fund (known by its Spanish acronym FUS), which had been created by Chávez to coordinate the distribution of resources to antipoverty programs. The law establishing the fund included a special provision to ensure that it would benefit from rising oil revenues. But when oil revenues started to go up, the Finance Ministry ignored the provision, allocating to the fund in the 2001 budget only $295 million—15 percent less than the previous year and less than a third of the legally mandated $1.1 billion. When my office pointed out this inconsistency, the Finance Ministry came up with the creative accounting gimmick of rearranging the law so that programs not coordinated by the FUS would nevertheless appear to be receiving resources from it. The effect was to direct resources away from the poor even as oil profits were surging. (Hard-liners in the government, incensed by my office's criticisms, immediately called for my ouster. When the last moderates, who understood the need for an independent research team to evaluate policies, left the Chávez camp in 2004, the government finally disbanded our office.)

Chávez's political success does not stem from the achievements of his social programs or from his effectiveness at redistributing wealth. Rather, through a combination of luck and manipulation of the political system, Chávez has faced elections at times of strong economic growth, currently driven by an oil boom bigger than any since the 1970s. Like voters everywhere, Venezuelans tend to vote their pocketbooks, and until recently, this has meant voting for Chávez. But now, his mismanagement of the economy and failure to live up to his pro-poor rhetoric have finally started to catch up with him. With inflation accelerating, basic foodstuffs increasingly scarce, and pervasive chronic failures in the provision of basic public services, Venezuelans are starting to glimpse the consequences of Chávez's economic policies—and they do not like what they see.

Fake Left

From the moment he reached office in 1999, Chávez presented his economic and social policies as a left-wing alternative to the so-called Washington consensus and a major departure from the free-market reforms of previous administrations. Although the differences were in fact fairly moderate at first, the pace of change accelerated significantly after the political and economic crisis of 2002–3, which saw a failed coup attempt and a two-month-long national strike. Since then, the Venezuelan economy has undergone a transformation.

The change can be broadly characterized as having four basic dimensions. First, the size of the state has increased dramatically. Government expenditures, which represented only 18.8 percent of GDP in

1999, now account for 29.4 percent of GDP, and the government has nationalized key sectors, such as electricity and telecommunications. Second, the setting of prices and wages has become highly regulated through a web of restrictions in place since 2002 ranging from rigid price and exchange controls to a ban on laying off workers. Third, there has been a significant deterioration in the security of property rights, as the government has moved to expropriate landholdings and private firms on an ad hoc basis, appealing to both political and economic motives. Fourth, the government has carried out a complete overhaul of social policy, replacing existing programs with a set of high-profile initiatives—known as the misiones, or missions—aimed at specific problems, such as illiteracy or poor health provision, in poor neighborhoods.

Views differ on how desirable the consequences of many of these reforms are, but a broad consensus appears to have emerged around the idea that they have at least brought about a significant redistribution of the country's wealth to its poor majority. The claim that Chávez has brought tangible benefits to the Venezuelan poor has indeed by now become commonplace, even among his critics. In a letter addressed to President George W. Bush on the eve of the 2006 Venezuelan presidential elections, Jesse Jackson, Cornel West, Dolores Huerta, and Tom Hayden wrote, "Since 1999, the citizens of Venezuela have repeatedly voted for a government that—unlike others in the past—would share their country's oil wealth with millions of poor Venezuelans. "The Nobel laureate economist Joseph Stiglitz has noted, "Venezuelan President Hugo Chávez seems to have succeeded in bringing education and health services to the barrios of Caracas, which previously had seen little of the benefits of that country's rich endowment of oil." Even The Economist has written that "Chávez's brand of revolution has delivered some social gains."

One would expect such a consensus to be backed up by an impressive array of evidence. But in fact, there is remarkably little data supporting the claim that the Chávez administration has acted any differently from previous Venezuelan governments—or, for that matter, from those of other developing and Latin American nations—in redistributing the gains from economic growth to the poor. One oft-cited statistic is the decline in poverty from a peak of 54 percent at the height of the national strike in 2003 to 27.5 percent in the first half of 2007. Although this decline may appear impressive, it is also known that poverty reduction is strongly associated with economic growth and that Venezuela's per capita GDP grew by nearly 50 percent during the same time period—thanks in great part to a tripling of oil prices. The real question is thus not whether poverty has fallen but whether the Chávez government has been particularly effective at converting this period of economic growth into poverty reduction. One way to evaluate this is by calculating the reduction in poverty for every percentage point increase in per capita income—in economists' lingo, the income elasticity of poverty reduction. This calculation shows an average reduction of one percentage point in poverty for every percentage point in per capita GDP growth during this recovery, a ratio that compares unfavorably with those of many other developing countries, for which studies tend to put the figure at around two percentage points. Similarly, one would expect pro-poor growth to be accompanied by a marked decrease in income inequality. But according to the Venezuelan Central Bank, inequality has actually increased during the Chávez administration, with the Gini coefficient (a measure of economic inequality, with zero indicating perfect equality and one indicating perfect inequality) increasing from 0.44 to 0.48 between 2000 and 2005.

Poverty and inequality statistics, of course, tell only part of the story. There are many aspects of the well-being of the poor not captured by measures of money income, and this is where Chávez's supporters claim that the government has made the most progress—through its misiones, which have concentrated on the direct provision of health, education, and other basic public services to poor communities. But again, official statistics show no signs of a substantial improvement in the well-being of ordinary Venezuelans, and in many cases there have been worrying deteriorations. The percentage of underweight babies, for example, increased from 8.4 percent to 9.1 percent between 1999 and 2006. During the same period, the percentage of households without access to running water rose from 7.2 percent to 9.4 percent, and the percentage of families living in dwellings with earthen floors multiplied almost threefold, from 2.5 percent to 6.8 percent. In Venezuela, one can see the misiones everywhere: in government posters lining the streets of Caracas, in the ubiquitous red shirts issued to program participants and worn by government supporters at Chávez rallies, in the bloated government budget allocations. The only place where one will be hard-pressed to find them is in the human development statistics.

Remarkably, given Chávez's rhetoric and reputation, official figures show no significant change in the priority given to social spending during his administration. The average share of the budget devoted to health, education, and housing under Chávez in his first eight years in office was 25.12 percent, essentially identical to the average share (25.08 percent) in the previous eight years. And it is lower today than it was in 1992, the last year in office of the "neoliberal" administration of Carlos Andrés Pérez—the leader whom Chávez, then a lieutenant colonel in the Venezuelan army, tried to overthrow in a coup, purportedly on behalf of Venezuela's neglected poor majority.

In a number of recent studies, I have worked with colleagues to look more systematically at the results of Chávez's health and education misiones. Our findings confirm that Chávez has in fact done little for the poor. For example, his government often claims that the influx of Cuban doctors under the Barrio Adentro health program is responsible for a decline in infant mortality in Venezuela. In fact, a careful analysis of trends in infant and neonatal mortality shows that the rate of decline is not significantly different from that of the pre-Chávez period, nor from the rate of decline in other Latin American countries. Since 1999, the infant mortality rate in Venezuela has declined at an annual rate of 3.4 percent, essentially identical to the 3.3 percent rate at which it had declined during the previous nine-year period and lower than the rates of decline for the same period in Argentina (5.5 percent), Chile (5.3 percent), and Mexico (5.2 percent).

Even more disappointing are the results of the government's Robinson literacy program. On October 28, 2005, Chávez declared Venezuela "illiteracy-free territory." His national literacy campaign, he announced, had taught 1.5 million people how to read and write, and the education minister stated that residual illiteracy stood at less than 0.1 percent of the population. The achievement received considerable international recognition and was taken at face value by many specialists as well as by casual observers. A recent article in the San Francisco Chronicle, for example, reported that "illiteracy, formerly at 10 percent of the population, has been completely eliminated." Spanish President Jose Luis Rodríguez Zapatero and UNESCO's general director, Koïchiro Matsuura, sent the Venezuelan government public letters of congratulation for the achievement. (After Matsuura's statement, the Chávez's administration claimed that its eradication of illiteracy had been "UNESCO-verified.")

But along with Daniel Ortega of Venezuela's IESA business school, I looked at trends in illiteracy rates based on responses to the Venezuelan National Institute of Statistics' household surveys. (A full presentation of our study will appear in the October 2008 issue of the journal Economic

Development and Cultural Change.) In contrast to the government's claim, we found that there were more than one million illiterate Venezuelans by the end of 2005, barely down from the 1.1 million illiterate persons recorded in the first half of 2003, before the start of the Robinson program. Even this small reduction, moreover, is accounted for by demographic trends rather than the program itself. In a battery of statistical tests, we found little evidence that the program had had any statistically distinguishable effect on Venezuelan illiteracy. We also found numerous inconsistencies in the government's story. For example, it claims to have employed 210,410 trainers in the anti-illiteracy effort (approximately two percent of the Venezuelan labor force), but there is no evidence in the public employment data that these people were ever hired or evidence in the government budget statistics that they were ever paid.

The Economic Consequences of Mr. Chávez

In fact, even as the conventional wisdom has taken hold outside of Venezuela, most Venezuelans, according to opinion surveys, have long been aware that Chávez's social policies are inadequate and ineffective. To be sure, Venezuelans would like the government's programs—particularly the sale of subsidized food—to remain in place, but that is a far cry from believing that they have reasonably addressed the nation's poverty problem. A survey taken by the Venezuelan polling firm Alfredo Kellery Asociados in September 2007 showed that only 22 percent of Venezuelans think poverty has improved under Chávez, while 50 percent think it has worsened and 27 percent think it has stayed the same.

At the same time, however, Venezuelan voters have given Chávez credit for the nation's strong economic growth. In polls, an overwhelming majority have expressed support for Chávez's stewardship of the economy and reported that their personal situation was improving. This is, of course, not surprising: with its economy buoyed by surging oil profits, Venezuela had enjoyed three consecutive years of double-digit growth by 2006.

But by late 2007, Chávez's economic model had begun to unravel. For the first time since early 2004, a majority of voters claimed that both their personal situation and the country's situation had worsened during the preceding year. Scarcities in basic foodstuffs, such as milk, black beans, and sardines, were chronic, and the difference between the official and the black-market exchange rate reached 215 percent. When the Central Bank board received its November price report indicating that monthly inflation had risen to 4.4 percent (equivalent to an annual rate of 67.7 percent), it decided to delay publication of the report until after the vote on the constitutional reform was held.

This growing economic crisis is the predictable result of the gross mismanagement of the economy by Chávez's economic team. During the past five years, the Venezuelan government has pursued strongly expansionary fiscal and economic policies, increasing real spending by 137 percent and real liquidity by 218 percent. This splurge has outstripped even the expansion in oil revenues: the Chávez administration has managed the admirable feat of running a budget deficit in the midst of an oil boom.

Such expansionary policies were appropriate during the deep recession that Venezuela faced in the aftermath of the political and economic crisis of 2002–3. But by continuing the expansion after the recession ended, the government generated an inflationary crisis. The problem has been compounded by efforts to address the resulting imbalances with an increasingly complex web of price and exchange controls coupled with routine threats of expropriation directed at producers and shopkeepers as a warning not to raise prices. Not surprisingly, the response has been a steep drop in food production and widening food scarcity.

A sensible solution to Venezuela's overexpansion would require reining in spending and the growth of the money supply. But such a solution is anathema to Chávez, who has repeatedly equated any call for spending reductions with neoliberal dogma. Instead, the government has tried to deal with inflation by expanding the supply of foreign currency to domestic firms and consumers and increasing government subsidies. The result is a highly distorted economy in which the government effectively subsidizes two-thirds of the cost of imports and foreign travel for the wealthy while the poor cannot find basic food items on store shelves. The astounding growth of imports, which have nearly tripled since 2002 (imports of such luxury items as Hummers and 15-year-old Scotch have grown even more dramatically), is now threatening to erase the nation's current account surplus.

What is most distressing is how predictable all of this was. Indeed, Cháveznomics is far from unprecedented: the gross contours of this story follow the disastrous experiences of many Latin American countries during the 1970s and 1980s. The economists Rudiger Dornbusch and Sebastian Edwards have characterized such policies as "the macroeconomics of populism." Drawing on the economic experiences of administrations as politically diverse as Juan Perón's in Argentina, Salvador Allende's in Chile, and Alan García's in Peru, they found stark similarities in economic policies and in the resulting economic evolution. Populist macroeconomics is invariably characterized by the use of expansionary fiscal and economic policies and an overvalued currency with the intention of accelerating growth and redistribution. These policies are commonly implemented in the context of a disregard for fiscal and foreign exchange constraints and are accompanied by attempts to control inflationary pressures through price and exchange controls. The result is by now well known to Latin American economists: the emergence of production bottlenecks, the accumulation of severe fiscal and balance-of-payments problems, galloping inflation, and plummeting real wages.

Chávez's behavior is typical of such populist economic experiments. The initial successes tend to embolden policymakers, who increasingly believe that they were right in dismissing the recommendations of most economists. Rational policy formulation becomes increasingly difficult, as leaders become convinced that conventional economic constraints do not apply to them. Corrective measures only start to be taken when the economy has veered out of control. But by then it is far too late.

My experience dealing with the Chávez government confirmed this pattern. In February 2002, for example, I had the opportunity of speaking with Chávez at length about the state of the Venezuelan economy. At that point, the economy had entered into a recession as a result of an unsustainable fiscal expansion carried out during Chávez's first three years in office. Moderates within the government had arranged the meeting with the hope that it would spur changes in the management of the public finances. As a colleague and I explained to Chávez, there was no way to avoid a deepening of the country's macroeconomic crisis without a credible effort to raise revenue and rationalize expenditures. The president listened with interest, taking notes and asking questions over three hours of conversation, and ended our meeting with a request that we speak with his cabinet ministers and schedule future meetings. But as we proceeded to meet with officials, the economic crisis was spilling over into the political arena, with the opposition calling for street demonstrations in response to Chávez's declining poll numbers. Soon, workers at the state oil company, PDVSA, joined the protests.

In the ensuing debate within the government over how to handle the political crisis, the old-guard leftists persuaded Chávez to take a hard line. He dismissed 17,000 workers at PDVSA and sidelined moderates within his government. When I received a call informing me that our future meetings with Chávez had been canceled, I knew that the hard-liners had gained the upper hand. Chávez's handling of the economy and the political crisis had significant costs. Chávez deftly used the mistakes of the opposition (calling for a national strike and attempting a coup) to deflect blame for the recession. But in fact, real GDP contracted by 4.4 percent and the currency had lost more than 40 percent of its value in the first quarter of 2002, before the start of the first PDVSA strike on April 9. As early as January of that year, the Central Bank had already lost more than $7 billion in a futile attempt to defend the currency. In other words, the economic crisis had started well before the political crisis—a fact that would be forgotten in the aftermath of the political tumult that followed.

The government's response to the crisis has had further consequences for the Venezuelan economy. The takeover of PDVSA by Chávez loyalists and the subordination of the firm's decisions to the government's political imperatives have resulted in a dramatic decline in Venezuela's oil-production capacity. Production has been steadily declining since the government consolidated its control of the industry in late 2004. According to OPEC statistics, Venezuela currently produces only three-quarters of its quota of 3.3 million barrels a day. Chávez's government has thus not only squandered Venezuela's largest oil boom since the 1970s; it has also killed the goose that lays the golden egg. Despite rising oil prices, PDVSA is increasingly strained by the combination of rising production costs, caused by the loss of technical capacity and the demands of a growing web of political patronage, and the need to finance numerous projects for the rest of the region, ranging from the rebuilding of Cuban refineries to the provision of cheap fuel to Sandinista-controlled mayoralties in Nicaragua. As a result, the capacity of oil revenues to ease the government's fiscal constraints is becoming more and more limited.

Plowing the Sea

Simón Bolívar, Venezuela's independence leader and Chávez's hero, once said that in order to evaluate revolutions and revolutionaries, one needs to observe them close up but judge them at a distance. Having had the opportunity to do both with Chávez, I have seen to what extent he has failed to live up to his own promises and Venezuelans' expectations. Now, voters are making the same realization—a realization that will ultimately lead to Chávez's demise. The problems of ensuring a peaceful political transition will be compounded by the fact that over the past nine years Venezuela has become an increasingly violent society. This violence is not only reflected in skyrocketing crime rates; it also affects the way Venezuelans resolve their political conflicts. Whether Chávez is responsible for this or not is beside the point. What is vital is for Venezuelans to find a way to prevent the coming economic crisis from igniting violent political conflict. As Chávez's popularity begins to wane, the opposition will feel increasingly emboldened to take up initiatives to weaken Chávez's movement. The government may become increasingly authoritarian as it starts to understand the very high costs it will pay if it loses power. Unless a framework is forged through which the government and the opposition can reach a settlement, there is a significant risk that one or both sides will resort to force.

Looking back, one persistent question (in itself worthy of a potentially fascinating study in international political economy) will be how the Venezuelan government has been able to convince so many people of the success of its antipoverty efforts despite the complete absence of real evidence of their effectiveness. When such a study is written, it is likely that the Chávez administration's strategy of actively lobbying foreign governments and launching a high-profile public relations campaign—spearheaded by the Washington-based Venezuela Information Office—will be found to have played a vital role. The generous disbursement of loans to cash-strapped Latin American and Caribbean nations, the sale of cheap oil and heating gas to support political allies in the developed and developing worlds, and the covert use of political contributions to buy the loyalty of politicians in neighboring countries must surely form part of the explanation as well.

But perhaps an even more important reason for this success is the willingness of intellectuals and politicians in developed countries to buy into a story according to which the dilemmas of Latin American development are explained by the exploitation of the poor masses by wealthy privileged elites. The story of Chávez as a social revolutionary finally redressing the injustices created by centuries of oppression fits nicely into traditional stereotypes of the region, reinforcing the view that Latin American underdevelopment is due to the vices of its predatory governing classes. Once one adopts this view, it is easy to forget about fashioning policy initiatives that could actually help Latin America grow, such as ending the agricultural subsidies that depress the prices of the regions exports or significantly increasing the economic aid given to countries undertaking serious efforts to combat poverty.

The American journalist Sydney Harris once wrote that "we believe what we want to believe, what we like to believe, what suits our prejudices and fuels our passions." The idea that Latin American governments are controlled by economic elites may have been true in the nineteenth century, but is wildly at odds with reality in a world in which every Latin American country except Cuba has regular elections with large levels of popular participation. Much like governments everywhere, Latin American governments try to balance the desire for wealth redistribution with the need to generate incentives for economic growth, the realities of limited effective state power, and the uncertainties regarding the effectiveness of specific policy initiatives. Ignoring these truths is not only anachronistic and misguided; it also thwarts the design of sensible foreign policies aimed at helping the region's leaders formulate and implement strategies for achieving sustainable and equitable development.

It would be foolhardy to claim that what Latin America must do to lift its population out of poverty is obvious. If there is a lesson to be learned from other countries' experiences, it is that successful development strategies are diverse and that what works in one place may not work elsewhere. Nonetheless, recent experiences in countries such as Brazil and Mexico, where programs skillfully designed to target the weakest groups in society have had a significant effect on their well-being, show that effective solutions are within the reach of pragmatic policymakers willing to implement them. It is the tenacity of these realists—rather than the audacity of the idealists—that holds the greatest promise for alleviating the plight of Latin America's poor.

FRANCISCO RODRÍGUEZ, Assistant Professor of Economics and Latin American Studies at Wesleyan University, was Chief Economist of the Venezuelan National Assembly from 2000 to 2004.

UNIT 5

Population, Resources, Environment, and Health

Unit Selections

Key Points to Consider

- What accounts for the demographic changes around the world?

- What are the implications of these trends in demography?

- What are the ways to decrease deforestation in the developing world?

- What is the controversy over water resources?

- What impact does climate change have on developing countries?

- Do rich countries bear some responsibility for the natural disasters that occur in the developing world?

- What are the ways to improve health care in the developing world?

- What is the link between a sustainable environment and health?

- How does illness contribute to poverty?

Student Web Site

www.mhcls.com/online

Internet References

Earth Pledge Foundation
http://www.earthpledge.org
EnviroLink
http://envirolink.org
Greenpeace
http://www.greenpeace.org
Linkages on Environmental Issues and Development
http://www.iisd.ca/linkages/
Population Action International
http://www.populationaction.org
The Worldwatch Institute
http://www.worldwatch.org

The developing world's population continues to increase at an annual rate that exceeds the world average. The average fertility rate (the number of children a woman will have during her life) for all developing countries is 2.9, while for the least developed countries the figure is 4.9. Although growth has slowed considerably since the 1960s, world population is still growing at the rate of over 70 million per year, with most of this increase taking place in the developing world. Increasing population complicates development efforts, puts added stress on the ecosystem, and threatens food security. Population migration patterns are shaped more and more by the trends in population growth in both the industrialized countries and the developing world.

World population surpassed 6 billion toward the end of 1999 and, if current trends continue, could reach 9.8 billion by 2050. Even if, by some miracle, population growth was immediately reduced to the level found in industrialized countries, the developing world's population would continue to grow for decades. Approximately one-third of the population in the developing world is under the age of 15, with that proportion jumping to almost 40 percent in the least developed countries. The population momentum created by this age distribution means that it will be some time before the developing world's population growth slows substantially. Some developing countries have achieved progress in reducing fertility rates through family planning programs, but much remains to be done. At the same time, reduced life expectancy, especially related to the HIV/AIDS epidemic, is having a significant demographic impact especially in sub-Saharan Africa.

Over a billion people live in absolute poverty, as measured by a combination of economic and social indicators. As population increases, it becomes more difficult to meet the basic human needs of the citizens of the developing world's citizens. Indeed, food scarcity looms as a major problem as the world struggles with a global food crisis, triggered by higher demand, skyrocketing oil prices, and the diversion of agricultural production to biofuels. Ironically, because of changes in food consumption patterns, obesity is becoming a health issue in wealthier developing countries. Larger population of poor people also places greater strains on the scarce resources and fragile ecosystems. Competition for the scarce water resources not only affects agricultural production but it also threatens to spark conflict. Deforestation for agriculture and fuel, as well as to meet demand for timber, has reduced forested areas and contributed to erosion, desertification, and global warming. In an effort to reduce illegal logging, some developing countries have initiated certification programs to ensure that timber is harvested sustainably. Intensified agricultural production, particularly of cash crops, has depleted soil. This necessitates increased fertilization, which is costly and also produces runoff that contributes to water pollution. Greenhouse gas emissions are accelerating climate change, the adverse effects of which will be felt first by the developing world.

Economic development, has not only failed to eliminate poverty but has actually exacerbated it in some ways. Ill-conceived

© Digital Vision/PunchStock

economic development plans have diverted resources from more productive uses and contributed to environmental degradation. There has also been a tendency to favor large-scale industrial plants that may be unsuitable to local conditions and that increase pollution. Where economic growth has occurred, the benefits are often distributed inequitably, widening the gap between the rich and the poor. If developing countries try to follow Western consumption patterns, sustainable development will be impossible. Furthermore, economic growth without effective environmental policies can lead to the need for more expensive clean-up efforts later in the future.

Divisions between the North and the South on environmental issues became more pronounced at the 1992 Rio Conference on Environment and Development. The conference highlighted the fundamental differences between the industrialized world and developing countries over the causes of and the solutions to global environmental problems. Developing countries pointed to consumption levels in the North as the main cause of environmental problems and called on the industrialized countries to pay most of the costs of environmental programs. Industrialized countries sought to convince developing countries to conserve their resources in their efforts to modernize and develop. Divisions have also emerged on the issues of climate and greenhouse gas emissions. The Johannesburg Summit on Sustainable Development, a follow-up to the Rio conference, grappled with many of these issues, achieving some modest success in addressing water and sanitation needs.

Rural-to-urban migration has caused an enormous influx of people to the cities, who are lured by the illusion of opportunity in cities and the attraction of urban life. In reality, opportunity is limited. Nevertheless, most choose marginal lives in the cities rather than a return to the countryside. As a result, urban areas in the developing world increasingly lack infrastructure to support this increased population, and also have rising rates of pollution, crime, and disease. Additional resources are diverted to the urban areas in an attempt to meet increased demands, further impoverishing rural areas. Meanwhile, food production may be affected, with those remaining in rural areas having to choose either to farm for subsistence, because of low prices, or to raise cash crops for export.

The fact that environmental factors account for about one-fifth of all diseases in developing countries illustrates the link between health and environmental issues. Disease also depletes family resources, contributing to poverty and debt. Environmental decline also make citizens more vulnerable to natural disasters. Sustainable development is essential to reduce poverty and curtail the spread of diseases. Improving access to affordable health care in the poor countries would also contribute to reducing poverty. The HIV/AIDS epidemic in particular has forced attention on public health issues, especially in Africa. Africans account for 70 percent of the over 40 million AIDS cases worldwide. Besides the human tragedy that this epidemic creates, its implications on development are enormous.

The loss of skilled and educated workers, the increase in the number of orphans, and the economic disruption that the disease causes will have a profound impact in the future. A WHO/UNAIDS initiative to get treatment for three million people suffering from AIDS fell short of the goal, but it did make some progress in treating the victims of this devastating disease. The development and availability of drugs to treat HIV/AIDS and malaria, which kills more children worldwide, is often constrained by patent and profitability concerns. Little of the spending on research and development of new drugs goes into finding therapies for the diseases that are prevalent in developing countries. Population, environment, and basic health care clearly represent huge challenges for the developing countries.

Booms, Busts, and Echoes

How the biggest demographic upheaval in history is affecting global development.

DAVID E. BLOOM AND DAVID CANNING

For much (and perhaps most) of human history, demographic patterns were fairly stable: the human population grew slowly, and age structures, birth rates, and death rates changed very little. The slow long-run growth in population was interrupted periodically by epidemics and pandemics that could sharply reduce population numbers, but these events had little bearing on long-term trends.

Over the past 140 years, however, this picture has given way to the biggest demographic upheaval in history, an upheaval that is still running its course. Since 1870 death rates and birth rates have been declining in developed countries. This long-term trend toward lower fertility was interrupted by a sharp, post–World War II rise in fertility, which was followed by an equally sharp fall (a "bust"), defining the "baby boom." The aging of this generation and continued declines in fertility are shifting the population balance in developed countries from young to old. In the developing world, reductions in mortality resulting from improved nutrition, public health infrastructure, and medical care were followed by reductions in birth rates. Once they began, these declines proceeded much more rapidly than they did in the developed countries. The fact that death rates decline before birth rates has led to a population explosion in developing countries over the past 50 years.

Even if the underlying causes of rapid population growth were to suddenly disappear, humanity would continue to experience demographic change for some time to come. Rapid increases in the global population over the past few decades have resulted in large numbers of people of childbearing age (whose children form an "echo" generation). This creates "population momentum," where the populations of most countries, even those with falling birth rates, will grow for many years, particularly in developing countries.

These changes have huge implications for the pace of economic development. Economic analysis has tended to focus on the issue of population numbers and growth rates as factors that can put pressure on scarce resources, dilute the capital-labor ratio, or lead to economies of scale. However, demographic change has important additional dimensions. Increasing average life expectancy can change life-cycle behavior affecting educa-

tion, retirement, and savings decisions—potentially boosting the financial capital on which investors draw and the human capital that strengthens economies. Demographic change also affects population age structure, altering the ratio of workers to dependents. This issue of *F&D* looks at many facets of the impact of demographic change on the global economy and examines the policy adjustments needed in both the developed and the developing world.

Sharp Rise in Global Population

The global population, which stood at just over 2.5 billion in 1950, has risen to 6.5 billion today, with 76 million new inhabitants added each year (representing the difference, in 2005, for example, between 134 million births and 58 million deaths). Although this growth is slowing, middle-ground projections suggest the world will have 9.1 billion inhabitants by 2050.

These past and projected additions to world population have been, and will increasingly be, distributed unevenly across the world. Today, 95 percent of population growth occurs in developing countries. The populations of the world's 50 least developed countries are expected to more than double by the middle of this century, with several poor countries tripling their populations over the period. By contrast, the population of the developed world is expected to remain steady at about 1.2 billion, with declines in some wealthy countries.

The disparity in population growth between developed and developing countries reflects the considerable heterogeneity in birth, death, and migration processes, both over time and across national populations, races, and ethnic groups. The disparity has also coincided with changes in the age composition of populations. An overview of these factors illuminates the mechanisms of population growth and change around the world.

Total fertility rate. The total world fertility rate, that is, the number of children born per woman, fell from about 5 in 1950 to a little over 2.5 in 2006 (see Figure 1). This number is projected to fall to about 2 by 2050. This decrease is attributable largely to changes in fertility in the developing world and can be ascribed to a number of factors, including declines in infant

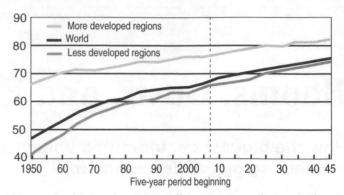

(total fertility rate; children per woman)

Figure 1 Smaller Families. Fertility rates are tending to converge at lower levels after earlier sharp declines.

Source: United Nations, *World Population Prospects,* 2004.

(life expectancy in years)

Figure 2 Living Longer. Life expectancy is continuing to rise, but there are big differences between rates in well-off and poorer countries.

Source: United Nations, *World Population Prospects,* 2004.

mortality rates, greater levels of female education and increased labor market opportunities, and the provision of family-planning services.

Infant and child mortality decline. The developing world has seen significant reductions in infant and child mortality over the past 50 years. These gains are primarily the result of improved nutrition, public health interventions related to water and sanitation, and medical advances, such as the use of vaccines and antibiotics. Infant mortality (death prior to age 1) in developing countries has dropped from 180 to about 57 deaths per 1,000 live births. It is projected to decline to fewer than 30 by 2050. By contrast, developed countries have seen infant mortality decline from 59 deaths per 1,000 live births to 7 since 1950, and this is projected to decline further still, to 4 by 2050. Child mortality (death prior to age 5) has also fallen in both developed and developing countries.

Life expectancy and longevity. For the world as a whole, life expectancy increased from 47 years in 1950–55 to 65 years in 2000–05. It is projected to rise to 75 years by the middle of this century, with considerable disparities between the wealthy industrial countries, at 82 years, and the less developed countries, at 74 years (see Figure 2). (Two major exceptions to the upward trend are sub-Saharan Africa, where the AIDS epidemic has drastically lowered life expectancy, and some of the countries of the former Soviet Union, where economic dislocations have led to significant health problems.) As a result of the global decline in fertility, and because people are living longer, the proportion of the elderly in the total population is rising sharply. The number of people over the age of 60, currently about half the number of those aged 15 to 24, is expected to reach 1 billion (overtaking the 15–24 age group) by 2020 and almost 2 billion by 2050. The proportion of individuals aged 80 or over is projected to rise from 1 percent to 4 percent of the global population by 2050.

> **"A new UN report says that in 2007 the worldwide balance will tip and more than half of all people will be living in urban areas."**

Age distribution: working-age population. Baby booms have altered the demographic landscape in many countries. As the experiences of several regions during the past century show, an initial fall in mortality rates creates a boom generation in which high survival rates lead to more people at young ages than in earlier generations. Fertility rates fall over time, as parents realize they do not need to give birth to as many children to reach their desired family size, or as desired family size contracts for other reasons. When fertility falls and the baby boom stops, the age structure of the population then shows a "bulge" or baby-boom age cohort created by the nonsynchronous falls in mortality and fertility. As this generation moves through the population age structure, it constitutes a share of the population larger than the cohorts that precede or follow. This creates particular challenges and opportunities for countries, such as a large youth cohort to be educated, followed by an unusually large working-age (approximately ages 15–64) population, with the prospect of a "demographic dividend," and characterized eventually by a large elderly population, which may burden the health and pension systems (see Figure 3).

Migration. Migration also alters population patterns. Globally, 191 million people live in countries other than the one in which they were born. On average during the next 45 years, the United Nations projects that over 2.2 million individuals will migrate annually from developing to developed countries. It also projects that the United States will receive by far the largest number of immigrants (1.1 million a year), and China, Mexico, India, the Philippines, and Indonesia will be the main sources of emigrants.

Urbanization. In both developed and developing countries, there has been huge movement from rural to urban areas since 1950. Less developed regions, in aggregate, have seen their population shift from 18 percent to 44 percent urban, while the corresponding figures for developed countries are 52 percent to 75 percent. A new UN report says that in 2007 the worldwide balance will tip and more than half of all people will be living in urban areas. This shift—and the concomitant urbanization of areas that were formerly peri-urban or rural—is consistent with the shift in most countries away from agriculturally based economies.

(ratio of working-age to non-working-age population)

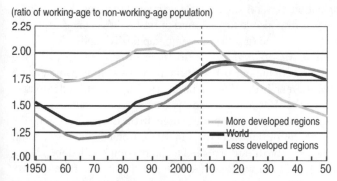

Figure 3 Tracking the Bulge. Developing countries are nearing the peak of their opportunity to benefit from a high ratio of workers to dependents.

Source: United Nations, *World Population Prospects,* 2004.

(world population, aged 80+; millions)

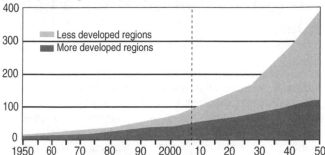

Figure 4 Retiree Boom. The number of people living past 80 is projected to rise sharply, but labor shortages could drive up living costs for retirees.

Source: United Nations, *World Population Prospects,* 2004.

The existence and growth of megacities (that is, those with 10 million or more residents) is a late-20th-century phenomenon that has brought with it special problems. There were 20 such cities in 2003, 15 in developing countries. Tokyo is by far the largest, with 35 million people, followed by (in descending order) Mexico City, New York, São Paulo, and Mumbai (all with 17 to 19 million). Cities in general allow for economies of scale—and, most often, for a salutary mix of activities, resources, and people—that make them centers of economic growth and activity and account, in some measure, for their attractiveness. As continued movement to urban areas leads to megacities, however, these economies of scale and of agglomeration seem to be countered, to some extent, by problems that arise in transportation, housing, air pollution, and waste management. In some instances, socioeconomic disparities are particularly exacerbated in megacities.

What Is the Impact on Economies?

The economic consequences of population growth have long been the subject of debate. Early views on the topic, pioneered by Thomas Malthus, held that population growth would lead to the exhaustion of resources. In the 1960s, it was proposed that population growth aided economic development by spurring technological and institutional innovation and increasing the supply of human ingenuity. Toward the end of the 1960s, a neo-Malthusian view, focusing again on the dangers of population growth, became popular. Population control policies in China and India, while differing greatly from each other, can be seen in this light. Population neutralism, a middle-ground view, based on empirical analysis of the link between population growth and economic performance, has held sway for the past two decades. According to this view, the net impact of population growth on economic growth is negligible.

Population neutralism is only recently giving way to a more fine-grained view of the effects of population dynamics in which demographic change does contribute to or detract from economic development. To make their case, economists and demographers point to both the "arithmetic accounting" effects of age structure change and the effects of behavioral change caused by longer life spans (see box).

Arithmetic accounting effects. These effects assume constant behavior within age and sex groups, but allow for changes in the relative size of those groups to influence overall outcomes. For example, holding age- and sex-specific labor force participation rates constant, a change in age structure affects total labor supply.

As a country's baby-boom generation gets older, for a time it constitutes a large cohort of working-age individuals and, later, a large cohort of elderly people. The span of years represented by the boom generation (which determines how quickly this cohort moves through the age structure) and the size of the population bulge vary greatly from one country to another. In all circumstances, there are reasons to think that this very dynamic age structure will have economic consequences. A historically high proportion of working-age individuals in a population means that, potentially, there are more workers per dependent than previously. Production can therefore increase relative to consumption, and GDP per capita can receive a boost.

Life cycle patterns in savings also come into play as a population's age structure changes. People save more during their working-age years, and if the working-age cohort is much larger than other age groups, savings per capita will increase.

Behavioral effects. Declining rates of adult mortality and the movement of large cohorts through the global population pyramid will lead to a massive expansion in the proportion of elderly in the world population (see the projections for 2050 in Figure 4). Some simple economic projections show catastrophic effects of this aging. But such projections tend to be based on an "accounting" approach, which assumes that age-specific behavior remains unchanged and ignores the potentially significant effects of behavior change.

The aging of the baby-boom generation potentially promotes labor shortages, creating upward pressure on wages and downward pressure on the real incomes of retirees. In response, people may adjust their behavior, resulting in increased labor force participation, the immigration of workers from developing countries, and longer working lives. Child mortality declines can also have behavioral effects, particularly for women, who tend to be the primary caregivers for children. When the reduced fertility effect of a decrease in child mortality is in place, more women participate in the workforce, further boosting the labor supply.

How Much Can the Human Life Span Be Stretched?

In most of the world, children born today can expect to live for many decades longer than their ancestors born in the 19th or early 20th centuries. In Japan, life expectancy at birth is now 82 years, and other regions have also made great progress as medical and public health advances, improved nutrition, and behavioral changes encouraged by improved education have combined to reduce the risk of death at all ages. But how far can these increases in longevity go?

Continuing increases in life expectancy in low-mortality populations have led some demographers to forecast further gains. Kenneth Manton, Eric Stallard, and H. Dennis Tolley, for example, estimate that populations with extremely healthy lifestyles—that is, with an absence or near-absence of risk factors such as infectious disease, smoking, alcohol abuse, and obesity, and the presence of health-promoting behaviors such as a healthy diet and exercise—could achieve a life expectancy of between 95 and 100 years.

But others have reached different conclusions. Nan Li and Ronald Lee estimate that life expectancy in the United States will rise from a 1996 figure of 76.3 to 84.9 by 2050, with that in Japan rising from 80.5 to 88.1. S. Jay Olshansky, Bruce Carnes, and Aline Desesquelles predicted in 1990 that life expectancy at birth would not surpass 85 years, even in low-mortality settings. Death rates, they argued, would not fall sufficiently for life expectancy to rise rapidly, and earlier increases were driven largely by dramatic reductions in infant and child mortality, which could not recur (Samuel Preston, on the other hand, observes that 60 percent of the life expectancy increase in the United States since 1950 is due to mortality declines in people over the age of 50). Perhaps more important, they saw no reason why the future should necessarily mirror the past—new threats to health such as influenza pandemics, antibiotic resistance, and obesity could reverse gains made in recent decades; technological improvements could stall and the drugs needed to counter the diseases of aging might not be found; and environmental disasters, economic collapse, or war could derail health systems at the same time that they weaken individuals' ability to protect their own health.

The Missing Link

Demographic effects are a key missing link in many macroeconomic analyses that aim to explain cross-country differences in economic growth and poverty reduction. Several empirical studies show the importance of demographics in explaining economic development.

East Asia's baby boom. East Asia's remarkable economic growth in the past half century coincided closely with demographic change in the region. As infant mortality fell from 181 to 34 per 1,000 births between 1950 and 2000, fertility fell from six to two children per woman. The lag between falls in mortality and fertility created a baby-boom generation: between 1965 and 1990, the region's working-age population grew nearly four times faster than the dependent population. Several studies have estimated that this demographic shift was responsible for one-third of East Asia's economic growth during the period (a welcome demographic dividend).

Labor supply and the Celtic Tiger. From 1960 to 1990, the growth rate of income per capita in Ireland was approximately 3.5 percent a year. In the 1990s, it jumped to 5.8 percent, well in excess of any other European economy. Demographic change contributed to the country's economic surge. In the decade following the legalization of contraceptives in 1979, Ireland saw a sharp fall in the crude birth rate. This led to decreasing youth dependency and a rise in the working-age share of the total population. By the mid-1990s, the dependency burden in Ireland had dropped to a level below that in the United Kingdom.

Two additional demography-based factors also helped fuel economic growth by increasing labor supply per capita. First, while male labor force participation rates remained fairly static, the period 1980–2000 saw a substantial increase in female labor force participation rates, particularly among those aged between 25 and 40. Second, Ireland historically had high emigration levels among young adults (about 1 percent of the population a year) because its economy was unable to absorb the large number of young workers created by its high fertility rate. The loss of these young workers exacerbated the problem of the high youth dependency rate. The decline in youth cohort sizes and rapid economic growth of the 1990s led to a reversal of this flow, resulting in net in-migration of workers, made up partly of return migrants and also, for the first time, substantial numbers of foreign immigrants.

Continued high fertility in sub-Saharan Africa. Demographic change of a very different type can account for slow economic development. Much of sub-Saharan Africa remains stalled at the first stage of a demographic transition. Fertility rates actually increased a bit from the 1950s through the 1970s and only recently have begun a slow fall. As swollen youth cohorts have entered the labor force, an inadequate policy and economic environment in most countries has prevented many young people from being able to engage in productive employment. The existence of large dependent populations (in this case, of children) has kept the proportion of working-age people low, making it more difficult for these economies to rise out of poverty.

Looking to the Future

Based on the indicators that are available, we can make a few important points:

- *All signs point to continued but slowing population growth.* This growth will result in the addition of roughly 2.5 billion people to the world population, before it stabilizes around 2050 at about 9 billion. Managing this increase will be an enormous challenge, and the economic consequences of failing to do so could be severe.
- *The world's population is aging rapidly.* The United Nations predicts that 31 percent of China's population in 2050—432 million people—will be age 60 or older. The corresponding figures for India are 21 percent and 330 million. No longer can aging be thought of as just a developed-world phenomenon.
- *International migration will continue, but the extent is unclear.* The pressures that encourage people to migrate—above all, the lure of greater economic well-being in the

developed countries—will undoubtedly persist, but the strength of countervailing policy restrictions that could substantially stanch the flow of migrants is impossible to predict.

- *Urbanization will continue, but the pace is also hard to predict.* Greater economic opportunities in the cities will surely continue to attract migrants from rural areas, but environmental and social problems may stymie growth.

Getting the Focus Right

Rapid and significant demographic change places new demands on national and international policymaking. Transitions from high mortality and fertility to low mortality and fertility can be beneficial to economies as large baby-boom cohorts enter the workforce and save for retirement. Rising longevity also tends to increase the incentives to save for old age.

The ability of countries to realize the potential benefits of the demographic transition and to mitigate the negative effects of aging depends crucially on the policy and institutional environment. Focusing on the following areas is likely to be key:

Health and nutrition. Although it has long been known that increased income leads to improved health, recent evidence indicates that good health may also be an important factor in economic development. Good nutrition in children is essential for brain development and for allowing them to become productive members of society. Health improvements—especially among infants and children—often lead to declines in fertility, above and beyond the heightened quality of life they imply. Focusing on the diseases of childhood can therefore increase the likelihood of creating a boom generation and certain positive economic effects. Countries wishing to accelerate fertility declines may benefit from focusing on access to family-planning services and education about fertility decisions.

> "The ability of countries to realize the potential benefits of the demographic transition and to mitigate the negative effects of aging depends crucially on the policy and institutional environment."

Education. Children are better able to contribute to economic growth as they enter the workforce if they have received an effective education. East Asia capitalized on its baby boom by giving its children a high-quality education, including both general schooling and technical skills, that equipped them to meet the demands of an ever-changing labor market. Ireland also profited from its baby boomers by introducing free secondary schooling and expanding tertiary education.

Labor market institutions. Restrictive labor laws can limit a country's ability to benefit from demographic change, particularly when they make it unduly difficult to hire and fire workers or to work part-time. International outsourcing, another controversial subject, may become an increasingly important means of meeting the demand for labor.

Trade. One way that East Asian countries provided their baby-boom cohorts with productive opportunities was by carefully opening up to international trade. By providing a new avenue for selling the region's output, this opening helped countries avoid the unemployment that could have arisen. We have found that open economies benefit much more from demographic change than the average, and that closed economies do not derive any statistically significant benefit from age structure changes.

Retirement. Population aging will require increased savings to finance longer retirements. This will likely affect financial markets, rates of return, and investment. In addition, as more people move into old age, health care costs will tend to increase, with the expansion of health care systems and growth in long-term care for the elderly. As nontradable, labor-intensive sectors with a low rate of technical progress, health care and elder care may slow economic growth. The ability of individuals to contribute to the financing of their retirement may be hampered by existing social security systems, many of which effectively penalize individuals who work beyond a fixed retirement age.

Although demographic changes are generally easier to predict than economic changes, the big picture outlook is nonetheless unclear. Indeed, many forces that affect the world's demographic profile are highly unpredictable. Will an outbreak of avian flu or another disease become pandemic, killing many millions and decimating economies? What happens if these diseases are, or become, drug-resistant? Conversely, scientific advances in areas such as genomics, contraceptive methods, or vaccines for diseases such as AIDS or malaria could save and improve millions of lives. Global warming and other environmental change could completely alter the context of demographic and economic predictions. Or—to take things to extremes—wars could result in massive premature mortality, thereby rendering irrelevant most predictions about demographic and related economic changes.

References

Bloom, David E., and David Canning, 2004, "Global Demographic Change: Dimensions and Economic Significance," in *Global Demographic Change: Economic Impacts and Policy Challenges,* proceedings of a symposium, sponsored by the Federal Reserve Bank of Kansas City, Jackson Hole, Wyoming, August 26–28, pp. 9–56.

Lee, Ronald, 2003, "The Demographic Transition: Three Centuries of Fundamental Change," *Journal of Economic Perspectives,* Vol. 17 (Fall), pp. 167–90.

National Research Council, 1986, *Population Growth and Economic Development: Policy Questions* (Washington: National Academies Press).

DAVID E. BLOOM is Professor of Economics and Demography and **DAVID CANNING** is Professor of Economics and International Health at the Harvard School of Public Health.

Forest Loss in Sumatra Becomes a Global Issue

Peter Gelling

Here on the island of Sumatra, about 1,200 miles from the global climate talks under way on Bali, are some of the world's fastest-disappearing forests.

A look at this vast wasteland of charred stumps and dried-out peat makes the fight to save Indonesia's forests seem nearly impossible.

"What can we possibly do to stop this?" said Pak Helman, 28, a villager here in Riau Province, surveying the scene from his leaking wooden longboat. "I feel lost. I feel abandoned."

In recent years, dozens of pulp and paper companies have descended on Riau, which is roughly the size of Switzerland, snatching up generous government concessions to log and establish palm oil plantations. The results have caused villagers to feel panic.

Only five years ago, Mr. Helman said, he earned nearly $100 a week catching shrimp. Now, he said, logging has poisoned the rivers snaking through the heart of Riau, and he is lucky to find enough shrimp to earn $5 a month.

Responding to global demand for palm oil, which is used in cooking and cosmetics and, lately, in an increasingly popular biodiesel, companies have been claiming any land they can.

Fortunately, from Mr. Helman's point of view, the issue of Riau's disappearing forests has become a global one. He is now a volunteer for Greenpeace, which has established a camp in his village to monitor what it calls an impending Indonesian "carbon bomb."

Deforestation, during which carbon stored in trees is released into the atmosphere, now accounts for 20 percent of the world's greenhouse gas emissions, according to scientists. And Indonesia releases more carbon dioxide through deforestation than any other country.

Within Indonesia, the situation is most critical in Riau. In the past 10 years, nearly 60 percent of the province's forests have been logged, burned and pulped, according to Jikalahari, a local environmental group.

"This is very serious—the world needs to act now," said Susanto Kurniawan, a coordinator for Jikalahari who regularly makes the arduous trip into the forest from the nearby city of Pekanbaru, passing long lines of trucks carting palm oil and wood. "In a few years it will be too late."

The rate of this deforestation is rising as oil prices reach new highs, leading more industries to turn to biodiesel made from palm oil, which, in theory, is earth-friendly. But its use is causing more harm than good, environmental groups say, because companies slash and burn huge swaths of trees to make way for palm oil plantations.

Even more significant, the burning and drying of Riau's carbon-rich peatlands, also to make way for palm oil plantations, releases about 1.8 billion tons of greenhouse gases a year, according to Greenpeace officials.

But it is also in Riau that a new global strategy for conserving forests in developing countries might begin. A small area of Riau's remaining forest will become a test case if an international carbon-trading plan called REDD is adopted.

REDD, or Reducing Emissions from Deforestation and Forest Degradation, is to be one of the central topics of discussion at the Bali conference. Essentially, it would involve payments by wealthy countries to developing countries for every hectare of forest they do not cut down.

Indonesia, caught between its own financial interest in the palm oil industry and the growing international demands for conservation, has been promoting the carbon-trading plan for months.

But there are plenty of skeptics, who doubt it will be possible to measure just how much carbon is being conserved—and who question whether the lands involved can be protected from illegal logging and corruption.

Illegal logging is commonplace in Indonesia, and though the government has prosecuted dozens of cases in recent years, it says it cannot be everywhere. Companies in this remote area are cultivating land legally sold to them by the Indonesian government, but maps of their projects obtained by Greenpeace indicate that many of them have also moved into protected areas.

Critics say corruption is their biggest concern. The most famous illegal logger in Indonesia, Adelin Lis, who operated in North Sumatra, was arrested this year, only to be acquitted by a court in Medan, the provincial capital. He then left the country.

The attorney general's office has opened a corruption investigation into judges and the police in Medan, and says there are many similar cases. "There are a number of ongoing investigations into corruption that has allowed illegal loggers from all over Indonesia to go free," said Thomson Siagian, a spokesman for the attorney general. "In such a lucrative industry, payoffs are common."

At the Bali conference, the Woods Hole Research Center, an environmental group based in the United States, has presented research showing that new satellite technology can make it more feasible to track illegal logging. Reports "show that radar imagery from new sensors recently placed in orbit can solve the problem of monitoring reductions in tropical deforestation, which previously was a major obstacle because of cloud cover that optical sensors can't see through," said John P. Holdren, the center's director.

Such developments are good news to Mr. Helman, the villager in Riau who, using his wooden boat, has been ferrying a steady stream of foreign environmentalists and journalists in and out of the forest in recent weeks.

"I am so thankful for the recent attention," he said, tinkering with the sputtering engine. "At times it seems too late. But I see some hope now."

Water Warriors

Declaring water a right, not a commodity, a global water justice movement is growing.

MAUDE BARLOW

Thousands have lived without love, not one without water.

—W.H. Auden, *First Things First*

A fierce resistance to the corporate takeover of water has grown in every corner of the globe, giving rise to a coordinated and, given the powers it is up against, surprisingly successful water justice movement. "Water for all" is the rallying cry of local groups fighting for access to clean water and the life, health and dignity that it brings. Many of these groups have lived through years of abuse, poverty and hunger. Many have been left without public education and health programs when their governments were forced to abandon them under World Bank structural adjustment policies. But somehow, the assault on water has been the great standpoint for millions. Without water there is no life, and for thousands of communities around the world, the struggle over the right to their own local water sources has been politically galvanizing.

A mighty contest has grown between those (usually powerful) forces and institutions that see water as a commodity, to be put on the open market and sold to the highest bidder, and those who see water as a public trust, a common heritage of people and nature, and a fundamental human right. The origins of this movement, generally referred to as the global water justice movement, lie in the hundreds of communities around the world where people are fighting to protect their local water supplies from pollution, destruction by dams and theft—be it from other countries, their own governments or private corporations such as bottled water companies and private utilities backed by the World Bank. Until the late 1990s, however, most were operating in isolation, unaware of other struggles or the global nature of the water crisis.

Latin America was the site of the first experiments with water privatization in the developing world. The failure of these projects has been a major factor in the rejection of the neoliberal market model by so many Latin American countries that have said no to the extension of the North American Free Trade Agreement to the Southern Hemisphere and that have forced the big water companies to retreat. A number of Latin American countries are also opting out of some of the most egregious global institutions. This past May Bolivia, Venezuela and Nicaragua announced their decision to withdraw from the World Bank's arbitration court, the International Centre for the Settlement of Investment Disputes (ICSID), in no small measure because of the way the big water corporations have used the center to sue for compensation when the countries terminated private delivery contracts.

Latin America, with its water abundance, should have one of the highest per capita allocations of water in the world. Instead, it has one of the lowest. There are three reasons, all connected: polluted surface waters, deep class inequities and water privatization. In many parts of Latin America, only the rich can buy clean water. So it is not surprising that some of the most intense fights against corporate control of water have come out of this region of the world.

The first "water war" gained international attention when the indigenous peoples of Cochabamba, Bolivia, led by a five-foot, slightly built, unassuming shoemaker named Oscar Olivera, rose up against the privatization of their water services. In 1999, under World Bank supervision, the Bolivian government had passed a law privatizing Cochabamba's water system and gave the contract to US engineering giant Bechtel, which immediately tripled the price of water. In a country where the minimum wage is less than $60 a month, many users received water bills of $20 a month, which they simply could not afford. As a result, La Coordinadora de Defensa del Agua y de la Vida (Coalition in Defense of Water and Life), one of the first coalitions against water privatization in the world, was formed and organized a successful referendum demanding the government cancel its contract with Bechtel. When the government refused to listen, many thousands took to the streets in nonviolent protest and were met with army violence that wounded dozens and killed a 17-year-old boy. On April 10, 2000, the Bolivian government relented and told Bechtel to leave the country.

The Bolivian government had also bowed to pressure from the World Bank to privatize the water of La Paz and in 1997 gave Suez, a French-based multinational, a thirty-year contract to supply water services to it and El Alto, the hilly region surrounding the capital, where thousands of indigenous peoples live. From the beginning, there were problems. Aguas del Illimani, a Suez subsidiary, broke three key promises: it did not deliver to all the residents, poor as well as rich, leaving about 200,000 without water; it charged exorbitant rates for water hookups, about $450, equivalent to the food budget of a poor family for two years; and it did not invest in infrastructure repair or wastewater treatment, choosing instead to build a series of ditches and canals through poor areas of La Paz, which it used to send garbage, raw sewage and even the effluent from the city's abattoirs into Lake Titicaca, considered by UNESCO a World Heritage site. To add insult to injury, the company located its fortresslike plant under the beautiful Mount Illimani, where it captured the snowmelt off the mountain and, after rudimentary treatment, piped it into the homes of families and businesses in La Paz that could pay. The nearest community, Solidaridad, a slum of about 100 families with no electricity, heat or running water, had its only water supply cut off. Its school and health clinic, built with foreign-aid money, could not operate because of a lack of water. It was the same all through El Alto.

An intense resistance to Suez formed. FEJUVE, a network of local community councils and activists, led a series of strikes in January 2005, which crippled the cities and brought business to a halt. This resistance was a prime factor in the ousting of presidents Gonzalo Sánchez de Lozada and Carlos Mesa. Their replacement, Evo Morales, the first indigenous president in the country's history, negotiated Suez's departure. On January 3, 2007, he held a ceremony at the presidential palace celebrating the return of the water of La Paz and El Alto after a long and bitter confrontation. "Water cannot be turned over to private business," said Morales. "It must remain a basic service, with participation of the state, so that water service can be provided almost for free."

Although they have received less international attention, similar battles over privatized water have raged in Argentina. Río de la Plata (Silver River) separates Buenos Aires, the Argentine capital, from Montevideo, the capital of Uruguay. For 500 years, it has also been called Mar Dulce (Sweet Sea) because its size made people think it was a freshwater sea. Today, however, the river is famous for something else: it is one of the few rivers in the world whose pollution can be seen from space. On March 21, 2006, the Argentine government rescinded the thirty-year contract of Aguas Argentinas, the Suez subsidiary that had run the Buenos Aires water system since 1993, in no small part because the company broke its promise to treat wastewater, continuing to dump nearly 90 percent of the city's sewage into the river. In another broken promise, the company repeatedly raised tariffs, for a total increase of 88 percent in the first ten years of operation. Water quality was another issue; water in seven districts had nitrate levels so high it was unfit for human consumption. An April 2007 report by the city's ombudsman stated that most of the population of 150,000 in the southern district of the city lived with open-air sewers and contaminated drinking water.

Yet as Food and Water Watch reports, the Inter-American Development Bank continued to fund Suez as late as 1999, despite the mounting evidence that the company was pulling in 20 percent profit margins while refusing to invest in services or infrastructure. Outrageously, with the backing of the French government, Suez is trying to recoup $1.7 billion in "investments" and up to $33 million in unpaid water bills at the ICSID. Suez had just (in December 2005) been forced out of the province of Santa Fe, where it had a thirty-year contract to run the water systems of thirteen cities. The company is also suing the provincial government at the ICSID for $180 million. Close on the heels of the Buenos Aires announcement, Suez was forced to abandon its last stronghold in Argentina, the city of Córdoba, when water rates were raised 500 percent on one bill.

In all cases, strong civil society resistance was key to these re treats. A coalition of water users and residents of Santa Fe, led by Alberto Múñoz and others, actually organized a huge and successful plebiscite, in which 256,000 people, about a twelfth of the population of the province, voted to rescind Suez's contract. They convened a Provincial Assembly on the Right to Water with 7,000 activists and citizens in November 2002, which set the stage for the political opposition to the company. The People's Commission for the Recovery of Water in Córdoba is a highly organized network of trade unions, neighborhood centers, social organizations and politicians with a clear goal of public water for all, and was instrumental in getting the government to break its contract with Suez. "What we want is a public company managed by workers, consumers and the provincial government, and monitored by university experts to guarantee water quality and prevent corruption," says Luis Bazán, the group's leader and a water worker who refused employment with Suez.

Mexico is a beachhead for privatization across the region, with its elites having access to all the water they need and also controlling governments at most levels of the country. Only 9 percent of the country's surface water is fit for drinking, and its aquifers are being drawn down mercilessly. According to the National Commission on Water, 12 million Mexicans have no access to potable water whatsoever and another 25 million live in villages and cities where the taps run as little as a few hours a week. Eighty-two percent of wastewater goes untreated. Mexico City has dried up, and its 22 million inhabitants live on the verge of crisis. Services are so poor in the slums and outskirts of the city that cockroaches run out when the tap is turned on. In many "colonias" in Mexico City and around the country, the only available water is sold from trucks that bring it in once a week, often by political parties that sell the water for votes.

In 1983 the federal government handed over responsibility for the water supply to the municipalities. Then in 1992 it passed a new national water bill that encouraged the municipalities to privatize water in order to receive funding. Privatization was supported by former President Vicente Fox, himself a former senior executive with Coca-Cola, and is also favored by the current president, Felipe Calderón. The World Bank and the Inter-American Development Bank are actively promoting water privatization in Mexico. In 2002 the World Bank provided $250 million for infrastructure repair with conditions that municipalities negotiate public-private partnerships. Suez is deeply entrenched in Mexico, running the water services for part of Mexico City, Cancún and about a dozen other cities. Its wastewater division, Degremont, has a large contract for San Luis Potosí and several other cities as well. The privatization of water has become a top priority for the Mexican water commission, Conagua. As in other countries, privatization in Mexico has brought exorbitant water rates, broken promises and cutoffs to those who cannot pay. The Water Users Association in Saltillo, where a consortium of Suez and the Spanish company Aguas de Barcelona run the city's water systems, reports that a 2004 audit by the state comptroller found evidence of contractual and state law violations.

A vibrant civil society movement has recently come together to fight for the right to clean water and resist the trend to corporate control in Mexico. In April 2005 the Mexican Center for Social Analysis, Information and Training (CASIFOP) brought together more than 400 activists, indigenous peoples, small farmers and students to launch a coordinated grassroots resistance to water privatization. The Coalition of Mexican Organizations for the Right to Water (COMDA) is a large collection of environmental, human rights, indigenous and cultural groups devoted not only to activism but also to community-based education on water, its place in Mexico's history and the need for legislation to protect the public's right to access. Their hopes for a government supportive of their perspective were dashed when conservative candidate Calderón won (many say stole) the 2006 presidential election over progressive candidate Andrés Manuel López Obrador. Calderón is working openly with the private water companies to cement private control of the country's water supplies.

Other Latin American cities or countries rejecting water privatization include Bogotá, Colombia (although other Colombian cities, including Cartagena, have adopted private water systems); Paraguay, whose lower house rejected a Senate proposal to privatize water in July 2005; Nicaragua, where a fierce struggle has been waged by civil society groups and where in January 2007 a court ruled against the privatization of the country's wastewater infrastructure; and Brazil, where strong public opinion has held back the forces of water privatization in most cities. Unfortunately, resistance in Peru, where increased rates, corruption and debt plague the system, has not yet reversed water privatization. Likewise, in Chile, resistance to water privatization is very difficult because of the entrenched commitment to market ideology of the ruling elites, although there is hope that the center-left government of Michelle Bachelet will be more open to arguments for public governance of Chile's water supplies.

From thousands of local struggles for the basic right to water—not just throughout Latin America but in Asia-Pacific countries, Africa and the United States and Canada—a highly organized international water justice movement has been forged and is shaping the future of the world's water. This movement has already had a profound effect on global water politics, forcing global institutions such as the World Bank and the United Nations to admit the failure of their model, and it has helped formulate water policy inside dozens of countries. The movement has forced open a debate over the control of water and challenged the "Lords of Water" who had set themselves up as the arbiters of this dwindling resource. The growth of a democratic global water justice movement is a critical and positive development that will bring needed accountability, transparency and public oversight to the water crisis as conflicts over water loom on the horizon.

MAUDE BARLOW is the author of *Blue Covenant: The Global Water Crisis and the Coming Battle for the Right to Water* (New Press), from which this article was adapted.

Why We Owe So Much to Victims of Disaster

At the G8 summit, Brown and Blair should think of our debts to Africans, not theirs to us. We have stolen their share of the planet's resources.

ANDREW SIMMS

If you want to know how to tackle global warming, try the simple wisdom of Wilkins Micawber in Dickens's David Copperfield. "Annual income twenty pounds, annual expenditure nineteen pounds nineteen and six, result happiness," he said. "Annual income twenty pounds, annual expenditure twenty pounds ought and six, result misery."

It is rarely understood this way, but climate change is really a problem of debt. Not a cash debt, but an ecological one. Environmentally, we're living way beyond our means, spending more than the bank of the earth and the atmosphere can replace in our accounts. It is this debt—not the hole in the nation's public spending plans—that ought to have been the subject of the election campaign. And it is this debt—not the financial debts of poor nations to rich—that should guide the thinking of the Chancellor and other western leaders as they approach the G8 summit in July.

Gordon Brown and Tony Blair have set Africa and global warming as the summit's key themes. Yet newly released documents reveal one of the government's more embarrassing oversights. It was agreed at an international summit, more than three years ago, to create a special pot of money to help poor countries cope with climate change. Britain, alone among major European aid donors, has failed to contribute to the "Least Developed Countries Fund".

For years, we have been pilfering from the natural resource accounts of the rest of the world. When the people of Asia, Africa and Latin America decide they want to spend their fair share of nature's equity, either it won't be there or we could be on the verge of a crash in its already overstretched banking system. If the whole world wanted to live like people in the UK, we would need the natural resources of three more planets. If the US were the model, we would need five.

It's not just that we owe these countries for our profligate use of the planet's resources. It is also that they suffer the worst effects of our overuse. The most vulnerable people in the poorest countries—particularly children and women—are in effect paying the interest on our ecological debts. According to the World Disasters Report, the number of mostly climate-related disasters rose from just over 400 a year in 1994–98 to more than 700 a year in 1999–2003, with the biggest rise in the poorest countries.

The sight of a Mozambican woman giving birth in a tree during the great storms of 2000 is seared into the world's consciousness. Mozambique was desperately poor and burdened with debt payments. The floods were the worst for 150 years. Not only had its potential to develop been mismanaged by western creditors, Mozambique was left more vulnerable because it had to choose between preparing for disasters or spending its meagre resources on health and education. Now, in a warming world, Africa's rainfall, so crucial to its farming, is about to become even more erratic.

The story is similar outside Africa. In the mid- to late 1990s, at the height of the Jubilee 2000 debt cancellation campaign, nearly half the Jamaican government's spending went on debt service. The island is rich in natural resources, but it was getting harder for it to earn a living from exporting crops such as sugar and bananas. Yet, under pressure from the IMF and the World Bank, the money available for social programmes in Jamaica was halved.

Angela Stultz-Crawle, a local woman who ran a project in Bennetlands, Kingston to provide basic health and education services, saw the consequences at first hand: reductions in health programmes, in education, in road repairs, in lights. "Just walking around," she said, "you see people living in dirt yards, scrap-board houses. It is repaying. Every day you hear the government come out and say, 'Oh, we have met our IMF deadlines, we have paid,' and everyone claps." Again, Jamaica is particularly vulnerable to the extreme weather that climate change will make more frequent. Last year alone, two major hurricanes, Ivan and Charley, skirted its shores.

So across the developing world, the poorest people suffer from two crises, to neither of which they contributed: financial debt (which their governments are repaying) and ecological debt (which our governments aren't repaying).

In case after case—the IMF-approved kleptocracy of Mobutu's Zaire, the collusion with corruption, asset-stripping and violence in Nigeria's oilfields—the responsibility for financial debts lies at least as much in western capitals as in developing countries in the south. Yet, to win paltry debt relief, poor countries had to swallow the economic-policy equivalent of horse pills. Even the Financial Times commented that the IMF "probably ruined as many economies as they have saved". Yet we still expect poor countries to repay most of their debts, despite the effects on their people's lifestyles. Rich countries, faced with ecological debt, will not even give up the four-wheel-drive school run.

The widening global gap in wealth was built on ecological debts. And today's economic superpowers soon became as successful in their disproportionate occupation of the atmosphere with carbon emissions as they were in colonial times with their military occupation of the terrestrial world. Until the Second World War, they managed this atmospheric occupation largely through exploiting their own fossil-fuel reserves. But from around 1950 they became increasingly dependent on energy imports. By 1998, the wealthiest fifth of the world was consuming 68 per cent of commercially produced energy; the poorest fifth, 2 per cent.

In 2002, many rich countries were pumping out more carbon dioxide per person than they were a decade earlier, when they signed the UN Framework Convention on Climate Change. Now, with Africa and climate change at the top of the G8 summit agenda, there couldn't be a better time for a little paradigm shift. If Blair and Brown want to show leadership, they could relabel the G8 as the inaugural meeting of the ecological debtors' club, and start discussing how to pay back their creditors down south.

But is there any chance that the advanced industrial economies could make the cuts in consumption needed to clear their debts? Perhaps we should ask the women recently seen reminiscing about VE Day, women who during the world war had to keep house under severe constraints. After all, global warming is now described as a threat more serious than war or terrorism. Drawing on articles in Good Housekeeping, and on guides with such titles as Feeding Cats and Dogs in Wartime or Sew and Save, they enormously reduced household consumption—use of electrical appliances, for example, dropped 82 per cent—while at the same time dramatically improving the nation's health.

The ecological debt problem of climate change, if it is to be solved, will still require a proper global framework, eventually giving everybody on the planet an equal entitlement to emit greenhouse gases, and allowing those who under-emit to trade with those who wish to over-emit. But such efforts will be hollow unless the argument to cut consumption can be won at household level.

To refuse the challenge would be the deepest hypocrisy. We have demanded that the world's poorest countries reshape their economies to pay service on dodgy foreign debts. It would be an appalling double standard now to suggest that we couldn't afford either to help developing countries adapt to climate change, or to cut our emissions by the 80–90 per cent considered necessary.

The language of restraint on public spending permeates our public discourse, yet the concept of living within our environmental means still escapes mainstream economics. That will have to change. "Balancing nature's books" could be the simple language that enables the green movement to resonate with the public. Imagine opening a letter from the bank over breakfast to learn that, instead of your usual overdraft, you had an ecological debt that threatened the planet. I wouldn't want to be there when the bailiffs called for that one.

ANDREW SIMMS's Ecological Debt: the health of the planet and the wealth of nations is published this month by Pluto Books ([pounds sterling]12.99 from www.plutobooks.com)

Population, Human Resources, Health, and the Environment

Getting the Balance Right

Anthony J. McMichael

The UN's World Commission on Environment and Development (WCED)—the "Brundtland Commission," chaired by Gro Harlem Brundtland—released its seminal report *Our Common Future* in 1987.[1] Much has changed on the global environment front since then, only some of which was (or could have been) anticipated by that report. As human population continues to grow and as human societies, cultures, and economies become more interconnected against the background crescendo of "globalization" in recent decades, the collective human impact on the biosphere has increasingly assumed a global and systemic dimension. While issues like climate change, freshwater deficits, and degradation of food-producing systems and ocean fisheries were appearing on the horizon in 1987, they have now moved to the foreground. Today, it is evident that these momentous changes pose threats not only to economic systems, environmental assets, infrastructural integrity, tourism, and iconic nature, but also to the stability, health, and survival of human communities. This realization—along with the fact that human-induced global environmental changes impinge unequally on human groups—heightens the rationale for seeking sustainable development.

While the WCED report explored the rationale and the path toward sustainable development, the extent of subsequent large-scale environmental problems arising from the scale and the energy and materials intensity of prevailing modes of development could not have been fully anticipated in 1987. Indeed, paradoxically, concern over world population growth had temporarily receded in the mid-1980s, reflecting the prevailing mix of politics and optimism. The optimism derived from the apparent alleviation of hunger that had been achieved by the Green Revolution of the 1970s and 1980s in much of the developing world, and from the downturn in fertility rates in at least some developing regions. Today, however, the population issue is reemerging in public discussion, reflecting renewed recognition that population growth, along with rising consumption levels, is exacerbating climate change and other global environmental changes.[2]

If the commission's assessment were re-run this decade, its updated terms of reference would necessarily focus more attention on the social and health dimensions of the "development" process, both as inputs and, importantly, as outcomes. The charge to the commission, which focused on the often-conflicted relationship between economic activity and environmental sustainability, was framed at a time when the orthodox Rostovian view (that economic development occurs in five basic stages from "traditional society" to "age of high mass consumption") still remained influential.[3] Today, human capital and social capital—both of which were first properly understood and factored into the development calculus in the 1990s, along with the need for sound governance—are better recognized as prerequisites for environmentally sustainable development. At the same time, realization is growing that the attainment of positive human experience is the core objective of human societies.[4] In contrast, the commission's primary mandated focus was on how to reconcile environmental sustainability with social-economic development. That orientation afforded little stimulus to considering why, in human experiential terms, achieving such a balance is not an end in itself, but is a prerequisite for attaining human security, well-being, health, and survival. Why else do we seek sustainability?

People, Resources, Environment, and Development

The UN General Assembly Resolution A/38/161 of 1983 establishing the WCED specified that the commission would "take account of the interrelationships between people, resources, environment and development."[5] The full text of the resolution emphasized—as did the commission's name—the dual need for long-sighted environmental management strategies and greater cooperation among countries in seeking a sustainable development path to the common future. Two words in the quoted phrase are of particular interest: "people" and "resources."

Reference to "people," rather than to "populations," seems to emphasize the *human* dimension. However, it also distracts from issues of fertility and population size—a distraction that probably reflected two prevailing circumstances. In the 1980s—when world population growth was at its historic high—the United States's conservative Reagan Administration withheld international aid from family planning because of its perceived links with abortion counseling. This ill-informed and culturally high-handed approach, coming from a powerful country with great financial influence over UN policies, was complemented by the fact that many low-income countries considered that issues of fertility and population size were their own business. Nevertheless, and to its credit, the WCED report directly addressed the question of population size and its environmental consequences, urging lower fertility rates as a prerequisite for both poverty alleviation and environmental sustainability.

The word "resources" is ambiguous; it could be taken to refer to natural environmental resources or to human resources (human capital, including education and health status). To what extent did the WCED consider human well-being and health in relation to changing environmental conditions, population size, and resources? "Many such changes are accompanied by life-threatening hazards," stated the WCED in its overview of the report,[6] suggesting that the report would indeed explore how the state of the natural environment, our basic habitat, sets limits on human well-being, health, and survival, both now—and of particular relevance to sustainability—in future. Indeed, in launching the report in Oslo, on 20 March 1987, Chair Brundtland said:

> Our message is directed towards people, whose wellbeing is the ultimate goal of all environment and development policies. . . . If we do not succeed in putting our message of urgency through to today's parents and decision makers, we risk undermining our children's fundamental right to a healthy, life-enhancing environment.[7]

Despite these promising statements, the report itself gave only limited attention to considering how environmental degradation and ecological disruption affect the foundations of human population health. The report focused primarily on the prospects for achieving an "ecologically sustainable" form of social and economic development that conserves the natural environmental resource base for future human needs. It paid little attention to the fact that the conditions of the world's natural environment signify much more than assets for production, consumption, and economic development in general; the biosphere and its component ecosystems and biophysical processes provide the functions and flows that maintain life processes and therefore good health. Indeed, all extant forms of life have evolved via an exquisite dependency on environmental conditions.

This somewhat restricted vision on the part of the WCED is not surprising. Indeed, such a perspective has been reflected often in subsequent forays of UN agencies into the rationale and objectives of sustainable development—forays that have consistently overlooked or sometimes trivialized the role of sustainable development as a precondition to attaining well-being, health, and survival (see the box on for the example of the UN's Millennium Development Goals).[8] In defense of the report, however, it does state:

It is misleading and an injustice to the human condition to see people merely as consumers. Their well-being and security—old age security, declining child mortality, health care, and so on—are the goal of development.[9]

In the 1980s and early 1990s, there was little evidence and understanding of the relationship between environmental conditions, ecological systems, and human health. For example, the First Assessment Report of the Intergovernmental Panel on Climate Change (IPCC), released in 1991, contained only passing reference to how global climate change would affect human health.[10] The IPCC report reviewed in detail the risks to farms, forests, fisheries, feathered and furry animals, to settlements, coastal zones, and energy generation systems. In contrast, it glossed cursorily over the risks to human health (and gave undue emphasis to solar ultraviolet exposure and skin cancer, which is very marginal to the climate change and health topic).

There was, then, only a rudimentary awareness that the profile and scale of environmental hazards to human health were undergoing a profound transformation. For instance, the human health risks due to stratospheric ozone depletion, first recognized during the late 1970s and early 1980s, had been easily understood. They belonged to the familiar category of direct-acting hazardous environmental exposures. An increase in ambient levels of ultraviolet radiation at Earth's surface would increase the risks of skin damage and skin cancer and would affect eye health (for example, cataract formation). Recognition of this straightforward risk to human biology facilitated the ready international adoption of the Montreal Protocol in 1987, requiring national governments to eliminate release of ozone-destroying gases (mostly chlorofluorocarbons, nitrous oxide, and methyl bromide).

In contrast, the great diversity of (mostly) less direct-acting but potentially more profound risks to human health from changes to Earth's climate system, agroecosystems, ocean fisheries, freshwater flows, and general ecosystem functioning (such as pollination, nutrient cycling, and soil formation) were only dimly perceived in the 1980s. Those health risks received relatively little attention in the WCED report, which focused instead on health hazards related to inadequate water supply and sanitation, malnutrition, drug addiction, and exposure to carcinogens and other toxins in homes and the workplace.

An Incomplete Model of Health Determinants

In discussing population health, the WCED report took a largely utilitarian view, discussing good health as an input to economic development and, specifically, as stimulus to the reduction of fertility and poverty. In this respect it was in good company: both the pioneering sanitary revolution of nineteenth-century England and World Health Organization's International Commission on Macroeconomics and Health, established in 2000, espoused the same rationale: good health fosters national wealth. To the extent that the WCED report addressed the determinants of population health, it focused mainly on the contributions of

Millennium Development Goals: How Much Progress Has Been Made?

By coincidence, the 20-year anniversary of the Brundtland report nearly coincides with the halfway mark of another UN project, the Millennium Development Goals (MDGs), 2000–2015.[1] The MDGs were launched in 2000 against a backdrop of increasing attention on what was termed "ecologically sustainable development" in large part stimulated by the WCED report. They encompass eight goals (each with associated targets): to eradicate extreme poverty and hunger; achieve universal primary education; promote gender equality and empower women; reduce child mortality; improve maternal health; combat HIV/AIDS, malaria, and other diseases; ensure environmental sustainability; and develop a global partnership for development.

Achievement of the MDGs is becoming increasingly improbable as time passes. Some headway has been made in relation to poverty reduction and child school enrollment. But there has been little alleviation of hunger and malnutrition, maternal mortality, and infant-child death rates (which have declined by around one sixth in poorer countries, well short of the two-thirds reduction target).

Inevitably, progress toward the goals has varied between regions and countries. China, for example, has made social and health advances on many fronts, albeit at the cost of increasingly serious environmental degradation. In contrast, in sub-Saharan Africa, no country is coming close to halving poverty, providing universal primary education, or stemming the devastating HIV/AIDS epidemic. More than 40 percent of persons in sub-Saharan Africa live in extreme poverty.

One quarter of the world's children aged less than 5 are underfed and underweight. This, as a proportion, is an improvement on the figure of one third in 1990. However, in sub-Saharan Africa and South Asia, nearly half the children remain underweight, and gains are minimal.

The total number of people living with AIDS has increased by nearly 7-million since 2001, to a total now of 40 million. Neither malaria nor tuberculosis is being effectively curtailed, with the attempt to reduce tuberculosis being threatened further by the recent emergence of strains with more extreme forms of antimicrobial resistance.

Perhaps this lack of progress is in part reflected in the UN's failure to explore and emphasize the primary interconnected role of Goal 7 for the achievement of the MDGs overall. Goal 7 seeks "environmental sustainability"—and achieving this particular goal is the bedrock for attaining most of the targets of the other seven goals. Without an intact and productive natural environment and its life-supporting global and regional systems and processes (such as climatic conditions, ocean vitality, ecosystem functioning, and freshwater circulation), the prospects are diminished for food production, safe drinking water adequate household and community energy sources, stability of infectious disease agents, and protection from natural environmental disasters.

The subsequent treatment by the UN of Goal 7 in relation to its health implications has been rather superficial, and mostly in relation to familiar, localized, environmental health hazards. For example, the UN's 2007 report on the MDGs focuses particularly on how Goal 7 relates to child diarrhoeal diseases. It states:

> The health, economic and social repercussions of open defecation, poor hygiene and lack of safe drinking water are well documented. Together they contribute to about 88 per cent of the deaths due to diarrhoeal diseases—more than 1.5 million—in children under age five. Infestation of intestinal worms caused by open defecation affects hundreds of millions of predominantly school-aged children, resulting in reduced physical growth, weakened physical fitness and impaired cognitive functions. Poor nutrition contributes to these effects.[2]

More encouraging is the recent, wider-visioned approach taken by the UN Millennium Project, undertaken for the Commission on Sustainable Development.[3] This project's definition of "environmental sustainability" refers explicitly to the health impacts of environmental changes, and states as follows:

> Achieving environmental sustainability requires carefully balancing human development activities while maintaining a stable environment that predictably and regularly provides resources such as freshwater, food, clean air, wood, fisheries and productive soils and that protects people from floods, droughts, pest infestations and disease.[4]

Notes

1. UN Secretary General, Millennium Development Goals (New York. United Nations, 2000), http://www.un.org/millenniumgoals/goals.html (accessed 23 August 2007).

2. United Nations, *The Millennium Development Goals Report 2007* (New York: United Nations, 2007).

3. J. Sachs and J. McArthur, "The Millennium Project: A Plan for Meeting the Millennium Development Goals," *Lancer* 365, no. 9456 (2005): 347–53.

4. Y. K. Nayarro, J. McNeely, D. Melnick, R. R. Sears, and G. Schmidt-Traub, *Environment and Human Wellbeing: A Practical Strategy* (New York: UN Millennium Project Task Force on Environmental Sustainability, 2005).

economic development, health care systems, and public health programs—and not on the fundamental health-supporting role of the natural environment and its ecosystem services.

The report noted the success of some relatively poor nations and provinces, such as China, Sri Lanka, and Kerala State in India, in lowering infant mortality and improving population health by investing in education (especially for girls), establishing primary health clinics, and enacting other health-care programs. The report extended this analysis, citing the history of the well-documented mortality decline in the industrial world—

which preceded the advent of modern drugs and medical care, deriving instead from betterment of nutrition, housing, and hygiene. Progressive policies, strong social institutions, and innovative health care and public health protection (especially against infectious diseases), without generalized gains in national wealth, the report's authors said, can be sufficient to raise population health markedly.

This important insight, though, makes no explicit reference to the role of wider environmental conditions. While the control of mosquito populations with window-screens and insecticides certainly confers some health protection, for example, land-use practices, surface water management, biodiversity (frogs and birds eat mosquitoes), and climatic conditions can affect mosquito ecology and mosquito-borne disease transmission more profoundly. The issue must be tackled at both levels.

In fairness, understanding the patterns and determinants of human population health within a wider ecological frame has been impeded by strong cultural and intellectual undercurrents. The rise of modern western science and medicine, in concert with the contemporary ascendancy of neo-liberalism and individualism, has recast our views of health and disease in primarily personal terms. The Christian biblical notion from two thousand years ago of the Four Horsemen of the Apocalypse as the major scourges of population health and survival—war, conquest, famine, and pestilence—has been replaced by today's prevailing model of health and disease as predominantly a function of individual-level consumer behaviors, genetic susceptibility, and access to modern health care technologies.

In addition to this cultural misshaping of our understanding, our increasing technological sophistication has created the illusion that we no longer depend on nature's "goods and services" for life's basic necessities. In this first decade of the twenty-first century, however, we are being forcibly reminded of that fundamental dependence. Hence, a repeat WCED report, written now, would give much higher priority to the relationship between biosphere, environmental processes, human biological health, and survival.

Footprints, Environmental Conditions, and Human Well-being

It is interesting that the WCED report was being drafted at about the time when, according to recent assessments, the demands and pressures of the global human population were first overreaching the planet's carrying capacity.[11]

In the time since the publication of the report, the "ecological footprint" has become a familiar concept. For any grouping of persons, it measures the amount of Earth's surface required to provide their materials and food and to absorb their wastes. Collectively, humankind reached a point in the mid-1980s when it began to exceed the limit of what Earth could supply and absorb on a sustainable basis. Since then, the human population has moved from having a precariously balanced environmental budget that left nothing in reserve to a situation today in which we are attempting to survive on a substantial, growing,

overdraft: our global standard-of-living is estimated to be at the level that requires approximately 1.3 Earths (see Table).[12] We are therefore consuming and depleting natural environmental capital. This explains the accruing evidence of climate change, loss of fertile soil, freshwater shortages, declining fisheries, biodiversity losses and extinctions. This is not a sustainable trajectory, and it is what, generically, the WCED report exhorted the world to avoid.

In the 1980s, there was more ambivalence about the population component of the "footprint" concept. The absolute annual increments in human numbers were at a historical high, and many demographers and some enlightened policymakers were concerned that population growth needed constraining. That view faced an emergent western political ethos that eschewed family planning, abortion counseling, and governmental intervention. In the upshot, population growth has begun to slow in a majority of countries. Meanwhile, this is being offset by the rapid rise in wealth and consumption in many larger developing countries, including China, India, Brazil, and Mexico.

This planet simply cannot support a human population of 8 to 10 billion living at the level of today's high-income country citizens. Each of those citizens, depending on their particular country, needs 4 to 9 hectares of Earth's surface to provide materials for their lifestyle and to absorb their wastes. Meanwhile, India's population of 1.2 billion has to get by with less than 1 hectare per person. With an anticipated world population of 8 to 10 billion living within Earth's limits, there would be no more than about 1.5 hectares of ecological footprint per average-person—and this arithmetic would limit the resources available for other species. To comply equitably with this limit will necessitate radical changes in value systems and social institutions everywhere.

Global Environment: Emerging Evidence

The Brundtland Commission foresaw at least some of the impending serious erosion of large-scale environmental resources and systems. Indeed, the WCED report judged that by early in the twenty-first century, climate change might have increased average global temperatures sufficiently to displace agricultural production areas, raise sea levels (and perhaps flood coastal cities), and disrupt national economies. This apparently has not yet happened, although very recent scientific reports point strongly to an acceleration in the climate change process,[13] as the global emissions of carbon dioxide from fossil-fuel combustion and of other greenhouse gases from industrial and agricultural activities alter the global climate faster than previously expected.

Several other adverse environmental trends have emerged since 1987. Accessible oil stocks may now be declining—thereby stimulating an (ill-judged) scramble to divert food-grain production into biofuel production as an alternative source of liquid energy.[14] It has also become apparent that human actions are transforming the global cycles of various elements other than carbon, particularly nitrogen, phosphorus, and sulfur.[15] Human agricultural and industrial activity now generates as much biologically activated nitrogen (nitrogenous

Table 1 Changes in Key Global Indicators of Environment and Population Health (1987–2007)

	1987 (1985–1989)	2007 (2005–2009)	Comments
World population size	4.9 billion	6.7 billion	Slight reduction in absolute annual increment
Annual population growth rate	1.7%	1.2%	
Fertility rate (births/woman)	3.4	2.4	
Percent over age 65 years	6%	8%	Low-income countries have increased from 4% to 5.5%
Life expectancy, years	65	68	
Maternal mortality (per 100,000 births)	430	400	
Under 5 mortality, per 1,000 births	115	70	
Infant mortality, per 1,000 births	68	48	
Primary schooling	~60%	82%	See also Figure 1
Malnutrition prevalence	870 million	850 million	Recent increase, relative to the turn of century (~ 820 million)
Child stunting, less than age 5, prevalence	~ 30%	25%	Down from 35% circa 1950, but a persistent and serious problem in sub-Saharan Africa (highest prevalence) and South Asia
HIV/AIDS, prevalent cases	10 million	40 million	
AIDS deaths per year	~ 0.2 million	3.2 million	
Lack safe drinking water	1.3 billion (27%)	1.1 billion (15%)	Percent of world population shown in brackets
Lack sanitation	2.7 billion (54%)	2.6 billion (40%)	Percent of world population shown in brackets
CO_2 atmospheric concentration	325 parts per million	385 parts per million	Approx 0.5% rise per year, currently accelerating. (Pre-industrial concentration 275 parts per million)
Increase in average global temperature relative to 1961–1990 baseline	0.1 degrees Celsius	0.5 degrees Celsius	Warming faster at high latitude, especially in northern hemisphere
Global ecological footprint	1.0 planet Earths	1.3 planet Earths	Estimate of number of planet Earths needed to supply, sustainably, the world population's energy, materials and waste disposal needs

Source: Compiled from various international agency reports, databases, and scientific papers.

compounds such as ammonia) as do lightning, volcanic activity, and nitrogen-fixation on the roots of wild plants. Meanwhile, worldwide land degradation, freshwater shortages, and biodiversity losses are increasing. Those environmental problems were all becoming evident in the mid-1980s and were duly referred to in the WCED report, albeit without particular connection to considerations of human health.

Some other large-scale environmental stresses, however, were not evident in the 1980s. The scientific community had not anticipated the acidification of the world's oceans caused by absorption of increasingly abundant atmospheric carbon dioxide. This acidification—global average ocean pH has declined by a little over 0.1 points during the past several decades—

endangers the calcification processes in the tiny creatures at the base of the marine food web. Nor was much attention paid to the prospect of loss of key species in ecosystems, such as pollinating insects (especially bees). Both those processes are now demonstrably happening, further jeopardizing human capital development, poverty alleviation, and good health.

During 2001–2006, the Millennium Eco-system Assessment (MA) was conducted as a comprehensive international scientific assessment with processes similar to those of IPCC. The MA documented the extent to which recent human pressures have accelerated the decline of stocks of many environmental assets, including changes to ecosystems.[15] The MA also projected likely future trends. This assessment documented how several other globally significant environmental graphs peaked in the mid-1980s. On land, the annual per capita production of cereal grains peaked and has subsequently drifted sideways and, recently, downwards. The harvest from the world's ocean fisheries also peaked at that time and has subsequently declined slowly—albeit with compensatory gains from aquaculture. These emergent negative trends in food-producing capacity jeopardize attempts to reduce hunger, malnutrition, and child stunting—a key target area of the Millennium Development Goals (see the box on next page).

The WCED report, if rewritten today, would presumably take a more integrative and systems-oriented approach to the topic of environmental sustainability and would incorporate greater awareness of the risks posed to human well-being and health.

Trends in Human Capital and Population Health

As discussed, the original UN resolution calling for the WCED report referred ambiguously to "resources." Within the overarching environmental context of the commission, the intended reference of that word may well have been to environmental resources (such as oil, strategic and precious metals, water supplies, etc.). Interestingly, the WCED treated the word as referring primarily to *human* resources in chapter 4, titled "Population and Human Resources."

The global population was 4.9 billion at the time the WCED report was published, and now exceeds 6.7 billion. It continues to increase by more than 70 million persons annually. Because overall fertility rates have declined a little faster than was previously expected, the current "medium" UN projection for population growth by 2050 is for a total of approximately 9.1 billion.[16] Most of that increase will occur in the low-income countries, predominantly in rapidly expanding cities.

Population growth necessarily increases demands on the local environment. But as the WCED report correctly argued, "the population issue is not solely about numbers."[17] Population size, density, and movement are part of a larger set of pressures on the environment. In some regions, resource degradation occurs because of the combination of poverty and the farming of thinly populated drylands and forests. Elsewhere, per-person levels of consumption and waste generation are the critical drivers of environmental stress. Extrapolation of current global economic trends foreshadows a potential five- to tenfold increase in economic activity by 2050. But this looks increasingly unachievable without radical changes in world technological choices and economic practices. The current experience of China is salutary in this regard: that country's rapid economic growth is engendering huge problems of freshwater supply, air quality, environmental toxins in food, desertification of western provinces—and, now, the world's largest national contribution to greenhouse gas emissions.

Is there an upside to population? "People," stated the WCED report, "are the ultimate resource. Improvements in education, health, and nutrition allow them to better use the resources they command, to stretch them further."[18] How have we progressed since 1987 in providing these improvements?

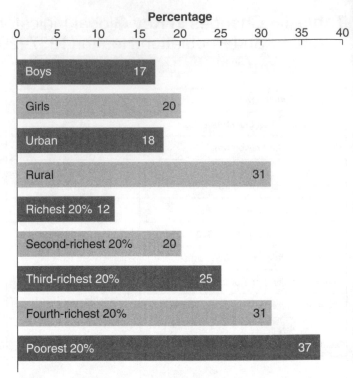

Figure 1 Children of primary school age not in school, by sex, place of residence, and household wealth, 2005

Source: United Nations, *Millennium Development Goals Report 2007* (New York: United Nations, 2007), http://www.un.org/millenniumgoals/goals.html (accessed 23 August, 2007).

Access to primary schooling has increased since 1987 (see Table 1). In particular, the proportion of young girls completing primary school has increased (starting from a lower base than for boys). Figure 1 on this page shows current proportions of the world's children not in primary schooling by key categories. Impediments persist in the form of poverty, parental illiteracy, civil war, and Islamic extremism (banning female education).

Beyond environmental stresses and deficits, the task of improving population health faces other, systemic difficulties. As my colleague C. D. Butler and I wrote last year:

The gap between rich and poor, both domestically and internationally, has increased substantially in recent decades. Inequality between countries has weakened the United Nations and other global organisations and institutions. Foreign aid has declined, replaced by claims that market forces and the removal of trade-distorting subsidies will reduce poverty and provide public goods, including health care and environmental stability.[19]

Hunger and malnutrition persist at high levels (see box). Famines in Africa remain frequent, and 300 million people in India are undernourished. Further, the almost 50 percent prevalence of underweight children in sub-Saharan Africa and South Asia causes widespread stunting of growth, intellectual development, and energy levels. Yet elsewhere, hundreds of millions of people in all continents are overfed and, via obesity, at increased risk of diabetes and heart disease.

Over the past two decades, demographic and epidemiological transitions have become less orderly than was anticipated

Recent Trends in Population Health

Human health experienced unprecedented gains last century. Globally, average life expectancy approximately doubled from around 35 years to almost 70 years.[1] Rises in life expectancy have slowed a little in recent years in high-income countries. Meanwhile, rises are continuing (from a lower base) in much of the rest of the world. However, the regional picture is very uneven, and some divergence has occurred. The rise in life expectancy has stalled in much of sub-Saharan Africa, various ex-Soviet countries, North Korea, and Iraq (see the figure on the next page). Meanwhile, health inequalities persist both between and within countries and reflect, variously, differences in economic circumstance, literacy, social institutions, and political regimen.

Improved food supply is the likely cause of much of the health gain in modern western populations. The second agricultural revolution, which began in eighteenth-century Europe, brought mechanization, new cultivars, and, eventually, fossil fuel power. Consequently, the millennia-old pattern of subsistence crises diminished and then disappeared. The greater security and abundance of food apparently explains why adult males in northern European countries have grown around 10 centimeters taller and 20–30 kilograms heavier than their eighteenth-century predecessors.[2] Others have argued that improved food quality and safety raised the resistance of better-nourished persons to infectious diseases.[3]

Despite these gains, an estimated 850 million persons remain malnourished. In absolute terms, that figure has grown since the time of the WCED report, including over the past decade.[4] Meanwhile, it has become increasingly evident in both high-income and lower-income countries that an abundance of food energy, especially in the form of refined and selectively produced energy-dense (high fat, high sugar) foods, poses various serious risks to health.

In the 1980s, the general assumption was that these non-communicable diseases appear in the later stages of economic development and would increase with further gains in wealth and modernity. However it has become clear in the past two decades that these diseases, particularly heart disease, hypertensive stroke, and type 2 diabetes, are increasing markedly in lower-income populations as they undergo urbanization, and dietary change. The burden of cardiovascular disease—which accounts for around 30 percent of all deaths in today's world—will continue this shift to low- and middle-income countries. This, plus the persistent infectious disease burden, particularly in poorer subpopulations, will further increase global health inequalities.[5]

Notes

1. A. J. McMichael, M. McKee, V. Shkolnikov, and T. Vaikonen, "Mortality Trends and Setbacks: Global Convergence or Divergence?" *Lancet* 363, no. 9415, (2004): 1155–59.

2. R. W. Fogel, *The Escape from Hunger and Premature Death, 1700–2100: Europe, American and the Third World* (Cambridge: Cambridge University Press, 2004).

3. T. McKeown, R. G. Brown, and R. Record, "An Interpretation of the Modern Rise of Population in Europe," *Population Studies* 26 no. 3 (1972): 345–82.

4. Food and Agriculture Organization of the United Nations (FAO), *The State of Food Insecurity in the World 2004* (Rome: FAO, 2005).

5. M. Ezzati et al., "Rethinking the 'Diseases of Affluence' Paradigm: Global Patterns of Nutritional Risks in Relation to Economic Development." *PLoS Medicine* 2, no.5 (2005), e133.doi.10.1371/journal.pmed.0020133.

by conventional demographic models. There has been considerable divergence between countries in trends in death rates (life expectancy) and fertility rates. National health trends (see box), particularly in poor and vulnerable populations, are falling increasingly under the shadow of climate change and other adverse environmental trends.

In many, but not all low-income countries, fertility rates have declined faster than might have been predicted. However, in some countries (such as East Timor, Nigeria, and Pakistan) fertility remains high (4–7 children per woman). In some regions, the fertility decline has led to an economically and socially unbalanced age structure, especially in China, where in the wake of their "one-child policy," the impending dependency ratio is remarkably high—many fewer young adults will have to provide economic support for an older, longer-living generation.

In some other countries, population growth has declined substantially because of rapid falls in life expectancy.[20] Russia and parts of sub-Saharan Africa have very different demographic characteristics, and yet common elements may underlie their downward trends in life expectancy. Both regions lack public goods for health.[21] In Russia there is a lack of equality, safety, and public health services—and many men have lost status and authority following the collapse of the Communist party structure. Meanwhile, in a number of sub-Saharan African countries, there is serious corruption in government, deficient governance structures, food insecurity, and inadequate public health services.

The conventional assumption, also evident in the WCED report, has been that a health dividend will flow from poverty alleviation. However, it is becoming clear that those anticipated health gains are likely to be lower because of the now-worldwide rise of various non-communicable diseases, including those due to obesity, dietary imbalances, tobacco use, and urban air pollution.[22]

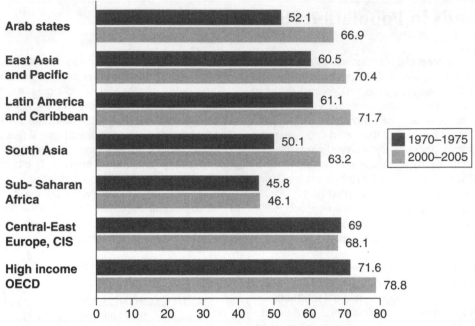

Changes in life expectancy by region, over the past three decades

Note: Differences are marked between regions—especially the lack of gains in sub-Saharan Africa and the central and eastern European (including ex-Soviet) countries.

Source: Based on M. Marmot, "Health in an Unequal World," *Lancet* 368, no. 9552 (2006): 2081–94.

Conclusion

The WCED was commissioned to examine critically the relationship between environmental resource use and sustainable development and to propose solutions for the tensions between environment (including the pressures of population growth and urbanization) and development. A prime task for the commission was to formulate a "global agenda for change" within the frame of ecologically sustainable development, while recognizing the aspirational goals of people and communities everywhere.[23]

During the time that the commission was developing its report, a widely held view, reinforced by the Green Revolution successes of the 1970s and early 1980s, was that continuing population growth need not have adverse environmental impacts. The commission was hesitant to embrace that view, which has recently been re-evaluated,[24] with renewed recognition of the adverse effects of rapid population growth, especially in developing countries, on both social and environmental conditions.[25]

In the 1980s, national governments and multilateral agencies began to see that economic development issues could not be separated from environment issues. Many forms of development erode the environmental resource base (including forests, fertile soils, and coastal zones) necessary for sustained development. And conversely, environmental degradation can jeopardize economic development. The WCED report rightly emphasized the futility of addressing environmental problems without alleviating poverty and international inequality. The report also recognized the needs for stronger social structures and legal processes to deal with tensions over environmental

commons, and for more enlightened public agency structures at the international level to address these issues. It advocated partnerships with the private sector—a sector in which there is now a growing recognition that business-as-usual is no longer an option.

Those formulations remain important and valid, but they are an incomplete basis for future strategic policy. They overlook the fundamental role that sustaining an intact biosphere and its component systems plays in enabling the social and human developmental processes that can reduce poverty, undernutrition, unsafe drinking water, and exposures to endemic and epidemic infectious diseases. The report, if updated today, would seek a better balance between these sets of relationships.

The idea of "ecologically sustainable development" was, in the latter 1980s, ahead of its time. We had, then, neither the evidence nor the insight to know just how fundamental that framework was to achieving the other human goals that would be embraced over the next two decades. Today, the ongoing growth of the global population and—with economic development and rising consumer expectations—the increasingly great environmental impact of that population means that we may be less than one generation away from exhausting much of the biosphere's environmental buffering capacity.[13] Unless we can constrain our excessive demands on the natural world, the demographic and epidemiological transitions (faltering in some regions) will be further affected and human fulfillment will thus be eroded.

Twenty years on from the report of the World Commission on Environment and Development, we can see additional layers to the environment challenge that were little understood in the 1980s. Clearly, some fundamental changes are needed in how we live, generate energy, consume materials, and dispose of wastes. Population arithmetic will impose a further dimension of challenge: 4.8 billion in 1987; 6.7 billion in 2007; perhaps 8 billion by 2027. Beyond that, the numbers and outcomes will be influenced by what current and future "Brundtland reports" formulate, and how seriously and urgently we and our governments take their formulations and recommendations.

Notes

1. World Commission on Environment and Development, *Our Common Future* (Cambridge, UK, and New York: Cambridge University Press, 1987).

2. A. C. Kelley, "The Population Debate in Historical Perspective: Revisionism Revised," in N. Birdsall, A. C. Kelley, and S. W. Sinding, eds., *Population Matters: Demographic Change, Economic Growth, and Poverty in the Developing World* (Oxford, UK: Oxford University Press, 2001), 24–54.

3. P. McMichael, *Development and Social Change: A Global Perspective* (Thousand Oaks, California: Pine Forge Press, 2004).

4. A. J. McMichael, M. McKee, V. Shkolnikov, and T. Valkonen, "Mortality Trends and Setbacks: Global Convergence or Divergence?" *Lancet* 363, no. 9415 (2004): 1155–59; and R. Eckersley, "Is Modern Western Culture a Health Hazard?" *International Journal of Epidemiology* 35, no 5 (2006): 252–58.

5. United Nations, "Process of Preparation of the Environmental Perspective to the Year 2000 and Beyond," General Assembly Resolution 38/161, 19 December 1983.

6. WCED, note 1 above, page 1.

7. G. H. Brundtland, speech given at the launch of the WCED report, Oslo, Norway, 20 March 1987.

8. D. G. Victor, "Recovering Sustainable Development," *Foreign Affairs* 85, no. 1 (January/February 2006): 91–103.

9. WCED, note 1 above, page 98.

10. Intergovernmental Panel on Climate Change, *Climate Change. The IPCC Scientific Assessment* (Cambridge, UK: Cambridge University Press, 1990).

11. Ibid.; and C. M. Wackernagel et al., "Tracking the Ecological Overshoot of the Human Economy," *Proceedings of the National Academy of Sciences* 99, no. 14 (2002): 9266–71.

12. Worldwide Fund for Nature International (WWF), *Living Planet Report 2006* (Gland, Switzerland: WWF, 2006), http://assets.panda.org/dowloads/living_planet_report.pdf (accessed 23 Aug 2007).

13. S. Rahmstorf et al., "Recent Climate Observations Compared to Projections," *Science* 316, no. 5825 (4 May 2007): 709.

14. See R. L. Naylor et al., "The Ripple Effect: Biofuels, Food Security, and the Environment," *Environment* 49, no. 9 (November 2007): 30–43.

15. Millennium Ecosystem Assessment, *Ecosystems and Human Wellbeing. Synthesis* (Washington, DC: Island Press, 2005).

16. UN Department of Economic and Social Affairs, Population Division: http://esa.un.org/unpp/p2k0data.asp (accessed Nov 1, 2007).

17. WCED, note 1 above, page 95.

18. WCED, note 1 above, page 95. This statement has faint resonance with the ideas of the late U.S. economist Julian Simon, whose book *The Ultimate Resource* made the tendentious argument that the more people on Earth the greater the probability of occurrence of important new ideas. J. L. Simon, *The Ultimate Resource* (Princeton, NJ: Princeton University Press, 1981).

19. A. J. McMichael and C. D. Butler, "Emerging Health Issues: The Widening Challenge for Population Health Promotion," *Health Promotion International* 21, no. 1 (2006): 15–24.

20. McMichael, McKee, Shkolnikov, and Valkonen, note 4 above.

21. R. Smith, R. Beaglehole, D. Woodward, and N. Drager, eds., *Global Public Goods for Health* (Oxford: Oxford University Press, 2003).

22. M. Ezzati et al., "Rethinking the 'Diseases of Affluence' Paradigm: Global Patterns of Nutritional Risks in Relation to Economic Development," *Plos Medicine* 2, no. 5 (2005): e133.

23. Brundtland, note 7 above.

24. Kelley, note 2 above.

25. M. Campbell, J. Cleland, A. Ezeh, and N. Prata, "Return of the Population Growth Factor," *Science* 315, no. 5818 (2 February 2007): 1501–2.

ANTHONY J. MCMICHAEL is a professor at the National Centre for Epidemiology and Population Health (NCEPH) at Australia National University in Canberra. From 2001 to 2007, he was director of NCEPH, where he has led the development of a program of epidemiological research on the environmental influences on immune disorders, particularly autoimmune diseases such as multiple sclerosis. Meanwhile, he has continued his pioneering research on the health risks of global climate change, developed in conjunction with his central role in the assessment of health risks for the Intergovernmental Panel on Climate Change. His work on climate and environmental change, along with longstanding interests in social and cultural influences on patterns of health and disease, also underlie his interests in understanding the determinants of the emergence and spread of infectious diseases in this seemingly "renaissant" microbial era. He may be contacted at Tony.McMichael@anu.edu.au.

From *Environment*, January/February 2008. Reprinted by permission of the Helen Dwight Reid Educational Foundation. Published by Heldref Publications, 1319 Eighteenth St., NW, Washington, DC 20036-1802. Copyright © 2008. www.heldref.org

A Lifelong Struggle for a Generation

Global Aids Campaign International AIDS conference, Toronto: the global AIDS industry needs to think strategically to meet the challenges of the next 25 years.

ALEX DE WAAL

The global AIDS industry put on its sixteenth bi-annual show in Toronto from 13–18 August 2006. The conference theme was "Time to Deliver"—with reference to the ever-more-ambitious pledges to tackle the AIDS pandemic made by world leaders, culminating in the G8 commitment at Gleneagles in 2005 to provide universal Aids treatment by 2010. But for the 30,000 participants who thronged Toronto's Metro Convention Centre, the speeches and debates were less important than the chance to meet and network. The crowded stalls set up by the activist groups in the "Global Village" and the sleek suites of the pharmaceutical companies in the main exhibition hall showed the breadth of the constituency mobilised by the virus barely twenty-five years since the first AIDS cases were diagnosed. This was as much a global trade fair as scientific conference.

One of the great success stories of the AIDS industry has been the creation of powerful anti-retroviral drugs.

Indeed, AIDS is a global industry. International aid for AIDS topped $8bn in 2005, more than twenty times what it commanded ten years ago. By volume, that still makes it a small business in comparison to the other sectors that warrant such international gatherings. If world leaders indeed recognize AIDS as one of the greatest catastrophes of our time, that recognition is still largely rhetorical, in comparison to what is spent on arms or oil. Far, far more is spent on domestic healthcare in developed nations; more on cosmetics. But the AIDS industry is now big enough and influential enough for us to legitimately ask: What are the products that it manufactures?

A Double Achievement

The AIDS industry has had two great successes. The first—and biggest—is medicines. The international AIDS conferences began as a forum where scientists could meet to compare notes about a frightening new disease. Since the early 1980s, more has been learned about the human immunodeficiency virus than about any other pathogen in history. Anti-retroviral therapy can, properly administered, make HIV infection a chronic and treatable condition rather than a death sentence. The fact that anti-retrovirals are now accepted as a normal regimen in developed countries, available to all, shows how sky-high are the expectations of the drugs industry.

In any other age, such progress would have been regarded as miraculous. The pace of roll-out in poor countries is lagging, but is still far faster than was dreamed of even in 2001, when Western governments and United Nations agencies were still debating whether any AIDS treatment would ever be possible in sub-Saharan Africa.

The world's, and AIDS professionals', expectations are still stellar. Virologists have long been warning that the extraordinary capacity of HIV to mutate and evade the normal evolutionary pressures towards lower virulence means that we must continually develop new lines of drugs to cope with the drug-resistant strains of HIV that are sure to evolve. In 2005 there was a scare over drug-resistant HIV in New York, and resistant cases emerge regularly in other parts of the world. Meanwhile, scientific opinion is still divided over whether a vaccine will be possible, ever.

The second great success is the unprecedented way in which a fatal, sexually-transmitted infection has not been an occasion for repression and control. Historically, public-health emergencies have led to crackdowns on civil liberties, and early indications were that sex workers, migrants, gay men and drug-users would all feel the full force of the repressive state. Give governments a free hand, and we see the coercive apparatus out in force.

For example, all African armies which have the capacity to enforce compulsory HIV testing of soldiers do so, and most of them automatically discharge any soldier found to be HIV-positive. Many governments admire Cuba's highly repressive—and so far, effective—approach to controlling AIDS, through population testing and the isolation of the infected. Some public health professionals regret the way in which AIDS has been "exceptional."

For example, they argue that the individual's right to privacy has been sanctified, overriding the right of that individual's sexual partners to know his or her HIV status. Better, they assert, to have obligatory testing and partner-tracing, sacrificing some confidentiality and risking the stigmatisation of those identified as HIV-positive, in order to help stop onward transmission.

The debate on human rights, confidentiality, stigma and testing rages on without conclusion. Some of the worst-hit countries, like Botswana (more than one in four adults has HIV), have introduced routine testing, which puts the burden on the individual patient to opt out of an HIV test, which is otherwise a routine activity. But epidemiological efficacy is not the only criterion for public-health policy. What about rights and democracy? What has been the political impact of the first-ever rights-based approach to tackling an epidemic?

A Liberal Dynamic

The AIDS pandemic coincided with global liberalisation. Indeed, it's possible that the increased movement of people and the relaxation of state and social control systems that accompanied the end of state socialism in many parts of the world, and apartheid in South Africa, actually facilitated the transmission of HIV. But it's also clear that the rights-based approach has helped to entrench political liberalism. In almost every country, civil-society organisations are leading the way in defining the problem, setting up prevention and care programmes, and mobilising people living with HIV and AIDS. It is particularly marked in Africa, where NGOs are represented on the "country coordinating mechanisms" whereby the Global Fund to Fight AIDS, TB and Malaria identifies the projects it will support.

The board of the Global Fund also includes people living with HIV and Aids; Peter Piot, executive director of Unaids, regularly meets with AIDS activists. An African activist who is blocked from directly influencing her government through parliament or the ministry of health may have more success through the roundabout route of linking up with international AIDS agencies, which can bring much more direct and powerful leverage to bear on the national government.

The global AIDS industry has done superbly well in giving a platform to activists across the world. Still faced with stigmatisation and discrimination, these activists need all the help they can get. Slowly the battle for the rights of people living with HIV and Aids is being won.

A Long-Wave Event

What is less clear is whether the fight against the virus is being won. The combination of pharmaceuticals and activists has led to some immense breakthroughs in providing treatment to the afflicted. But there is much less evidence for progress on preventing new infection and on providing care and support to the tens of millions of children affected by AIDS. Although HIV prevalence rates appear to have stabilised in many African countries, there is little reason for self-congratulation—a 10% adult prevalence rate still represents an immense human tragedy. Today less than 5% of African children affected by AIDS receive any support from national governments or international agencies.

Missing are organised political interests to promote HIV prevention and assistance to children. Pharmaceutical companies have clear financial incentives in developing and selling new drugs. People living with HIV and AIDS have clear incentives in expanding cheaper treatment. Governments of highly affected countries need no special programmes to help them respond to the political threats posed by AIDS they have smartly, if often surreptitiously, made sure treatment is available for the elite.

But at the moment there's no reward to a government that cuts down the number of new HIV infections. The standard measure of HIV level in a population is prevalence—the overall number of people infected. The link between new infections and overall prevalence is a complicated one, depending on the numbers of people dying, migration rates, and technical aspects of how statistics for the prevalence rate are estimated. And if the rate of new infections begins to fall, it can take six or eight years before that registers in prevalence data—enough to switch off any politician's interest. Rapid and reliable tests for new infections are available but rarely used so the most important indicator of success or failure in tackling AIDS is simply not being measured. If we are not measuring it, we cannot reward the policies that make a difference.

Children affected by unmeasured statistics are the hidden face of the epidemic. We are moved by the 14m children orphaned, but their harrowing stories of distress are not a factor in governments' calculations. There is still no serious commitment by national governments in poor countries, or from international donors, to mobilise the kinds of resources needed to provide for the basic welfare of children in societies affected. Perhaps the time lag between action today and measurable results is simply too long to attract political leaders concerned with winning the next election.

The HIV/AIDS pandemic is a long-wave event. After a quarter of a century, it has still not reached its peak. Only when political leaders are ready to act with similar generation-long time horizons, can we expect serious action to overcome it. And only when political interests are served by such long-term actions, can we expect leaders to act. The global Aids industry has come a long way: it needs to plan for its next twenty-five years.

Reversal of Fortune
Why Preventing Poverty Beats Curing It

ANIRUDH KRISHNA

Lifting people out of poverty has become a mantra for the world's political leaders. The first U.N. Millennium Development Goal is to halve the number of people whose income is less than $1 per day, currently about 1 billion people. And, in the past decade, millions around the world have been pulled out of poverty by economic growth, effective development aid, and sheer hard work.

Four years ago, I set out to discover which countries—and which local communities—were doing the best job of ending poverty. Using a varied sample of more than 25,000 households in 200 diverse communities in India, Kenya, Peru, Uganda, and the U.S. state of North Carolina, my colleagues and I traced which households have emerged from poverty and attempted to explain their success. At first, the data were very encouraging. In 36 Ugandan communities, 370 households (almost 15 percent of the total) moved out of poverty between 1994 and 2004. In Gujarat, India, 10 percent of a sample of several thousand households emerged from poverty between 1980 and 2003. In Kenya, 18 percent of a sample of households rose out of poverty between 1980 and 2004.

Looking at these figures, one could be forgiven for feeling a sense of satisfaction. But pulling people out of impoverishment is only half the story. Our research revealed another, much darker story: In many places, more families are falling into poverty than are being lifted out. In Kenya, for example, more households, 19 percent, fell into poverty than emerged from it. Twenty-five percent of households studied in the KwaZulu-Natal province of eastern South Africa fell into poverty, but fewer than half as many, 10 percent, overcame poverty in the same period. In Bangladesh, Egypt, Peru, and every other country where researchers have conducted similar studies, the results are the same. In many places, newly impoverished citizens constitute the majority of the poor. It's a harsh fact that calls into question current policies for combating poverty.

All sorts of factors—including financial crises and currency collapse—can push people into poverty. But our research indicates that the leading culprit is poor healthcare. Tracking thousands of households in five separate countries, my colleagues and I found that health and healthcare expenses are the leading cause for people's reversal of fortune. The story of a woman from Kikoni village in Uganda is typical. She and her husband lived relatively well for many years. "Then my husband was sick for 10 years before he died, and all the money that we had with us was spent on medical charges," she said. "My children dropped out of school because we could not pay school fees. Then my husband died. I was left with a tiny piece of land. Now I cannot even get enough food to eat."

Among newly poor households in 20 villages of western Kenya, 73 percent cited ill health and high medical costs as the most important cause of their economic decline. Eighty-eight percent of people who fell into poverty in 36 villages in Gujarat placed the blame on healthcare. In Peru, 67 percent of recently impoverished people in two provinces cited ill health, inaccessible medical facilities, and high healthcare costs. When families are hit by a health crisis, it's often hard to recover. In China, one major illness typically reduces family income by 16 percent. Successive illnesses ensure an even faster spiral into lasting poverty. Surveys in several African and Asian countries show that a combination of ill health and indebtedness has sent tens of thousands of households into poverty, including many that were once affluent. The phenomenon exists in the rich world as well; half of all personal bankruptcies in the United States are due to high medical expenses.

Millions of people are living one illness away from financial disaster, and the world's aid efforts are ill-suited to the challenge. An intense focus on stimulating economic growth isn't enough. Healthcare is not automatically better or cheaper where economic growth rates have been high. In Gujarat, a state in India that has achieved high growth rates for more than a decade, affordable healthcare remains a severe problem, and thousands have fallen into poverty as a result. Healthcare in fast growing Gujarat is no better than in other, often poorer, states of India. Indeed, Gujarat ranked fourth from the bottom among 25 states in terms of proportion of state income spent on healthcare. Perversely, rapid economic growth often weakens existing social safety nets and raises the danger of backsliding. In places as diverse as rural India, Kenya, Uganda, and North Carolina, we observed how community and family support crumbles as market-based transactions overtake traditional networks.

As economic growth helps lift people out of poverty, governments must stand ready to prevent backsliding by providing affordable, accessible, and reliable healthcare. Japan's recent history offers hope that enlightened policy can prevail. At 4 percent, Japan's poverty rate is among the lowest in the world. Sustained economic growth undoubtedly helped, but so too did an entirely different set of policies. Quite early in the country's post-World War II recovery, Japanese officials recognized the critical relationship between illness, healthcare services, and poverty creation, and they responded by implementing universal healthcare as early as the 1950s.

Regrettably, that insight hasn't traveled nearly as well as Japan's many other exports. It's well past time that political leaders put as much effort into stopping the slide into poverty as they do easing the climb out of it.

ANIRUDH KRISHNA is assistant professor of public policy and political science at Duke University.

From *Foreign Policy*, May/June 2006, pp. 62–63. Copyright © 2006 by the Carnegie Endowment for International Peace. Reprinted with permission. www.foreignpolicy.com

UNIT 6

Women and Development

Unit Selections

Key Points to Consider

- Has there been progress on the women's agenda established at the 1994 International Conference on Population and Development?

- In what ways does educating girls contribute to development?

- What accounts for lagging school attendance rates for girls?

- How are girls from socially excluded groups further disadvantaged in getting an education?

- How has women's political participation in Afghanistan been increased?

Student Web Site

www.mhcls.com/online

Internet References

WIDNET: Women in Development NETwork
http://www.focusintl.com/widnet.htm
Women Watch/Regional and Country Information
http://www.un.org/womenwatch/

There is widespread recognition of the crucial role that women play in the development process. Women are critical to the success of family planning programs, bear much of the responsibility for food production, account for an increasing share of wage labor in developing countries, are acutely aware of the consequences of environmental degradation, and can contribute to the development of a vibrant, civil society and good governance. Despite their important contributions, however, women lag behind men in access to health care, nutrition, and education while continuing to face formidable social, economic, and political barriers. Women's lives in the developing world are invariably difficult. Often female children are valued less than male offspring, resulting in higher female infant and child mortality rates. In extreme cases, this undervaluing leads to female infanticide. Those females who do survive face lives characterized by poor nutrition and health, multiple pregnancies, hard physical labor, discrimination, and in some cases violence.

Clearly, women are central to any successful population policy. Evidence shows that educated women have fewer and healthier children. This connection between education and population indicates that greater emphasis should be placed on educating women. In reality, female school enrollments are lower than those of males because of state priorities, insufficient family resources that are not enough to educate both boys and girls, female socialization, and cultural factors. Although education is probably the largest single contributor to enhancing the status of women, and thereby promoting development, access to education is still limited for many women. Sixty percent of children worldwide not enrolled in schools are girls. Girls from socially excluded groups face even greater obstacles to obtaining an education. Education for women provides improved health, better wages, and greater influence in decision making, which benefits not only women but the broader society as well. Women make up a significant portion of the agricultural workforce. They are heavily involved in food production right from planting to cultivation, harvesting, and marketing. Despite their agricultural contribution, women frequently do not have adequate access to advances in agricultural technology or the benefits of extension and training programs. They are also discriminated against in land ownership. As a result, important opportunities to improve food production are lost when women are not given access to technology, training, and land ownership commensurate with their agricultural role.

The industrialization that has accompanied the globalized production has meant more employment opportunities for women, but often these are low-tech, low-wage jobs. The lower labor costs in the developing world that attract manufacturing facilities are a mixed blessing for women. Increasingly, women are recruited to fill these production jobs because wage differentials allow employers to pay women less. On the other hand, expanding opportunities for women in these positions contributes to family income. The informal sector, where jobs are small scale, more traditional, and labor-intensive, has also attracted

© Getty Images

more women. These jobs are often their only employment option, due to family responsibilities or discrimination.

Women also play a critical role in the economic expansion of developing countries. Nevertheless, women are often the first to feel the effects of an economic slowdown. The consequences of the structural adjustment programs that many developing countries have to adopt have also fallen disproportionately on women. When employment opportunities decline because of austerity measures, women lose jobs in the formal sector and face increased competition from males in the informal sector. Cuts in spending on health care and education also affect women, who already receive fewer of these benefits. Currency devaluations further erode the purchasing power of women.

Because of the gender division of labor, women are often more aware of the consequences of environmental degradation. Depletion of resources such as forests, soil, and water are much

175

more likely to be felt by women, who are responsible for collecting firewood and water, and who raise most of the crops. As a result, women are an essential component of successful environmental protection policies, but they are often overlooked in planning environmental projects.

Enhancing the status of women has been the primary focus of several international conferences. The 1994 International Conference on Population and Development (ICPD) focused attention on women's health and reproductive rights, and the crucial role that these issues play in controlling population. The 1995 Fourth World Conference on Women held in Beijing, China, proclaimed women's rights to be synonymous with human rights. These developments represent a turning point in women's struggle for equal rights, and have prompted efforts to pass legislation at the national level to protect women's rights. International conferences have not only focused attention on gender issues, but also provided additional opportunities for developing leadership and encouraging grassroots efforts to realize the goal of enhancing the status of women. A 2004 review of the women's agenda established at the 1994 ICPD showed mixed results in the evaluation of women's access to contraceptives and sex education, and in improving women's reproductive health

There are indications that women have made progress in some regions of the developing world. The election of Ellen John-Sirleaf as president of Liberia and Africa's first female head of state is the most visible indicator of a trend toward greater political involvement of women in Africa. In the Middle East, the 2002 Arab Human Development Report highlighted the extent to which women in the region lagged behind their counterparts in other parts of the world. The influence of religious conservatives threatens to limit women's political participation in Iraq, raising further concerns about whether the country can be used as a model for democratic reform in the region. While there has been some progress recently, the gap in gender equality between the Middle East and the rest of the world remains wide. There remains a wide divergence in the status of women worldwide, but the recognition of the valuable contributions they can make to society is increasing the pressure to enhance their status.

Ten Years' Hard Labour

More money and less ideology could improve the reproductive health of millions

A decade ago, the world's leaders met in Cairo at the International Conference on Population and Development (ICPD). There, they crafted a plan to achieve "reproductive health and rights for all" by 2015. That plan was wide-ranging—from more contraception and fewer maternal deaths to better education for girls and greater equality for women. But more than just setting targets, the ICPD plan also aimed to change the way those at the sharp end of making policy and delivering services thought about reproduction. It wanted to move away from a focus on family planning (and, by extension, government policies on population control) towards a broader view of sexual health, and systems and services shaped by individual needs.

Over the past week, hundreds of government officials, public-health experts and activists met in London to mark the anniversary of the ICPD and to take stock of progress towards achieving its goals. On paper, that progress has been impressive. Governments around the world have introduced legislation that reflects the ICPD's aims. But when it comes to turning policy into practice, "mixed success" is the verdict of a report card just released by Countdown 2015, a coalition of voluntary bodies involved in the field.

Take contraception, for example. According to the United Nations' Population Fund (UNFPA), 61% of married couples now use contraception, an 11% increase since 1994. This has helped push global population growth down from 82m to 76m people a year over the past decade. But in some places—particularly in sub-Saharan Africa and parts of Asia—birth rates remain high (see chart). That has spurred some governments to offer incentives to those who have fewer children, and others to inflict penalties on those who do not.

Sometimes, a high birth rate is a result of people wanting large families. But often it is due to a lack of affordable contraception. UNFPA estimates that 137m women who want to use contraception cannot obtain it. As Amare Bedada, the head of the Family Guidance Association of Ethiopia, points out, "We don't need to tell our clients about contraception. They see their plots of land diminishing, and they tell us they want to limit their family size."

Maternal health is another area where much more needs to be done. Poor women still die in huge numbers from the complica-

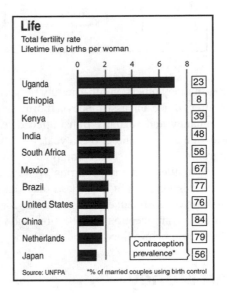

Life
Total fertility rate
Lifetime live births per woman

Country	Contraception prevalence*
Uganda	23
Ethiopia	8
Kenya	39
India	48
South Africa	56
Mexico	67
Brazil	77
United States	76
China	84
Netherlands	79
Japan	56

Source: UNFPA   *% of married couples using birth control

tions of pregnancy and childbirth. According to UNFPA, 920 women die for every 100,000 live births in sub-Saharan Africa. In Europe, by contrast, the figure is 24 (see the chart on the next page of this article). However, these numbers are, at best, only rough estimates gleaned from hospital statistics. Many women go uncounted because they never reach the health-care system for treatment in the first place.

Plenty of studies have shown what it takes to reduce maternal sickness and death. Good ante-natal health care is vital. So are cheap and simple drugs, such as oxytocin, to prevent haemorrhaging during birth. Trained midwives (or "birth attendants" as they are known in medical parlance) help, too. And so do local emergency obstetric centres that can handle complicated deliveries. Some countries, such as Sri Lanka, have managed to cut maternal mortality by careful spending on such measures. The challenge is to translate these successes to other places.

Yet another subject that needs to be tackled more effectively is youth sex. The largest generation of teenagers in history—a whopping 1.3 billion 10–19-year-olds—is now making its sexual debut. How it behaves, and what it learns, is crucial.

The ICPD plan was the first international agreement to acknowledge the sexual and reproductive rights of teenagers. A few countries, such as Panama, have introduced laws to safeguard

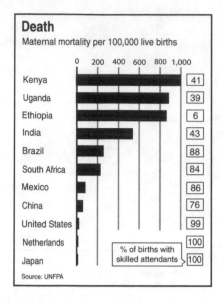

Death
Maternal mortality per 100,000 live births

	% of births with skilled attendants
Kenya	41
Uganda	39
Ethiopia	6
India	43
Brazil	88
South Africa	84
Mexico	86
China	76
United States	99
Netherlands	100
Japan	100

Source: UNFPA

some of these. In many others, youth-friendly programmes have sprung up to offer advice and assistance on thorny issues such as unwanted pregnancy and sexually transmitted diseases—now soaring worldwide at 340m infections a year.

Such programmes, of course, are complicated by fierce—if probably futile—battles in many countries over whether young people should be having sex at all. These play out in international skirmishes over abstinence versus condoms for the young, parental consent to contraception and abortion, and what, if any, sex education should be provided by the state.

Sex and Money

One significant obstacle to tackling these problems is money, or rather the lack of it. Ten years ago, the ICPD estimated the cost of implementing its recommended programmes at $18.5 billion by 2005—or $23.7 billion in today's dollars. The goal was to mobilise one-third of that money from rich donors, and the rest from developing countries themselves. But current spending is well below the mark.

Few poor countries have earmarked enough of their budgets to meet their citizens' reproductive-health needs. Nor have donors lived up to expectations. In 2003, they spent an estimated $3.1 billion on reproductive health. Although contributions have increased over recent years, with a few European countries, such as the Netherlands, chipping in more, and private donors, such as the Gates Foundation, entering the field, this is still far off even the inflation-devalued $6.1 billion expected from donors by 2005.

Reproduction, it seems, is no longer a sexy subject. As Steve Sinding, the head of the International Planned Parenthood Federation (IPPF), points out, donor interest in the past was stimulated largely by fears of a population crisis. When the Cairo Conference reframed the issues in terms of women's health and reproductive rights, that demographic rationale was lost, taking funding with it.

Moreover, there are other causes competing for international funding, most notably AIDS. At the time of the Cairo Confer-

ence, 20m people were infected with HIV, the virus that causes AIDS. Today, that number has doubled. Indeed, AIDS threatens to derail the ICPD strategy. For, although billions of dollars are now pouring in to fight the disease, much of this money is going into AIDS-specific programmes that do not address reproductive health more broadly.

As Nafis Sadik, a former head of UNFPA and now the UN secretary-general's special envoy for HIV in Asia, observes, ten years ago those working in family planning shied away from the field of HIV, with its heavy burden of social stigma. Today, the roles are reversed, as reproductive health is engulfed in a storm of religious and political controversy. One consequence is that organisations concerned with fighting AIDS are failing to make use of valuable infrastructure and expertise already on the ground in places where the disease hits hardest. Given that more than half of HIV infections in sub-Saharan Africa are among women, and that for many African women family-planning services are their main contact with the formal health-care system, such services need to be drafted into the wider battle against HIV. Many family-planning clinics already offer HIV testing and counselling, as well as condoms (against the double whammy of unwanted pregnancy and HIV infection), and also a broad based message of sexual health.

What the field of reproductive health lacks in resources, however, it makes up in ideology. Over the past ten years, battles have broken out between contending views of sexuality, pitting religious conservatives—primus inter pares, the Vatican—against social liberals. The fight has become particularly fierce since the election of George W. Bush as America's president. Mr Bush's socially conservative views are reflected in the way America, the world's leading donor for reproductive health, spends its money at home and abroad.

Breeding Trouble

The main battles are over abortion. Austin Ruse, the president of the Catholic Family and Human Rights Institute (C-FAM), an American Christian lobby group, argues that the shift in talk from fertility control to reproductive rights and services is just code for making abortion universally available. He regards this as wrong, and believes that the ICPD plan of action and those agencies which support it—particularly UNFPA—should be opposed at every turn by a growing coalition of "pro-family" groups worldwide. "Over the next five years, I see everything coming our way, especially on the question of abortion," says Mr Ruse.

UNFPA, not surprisingly, has a different view. Thoraya Obaid, its head, reckons that those who oppose the ICPD plan of action are not just against legalising abortion, but are fighting against women's rights in general. She points to the text of the plan, which states that abortion should never be promoted as a form of family planning and that women should be helped to avoid abortion through better access to contraception. (It also says that those who have sought abortions are entitled to the best possible medical treatment to deal with the complications.)

All sound stuff, but trouble lies in the plan's statement that abortion policy should be up to national governments to decide.

Since 1994, more than a dozen countries have liberalised their laws on abortion (with a couple of countries tightening them up). But none of this comes without a fight, often led by the Catholic Church. Kenya has seen a particularly nasty debate over the past six months. There have been street protests, graphic television "docudramas" showing the perils of abortion, and even the arrests of health-care workers who are alleged to have performed more than a dozen abortions whose fetuses recently ended up in a ditch outside Nairobi. The government, which was looking at its abortion laws as part of a broader constitutional review, has made no changes to the current provision, which bans abortion unless the mother's life is at stake.

In many developing countries, Christian anti-abortion groups such as America's Human Life International—a sister organisation to C-FAM—have been pitching in to help organise resistance to changes in abortion laws. But American officials have entered the fray as well. Delegates to regional meetings held in Latin America during the past year to re-affirm their commitment to the ICPD plan of action have complained about pressure from American officials to reject the plan's calls for broad-based reproductive rights and services.

While pressure by the Catholic Church and other opponents of legal abortion can shape official policy, Tim Black, the head of Marie Stopes International (MSI), a voluntary organisation providing reproductive services, argues it does little to stop women seeking abortions, legal or illegal. Surveys from hospitals in Ethiopia, Uganda and Kenya suggests that anywhere from 20-50% of maternal deaths are due to complications resulting from unsafe backstreet abortions. But these numbers are challenged by the opponents of abortion, who argue that it is a rare phenomenon in the developing world, and that legalising it will make it more common.

The American government's views on abortion are expressed in the Mexico City Policy, which was re-introduced by Mr Bush in 2001. This policy, first implemented by Ronald Reagan in 1984, forbids American government funding of foreign organisations which in any way promote, endorse or advocate abortion. American law has banned foreign assistance for the direct performance of abortions since 1973. But the Mexico City Policy, or "Global Gag Rule" as its critics often refer to it, means that groups which want to perform abortions with money from other sources must also toe the United States' line, or else forfeit American assistance.

Opponents of this policy argue that it imposes on foreigners restrictions which are unconstitutional in America. Indeed, Frances Kissling, the head of Catholics for a Free Choice, an American voluntary organisation which opposes banning abortion, argues that Mr Bush is flexing his conservative muscles abroad—and therefore appeasing his supporters at home—precisely because he cannot deliver a domestic anti-abortion agenda. Last week, for example, a court in New York declared unconstitutional a ban on so-called partial-birth abortion that Mr Bush signed into law in 2003.

Several prominent family-planning organisations, such as MSI and the IPPF, have refused to agree to the Mexico City Policy, saying it compromises their ability to offer women in poor countries the full range of services available in the rich world. In Ethiopia, for example, these groups have had to trim their services and shelve expansion plans as a result of losing both money and contraceptive supplies from the American government.

Such arguments, however, cut little ice with Jeanne Head, the United Nations representative for National Right to Life, an American anti-abortion group. As she puts it, "if they refuse these funds and they can't keep functioning, then they don't care about these women, they only care about abortion. I think the blame lies on the organisations, not on the US government."

John Kerry has said he will rescind the Mexico City Policy if elected. The Democratic candidate has also promised to restore American funding to UNFPA. This has been withheld by the Bush administration for the past three years under a piece of legislation called the Kemp-Kasten amendment. This amendment authorises the president to restrict funding to any group that "supports or participates in the management of a programme of coercive abortion or involuntary sterilisation."

The White House accuses UNFPA of abetting coercive reproductive practices in China—a claim that UNFPA denies. Several international delegations, including ones from Britain's parliament and the American State Department, have investigated UNFPA's activities in China and failed to find evidence to support such allegations. On the contrary, they argue that where UNFPA operates, policies in China are improving. But these findings are contested. The Bush administration says UNFPA has yet to mend its ways, and refuses to pay the $34m appropriated by Congress. The agency says it has managed to fill the gap this year, from big donors such as Britain, which is raising its annual contribution to £20m ($36m), and tiny ones such as Afghanistan, which chipped in $100.

But making up the money is the easy part. Today's battles over abortion, abstinence and condoms are casting a pall over the field, and complicating what is already a formidable task. Making sex safer and reproduction less risky in the 21st century requires all the tools to hand. Policies that restrict people's choices should not be a fact of life.

Educating Girls, Unlocking Development

"Compelling evidence, accumulated over the past 20 years . . . , has led to an almost universal recognition of the importance of focusing on girls' education as part of broader development policy."

RUTH LEVINE

One of the most important public policy goals in the developing world is the expansion and improvement of education for girls. Vital in its own right for the realization of individual capabilities, the education of girls has the potential to transform the life chances of the girls themselves, their future families, and the societies in which they live. Girls with at least a primary school education are healthier and wealthier when they grow up and their future children have much greater opportunities than they otherwise would; even national economic outcomes appear to be positively influenced by expanded girls' education.

Unlike some development outcomes that depend on multiple factors outside the control of policy makers (either in developing countries or among donor nations), significant improvement in girls' education can be achieved through specific government actions. Expansion of basic education, making school infrastructure and curriculum more girl-friendly, and conditional cash transfers and scholarships to overcome household barriers have all been used to improve key outcomes, with demonstrable success. Lessons from regions that have made rapid advances with girls' education, and from programs that have introduced successful financing and teaching innovations, can be applied to accelerate progress.

While public policy can make the difference, policies that ignore important gender-related constraints to education at the primary and, particularly, at the postprimary educational levels can have the opposite effect, reinforcing existing patterns of gender discrimination and exclusion. Those patterns are often deep-seated. Families in many societies traditionally have valued schooling less for girls than for boys. In most households, the domestic workload falls more to females than to males, leaving less time for school. If families are struggling to find income, the demand for girls' help around the house (or in wage labor) may increase. Many parents believe that the return on educational investments varies according to gender—particularly if girls, when they marry, leave their parents' households to join the husbands'.

When girls in developing countries do enroll in school, they frequently encounter gender-based discrimination and inadequate educational resources. Large numbers of girls in sub-Saharan Africa drop out, for example, when they reach puberty and the onset of menstruation simply because schools lack latrines, running water, or privacy. Parental concerns about girls' security outside the home can limit schooling where girls are vulnerable in transit and male teachers are not trusted. And in some countries, cultural aversion to the education of girls lingers. Afghanistan's Taliban insurgents, who believe that girls' education violates Islamic teachings, have succeeded in closing numerous schools, sometimes by beheading teachers. Afghanistan is an extreme case, but a reminder nonetheless of the challenges that remain on the path toward achieving the high payoffs from girls' education.

The Benefits

Why is the schooling of girls so critical? Education in general is among the primary means through which societies reproduce themselves; correspondingly, changing the educational opportunities for particular groups in society—girls and minority groups—is perhaps the single most effective way to achieve lasting transformations. A considerable body of evidence has shown that the benefits of educating a girl are manifested in economic and social outcomes: her lifetime health, labor force participation, and income; her (future) children's health and nutrition; her community's and her nation's productivity. Most important, education can break the intergenerational transmission of poverty.

Female participation in the formal labor market consistently increases with educational attainment, as it does for males. In at least some settings, the returns to education of girls are superior to those for boys. Several studies have shown that primary schooling increases lifetime earnings by as much as 20 percent for girls—

higher than for their brothers. If they stay in secondary school, the returns from education are 25 percent or higher.

The inverse relationship between women's education and fertility is perhaps the best studied of all health and demographic phenomena. The relationship generally holds across countries and over time, and is robust even when income is taken into account. Completion of primary school is strongly associated with later age at marriage, later age at first birth, and lower lifetime fertility. A study of eight sub-Saharan countries covering the period from 1987 to 1999 found that girls' educational attainment was the best predictor of whether they would have their first births during adolescence.

Another study examined surveys across the developing world to compare female education and fertility by region. The higher the level of female education, the lower desired family size, and the greater the success in achieving desired family size. Further, each additional year of a mother's schooling cuts the expected infant mortality rate by 5 to 10 percent.

Maternal education is a key determinant of children's attainment. Multiple studies have found that a mother's level of education has a strong positive effect on daughters' enrollment—more than on sons and significantly more than the effect of fathers' education on daughters. Studies from Egypt, Ghana, India, Kenya, Malaysia, Mexico, and Peru all find that mothers with a basic education are substantially more likely to educate their children, especially their daughters.

Children's health also is strongly associated with mothers' education. In general, this relationship holds across countries and time, although the confounding effect of household income has complicated the picture. One study, for instance, compared 17 developing countries, examining the relationship between women's education and their infants' health and nutritional status. It found the existence of an education-related health advantage in most countries, although stronger for postneonatal health than for neonatal health. (In some countries the "education advantage" did appear to be eliminated when controlling for other dimensions of socioeconomic status.)

Other studies have found clear links between women's school attainment and birth and death rates, and between women's years of schooling and infant mortality. A 1997 study for the World Bank, which focused on Morocco, found that a mother's schooling and functional literacy predicted her child's height-for-age, controlling for other socioeconomic factors.

Although the causal links are harder to establish at the macrolevel, some researchers have made the attempt, with interesting results. For example, in a 100-country study, researchers showed that raising the share of women with a secondary education by 1 percent is associated with a 0.3 percent increase in annual per capita income growth. In a 63-country study, more productive farming because of increased female education accounts for 43 percent of the decline in malnutrition achieved between 1970 and 1995.

In short (and with some important nuances set aside), girls' education is a strong contributor to the achievement of multiple key development outcomes: growth of household and national income, health of women and children, and lower and wanted fertility. Compelling evidence, accumulated over the past 20 years using both quantitative and qualitative methods, has led to an almost universal recognition of the importance of focusing on girls' education as part of broader development policy.

The Trends

Given the widespread understanding about the value of girls' education, the international community and national governments have established ambitious goals for increased participation in primary education and progress toward gender parity at all levels. The Millennium Development Goals (MDG), approved by all member states of the United Nations in 2000, call for universal primary education in all countries by 2015, as well as gender parity at all levels by 2015.

There is good news to report. Impressive gains have been made toward higher levels of education enrollment and completion, and girls have been catching up rapidly with their brothers. As primary schooling expands, girls tend to be the main beneficiaries because of their historically disadvantaged position.

The rate of primary school completion also has improved faster for girls than for boys, again in large part because they had more to gain at the margins. Across all developing countries, girls' primary school completion increased by 17 percent, from 65 to 76 percent, between 1990 and 2000. During the same period, boys' primary completion increased by 8 percent, from 79 to 85 percent. Global progress is not matched, however, in every region. In sub-Saharan Africa, girls did only slightly better between 1990 and 2000, with primary completion increasing from 43 to 46 percent. (The primary completion rate for boys went in the opposite direction, from 57 to 56 percent.)

The overall good news about girls' progress must be tempered by realism, and a recognition that the goal is not to have boys' and girls' educational attainment "equally bad." Today, a mere nine years from the MDG deadline, it is clear that the important improvements over the past several decades in the developing world—in many instances, unprecedented rates of increase in primary school enrollment and completion—still leave a large number of poor countries very far from the target. While girls are making up ground rapidly, in many of the poorest countries the achievements on improved gender parity must be seen in the context of overall low levels of primary school completion.

An estimated 104 million to 121 million children of primary school age across the globe are not in school, with the worst shortfalls in Africa and South Asia. Completion of schooling is a significant problem. While enrollment has been increasing, many children drop out before finishing the fifth grade. In Africa, for example, just 51 percent of children (46 percent of girls) complete primary school. In South Asia, 74 percent of children (and just 63 percent of girls) do so.

Low levels of enrollment and completion are concentrated not only in certain regions but also among certain segments of the population. In every country completion rates are lowest for children from poor households. In Western and Central Africa, the median grade completed by the bottom 40 percent of the income distribution is zero, because less than half of poor children complete even the first year of school.

The education income gap also exacerbates gender disparities. In India, for example, the gap between boys and girls from the richest households is 2.5 percent, but the difference for children from the poorest households is 24 percent.

Girls are catching up quickly in most countries, but the level they are catching up to is still quite low.

In some countries the main reason for low educational attainment is that children do not enroll in school. In Bangladesh, Benin, Burkina Faso, Ivory Coast, India, Mali, Morocco, Niger, and Senegal, more than half of children from the bottom 40 percent of the income distribution never even enroll. Elsewhere, particularly in Latin America, enrollment may be almost universal, but high repetition and dropout rates lead to low completion rates. In both cases poor students are much more likely not to complete school.

In many countries the rural/urban education gap is a key factor explaining education differentials. In Mozambique, the rural completion rate is 12 percent, while at the national level 26 percent of children complete school. Burkina Faso, Guinea, Madagascar, Niger, and Togo all demonstrate a similar pattern. In rural areas, the gender gap in completion is pronounced in Africa: in Benin, Burkina Faso, Guinea, Madagascar, Mozambique, and Niger, a mere 15 percent of girls who start primary school make it to the end.

Policy makers increasingly are recognizing the importance of addressing the special needs and vulnerabilities of marginal populations, even in relatively well-off countries with education levels that, on average, look quite good. As my colleagues Maureen Lewis and Marlaine Lockheed at the Center for Global Development highlight in a forthcoming book, girls who are members of marginalized groups—the Roma in Eastern Europe, the indigenous populations in Central America and elsewhere, the underprivileged castes and tribes in India—suffer a double disadvantage. Low educational attainment for girls is an obvious mechanism through which historical disadvantage is perpetuated. In Laos, for example, more than 90 percent of men in the dominant Laotai group are literate, while only 30 percent of the youngest cohort of women belonging to excluded rural ethnic groups can read and write.

Beyond the primary school enrollment and completion trends, a complex problem is the quality of education. Although measurement of learning outcomes is spotty at best, analyses of internationally comparable assessments of learning achievement in mathematics, reading, and science indicate that most developing countries rank far behind the industrialized nations. This is all the more of concern because the tests are taken by the children in school who, in low-enrollment countries, are the equivalent in relative terms to the top performers in the high-enrollment developed nations. The data on national examinations is equally alarming. Student performance on national exams in South Asian and African countries shows major gaps in acquisition of knowledge and skills.

Thus, the picture of progress and gaps is a complex one: rapid improvements relative to historical trends, but far off the ideal mark in the poorest countries. Girls are catching up quickly in most countries, but the level they are catching up to is still quite low. In many nations, the "lowest hanging fruit" has already been reached; for all children, and for girls in particular, the ones now out of school come from the most economically and socially disadvantaged backgrounds, and will be the hardest to reach. Finally, even among those children in school, evidence about poor learning outcomes should be cause for alarm.

The Challenges

The central imperative for improving educational opportunities and outcomes for girls in the low enrollment countries, including in sub-Saharan Africa and parts of South Asia, is to improve overall access and the quality of primary schooling. In doing so, planners and policy makers should ensure that they are not perpetuating barriers to girls' participation.

Getting to universal primary education (either enrollment or the more ambitious goal of completion) in sub-Saharan Africa and South Asia will require large-scale expansion in physical infrastructure, the number of teachers, and teaching/learning materials. Moreover, it will require fundamental improvements in the education institutions: more attention to learning outcomes rather than enrollment numbers, greater incentives for quality teaching, and more responsiveness to parents. This is a huge agenda. The donor and international technical community can support it, but it must be grounded in the political commitment of national and subnational governments.

Secondary to the "more and better education for all" agenda, and of particular relevance in countries that have already made significant progress so that most children go to school, is the need to understand and address the needs of particular disadvantaged groups, where gender differentials are especially pronounced. Beyond the efforts to reach children from poor and rural households, public policy makers need to understand and pay attention to ethnic and linguistic minorities, reaching them with tailored approaches rather than simply an expansion of the types of educational opportunities provided to the majority population. In addressing this challenge, policy makers must accept that reaching these key populations implies higher unit costs, as well as the adoption of potentially controversial measures, such as bilingual curriculum.

Finally, success in moving close to universal primary school enrollment generates its own new challenges. As more children complete primary school, the private benefits, in higher wages, decline (though the social benefits remain high). Private rates of return—perceived and real—cease to be seen as much of a reason for sending children to primary school, unless there is access to postprimary education. In addition, both the expansion of the existing education systems in many developing countries and the "scaling-up" of other public sector functions (such as health services, water management, and general public administration) require a larger cadre of educated and trained workers, the products of postprimary education. For these reasons, attention must be given to expanded opportunities for girls at the secondary level.

While international attention and goal-setting have been directed almost exclusively at the primary level, and the donor community has been persuaded by arguments about greater economic returns from primary education and the potentially regressive effects of investments at the secondary level, a large agenda remains unattended. It is at the secondary level that many of the microeconomic, health, and fertility outcomes of girls' education are fully realized. And common sense alone suggests that the large (and growing) cohort of children moving through primary schooling will create unsustainable pressures for postprimary education opportunities. If those are severely rationed, as they are in much of sub-Saharan Africa, the negative feedback to parents who sacrificed to send their children through primary school may be profound. Sorting out the design, financing, and institutional arrangements for effective secondary schooling—that is also responsive to labor market demand—is an essential part of good policy making today.

The Way Forward

Beyond general expansion of enrollment, governments can get out-of-school children into school by crafting specific interventions to reach them, and by increasing educational opportunities (formal and informal) for girls and women. In designing these initiatives, success depends on understanding and taking into account powerful demand-side influences that may constrain girls' school participation.

Specific interventions have been shown, in some settings, to get hard-to-reach children into school. These include eliminating school fees, instituting conditional cash transfers, using school feeding programs as an incentive to attend school, and implementing school health programs to reduce absenteeism. Several interventions have proved particularly successful where girls' participation is low. These include actions that increase security and privacy for girls (for example, ensuring that sanitation facilities are girl-friendly), as well as those that reduce gender-stereotyping in curriculum and encourage girls to take an active role in their education.

While few rigorous evaluations have been undertaken, many experts suggest that literacy programs for uneducated mothers may help increase school participation by their children. Adult literacy programs may be particularly useful in settings where there are pockets of undereducated women, such as ethnic or indigenous communities.

It is tempting for policy makers to focus on specific programmatic investments. But sustained improvements in education are impossible to achieve without improving the way in which key institutions in the sector function, and without increasing parental involvement in decisions affecting their children's education. Many countries with poorly performing educational systems suffer from institutional weaknesses, including low management capacity, nontransparent resource allocation and accounting practices, and substandard human resources policies and practices. Incentive structures that fail to reward good performance create and reinforce the most deleterious characteristics of weak institutions.

Parents who are well informed of policies and resource allocations in the education sector and who are involved in decisions regarding their children's schooling exert considerable influence and help contribute solutions. Involved communities are able to articulate local school needs, hold officials accountable, and mobilize local resources to fill gaps when the government response is inadequate.

In Benin, Burkina Faso, Guinea, Madagascar, Mozambique, and Niger, a mere 15 percent of girls who start primary school make it to the end.

A Modest Proposal

Donor agencies have been at the leading edge of the dialogue about the importance of girls' education, often providing the financial support, research, and political stimulus that may be lacking in countries that have more than their hands full with the basics of "Education for All." There is a broad consensus in the international donor community about the value of girls' education, and innovations have been introduced through donor-funded programs under the auspices of UNICEF, the World Food Program, the US Agency for International Development, and other key agencies. These have been valuable contributions, and have supported the work of champions at the national and local levels.

The donor community could come together now to accelerate progress in a very particular way. Working with both governments and nongovernmental organizations in countries where specific excluded groups—ethnic and/or linguistic minorities—have much poorer education outcomes, donors could finance the design, introduction, and rigorous evaluation of targeted programs to improve access to appropriate educational opportunities, with a particular emphasis (if warranted by the baseline research) on the needs and characteristics of girls. While different bilateral and multilateral donors could take the lead in funding specific types of programs or working in particular countries on the challenge of the "doubly disadvantaged," a shared learning agenda could be coordinated across agencies to generate much more than the spotty anecdotes and case studies on which we currently depend.

The learning agenda would include three components: first, the enduring questions to be examined—for example, determining the most effective strategies to improve learning outcomes among children who come from households where the language spoken is not the language of instruction; second, the use of methods that permit observed results to be attributed to the program; and third, the features that will ensure maximum credibility of the evaluations, such as independence, dissemination of results (whether the findings are favorable or not), and wide sharing of the data for reanalysis.

Just as education can transform individuals' lives, learning what works can transform the debates in development policy. The beneficiaries in developing countries would include not only girls who receive the education they deserve and need, but also families and communities and future generations thereby lifted over time out of poverty.

RUTH LEVINE is director of programs and a senior fellow at the Center for Global Development.

Getting All Girls into School

New ways are needed to educate "excluded girls" in developing countries.

MAUREEN A. LEWIS AND MARLAINE E. LOCKHEED

Since 1960, primary school enrollment rates in the developing world have risen steeply for boys and girls, with girls' participation converging with that of boys in most countries. Yet UNESCO (2006) recently estimated that 43 million school-age girls are not enrolled in school, many more complete fewer than six years of schooling, and a gap between boys and girls remains in some countries. This gap is due overwhelmingly to the lag in schooling of socially excluded groups, often minority groups that are on the margins of society (see box and table) and in which girls are at a distinct disadvantage relative to boys. Indeed, we estimate that approximately 70 percent of these out-of-school girls come from such groups.

Where are these out-of-school girls? By far the greatest number are in sub-Saharan Africa (47 percent) and South Asia (25 percent), followed by East Asia and the Pacific (11 percent); the Middle East and North Africa (9 percent); and Latin America and the Caribbean, Eastern Europe and Central Asia, and North America and Western Europe (all close to 3 percent). However, the Latin American and Caribbean region scores highest when the focus is on the percentage of out-of-school girls coming from excluded groups (see Chart 1).

The educational consequences for the socially excluded—girls in particular—are real. They range from teachers ignoring students in class to the destruction of schools and violence against teachers and communities. Compounding the problem, socially excluded groups are often less likely to send their daughters to school and more likely to allow their daughters than their sons to drop out early.

Over the past decade, much has been learned about how to reach poor children and those from excluded groups. Most of this experience is from developed and middle-income developing countries. Programs have been designed that raise enrollments, sustain attendance, and equalize learning outcomes of excluded children. Similarly, much is known about how to reach girls. But relatively little is known about how to reach excluded girls specifically. This article highlights some of the lessons from our recent Center for Global Development study, which looks at why girls from socially excluded groups are not in school and what can be done about it.

Who's Excluded and Why?

Socially excluded groups are population subgroups that are prevented by discrimination and indifference in their own countries from receiving the social rights and protection meant for all citizens. These groups—ethnic minorities, isolated clans, and groups in which the majority language is not predominant—are marginalized for various reasons:

- Stigmatization at the hands of the majority population, such as a history of slavery (blacks in Brazil, Cuba, and the United States) or dispossession of a homeland (native peoples of Canada and the United States).
- Differences in ethnic group, language, and religion, such as the hill tribes in Laos and indigenous groups in Latin America.
- Low status, whereby excluded groups are subordinated in the social hierarchy to the majority population, such as the Roma in Europe and lower-caste groups in India and Nepal.
- Involuntary minority status (in contrast to immigrant groups that accept minority status voluntarily in exchange for economic opportunity in the labor market).

Source: Meerman (2005).

The Extent of the Problem

To begin with, it is helpful to think of countries as highly homogeneous (like South Korea and Tunisia, which have a single ethnic group with a common language and a shared cultural heritage) or heterogeneous—with multiple ethnic groups that speak different languages and often have distinct cultures. In the latter group, communities that are "different" from the mainstream society and economy tend to become excluded, and it is the parents in these communities who are likely to keep their children out of school, in contrast to parents in majority communities, who are increasingly sending both boys and girls to school.

Who They Are

Excluded groups differ across regions and countries.

Region	Who they are
Sub-Saharan Africa	Populations other than the dominant tribe
South Asia	India's dalits, lower castes, and tribes; rural tribes in Pakistan; lower castes in Nepal; rural populations in Afghanistan
Middle East and North Africa	Berbers, rural populations
Latin America and Caribbean	Indigenous and Afro-Latino populations
East Asia and Pacific	Hill Tribes; Muslim minorities; other ethnic minorities
Eastern Europe and Central Asia/ Commonwealth of Independent States	Roma; Turkey's rural populations

Source: Lewis and Lockheed (2006).

(excluded girls as estimated share of all girls out of school, percent)

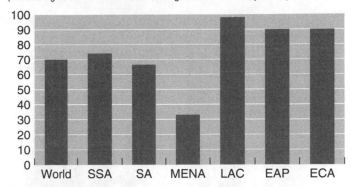

Chart 1   Not Even Enrolled in School.   Most out-of-school girls come from socially excluded groups.

Source: Lewis and Lockheed (2006).
Notes: SSA = Sub-Saharan Africa, SA = South Asia, MENA = Middle East and North Africa, LAC = Latin America and the Caribbean, EAP = East Asia and the Pacific, ECA = Europe and Central Asia.

(average year of schooling)

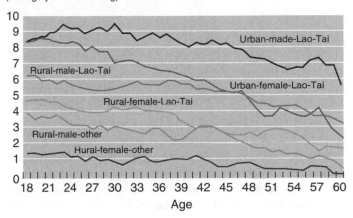

Chart 2   Less Schooling for Excluded Girls.   Rural tribal girls in Laos complete far less schooling than urban majority children.

Source: Lewis and Lockheed (2006).
Notes: The figures are on a three-age-moving average. The urban non-Lao-Tai are too small a group to include.

Why do minority parents keep children at home? The reasons are complex and many. They include a general resistance to change; a desire to retain a separate ethnic identity; a lack of interest in what schools offer; a worry about discrimination and mistreatment (children might be beaten or simply sidelined); a need for child labor and apprenticeships within the family; the direct costs of fees, books, and uniforms; limited employment opportunities upon graduation; low economic returns to those who have attended school; a lack of accessible and acceptable schools; and concerns for safety (especially for adolescent girls). And minority communities are more likely to educate boys than girls because boys have better labor market opportunities, and girls in many societies are "married away" and join their husband's family. Moreover, when excluded children do attend school, they are more likely to drop out and less likely to complete primary school.

Although concrete data are available for relatively few countries, the following examples give a sense of the extent and degree of the problem of girls' exclusion.

- In India, 37 percent of girls aged 7–14 belonging to the lowest castes or tribes do not attend school, compared with 26 percent of majority girls of the same age. School attendance for tribal girls is 9 percentage points below that of tribal boys.
- In Laos, Hill Tribe girls from rural communities complete fewer than two years of school, whereas majority Lao-Tai girls from urban communities complete eight years (see Chart 2).
- In Guatemala, indigenous girls are the least likely to have ever enrolled in primary school (see Chart 3), and

(percent enrolled)

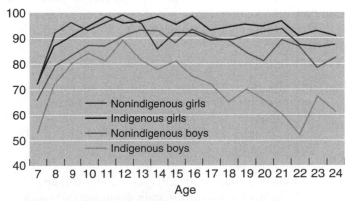

Chart 3   Falling through the Cracks.   Indigenous girls in Guatemala are least likely to have ever been enrolled in school.

Source: Lewis and Lockheed (2006).

185

(reported test scores, 2000)

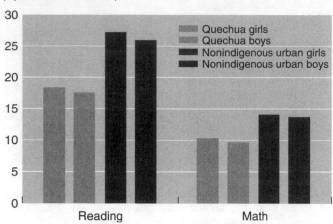

Chart 4   Lower Achievement of the Excluded. In Peru, rural Quechua children perform far worse in school than nonindigenous children in urban areas.

Source: Lewis and Lockheed (2006).

only 26 percent of indigenous non-Spanish-speaking girls complete primary school, compared with 62 percent of Spanish-speaking girls.
• In the Slovak Republic, only 9 percent of Roma girls compared with 54 percent of Slovak girls attend secondary school.

But all available evidence suggests that, once in school, excluded girls perform as well as, or even better than, excluded boys at the primary level (although the achievement levels of excluded children as a whole lag behind those of majority children). This difference between girls' and boys' performance holds true in industrial countries, where girls outpace boys in schooling completion among the majority population. It also holds true among minority groups—the Maori in New Zealand and African-Americans and indigenous groups in the United States—once concerns about language, culture, and treatment in schools have been addressed and access to quality schools has improved. Most studies in developing and transition countries do not disaggregate achievement results, but some country studies yield encouraging findings on girls' achievement:

• In Peru, the fifth-grade reading and mathematics scores of rural Quechua girls were no different from those of rural Quechua boys, although the performance of Quechua children was substantially lower than that of nonindigenous urban children (see Chart 4).
• In Ecuador, indigenous girls scored higher than indigenous boys on fifth-grade mathematics tests, with scores nearly as high as those of nonindigenous children.

Reaching and Teaching Excluded Girls

We infer from what we have learned about reaching poor and excluded children that getting and keeping excluded girls in school requires different approaches and entails higher costs. Cultural variations, linguistic differences, and girls' special needs (for example, safety and hygiene) drive up costs because they require new methods tailored to each group. Investment on two fronts is essential for enrolling and retaining excluded children in general, and girls in particular.

First, many countries still lack good-quality educational opportunities for all students. Thus, *the first line of attack is to improve the quality of schooling* through three key actions:

Make education policies more fair. Policies that appear fair may be subtly biased against girls from excluded groups. For example, policies requiring use of a majority language in school may be particularly disadvantageous to girls from excluded groups because they often have less exposure than boys to the majority language. Similarly, policies that require either single-sex schools or coeducation may limit girls' opportunities, when, as a result of such policies, only schools for boys are established, as in some areas of Pakistan, or parents restrict older girls' attendance in coeducational schools.

Expand schooling options. Parents' concern for their daughters' safety may mean that nearby community schools and informal alternative schools can attract and retain girls from excluded groups more easily than formal schools located at a distance. For example, in Rajasthan, India, community schools that employed paraprofessional teachers, allowed the community to select and supervise teachers, and hired part-time workers to escort girls from excluded groups to school had higher enrollment, attendance, and test scores than public schools. Preschools can help excluded children transition more easily to formal schools. In Brazil, Turkey, Bolivia, and India, preschool programs involving both mothers and children from excluded groups have reduced primary school dropout rates and boosted achievement. Compensatory programs also help. Brazil, India, and Spain have offered targeted, compensatory in-school or after-school programs to help disadvantaged students stay in school, raising their achievement. In India, where young women were hired to tutor children who were lagging behind, the largest achievement gains were recorded for the most economically disadvantaged children. Radio, television, and computers can also expand opportunities for girls, particularly those kept home after primary school.

Improve the physical environment and instructional materials. Girls are less likely than boys to enroll in, and more likely to drop out of, schools that are in poor physical condition (for example, with leaky roofs), whose teachers are often absent, and with inadequate materials. And those who stay in school under these circumstances—especially if only the majority language is taught—tend to perform more poorly. In fact, studies show that school quality matters more for excluded girls than for boys and children from mainstream families because minority parents often have higher standards for the state of the school and the quality—and often gender—of the teachers. What can be done? One solution lies in offering bilingual education. Other solutions encompass targeting additional resources to schools where average performance is low, repairing school buildings, strengthening the curriculum, and hiring knowledgeable teachers, something that cannot be taken for granted.

The *second line of attack is to create incentives for households to send girls to school*. Evidence on what incentives might work is less clear and needs more focused evaluation.

Offer conditional cash transfers. Such transfers help households defray some education costs, tying assistance payments to desirable behaviors. They are often challenging to administer but do motivate families to send children to school. Programs in Bangladesh, Ecuador, and Mexico, among others, have been successful, although their specific impact on excluded groups has not been assessed. A conditional cash transfer program in Ecuador boosted school enrollment overall by 3.7 percentage points but did not benefit girls or minority students in a significant way.

Offer scholarships and stipends for girls. Secondary school scholarship programs offer girls financing and encouragement to stay in school and compensate families for the direct and indirect costs of education. They have been highly effective in several countries, notably Bangladesh, where scholarships for girls increased their enrollment to twice the national average for females. Stipend programs also compensate parents for the cost of schooling but are tied to such school inputs as uniforms, books, materials, and transportation. Even the opportunity to earn a scholarship has been found to boost student achievement.

Introduce school feeding programs. Various feeding programs are associated with higher enrollment and attendance. In Kenya, free meals raised attendance in program schools 30 percent relative to schools without free meals, and test scores rose substantially. But rigorous evaluations found that the feeding programs benefited boys rather than girls and did little to reduce the gender gap.

How to Make It Happen

Practical actions to promote education for excluded girls entail tailoring programs that appeal to parents and students, drawing on the kinds of successful efforts discussed above. These are generally expensive alternatives but have been shown to be necessary to bring excluded children, particularly girls, into school and ensure that they remain and graduate. The United States' Head Start program is one such example, and middle-income countries like Chile, Malaysia, and Mexico have pioneered similar programs.

But lower-income countries cannot afford the extra efforts required to reach excluded groups and the out-of-school girls in those communities. For them, external support will be needed. First, bilateral, multilateral, and private donors should direct their support to programs that have demonstrated positive effects for excluded girls. A trust fund could be established to provide the financial basis for expanding successful efforts in reaching, retaining, and teaching excluded girls. Second, a girls' education evaluation fund could help expand the knowledge base about what works, particularly in Africa, where evidence is slim and more than 40 percent of excluded girls reside. Finally, the UNESCO Institute for Statistics should report school participation and achievement data disaggregated by gender and exclusion, which will be essential for monitoring improvements and determining what approaches are most effective.

References

Lewis, Maureen A., and Marlaine E. Lockheed, 2006, *Inexcusable Absence* (Washington: Center for Global Development); see http://www.cgdev.org/content/publications/detail/11898

Meerman, Jacob, 2005, "Oppressed People: Economic Mobility of the Socially Excluded," *Journal of Socioeconomics,* Vol. 34 (August), pp. 542–67.

UNESCO, 2006, *2007 Global Monitoring Report: Strong Foundations: Early Childhood Education* (Paris).

MAUREEN A. LEWIS is Acting Chief Economist for Human Development at the World Bank, and **MARLAINE E. LOCKHEED** is a Visiting Fellow at the Center for Global Development and formerly Education Sector Manager at the World Bank. This article draws largely from their book *Inexcusable Absence*.

Women and Warlords

Ann Jones

To the Bush bunch, an election seems to equal "democracy." Yet five months after elections in Iraq, that country has no government. And nine months after parliamentary elections in Afghanistan, it's unclear who the new legislature represents and where it's headed.

I recently visited the Afghan Parliament, just finishing its third month in session, to interview twenty members of the lower house who seem to many Afghans to be the last, best hope for a democratic future. They are certainly not typical. Standard issue parliamentarians are familiar mujahedeen commanders and cronies previously defeated, discredited and driven from the country. But these twenty parliamentarians are different: They're women.

Trumpeted as "the first democratically elected Parliament in over thirty years," this one was planned at the December 2001 Bonn conference that followed the fall of the Taliban, and was brought into being at fabulous expense by an army of some 130,000 internationally paid election workers. The United States' inexplicable pressure to invite those mujahedeen commanders to Bonn plays out now in a Parliament where every other member is a former jihadi, and nearly half are affiliated with fundamentalist or traditionalist Islamist parties, including the Taliban.

The presence of so many of the country's notorious bad guys is certainly the most peculiar feature of this "democratic" Parliament (another is the new Parliament building itself, which has plenty of room for prayer mats but no office space). One international analyst reports that among the 249 members of the Wolesi Jirga (lower house) are forty commanders (warlords) of armed militias, twenty-four members of criminal gangs, seventeen drug traffickers and nineteen men facing serious allegations of war crimes and human rights violations. The deputy chairman of the Afghan Independent Human Rights Commission charges that "more than 80 percent of winning candidates in provinces and more than 60 percent in the capital, Kabul, have links to armed groups." Plenty of parliamentarians parade around town in armored cars packed with bodyguards flourishing automatic weapons. "How can I stand up to that?" asked one woman delegate. "I am only one small lady arriving on the bus."

Warlords and criminals got into Parliament by the usual tactics: intimidation, bribery, theft and the occasional murderous assault. Many spent lavishly on campaigns, running up six-figure bills despite an official spending cap of about $15,000 (750,000 afghanis). Many gave away coveted products—from cell phones to motor bikes—to inspire voter loyalty. Some allegedly stuffed ballot boxes, using voter-registration cards confiscated from women. The highest percentages of women's votes were recorded in precisely those provinces where women are not allowed to leave the house. In Kandahar province, brimming ballot boxes were returned from women's voting centers, although few women had been seen visiting the polls.

The presence on the ballot of the usual suspects—especially the commanders who wrecked the country—kept many voters from last September's polls. (The low voter turnout, also attributed to widespread disillusionment with President Hamid Karzai, further dims the democratic credentials of the new Parliament.) But many voters filed a protest vote that produced Parliament's other startling statistic: Better than one in four members of the Wolesi Jirga is a woman.

What made that result possible is a national policy of "affirmative discrimination," a quota system endorsed and encouraged by the international community. The Afghan Constitution of 2004 provides that "from each province on average at least two female delegates shall have membership to the Wolesi Jirga." That's a total of sixty-eight women, or 27 percent of the lower house, a figure that catapults Afghanistan into the ranks of nations with the highest proportion of female representation. Sweden is number one, with 44 percent, and Afghanistan a respectable number twenty. (The United States, at roughly 15 percent, is a conspicuous disgrace.)

Surprisingly, when the votes were counted last September, nineteen women had received enough votes to win seats even without the quota system. In Herat, Fauzia Gailani, a political unknown who runs a gym for women, took first place, though she faced rivals backed by the former mujahedeen commander and provincial governor (and current Cabinet minister) Ismail Khan. In Farah province, second place went to Malalai Joya, the young woman who, as a delegate to the constitutional loya jirga in 2004, became dangerously famous for denouncing the warlords and war criminals in President Karzai's Cabinet.

One female parliamentarian insists the warlords 'won't oppose women or liberals on everything. They will pick their battles.'

The performance of female candidates for the provincial councils, elected at the same time, was even more amazing. Women won the most votes in three provinces (Balkh, Ghazni and Kunduz) and won seats in eighteen of thirty-four provinces. In Kabul women won ten seats, two more than the quota prescribed. And this despite the fact that most female candidates had little money or time to spend on campaigning, while husbands and social customs kept many from campaigning at all. Many reported death threats. A rival parliamentary candidate attacked Dr. Roshanak Wardak's home in Wardak province with automatic weapons and rockets. A local warlord is suspected in an attack in Nuristan that seriously wounded parliamentary candidate Hawa Nuristani and three of her staff just days before the election. Both women won.

From the time the election results were announced last fall, commentators worried aloud about what would happen when women met warlords. The smart, cynical money was on the warlords, while international NGOs and UN agencies hastened to offer the women coaching and technical support. But after the Wolesi Jirga was in session three months, its chairman (and former presidential candidate), Yunus Qanooni, told this reporter that there are strong and outspoken parliamentarians on both sides of the gender gap. He thinks the women are doing just fine. On the whole, the women members are better educated than the men, many of whom are illiterate; and most have careers as teachers, doctors or civil servants, while taking care of five children (on average) at home.

Qanooni argues that because Parliament is a new institution, both men and women should receive international training. Maybe in communication skills: Men complain that women interrupt them. Women say men need lessons in "democratic conversation."

During the first full-scale parliamentary debate—on the issue of whether women parliamentarians would be allowed to travel abroad without *mahrams* (male escorts)—women held their own. "We no longer cross the desert by camel, you know," said Shinkai Karokhail. "We take airplanes." Warlords asked, "Why are these women yelling at us?" Qanooni quickly sent the issue to an administrative committee.

Women parliamentarians, who were expected to quail before the warlords, already claim to be changing them for the better. Unfortunately, the female quota system gave warlords the chance to buy loyalty in exchange for protection and financial support. One female parliamentarian claims off the record that "half the women in Parliament belong to some warlord." So when a female parliamentarian reports that some well-known war criminal has become "a very good man," it's hard to know what to make of her opinion.

Nevertheless, the independent Kabul member Karokhail says it's possible to work with the commanders. "They're called warlords," she says, "but they've survived by being very shrewd factional leaders. Politicians. They won't oppose women or liberals on everything. They will pick their battles, and we will pick ours." And Roshanak Wardak notes that the ground has shifted. "The commanders could be outside running around with the Taliban and Al Qaeda, but they're inside talking to us," she says. "They used to be gunmen, but what good is a gun in the Parliament?"

That's the hopeful view. But skeptics in the international community note the ease with which Afghan thugs adopt Western vocabulary. Armed militia commanders talk peace and democracy, and fundamentalist mullahs spout feminism. Internationals say, "The leopard doesn't change its spots." In the parliamentary cafeteria, women members caucus over cups of tea. In the corridor strolls gray-bearded parliamentarian Abdul Rasul Sayyaf, Islamic cleric and scholar, militia commander, leader of the Wahhabi fundamentalist faction, friend of Osama bin Laden, accused war criminal and the purported choice of President Karzai (read Bush) for chairman of the Wolesi Jirga. Optimists take his narrow loss to Qanooni (himself a former mujahid and right hand to the assassinated national hero Ahmed Shah Massoud, but no extremist) as a sign of political change.

But the strolling Sayyaf is trailed day after day by fellow parliamentarians from the provinces. They parade in cloaks and shawls, their turbans tightly wrapped or trailing tails, their beards dyed jet black or bright red in the fashion of this or that part of the countryside. Unmistakably, they are drawn to the scent of power. But if Sayyaf lost, why are they still following him?

The answer lies outside the walls of Parliament, in the countryside. There, in the south and east, where warfare that followed the American bombardment of 2001 has never stopped, violence increases every day. Schools have been attacked; teachers beheaded. It is estimated that in Kandahar 200 schools have closed; in Helmand 165; in Zabul all but five of 170. Murders are reported almost every day: police officers, village officials, former political or military leaders. Americans say the attackers are Taliban, though many Afghans say the Taliban are busy working as drivers or translators for Americans who don't know their history. Others say the attackers are drug smugglers, inciting insecurity to cover their illegal operations.

But many Afghans say that the same familiar militia men are behind the violence, settling old scores.

In a sense, the countryside is supposed to belong to parliamentarians. Every Thursday they're expected to visit their constituents and report problems back to Kabul. Women members generally have less money and more obstacles to travel, but most of them go. Dr. Gulalai Noor Safi sets off by car over the arduous Salang Pass. Safora Yalkhani boards a battered bus to Bamiyan. Roshanak Wardak takes me into the mountains of Wardak in a Russian jeep for meetings with village elders and Kuchi nomads huddling around grass-fed fires. At Abdura, twenty male elders recite the needs of the village. *A school.* More than 250 boys meet daily in a field, weather permitting. A like number of girls stay home. *A clinic.* Pregnant women walk all day to reach Dr. Roshanak's surgery, and then they walk back with their newborns. *Jobs.* Twenty-five ablebodied young men have gone to work in Iran, leaving families behind. This village is lucky enough to have water, supplied most of the year by mountain snowmelt. They've terraced and cultivated small plots, but the rocky soil yields only enough food to last the villagers fifteen days. Then men must find paid work to feed their families. Looking out across the rocky, high-desert waste, one wonders where.

"Why don't they pool their resources and build a school?" I ask Dr. Roshanak. "They have no resources," she says. "I think you cannot understand what it is to have nothing."

Making justice for such villagers throughout the country—who so far have seen no benefits of the reported billions in foreign aid to Afghanistan—is the job that many women parliamentarians are undertaking. As more and more posh palaces of drug lords and corrupt officials rise in the capital, women members speak in Parliament of the deep and widening chasm between rich and poor. Warlords claim benefits for their own fiefdoms, but women—and Chairman Qanooni—press for equality among all regions and ethnic groups.

Current power struggles don't bode well. In late April President Karzai—Afghanistan's own "unitary executive"—won confirmation for twenty of his twenty-five Cabinet nominees, including a previously unknown personal adviser to replace veteran Foreign Minister Abdullah Abdullah. Among the losers were the culture minister, attacked for permitting women and "racy" Indian films to appear on state TV, and Suraya Raheem Sabarnag, named to be women's affairs minister—Karzai's only female nominee. An anonymous Karzai aide explained that women don't need "special appointments" to the Cabinet or the courts because they're already represented in Parliament.

Clearly, the only effective challenge to Karzai came not from Yunus Qanooni and colleagues but from right-wing jihadis who'd like to do away with female TV performers and ministers altogether. Karzai bowed to them (again) in naming the over-aged Islamic cleric Fazle Hadi Shinwari to continue as Chief Justice of the Supreme Court and effective head of the judiciary system. (Shinwari, who is on record opposing women on TV and equal education for girls, forced the first women's affairs minister from office by charging her with blasphemy, an offense punishable by death.)

How can women parliamentarians stand up to that? Maybe they're not meant to accomplish something like justice—or democracy—for Afghanistan. Maybe the new Parliament is just another foreign invention, like Kabul's new luxury hotel, designed to gratify the international community while serving no constructive Afghan purpose. Or maybe the new Parliament, such as it is, simply belongs already to the bad old boys.

ANN JONES (www.annjonesonline.com) is the author of *Kabul in Winter: Life Without Peace in Afghanistan* (Metropolitan).

Test-Your-Knowledge Form

We encourage you to photocopy and use this page as a tool to assess how the articles in *Annual Editions* expand on the information in your textbook. By reflecting on the articles you will gain enhanced text information. You can also access this useful form on a product's book support Web site at *http://www.mhcls.com/online/*.

NAME:

DATE:

_____

TITLE AND NUMBER OF ARTICLE:

_____

BRIEFLY STATE THE MAIN IDEA OF THIS ARTICLE:

_____

LIST THREE IMPORTANT FACTS THAT THE AUTHOR USES TO SUPPORT THE MAIN IDEA:

_____

WHAT INFORMATION OR IDEAS DISCUSSED IN THIS ARTICLE ARE ALSO DISCUSSED IN YOUR TEXTBOOK OR OTHER READINGS THAT YOU HAVE DONE? LIST THE TEXTBOOK CHAPTERS AND PAGE NUMBERS:

_____

LIST ANY EXAMPLES OF BIAS OR FAULTY REASONING THAT YOU FOUND IN THE ARTICLE:

_____

LIST ANY NEW TERMS/CONCEPTS THAT WERE DISCUSSED IN THE ARTICLE, AND WRITE A SHORT DEFINITION:

We Want Your Advice

ANNUAL EDITIONS revisions depend on two major opinion sources: one is our Advisory Board, listed in the front of this volume, which works with us in scanning the thousands of articles published in the public press each year; the other is you—the person actually using the book. Please help us and the users of the next edition by completing the prepaid article rating form on this page and returning it to us. Thank you for your help!

ANNUAL EDITIONS: Developing World 09/10

ARTICLE RATING FORM

Here is an opportunity for you to have direct input into the next revision of this volume.
We would like you to rate each of the articles listed below, using the following scale:

1. **Excellent: should definitely be retained**
2. **Above average: should probably be retained**
3. **Below average: should probably be deleted**
4. **Poor: should definitely be deleted**

Your ratings will play a vital part in the next revision.
Please mail this prepaid form to us as soon as possible.
Thanks for your help!

RATING	ARTICLE	RATING	ARTICLE
	1. The New Face of Development		24. The Somali Catastrophe
	2. The Ideology of Development		25. Dangerous Liaisons
	3. Africa's Village of Dreams		26. Call in the Blue Helmets
	4. Today's Golden Age of Poverty Reduction		27. The Democratic Rollback
	5. Devising a Shared Global Strategy for the MDGs		28. Turkey Face West
	6. Development as Poison		29. The Practice—and the Theory
	7. Why God Is Winning		30. South Africa After the Age of Heroes
	8. Industrial Revolution 2.0		31. Congo's Peace
	9. Governing Global Trade		32. Africa: How We Killed Our Dreams of Freedom
	10. Social Justice and Global Trade		33. Lula's Brazil
	11. Cotton: The Huge Moral Issue		34. An Empty Revolution
	12. Ranking the Rich		35. Booms, Busts, and Echoes
	13. Foreign Aid II		36. Forest Loss in Sumatra Becomes a Global Issue
	14. The Debt Frenzy		37. Water Warriors
	15. Across Globe, Empty Bellies Bring Rising Anger		38. Why We Owe So Much to Victims of Disaster
	16. The Micromagic of Microcredit		39. Population, Human Resources, Health, and the Environment
	17. The Coming Revolution in Africa		
	18. The End of War?,		40. A Lifelong Struggle for a Generation
	19. The Shiite "Threat" Revisited		41. Reversal of Fortune
	20. Letter From Afghanistan		42. Ten Years' Hard Labour
	21. Again		43. Educating Girls, Unlocking Development
	22. Will the Kenyan Settlement Hold?		44. Getting All Girls into School
	23. Zimbabwe Goes to the Brink		45. Women and Warlords

BUSINESS REPLY MAIL
FIRST CLASS MAIL PERMIT NO. 551 DUBUQUE IA

POSTAGE WILL BE PAID BY ADDRESSEE

McGraw-Hill Contemporary Learning Series
501 BELL STREET
DUBUQUE, IA 52001

NO POSTAGE
NECESSARY
IF MAILED
IN THE
UNITED STATES

ABOUT YOU

Name   Date
_____

Are you a teacher? ☐ A student? ☐
Your school's name
_____

Department
_____

Address   City   State   Zip
_____

School telephone #
_____

YOUR COMMENTS ARE IMPORTANT TO US!

Please fill in the following information:
For which course did you use this book?
_____

Did you use a text with this ANNUAL EDITION? ☐ yes ☐ no
What was the title of the text?
_____

What are your general reactions to the Annual Editions concept?
_____

Have you read any pertinent articles recently that you think should be included in the next edition? Explain.
_____

Are there any articles that you feel should be replaced in the next edition? Why?
_____

Are there any World Wide Web sites that you feel should be included in the next edition? Please annotate.
_____

May we contact you for editorial input? ☐ yes ☐ no
May we quote your comments? ☐ yes ☐ no